I0828434

HISTORIC PHOTOS OF
MADISON

TEXT AND CAPTIONS BY
DONALD J. JOHNSON

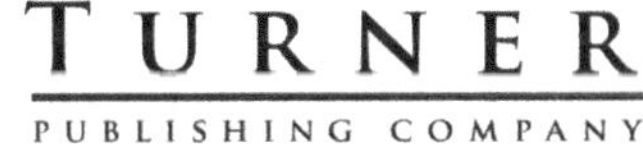

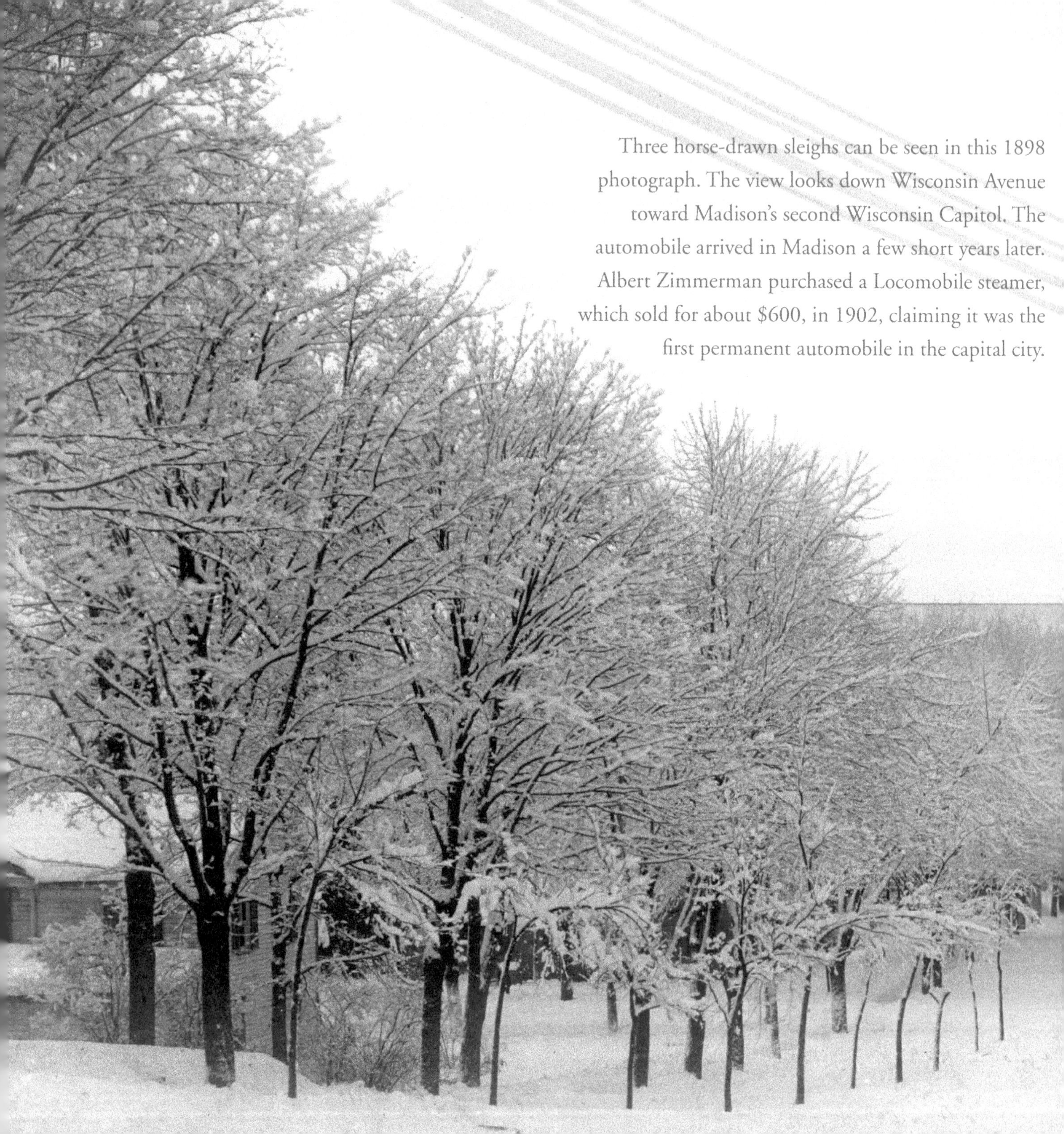

Three horse-drawn sleighs can be seen in this 1898 photograph. The view looks down Wisconsin Avenue toward Madison's second Wisconsin Capitol. The automobile arrived in Madison a few short years later. Albert Zimmerman purchased a Locomobile steamer, which sold for about $600, in 1902, claiming it was the first permanent automobile in the capital city.

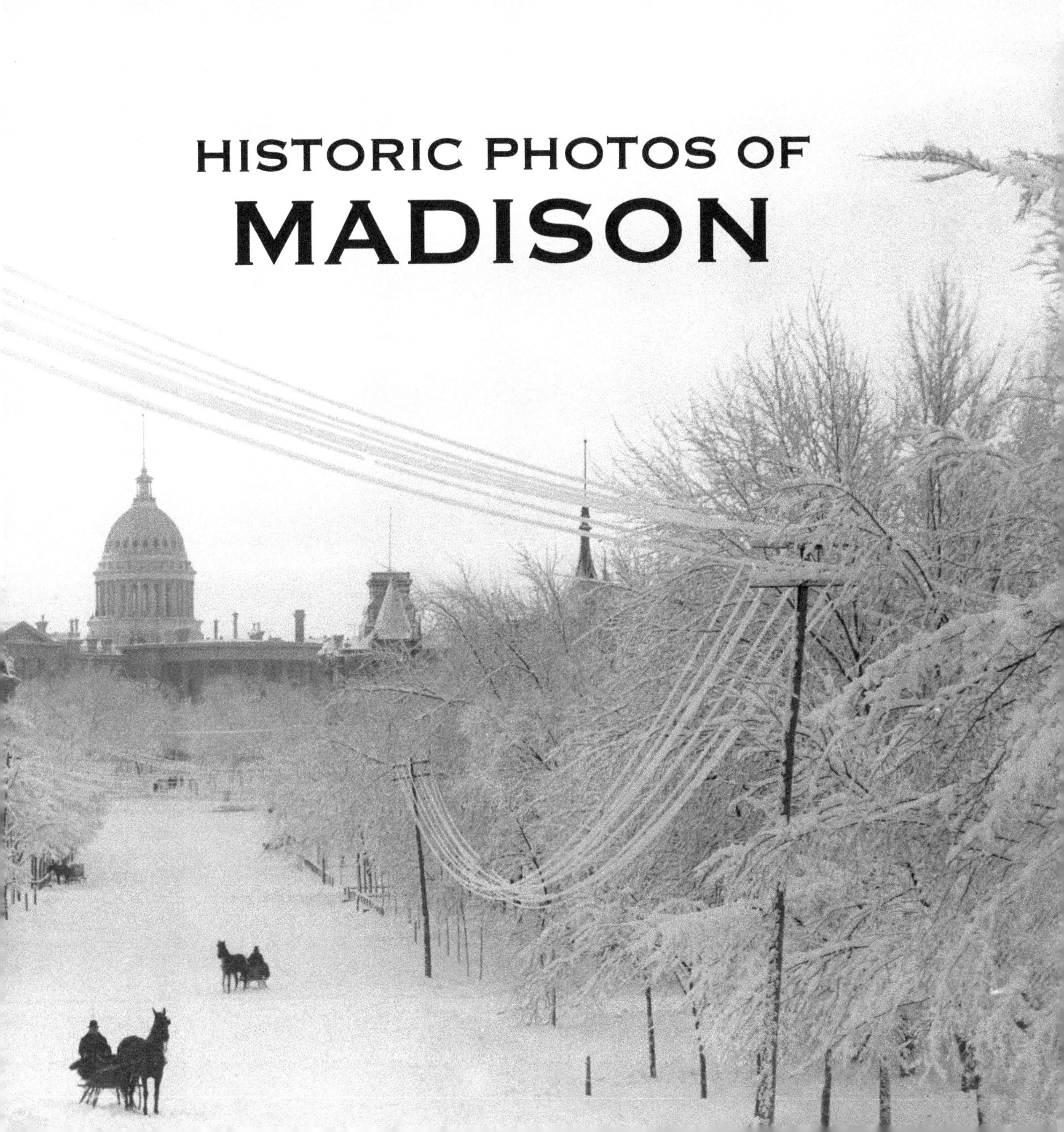

HISTORIC PHOTOS OF
MADISON

Turner Publishing Company
www.turnerpublishing.com

Historic Photos of Madison

Library of Congress Control Number: 2007923668

ISBN-13: 978-1-59652-335-7
ISBN: 1-59652-335-2

Printed in the United States of America

ISBN 978-1-68336-949-3 (hc)

Contents

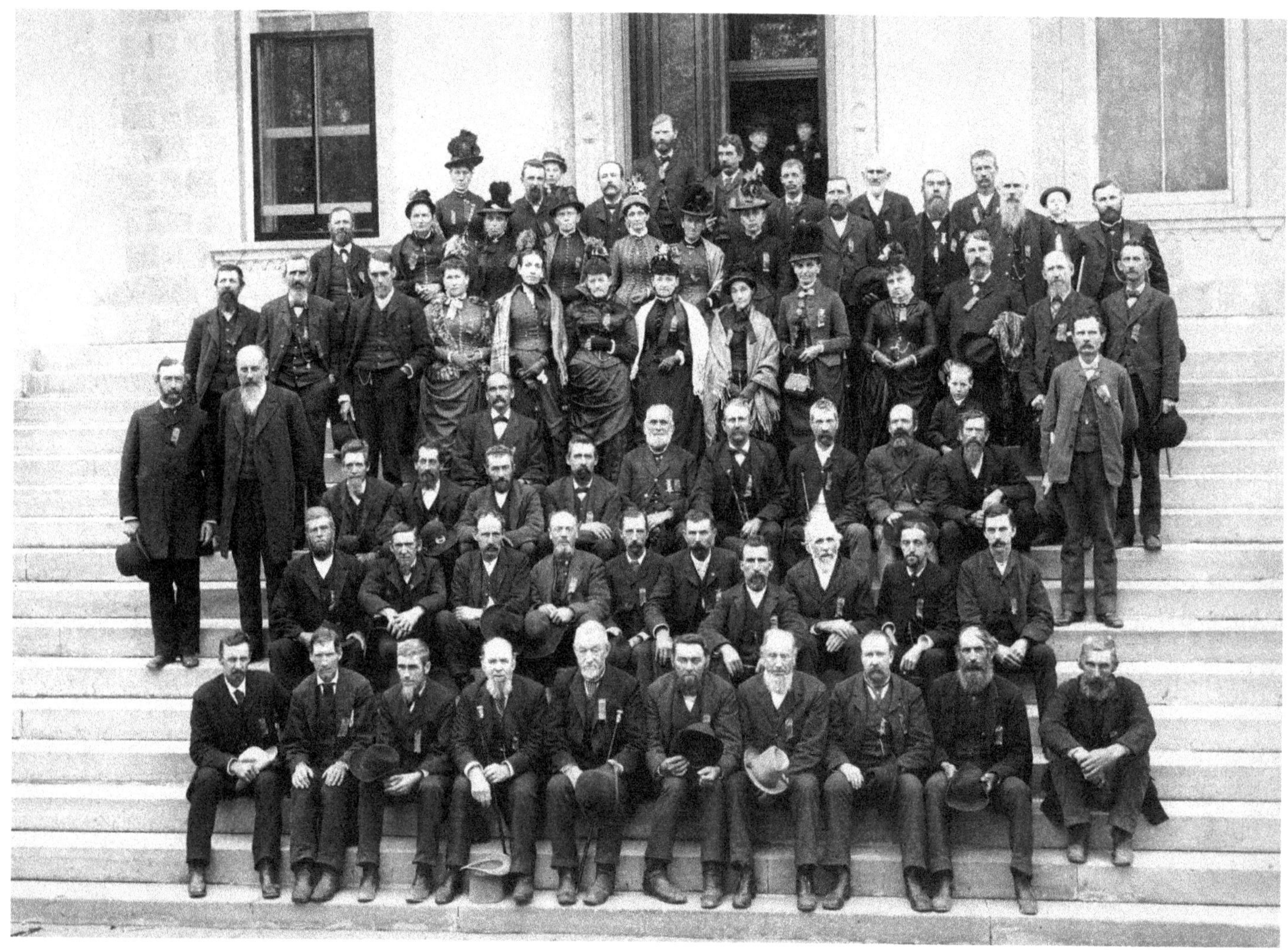

H. H. Bennett, one of the premier photographers of the era, took this group portrait of the 16th Wisconsin Volunteer Infantry, together with their wives and families, during their first reunion in Madison on September 7, 1887, twenty-two years after they were mustered out. Bennett, a veteran of the 12th Wisconsin Volunteer Infantry, may have included some members of his regiment as well.

Acknowledgments

This volume, *Historic Photos of Madison,* is the result of the cooperation and efforts of many individuals and organizations. In particular, its creation would not be possible without the world-class resources of the Wisconsin Historical Society and the University of Wisconsin-Madison libraries, which include the University Archives. It is with great thanks that we acknowledge those valuable contributions.

This project represents countless hours of review and research. The researchers and writer have reviewed thousands of photographs. We greatly appreciate the generous assistance of the archives listed here, without whom this project could not have been completed.

The goal in publishing this work is to provide broader access to a set of extraordinary photographs. The aim is to inspire, provide perspective, and evoke insight that might assist officials and citizens, who together are responsible for determining Madison's future. In addition, the book seeks to preserve the past with respect and reverence.

With the exception of touching up imperfections caused by the vicissitudes of time and cropping where necessary, no other changes have been made. The focus and clarity of many images is limited to the technology of the day and the skill of the photographer who captured them.

We encourage readers to reflect as they explore Madison, stroll along its streets, or wander its neighborhoods. It is the publisher's hope that in making use of this work, longtime residents will learn something new and that new residents will gain a perspective on where Madison has been, so that each can contribute to its future.

—Todd Bottorff, Publisher

This book is a tribute with love to my family and to Madison.
To my wife, Debra, and to my son, Jared,
and to my father and mother, Rodney and Frances Johnson.

—Donald J. Johnson, Author

Preface

In less than thirty years, Madison will touch upon its 200th anniversary. The land that is now the home of the capital city of Wisconsin was surveyed in 1834. It was put up for sale in 1835 by the federal government, and the first road was built through the area by soldiers under the command of a future president, Zachary Taylor. Within two years after being surveyed, Madison appeared on paper when James Doty drew up the plat map for "Madison," named for the former president and author of the U.S. Constitution; streets were named after Madison's colleagues, who worked with him in crafting the world's first blueprint for democracy.

Later that same year, the legislature of the newly created Wisconsin territory selected Madison, which had no permanent residents, as the territorial capital, replacing Belmont. The first settler arrived the next year in 1837. By 1848, barely fourteen years after being surveyed, the land hosted more than a thousand settlers and had since become the capital city of a newly christened state in the union.

The story that evolved since then is as intricate as any complex family history. The photographs selected for this volume after countless hours of work by researchers and editors constitute one of many possible albums showing that history. Although other collections could be equally interesting, none, including this one, can promise to be more than a series of glimpses into that past and what we think was true. We try to provide a balanced sample, drawing from the principal forces that affected people's lives—commerce, politics, religion, education, and transportation.

Many writers, too many to mention, have worked with great care to preserve parts, if not the whole, of the city's history in books, pamphlets, and web sites. Our most reliable sources can be found among the rich primary source documents and treasures in the Wisconsin Historical Society and in the state's many libraries. This book does not attempt to compete as a comprehensive historical record. For such accounts, both collective and personal, there are histories and daily stories by historians and journalists such as Stuart Levitan, Reuben Gold Thwaites, David Mollenhoff, William Wineke, Susan Lampert Smith, Frank Custer.

The inspiration for the book does, however, match their love for a place and for the people who make it unique—rich with history and diverse experiences—a home that few want to leave and to which many return. Like other families, we have argued fervently among ourselves about how we should care for our beloved Madison and what its future should hold. Future debates promise to be just as ardent. Will such discussions ever settle at an "angle of repose" as in the title from the Pulitzer Prize–winning novel by former Madisonian Wallace Stegner? Probably not soon. Although we can reflect, sometimes with awe and at other times with amusement, our story is yet still too young to look back for long. Perhaps our best tack is to remember what we hold dear about Madison and let that be our guide in building our future community.

—Donald J. Johnson

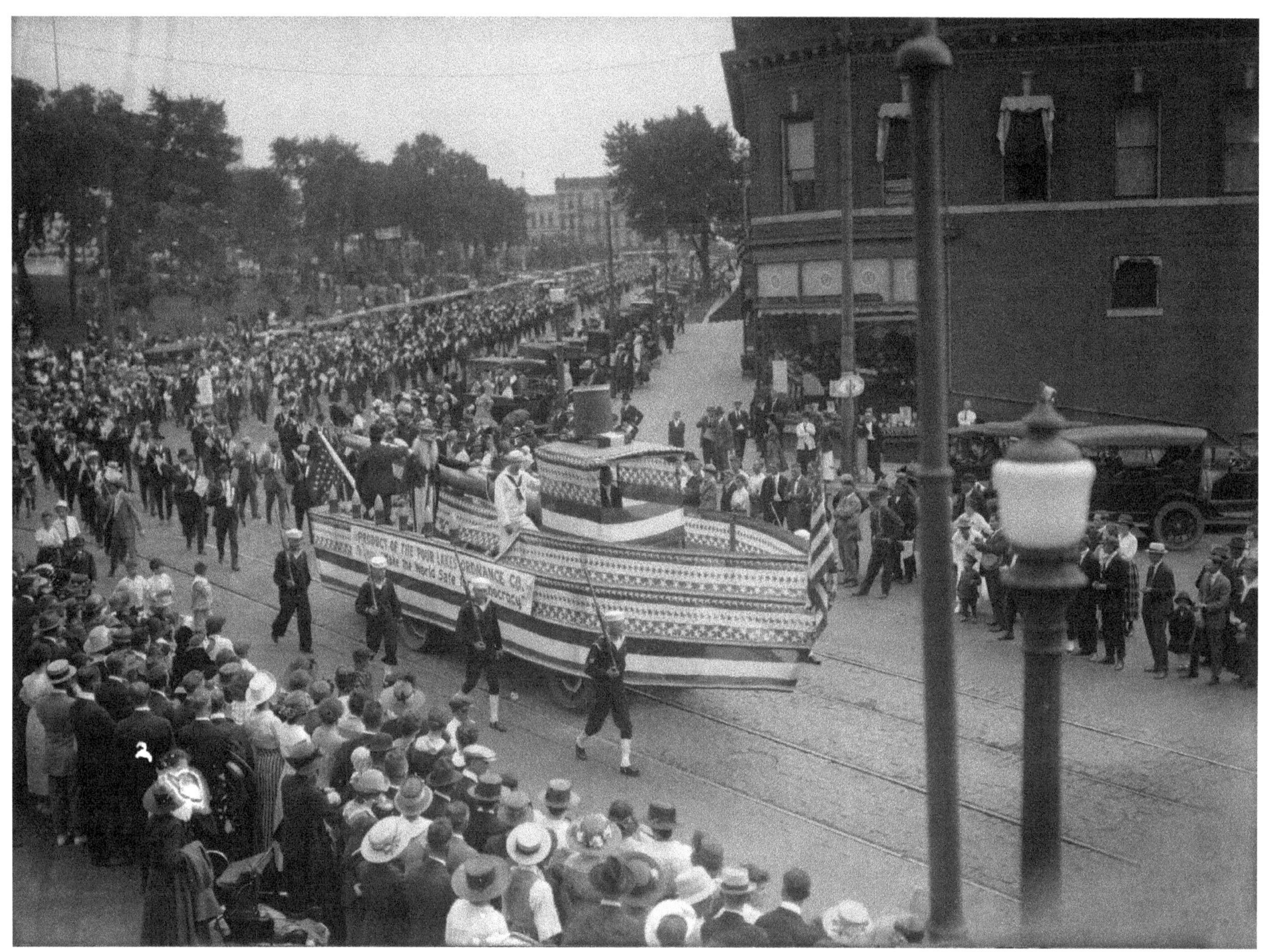

Part of a Labor Day parade featuring a float shaped like a boat turns off the Capitol Square in 1918. The photograph was taken by William Meuer, a well-known Madison photographer, who chronicled the famous and not-so-famous in Madison's history from the late 1800s through 1934. His collection of more than 28,000 black-and-white photographs is housed in the University Archives of the University of Wisconsin-Madison libraries. Topics range from faculty portraits, new scientific discoveries, athletics, students, governors of Wisconsin, and images of Madison.

A Young City Comes into Its Own

(1860–1899)

Madison was named for the "Father of the United States Constitution" and the fourth president of the United States. The man incorporated a belief in debate, the role of individual rights, and the importance of holding government accountable to its people as founding principles in this blueprint for democracy. In a distinction keeping with its prestigious namesake, even though it had no permanent residents, Madison was named the capital of the Wisconsin territory in 1836. Within two decades it had been incorporated as a city and boasted a population of about 11,000.

By 1860, however, the 1857 economic panic had taken its toll, and the population had dropped a few thousand. That was compounded by actions of the city council, through a series of bad decisions on spending and borrowing, that had left the city bankrupt.

In spite of this uneven start to the decade, the city would soon boast a new state capitol, the second in Madison and the third for the state, the start of its own Mansion Hill, its first suburb, and a first-class hotel.

During this last half of the nineteenth century, Madison saw rapid expansion of its role in commerce and tourism, where railroads, manufacturing, education, breweries, and religion became significant enterprises. By century's end, Madison had a population of nearly 20,000 and was deeply engaged in preserving the quality of life through city planning.

By then it had sent men off to the Civil War; those who survived returned as heroes. The Attic Angels had begun their philanthropic work, Madison was hosting the most successful Chautauqua in the West, and the city council had passed a resolution about affairs in faraway Ireland—the beginning of a long-standing tradition of righteous commentary from a municipality on national and international affairs.

These anecdotal pieces of history may not be significant as discrete events, but they represent themes in the character of a growing city. These civic roles continue to this day: Madisonians believe they should and must speak out on local, state, national, and international affairs.

As much by accident as by design, Madison became a community that recognized the individual citizen's unique place in the landscape, a perspective that fits its name.

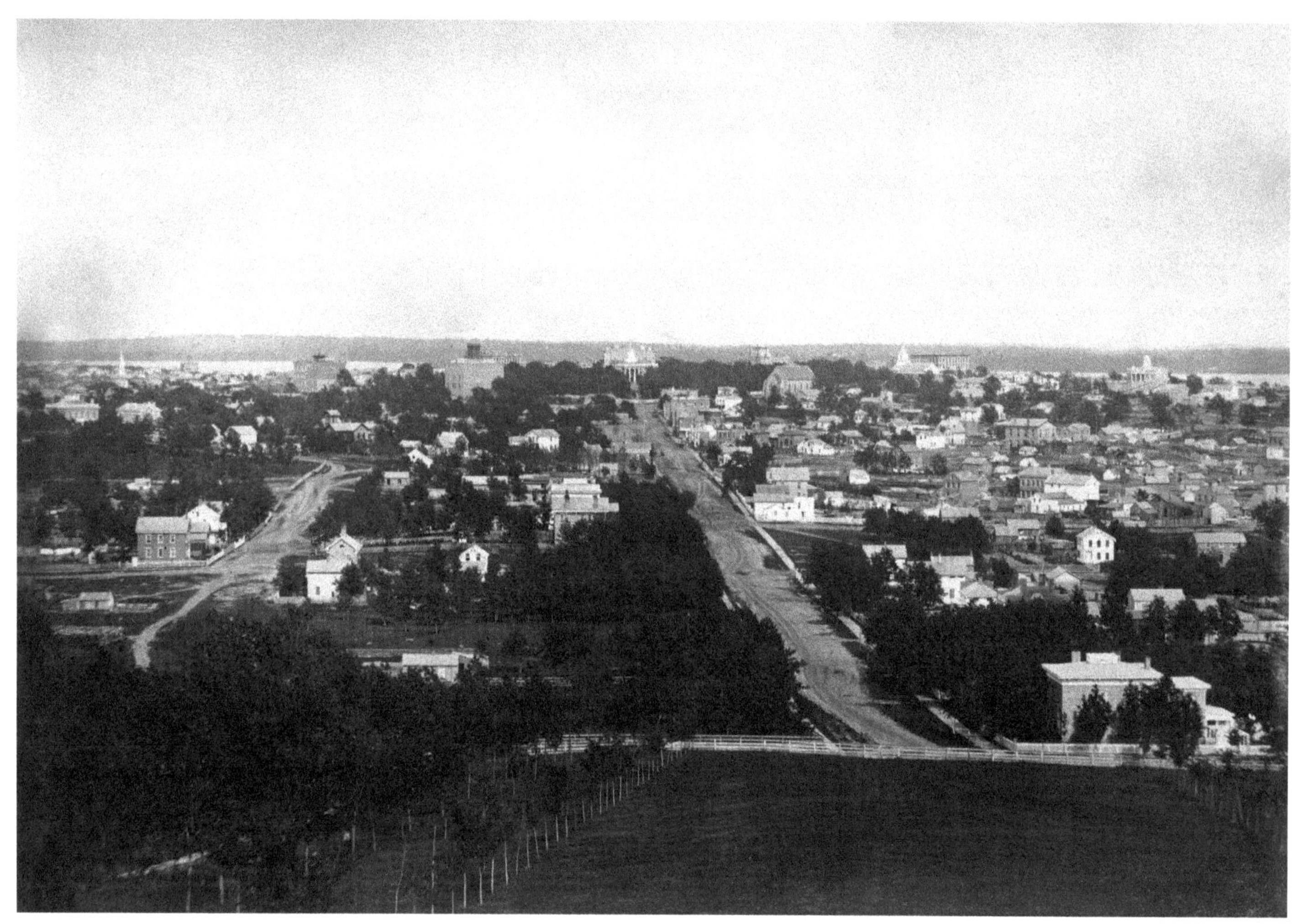

The first Wisconsin Capitol constructed in Madison, visible in this 1861 photograph, sits at the top of State Street in this view from Bascom Hill on the University of Wisconsin campus.

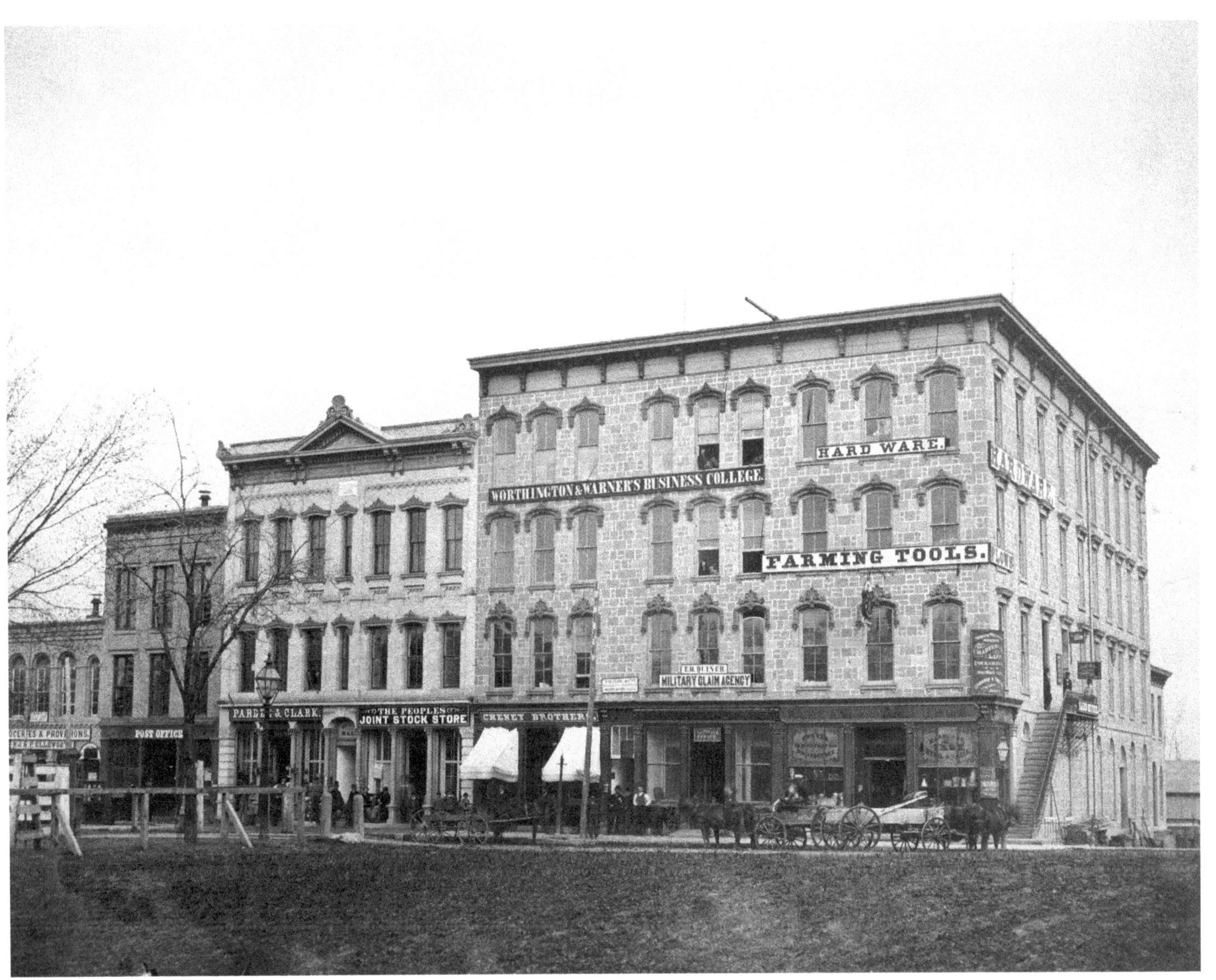

In little more than a decade after its creation from wilderness in 1836, Madison had become a thriving small metropolis. The busy corner of West Main and South Carroll streets shows businesses and horse-drawn wagons during the pre–Civil War era (ca. 1860).

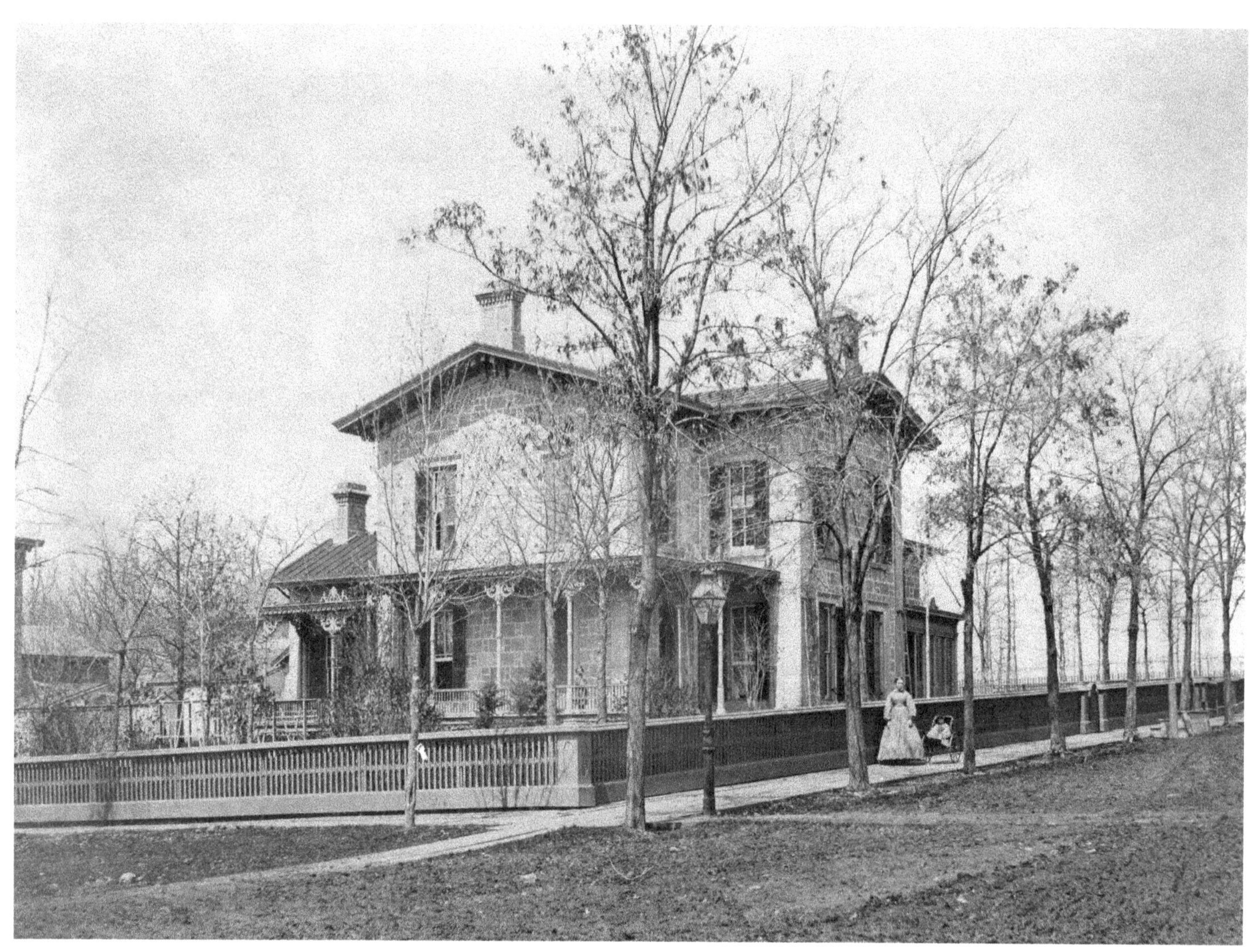

The Van Slyke residence at 510 North Carroll Street in May 1867. This sandstone Italianate was built for hardware merchant Samuel Fox about 1856, but was soon sold to Napoleon Bonaparte Van Slyke, a banker and one of the first University of Wisconsin regents.

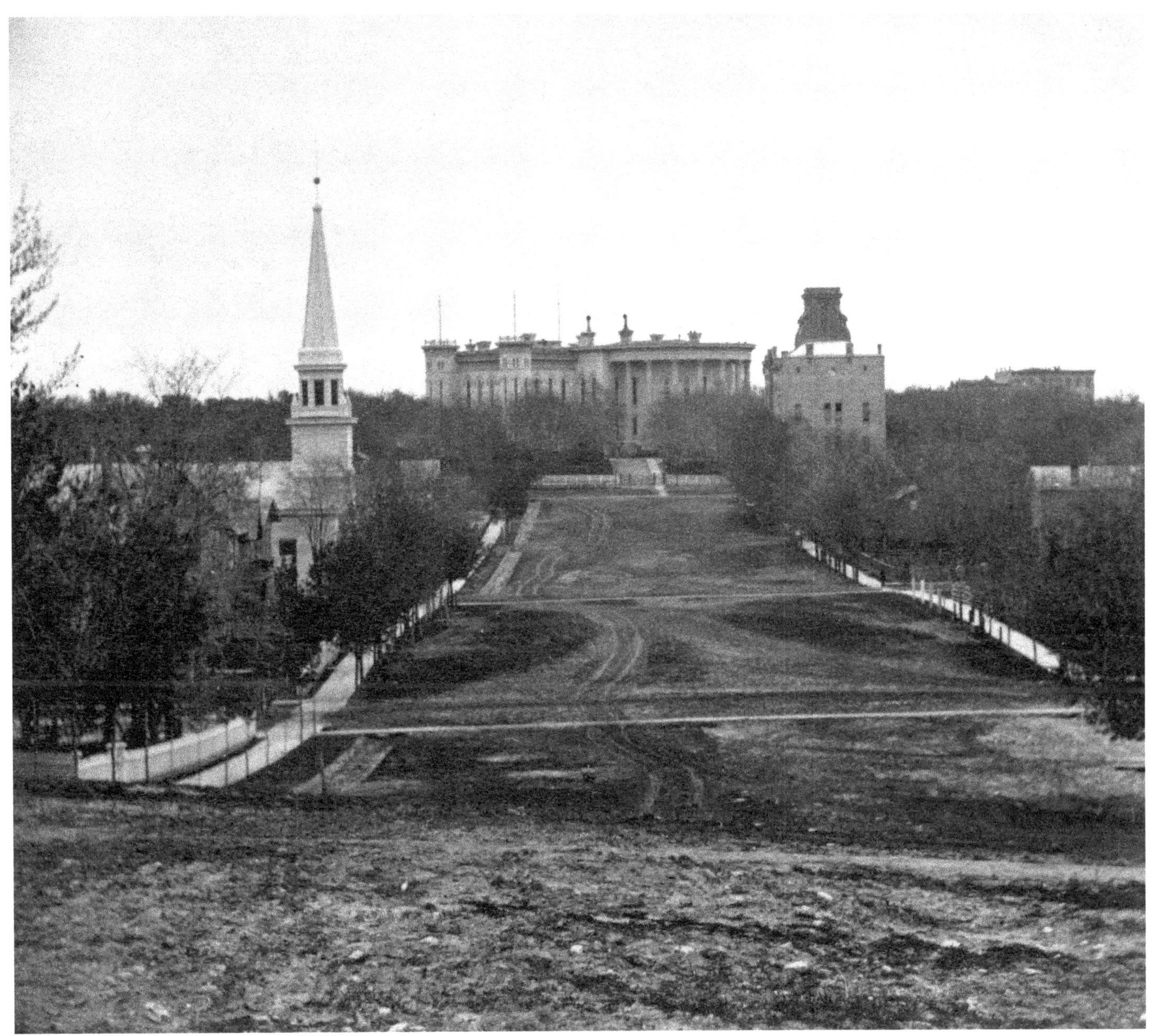

The state's third Capitol (the second located in Madison), designed by August Kutzbock and Samuel Donnel, appears in this rare photograph before its dome was added in 1869. The architects intended a smaller dome, to fit the scale of the building, but state officials pressed for a more impressive structure, with in mind the new dome on the U.S. Capitol. A new architect was selected to design a rotunda. Shortly afterward in 1868, Kutzbock, believed to be distressed over the rejection of his design, committed suicide by filling his pockets with rocks and walking into the waters off Picnic Point on Lake Mendota.

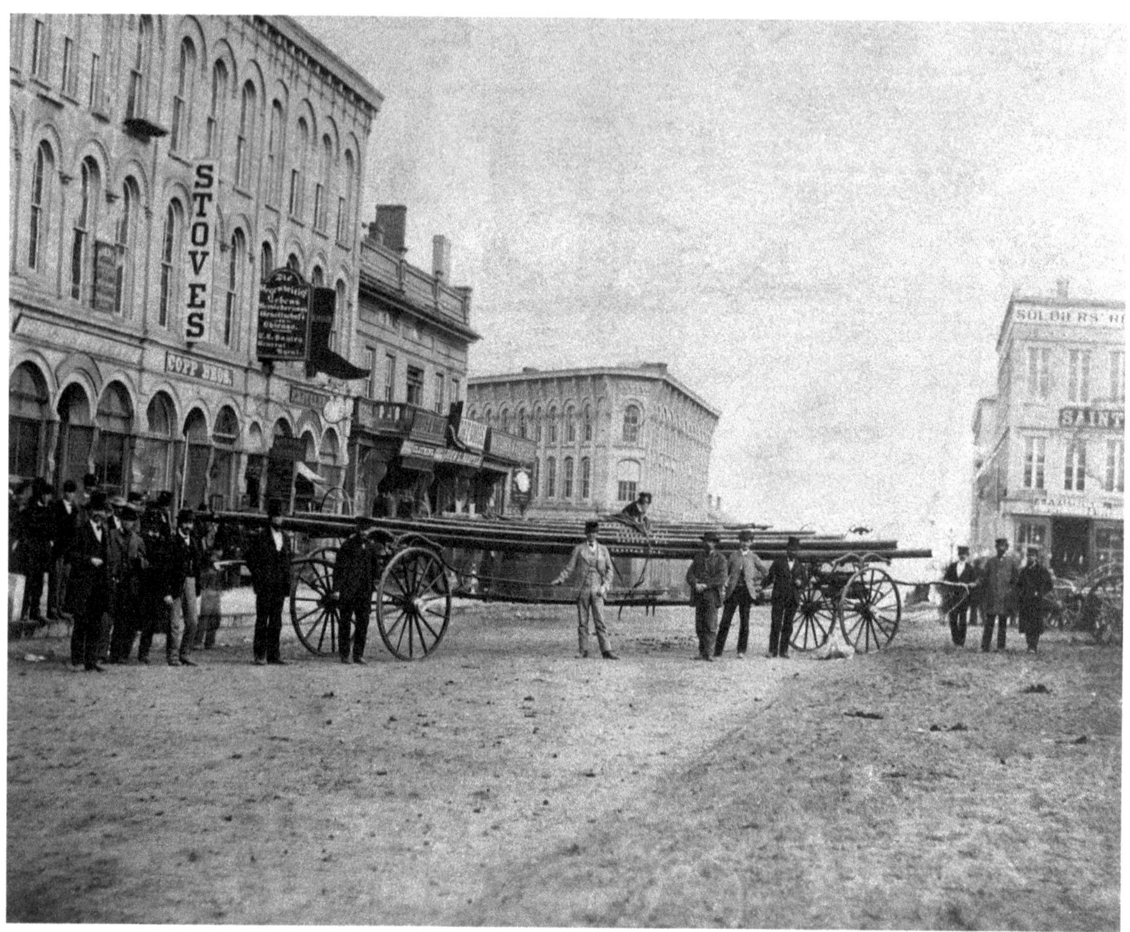

The all-volunteer firefighting company of Capitol Hook and Ladder Company #1 display their first ladder wagon and its 48-foot ladders at the corner of Pinckney and Main streets. The group of young men formed the company in September 1857. Their $685 truck equipped with five ladders arrived seven months later. Four men were required to push the wagon to a fire. In 1885 it was the last company absorbed into the Madison fire department. Six years later Madison bought a new $2,400 horse-drawn truck.

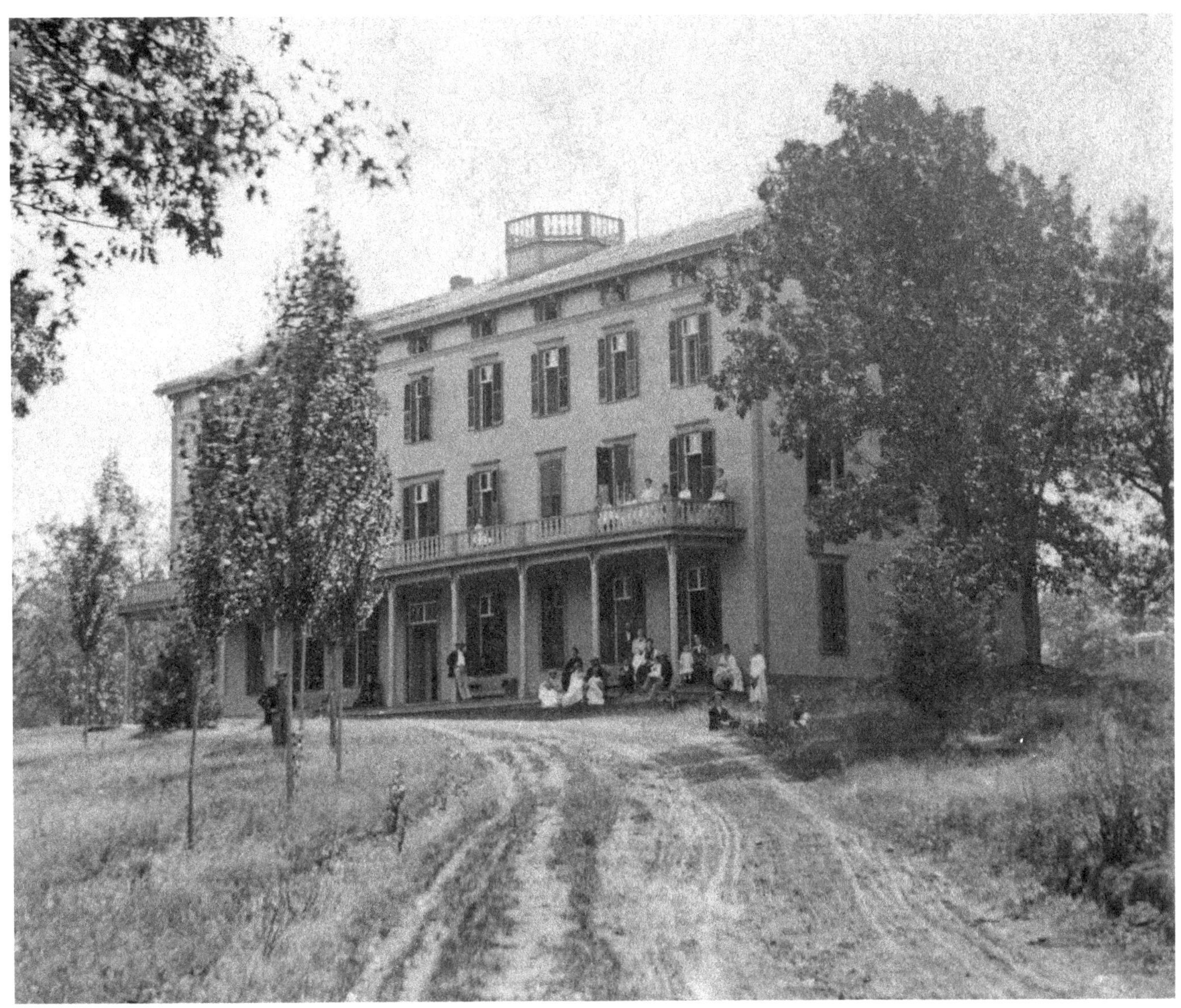

The Lakeside House, the renovated and expanded Water Cure building built on the shore of Lake Monona in 1855, became a centerpiece of a thriving tourism trade. The cream-colored resort overlooking the city's growing skyline catered to the well-heeled carriage trade, particularly travelers from St. Louis. It burned about 1870.

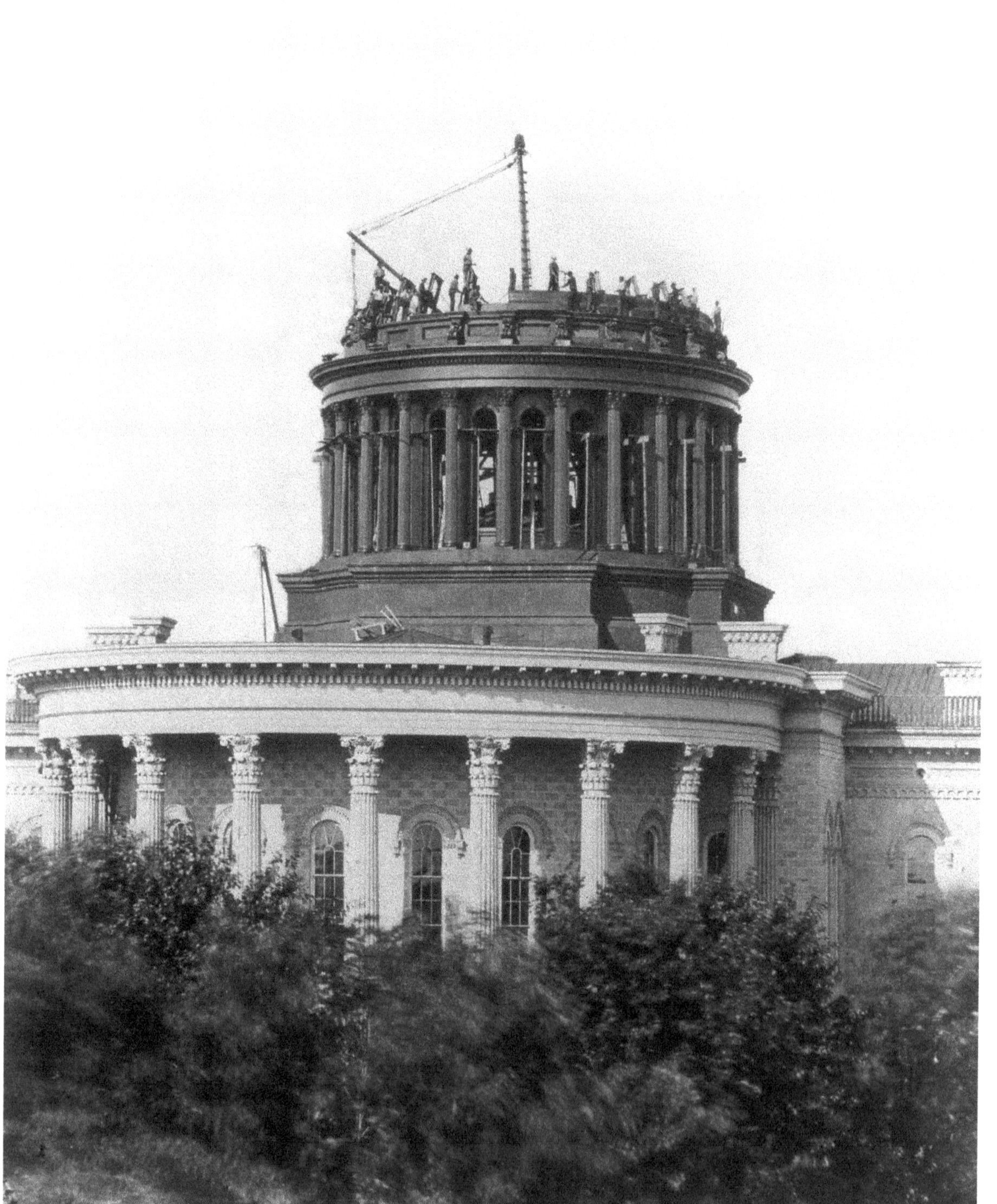

Workmen and the equipment they used to hoist material into place for the dome on the state's third Capitol in 1869. The dome, an oversized design 225 feet tall at the top of its flagstaff, replaced the plans of the original architects. It was built of cast iron and painted white.

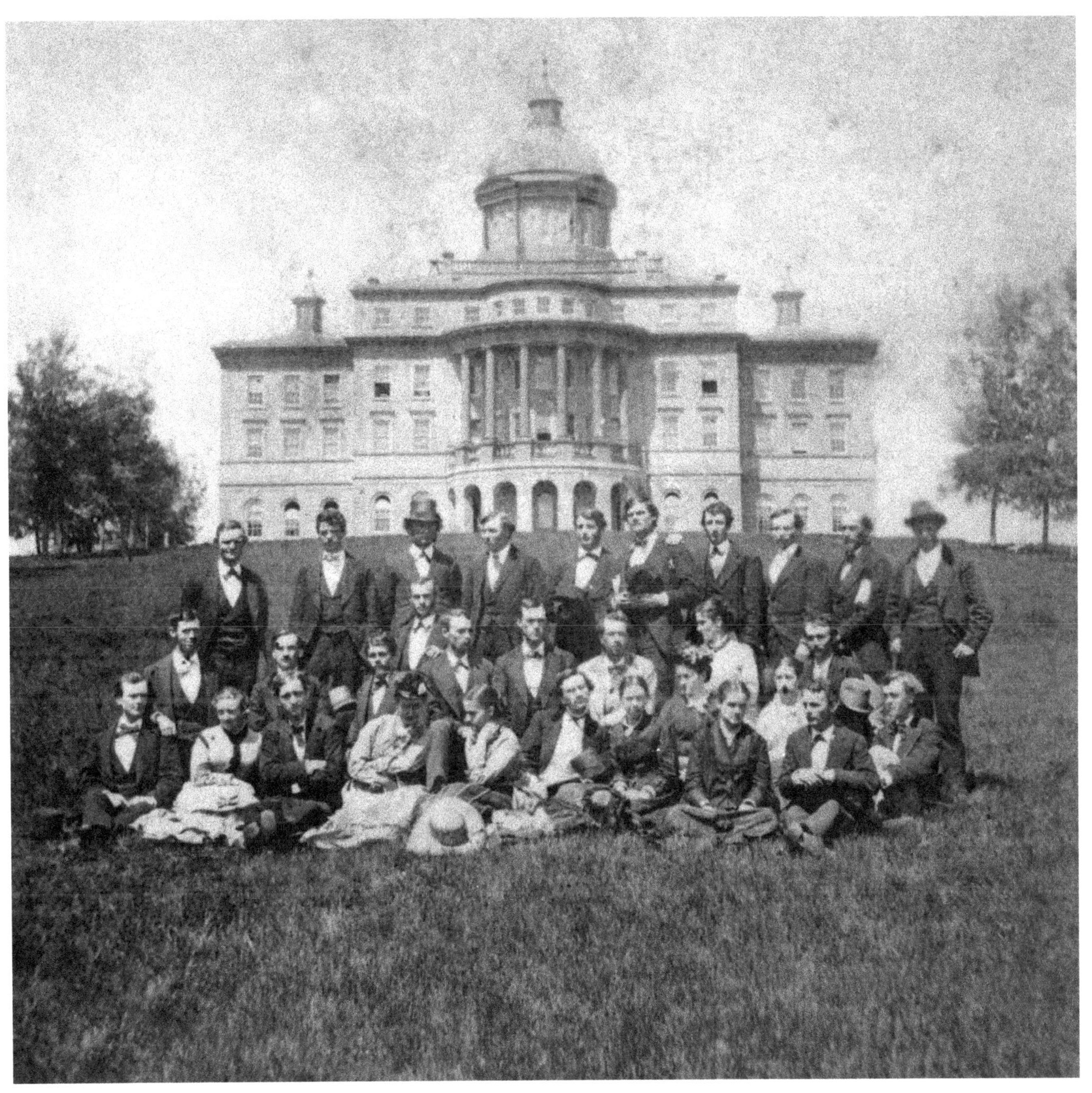

University of Wisconsin students pose on the lawn of Main Hall (later Bascom Hall) about 1869. Main Hall opened in 1859 and was the first building on the growing campus devoted entirely to instruction.

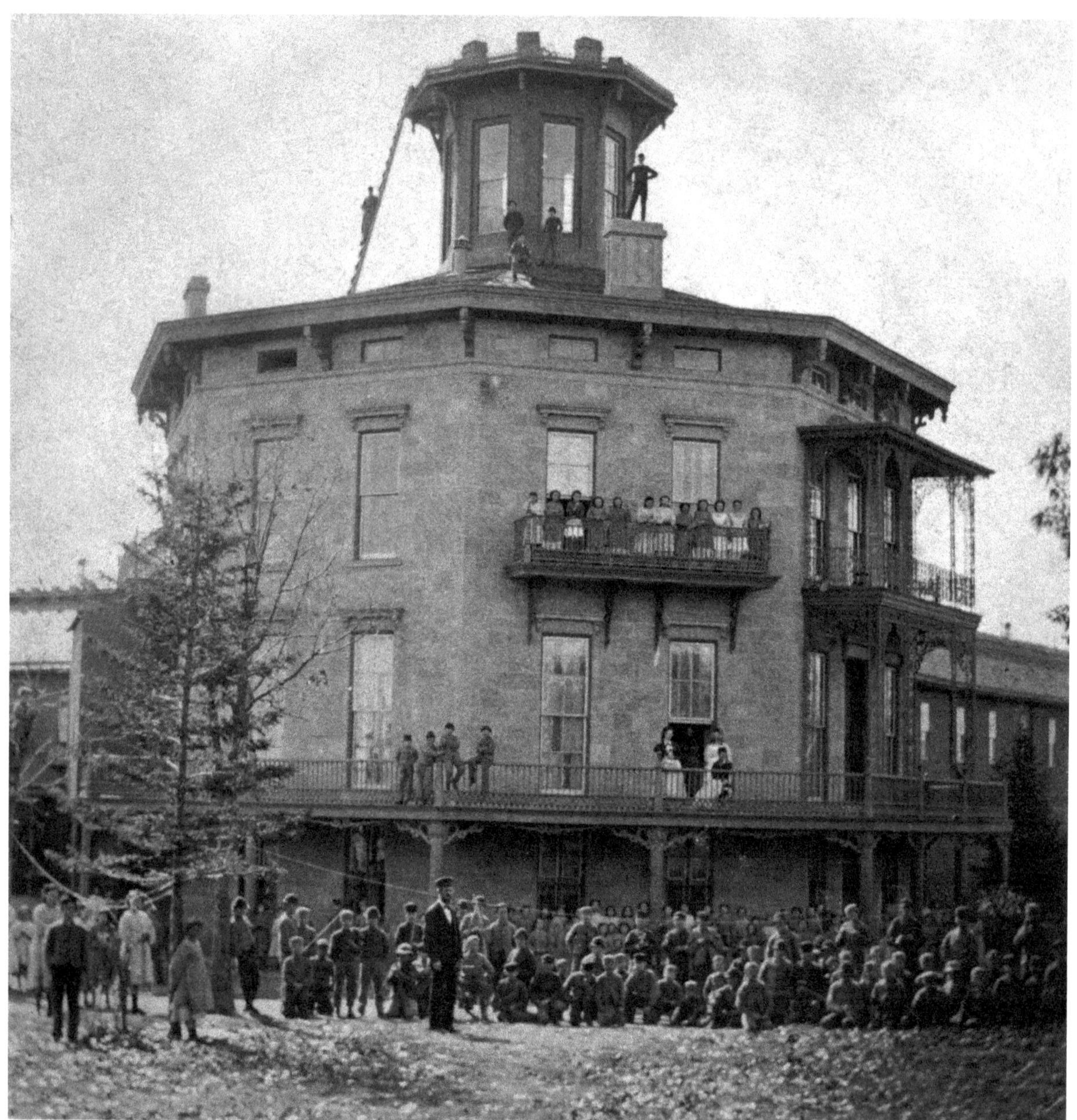

This breathtaking 9,000-square-foot, three-story octagon house was designed for Governor Leonard Farwell by the same architects who created the plans for the third Wisconsin Capitol. Completed in 1854, it occupied a lakefront block on Brearly and Spaight streets. Farwell lost the mansion along with his other holdings in the panic of 1857. The house became the Harvey Hospital and later the Soldiers' Orphans home.

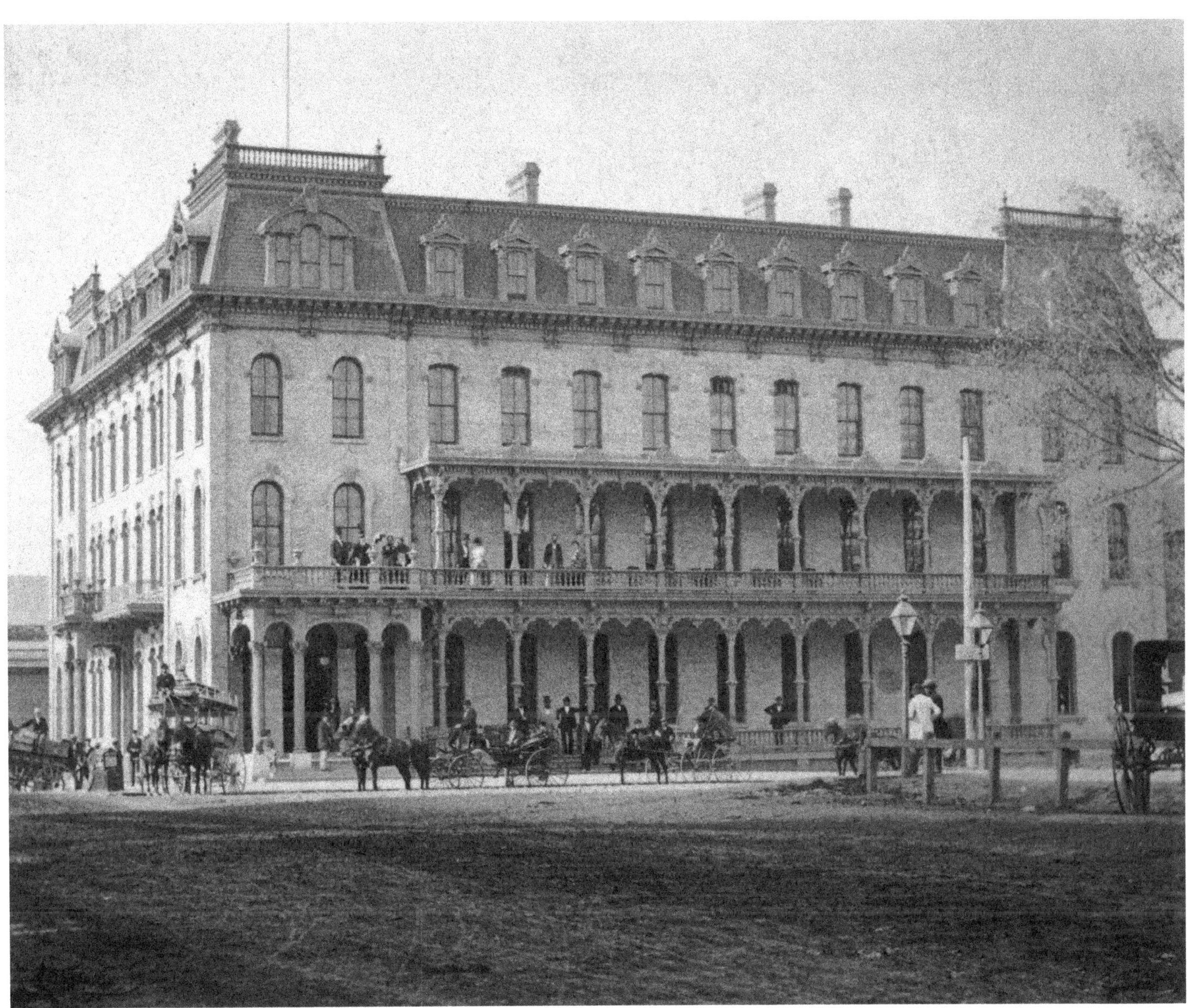

The Park Hotel was built in 1871 at the corner of South Carroll and West Main streets by investors worried by an attempt to move the state's capital from Madison. It was one of Madison's earliest first-class hotels and the first building on the Capitol Square to have water closets. The four-story hotel had 118 sleeping rooms with walnut trim, marble fireplaces, and spring beds. The building was demolished in 1961 to make way for the Park Motor Inn, now called the Inn on the Park.

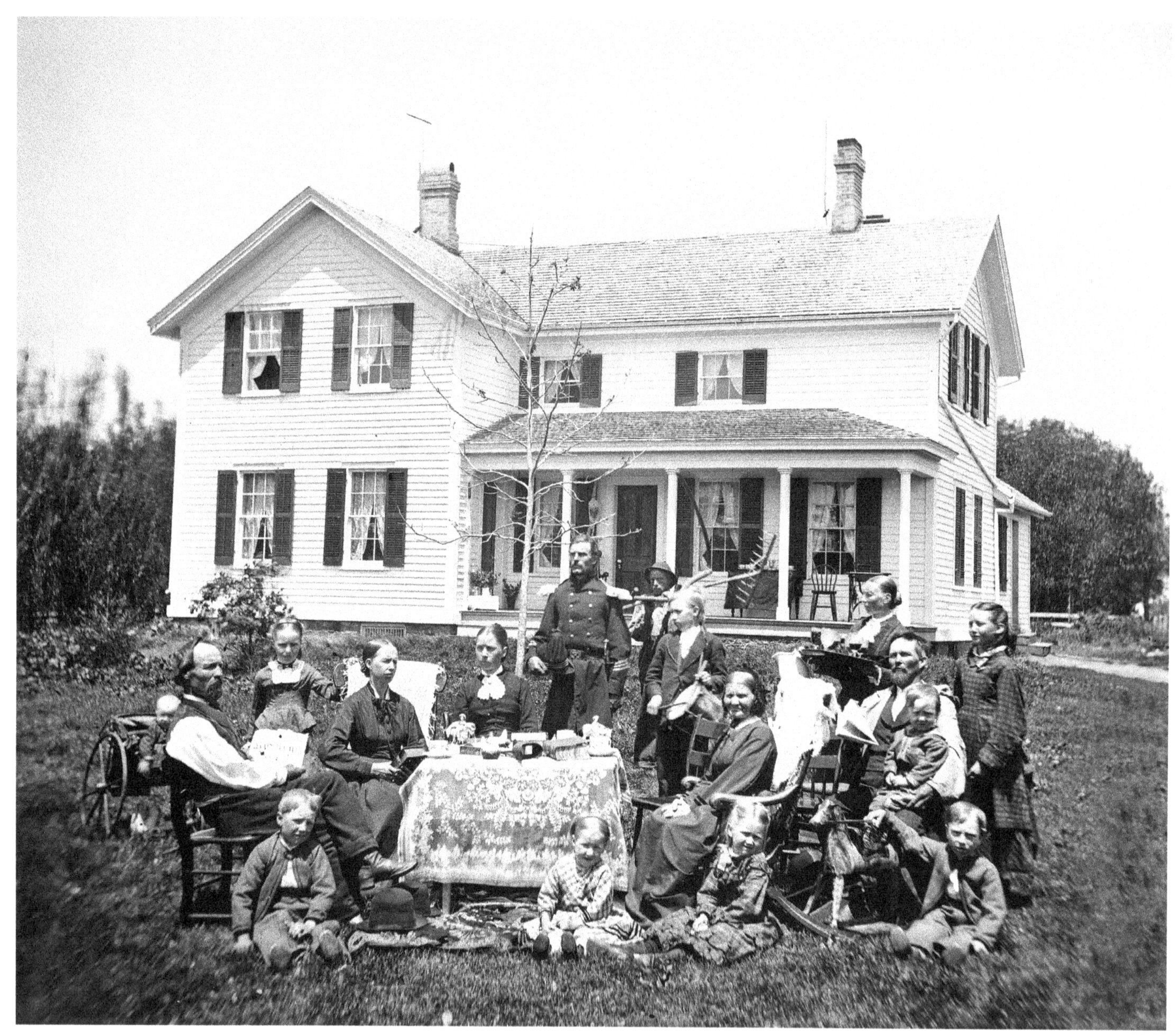

This 1870s image documents a Norwegian family's significant possessions—a lace-covered table, coffee cups, books, figurines—carefully arranged in front of their home near Madison. The man in uniform (center) is a Civil War veteran.

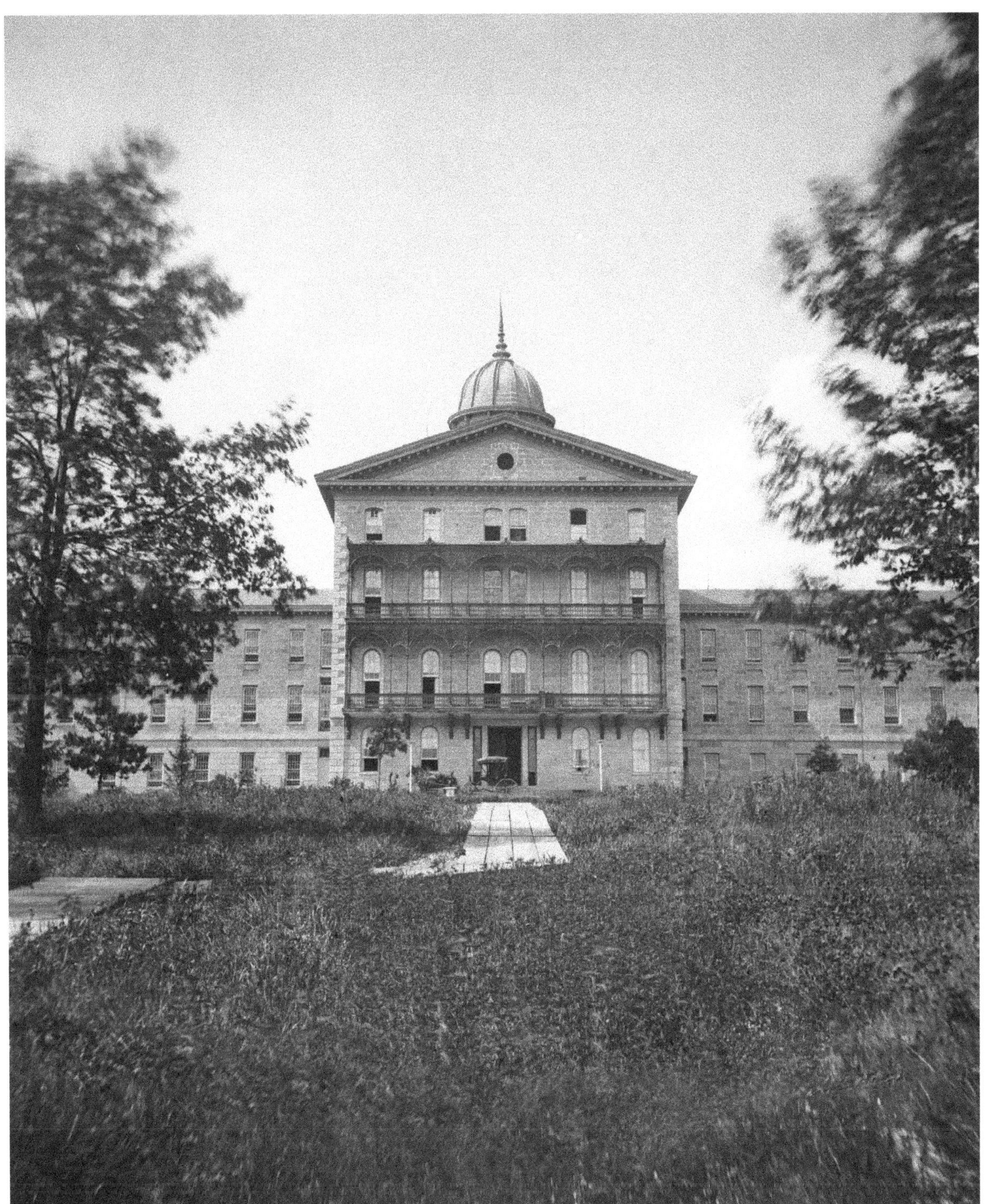

The stone four-story Wisconsin State Hospital for the Insane opened in July 1860 on the north shore of Lake Mendota. The building was surrounded by 393 acres of ornamental grounds, woods, and farming lands. It later became known as Mendota State Hospital.

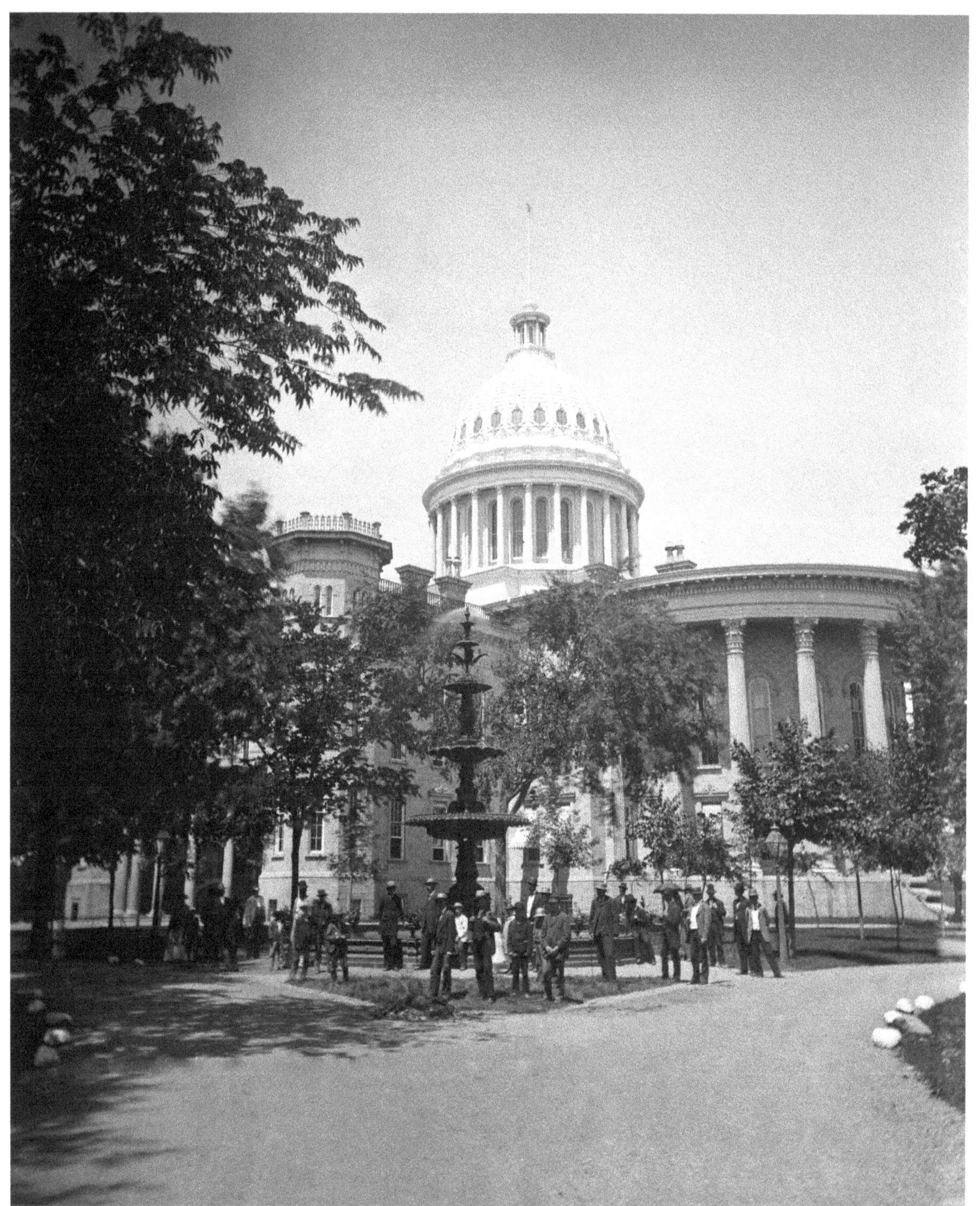

The Centennial Fountain, on the Capitol Square as seen from Monona Avenue, was modeled on a fountain by the same name erected in Philadelphia in 1876. Before 1877, Monona Avenue was known as South Wisconsin Avenue. It kept the name Monona for more than 100 years before being renamed Martin Luther King Jr. Boulevard in the 1990s.

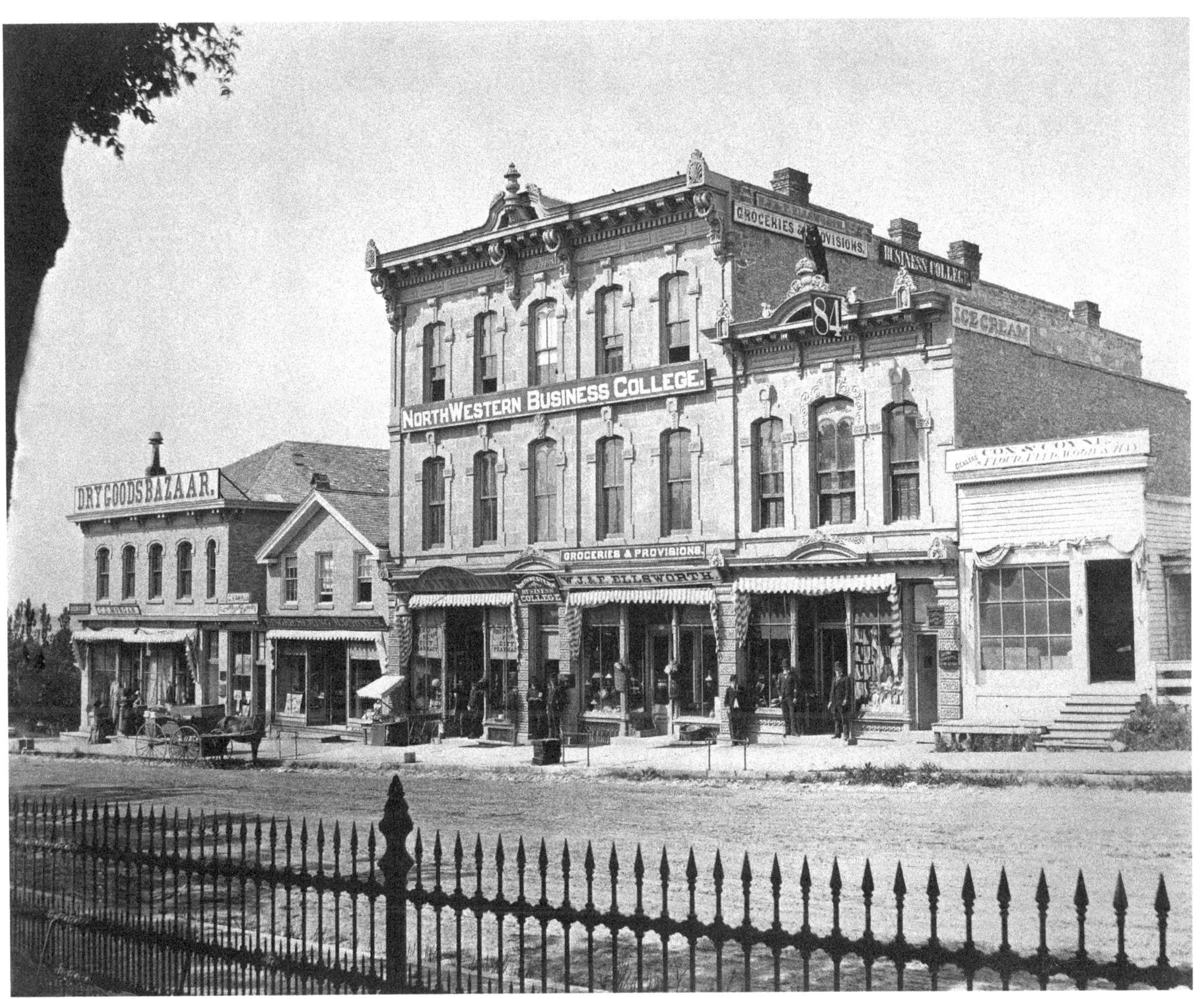

This view across the iron fence built around the Capitol Park in 1873 shows the Ellsworth Block on North Pinckney Street between East Washington Avenue and East Mifflin Street. Storefronts include the Dry Goods Bazaar, Singer Sewing Machines, the Hollister & Wittman Pharmacy, the Ellsworth Grocery Store, and the NorthWestern Business College.

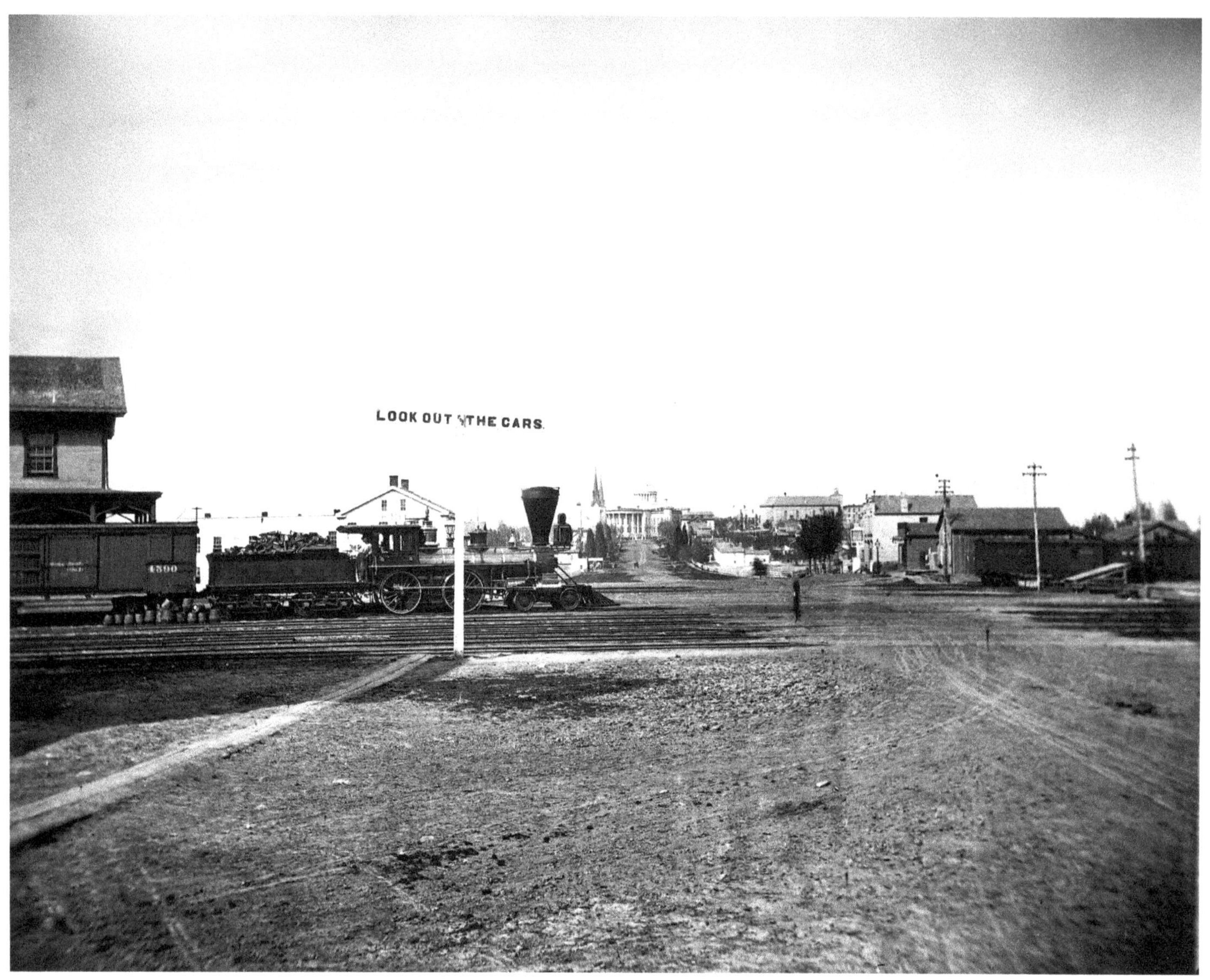

The Northwestern Railroad depot (behind the locomotive) was built in 1871. The view looks east along West Washington Avenue toward the Capitol.

A family poses with farm implements in a field outside Madison in the mid 1870s.

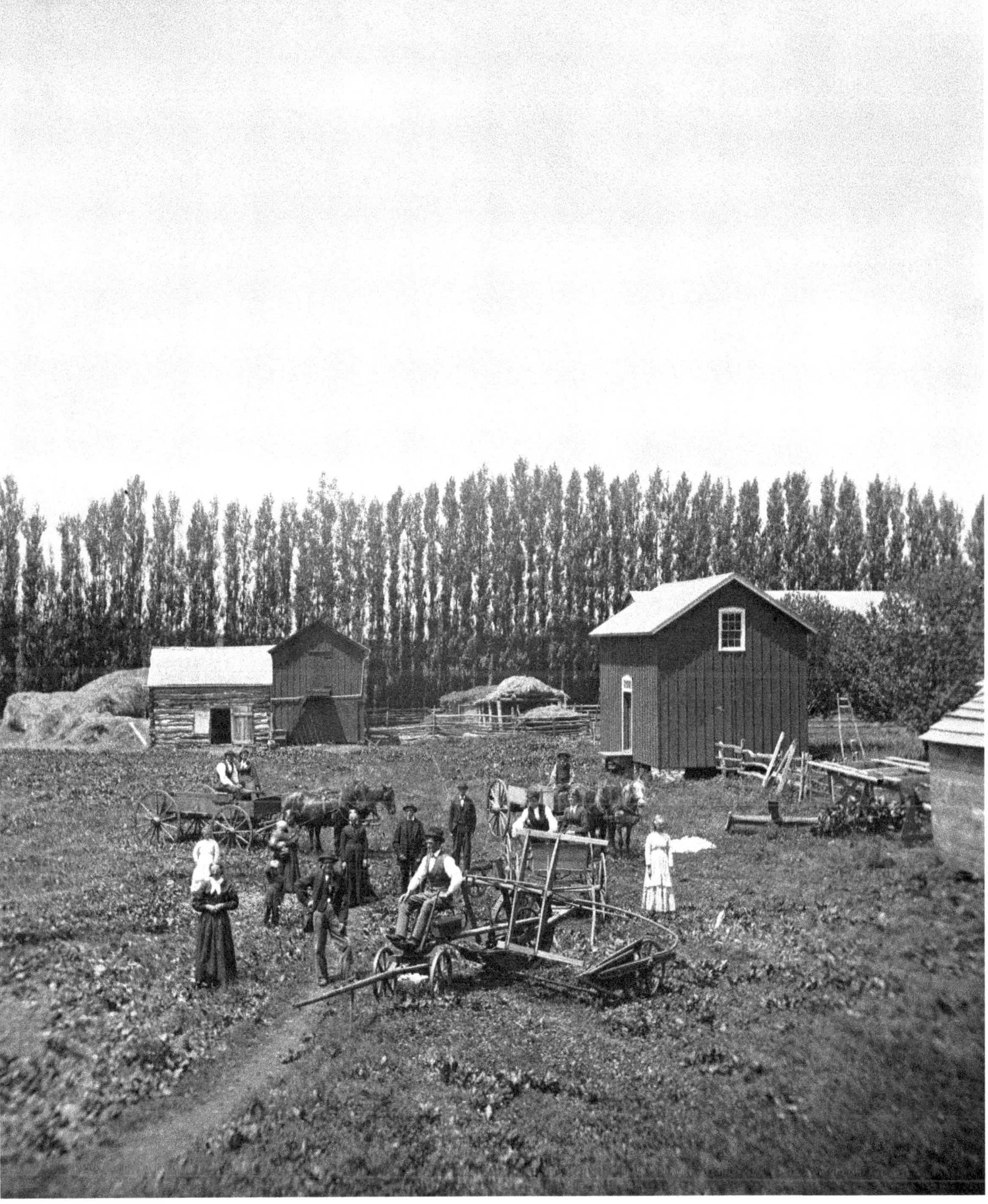

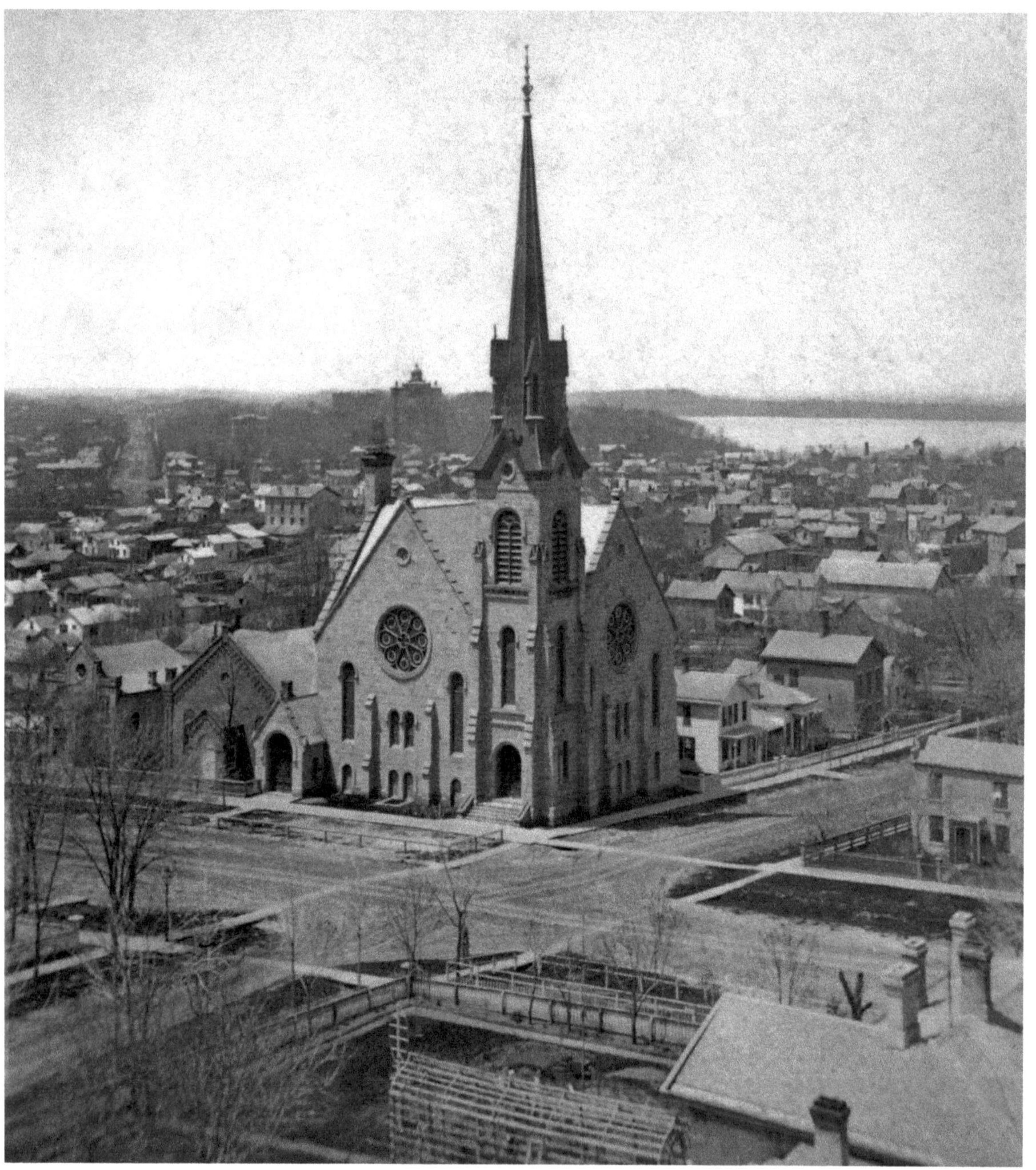

This image looking northwest across West Washington Avenue features the Congregationalist Church in the mid 1870s. At center-left is Main Hall, now Bascom Hall on the university campus.

Steamboats plied Madison's lakes in the late nineteenth century, particularly on the more peaceful Lake Monona, which appealed to Victorian tastes more than the rougher and larger Lake Mendota. A barge in the foreground, with two sidewheel excursion boats behind, is shown here around 1875. Steamboat operators built pleasure parks along both lakeshores, to which they ferried tourists.

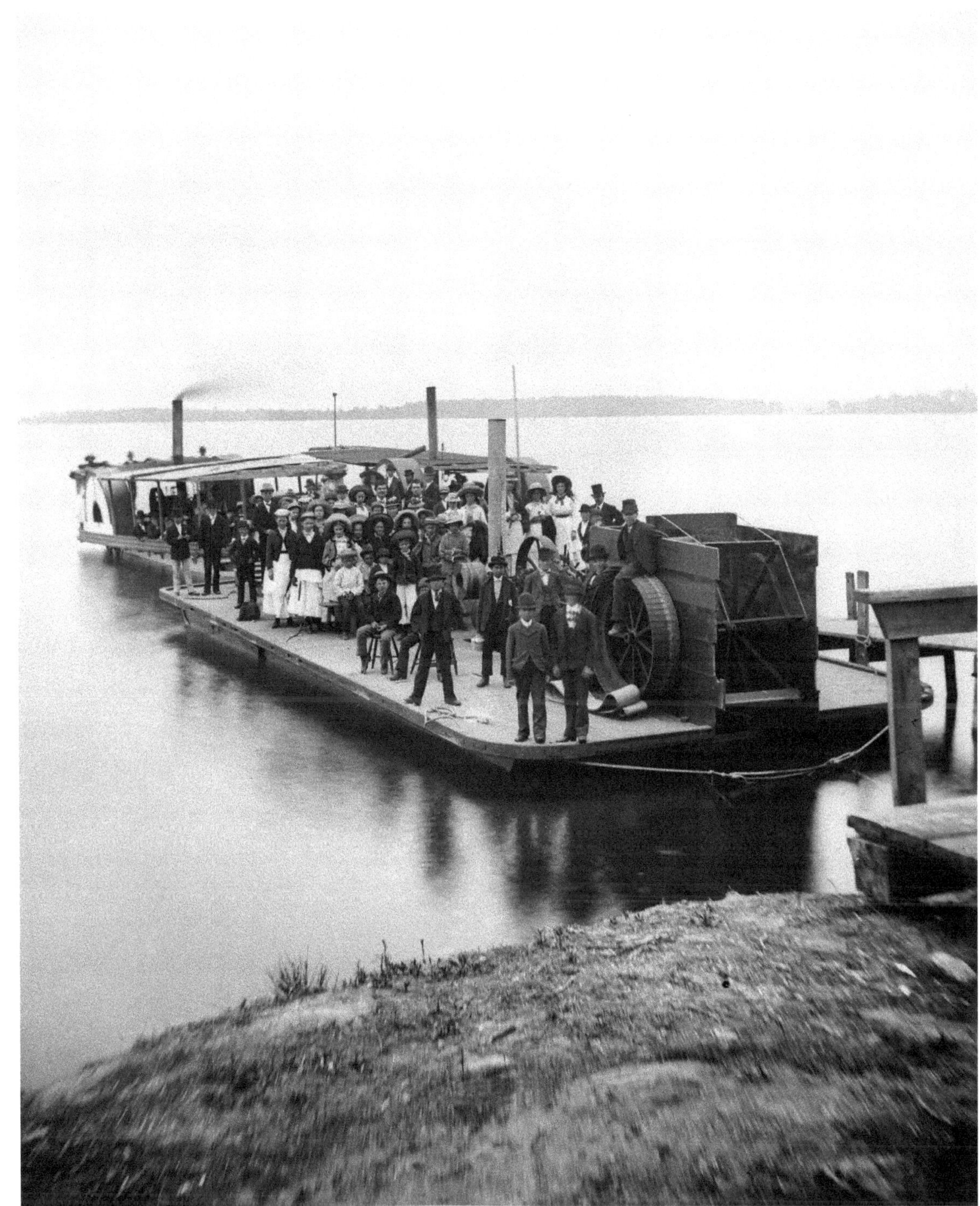

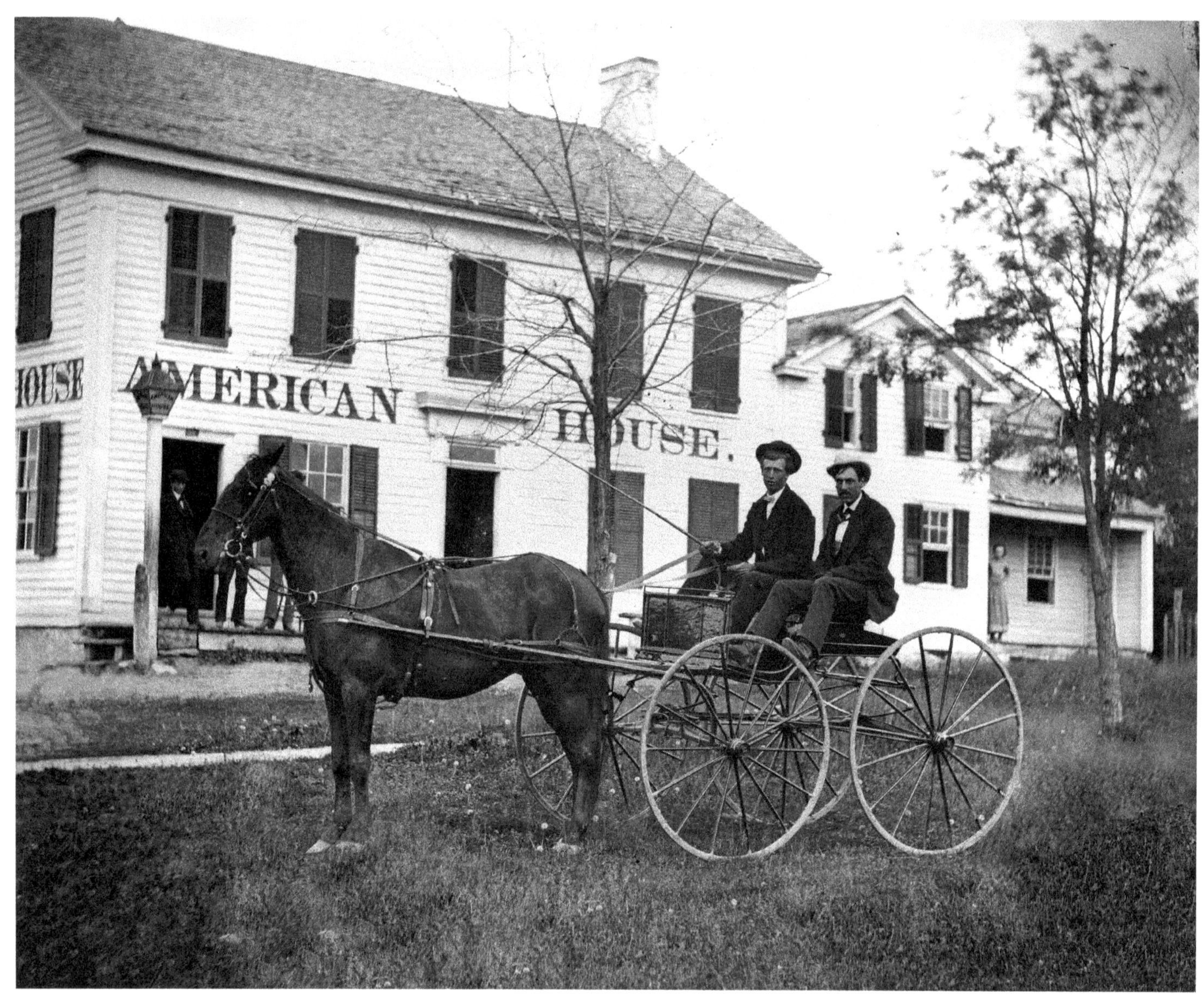

The American House, a hotel across the street from the Capitol, was run by a U.S. president's grandson, John W. Jefferson (1835–1892), in the late 1850s. John led Wisconsin's 8th Infantry during the Civil War. In 2000, DNA research confirmed that Eston, John's father, was very likely the son of President Thomas Jefferson and his slave Sally Hemmings. After moving to Wisconsin, Eston added Jefferson to his name. The entire Eston Hemmings family is buried in Madison's Forest Hill Cemetery.

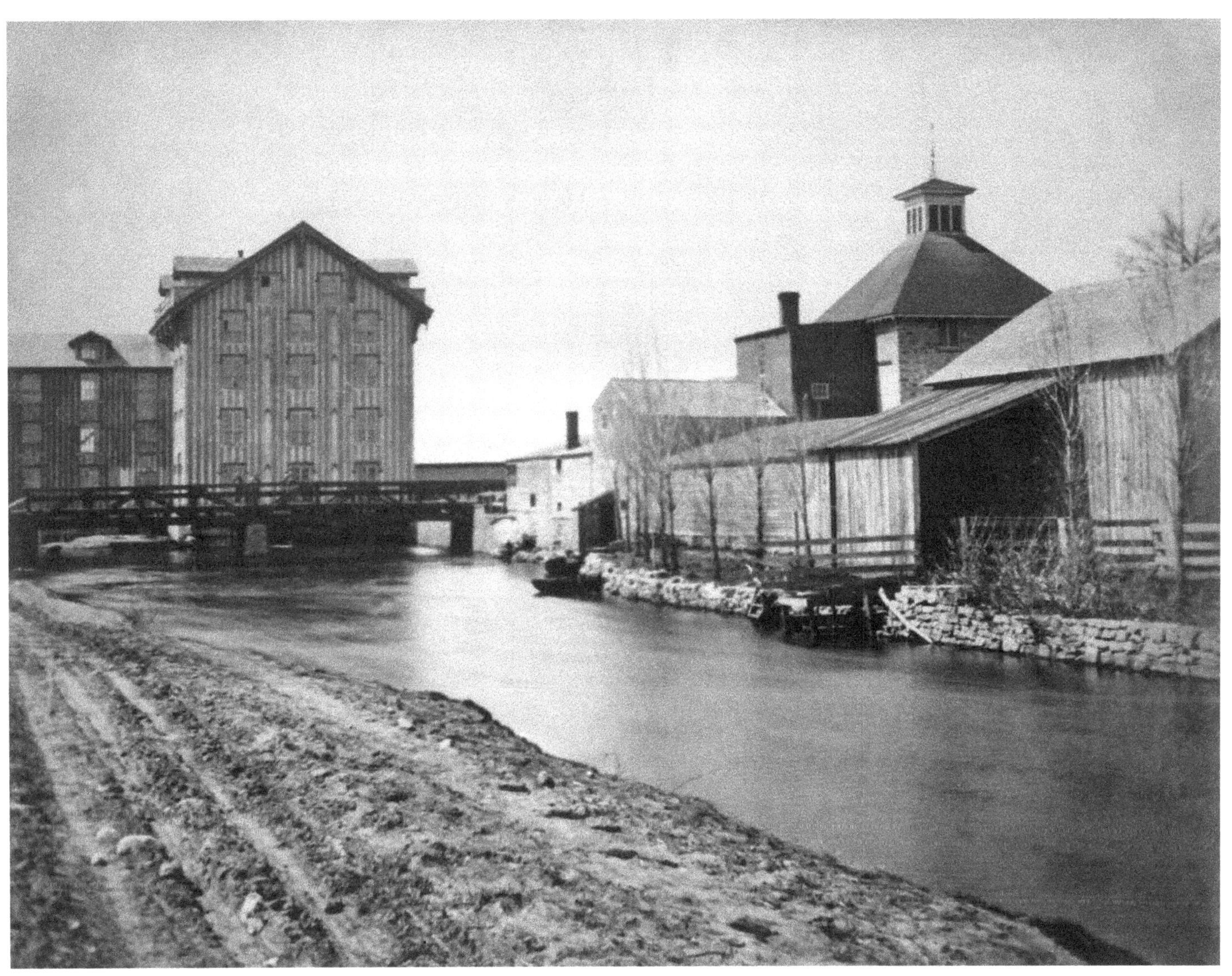

Farwell's Mill, also known as Madison Mills, was established when Leonard J. Farwell (Wisconsin's second governor from 1852 to 1854) straightened the Catfish (Yahara) River and established the mill at the mouth of the river on Fourth (Mendota) Lake. It was described as the best flour mill in the state by the *Wisconsin Gazetteer* in 1853.

Although partly blocked by the U.S. Post Office, the third Wisconsin Capitol can be seen center-left in this 1870s view from the William F. Vilas House on the corner of Wisconsin Avenue and East Gilman.

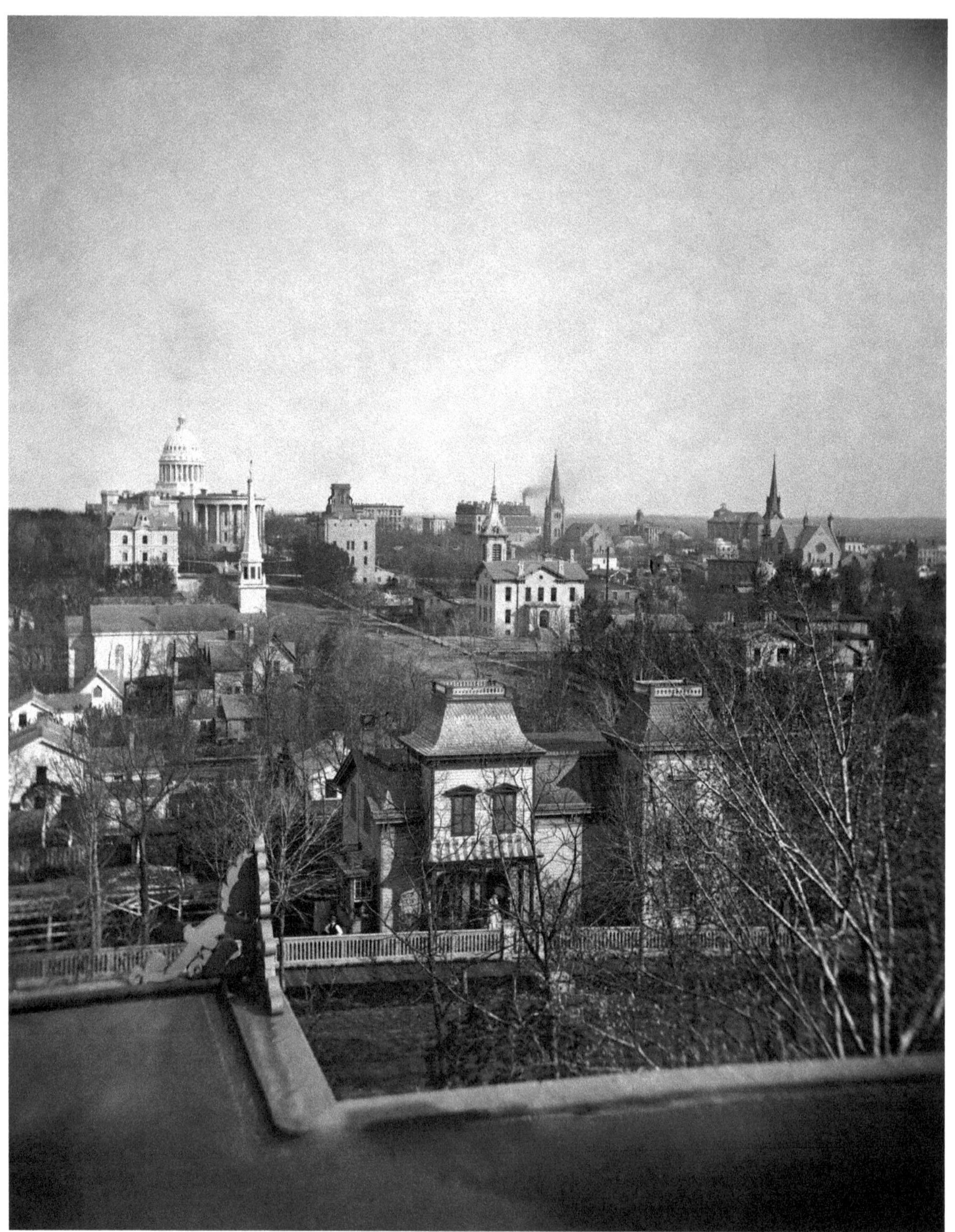

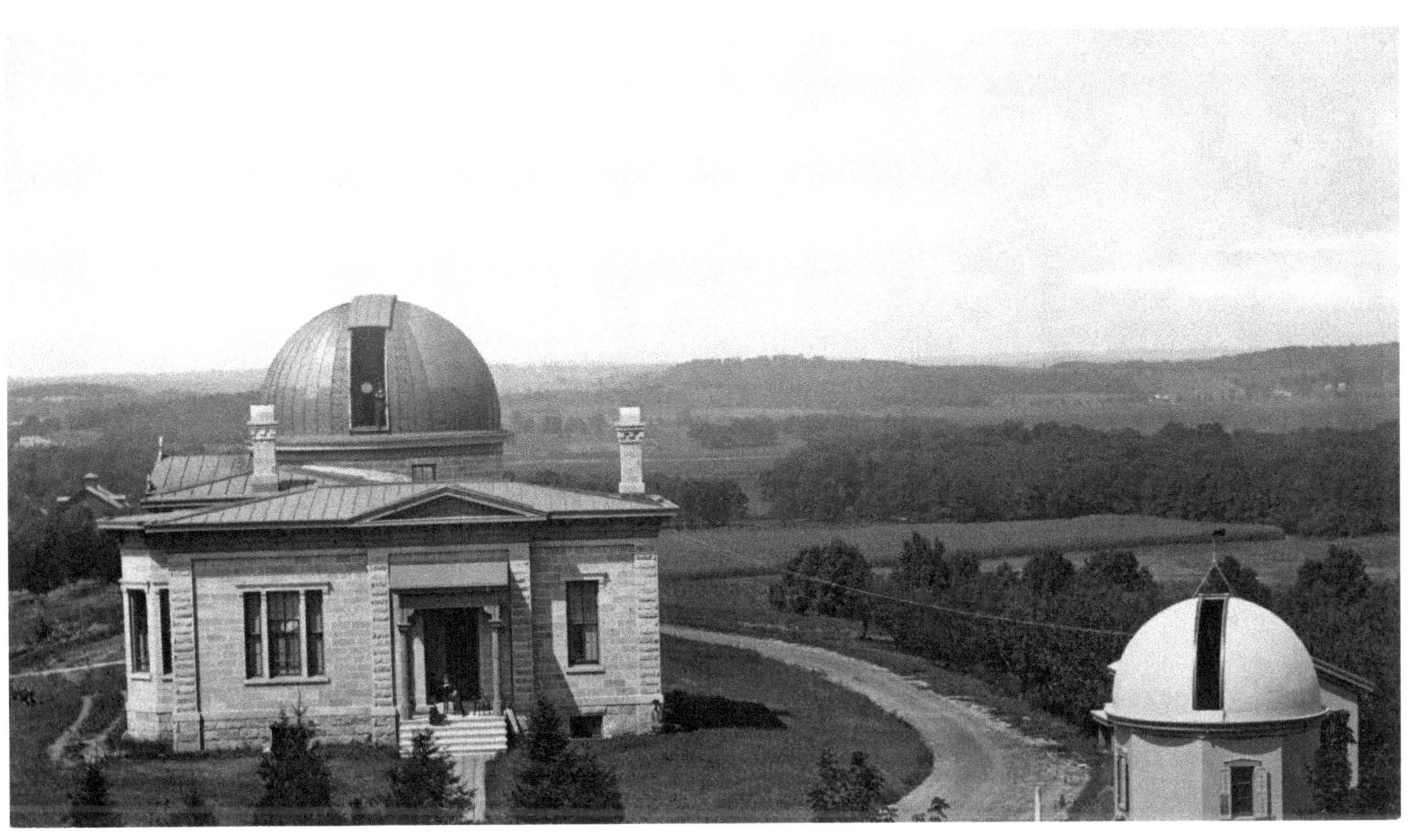

The Washburn Observatory, completed in 1881, was named for Wisconsin governor Cadwallader C. Washburn, who allocated the funds—$3,000 a year for three years—around one-seventh of the university's state-funded budget. At the time, the 15.6-inch diameter telescope was the third largest in the United States.

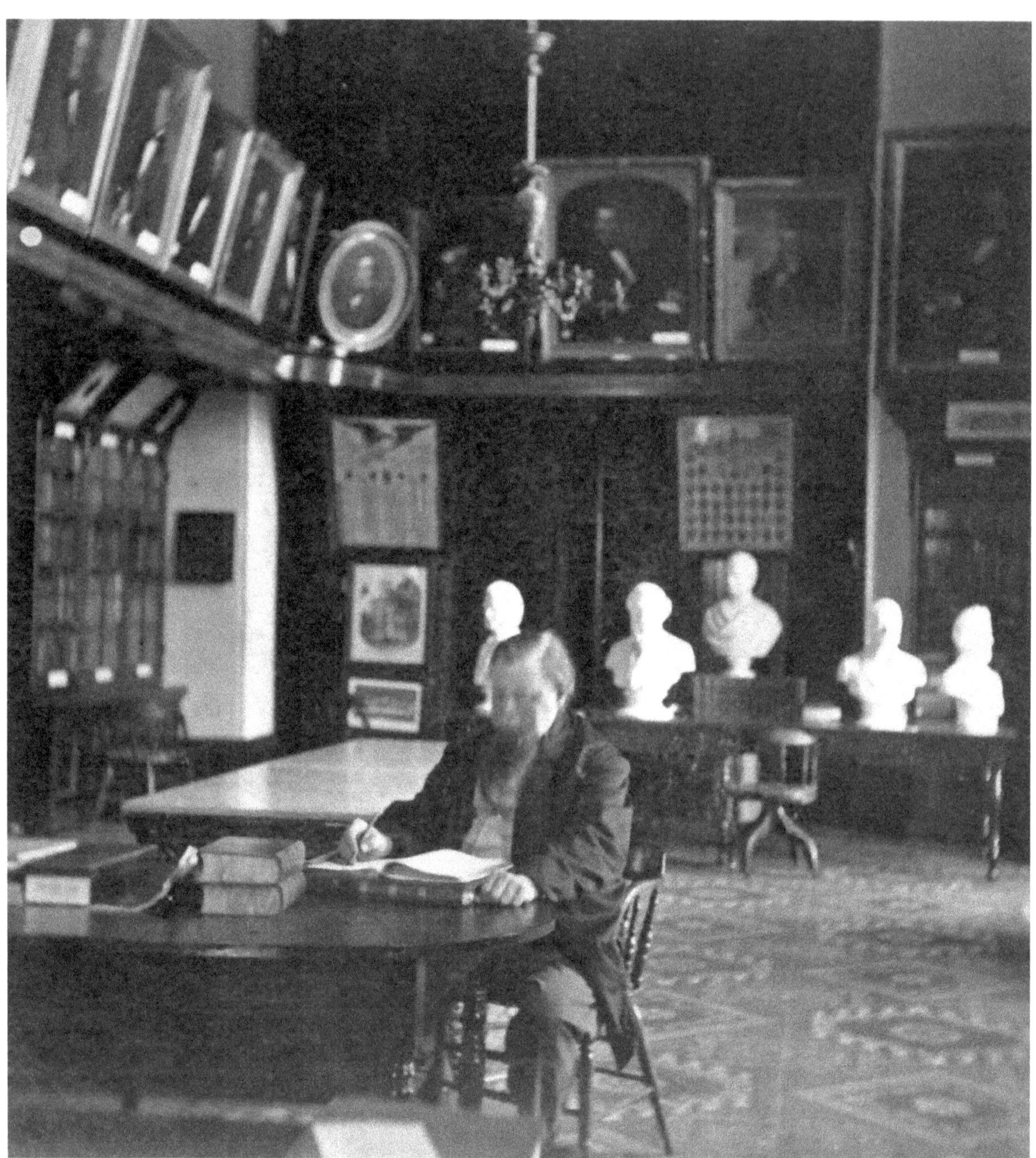

The Wisconsin Historical Society occupied this two-story room in the South Wing of the third Capitol as well as the entire second floor of the South Wing from 1866 to 1883. In 1900 the Historical Society moved to a building on State Street, presciently citing the need for additional space and fireproof quarters. Four years later, all but the North Wing of the Capitol burned down after a gas jet ignited the newly varnished Capitol ceiling.

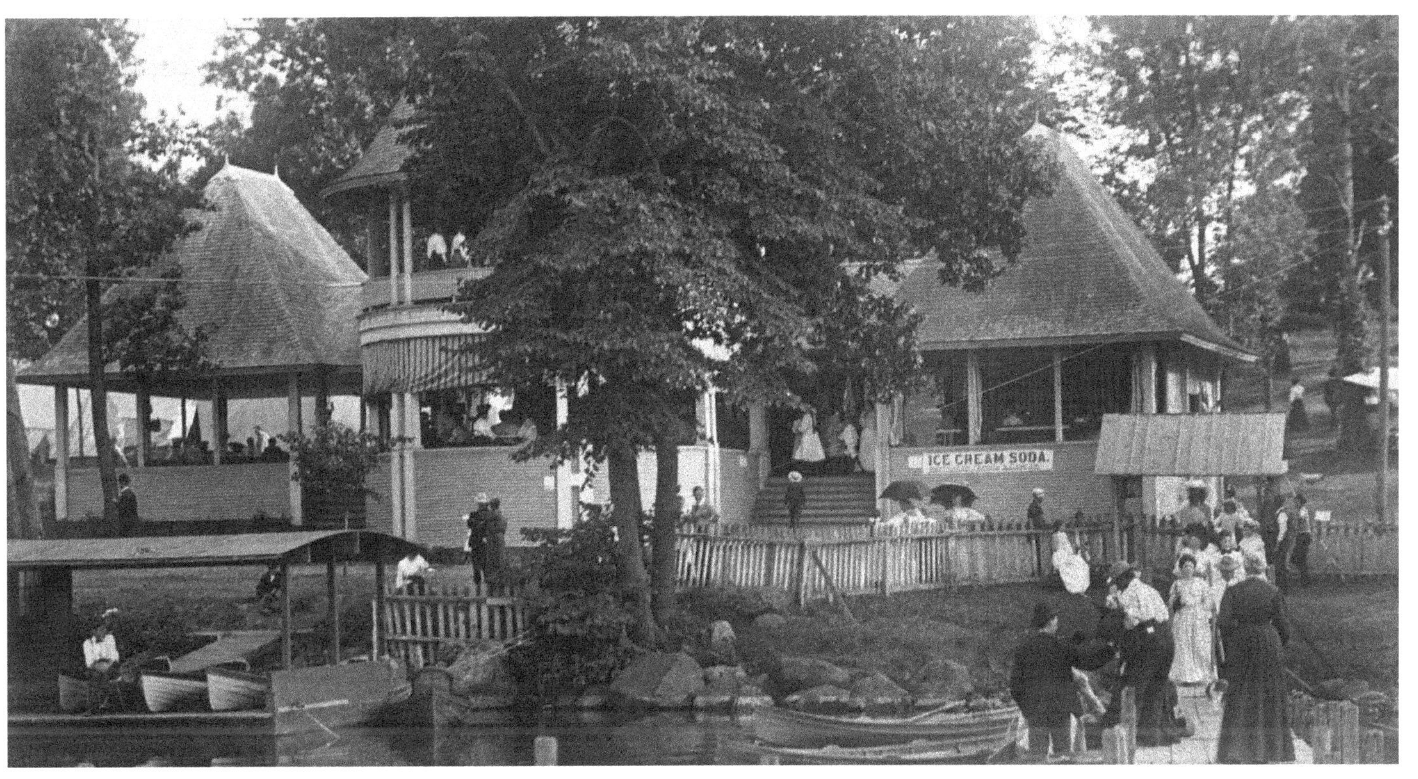

At Chautauqua, a lakeside town in southwestern New York, an outdoor summertime gathering to train Sunday school teachers rose to popularity. In Madison, Monona Lake Assembly began what became a well-known "Chautauqua of the West." The highly popular two-week programs of lectures and concerts started in 1881 and ran for nearly thirty years. James E. Moseley, founder of a bookstore on Pinckney Street, became a driving force as the "father of the Assembly." After the Assembly's popularity declined, the city purchased the land, which has since become Olin-Turville Park.

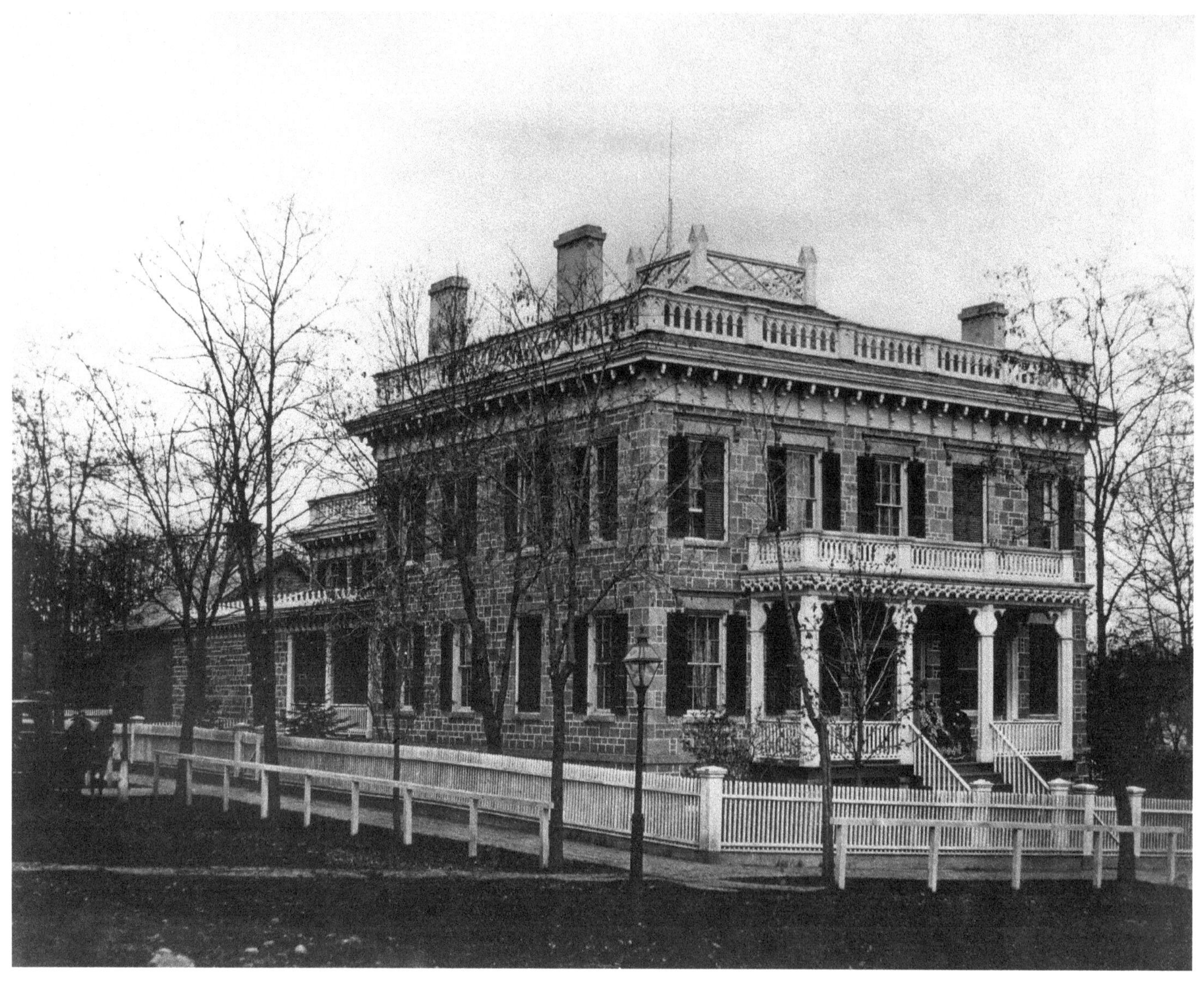

The Levi Vilas House was built in 1853 at the corner of Henry and Langdon streets after Vilas brought his family and his fortune to Wisconsin in 1851. He established a law practice, invested heavily in Madison real estate, and became the first president of the Dane County Bank, later First National Bank. He also continued his political career, was mayor of Madison, served in the state assembly, and was a regent of the University of Wisconsin. His son was U.S. Senator William F. Vilas.

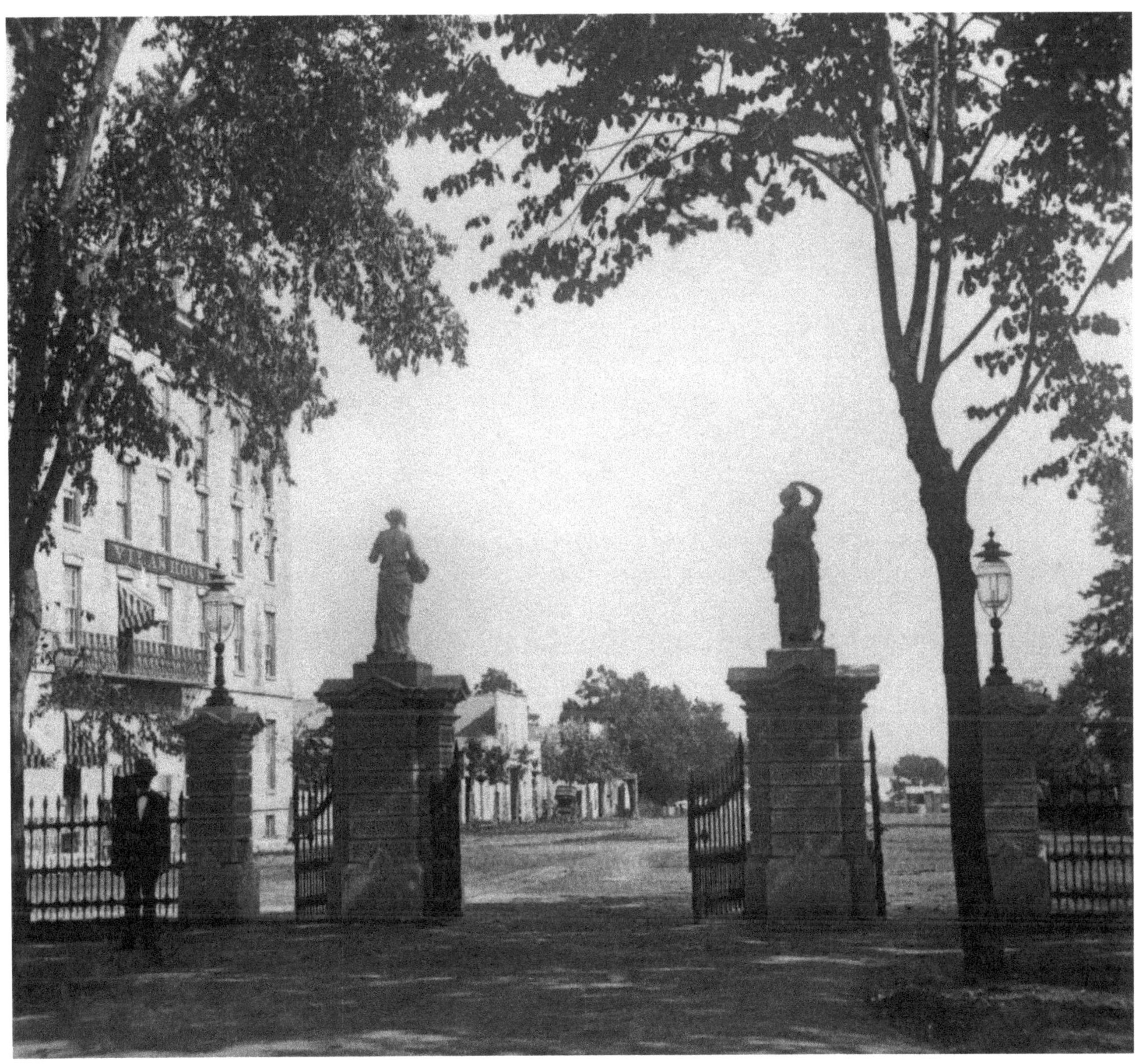

An iron fence with gates, as seen here, surrounded the Capitol grounds from 1873 until 1899, when Governor Edward Scofield had it removed. Part of that fence now stands at the entrance of the Governor's Mansion in Maple Bluff on Lake Mendota.

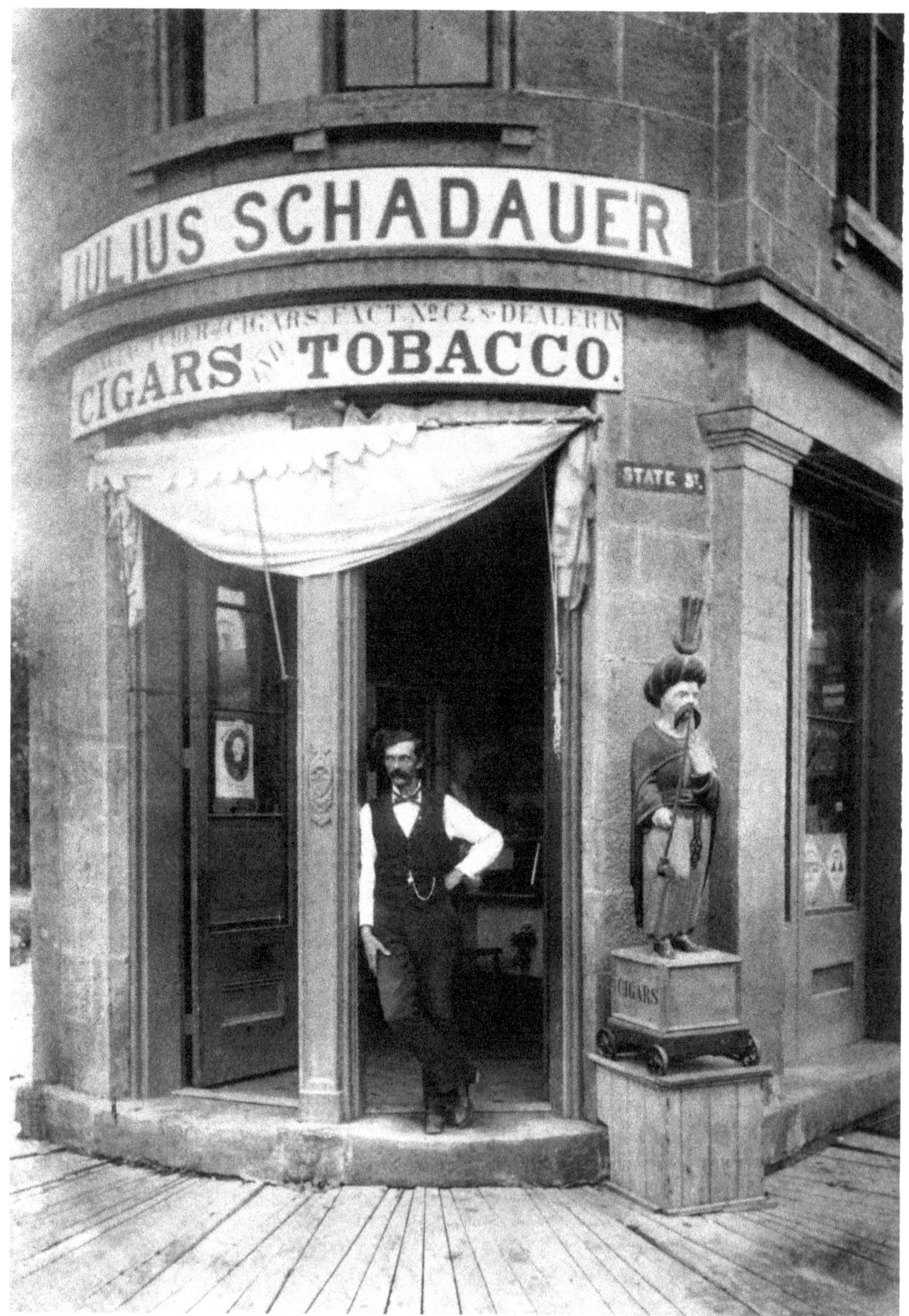

A man poses in the doorway of Julius Schadauer's tobacco shop at 101 State Street in 1880. The triangular building pointing at the Capitol Square was constructed in 1855 by Stephen Vaughn Shipman, designer of the third Capitol dome, using stone transported by horse from quarries in the Town of Westport. Now known as the Caputo-Milsted building, it has been recognized by the Madison Trust for Historic Preservation.

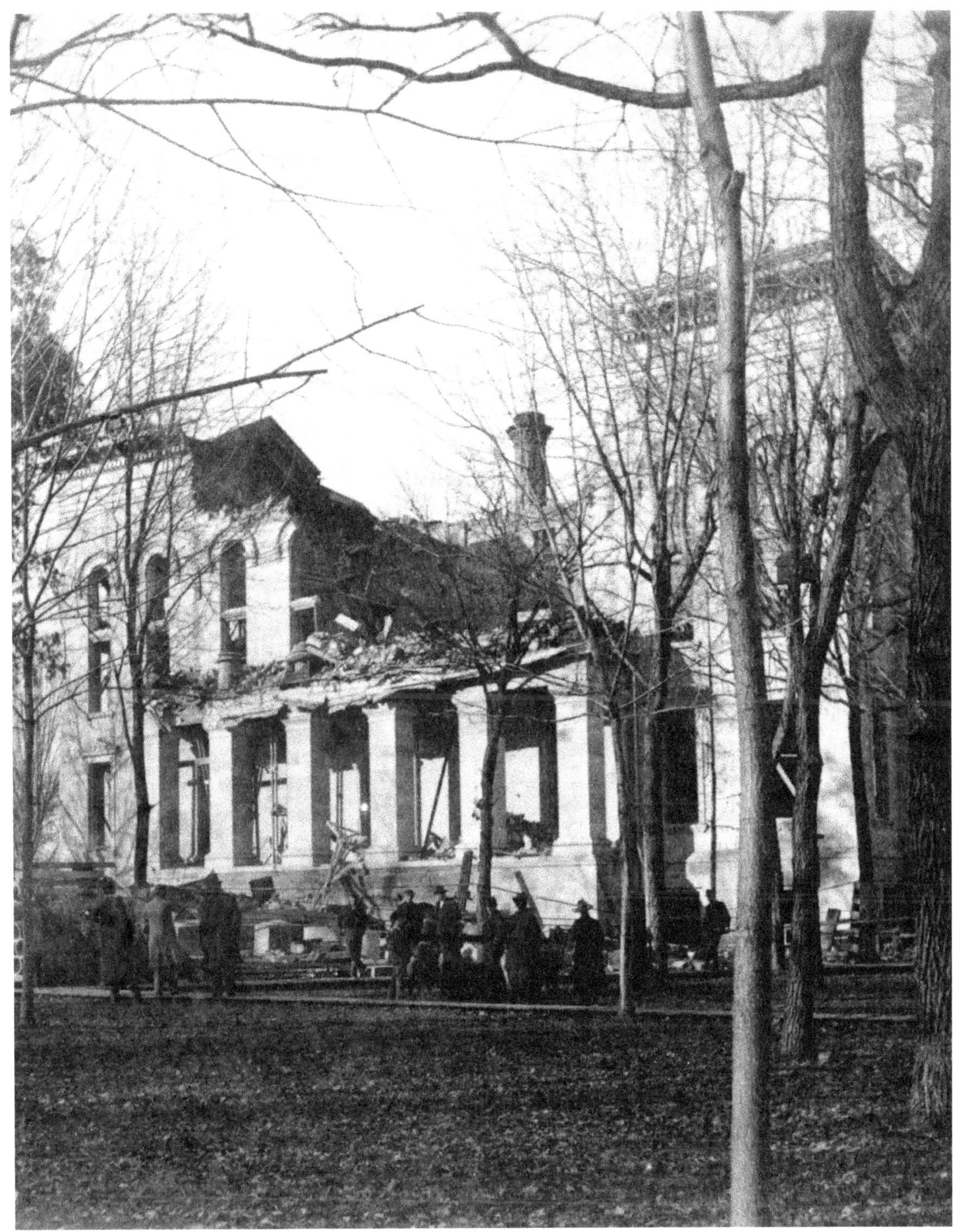

The nearly finished South Wing of the third Wisconsin State Capitol collapsed during construction in 1883, killing six workers and injuring twenty others. Since Madison did not have a hospital, the wounded and dying were carried to offices of the governor, the insurance commissioner, and the quartermaster general, or to their own homes. Shoddy construction was blamed, creating a scandal and public investigation. World-renowned architect Frank Lloyd Wright witnessed the collapse as a schoolboy and recalled it in his autobiography.

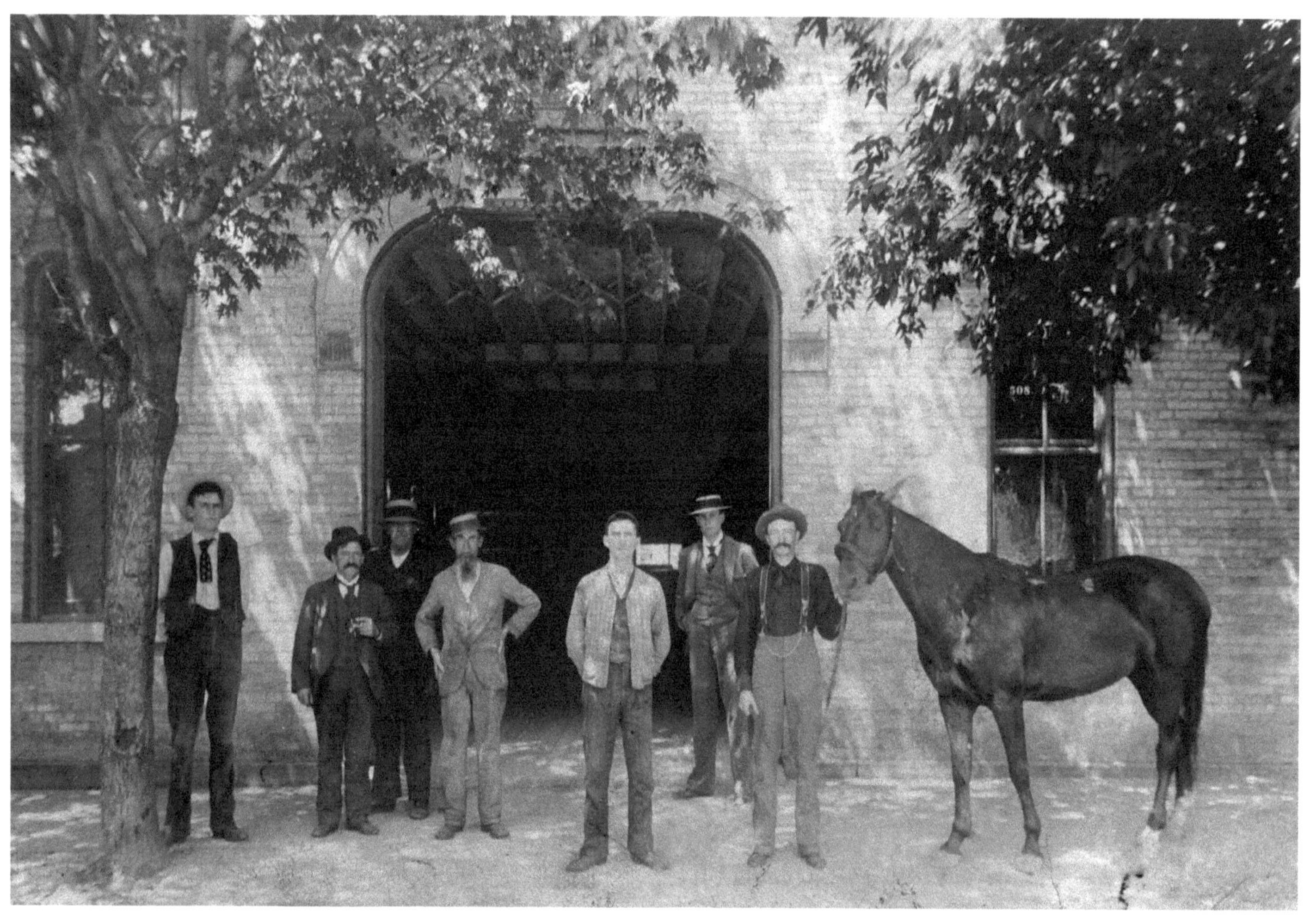

In 1883, John Hess and Froderick Schmitz stand with horse at the entrance to 508 State Street, now the location of Nadia's French restaurant and a popular music store called the Exclusive Company.

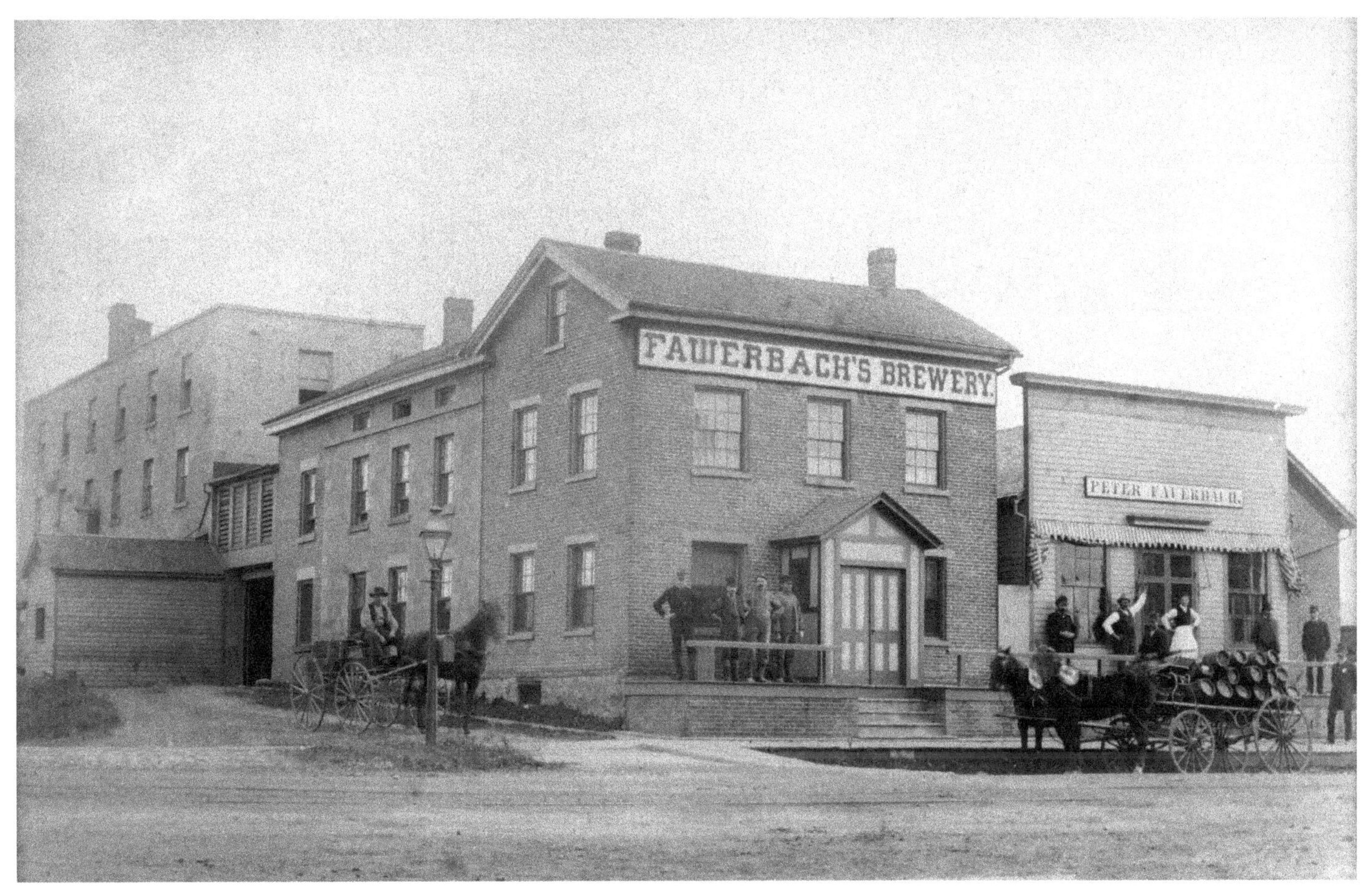

Fauerbach's Brewery at 651-3 Williamson Street, shown here in 1885, was founded in 1848. The brewery, sitting on the shore of Third Lake (Monona), was a popular launching site for the excursion steamboat trade that took customers to picnic spots along the lakeshores. The brewery also maintained an ice house on the shore, from the company's founding to 1917.

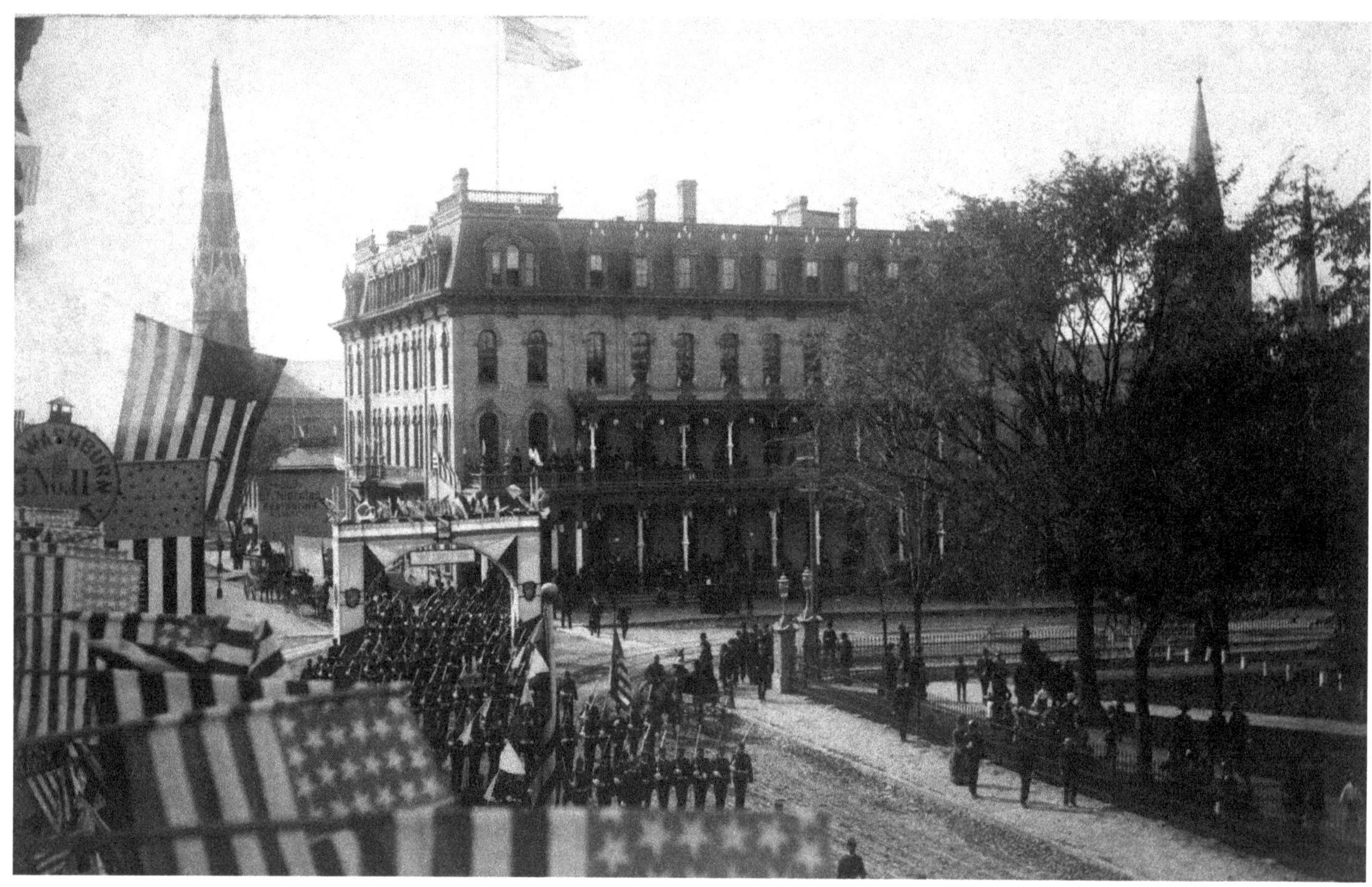

President Grover Cleveland, the only U.S. president to serve two non-consecutive terms, visited Madison October 7-9, 1887, during his first term before being unseated by Benjamin Harrison the following year. He was a personal friend of Madisonian William F. Vilas, a leader in the Democratic Party, who served in Cleveland's cabinet first as postmaster general and later as secretary of the interior. The Park Hotel, the Capitol Park, and the steeple of St. Raphael's Catholic Church are visible. Soldiers of the University Battalion are marching along Main Street on their way to meet Cleveland.

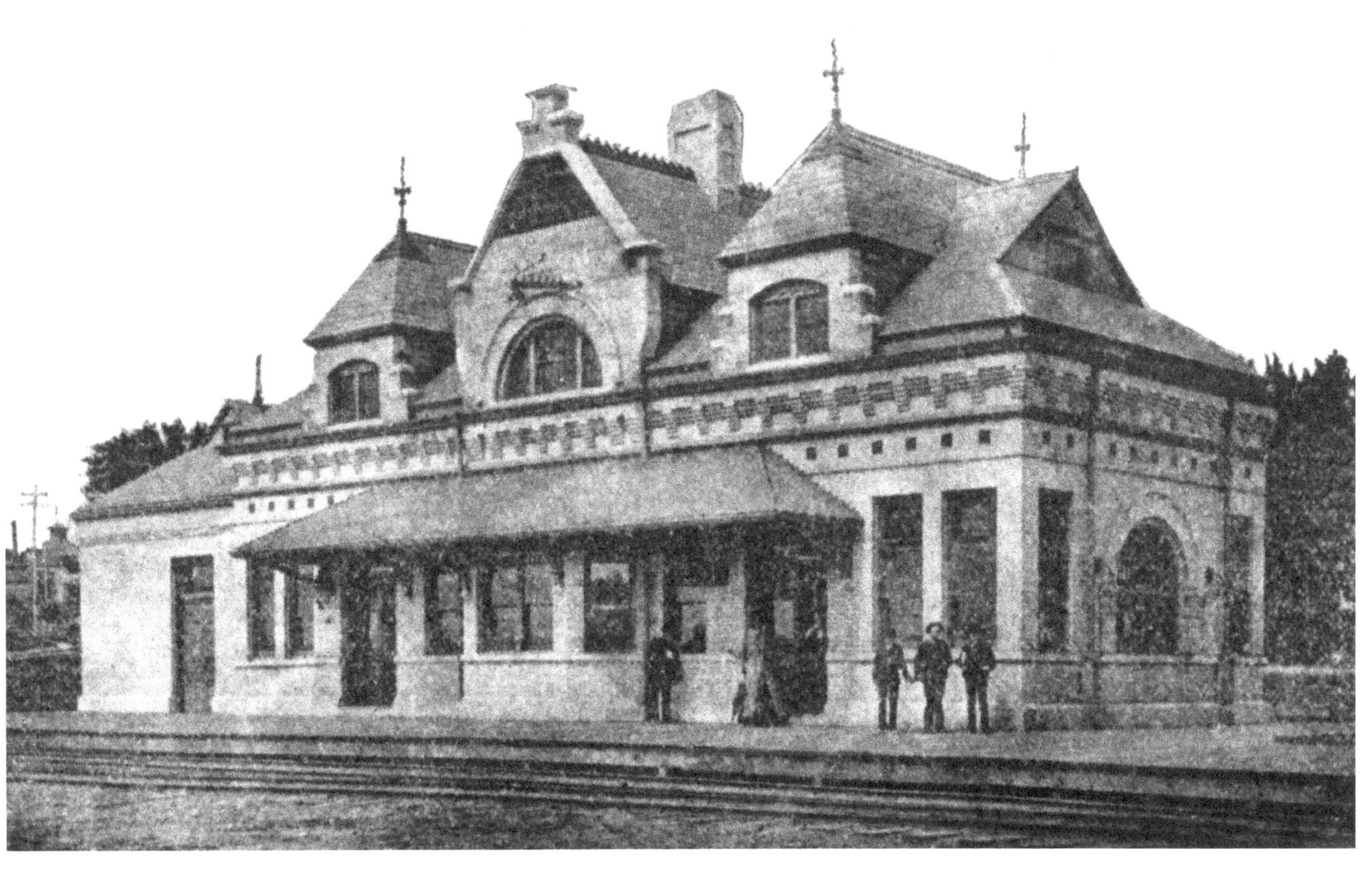

At one time Madison had six railroad stations. Shown here in 1889 is the Milwaukee Road's Franklin Street station on East Wilson Street.

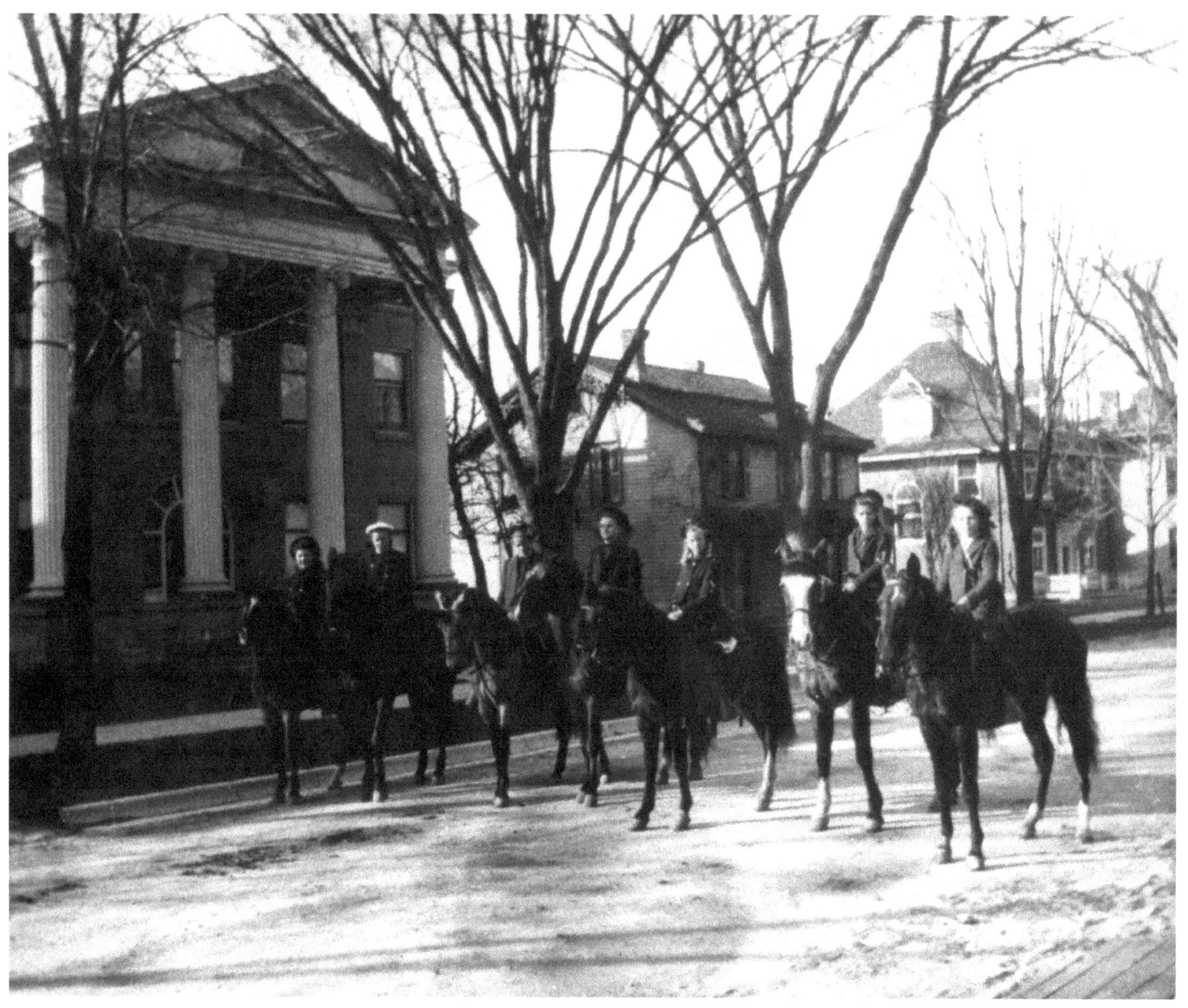

The Riding Club poses in the 1890s on Langdon Street near Wisconsin Avenue. Riders include Elizabeth Proudfit, Mary Conklin, Mary Brown, Margaret Head, Catherine Brandenburg, Eleanore Brown, and Catherine Trobridge.

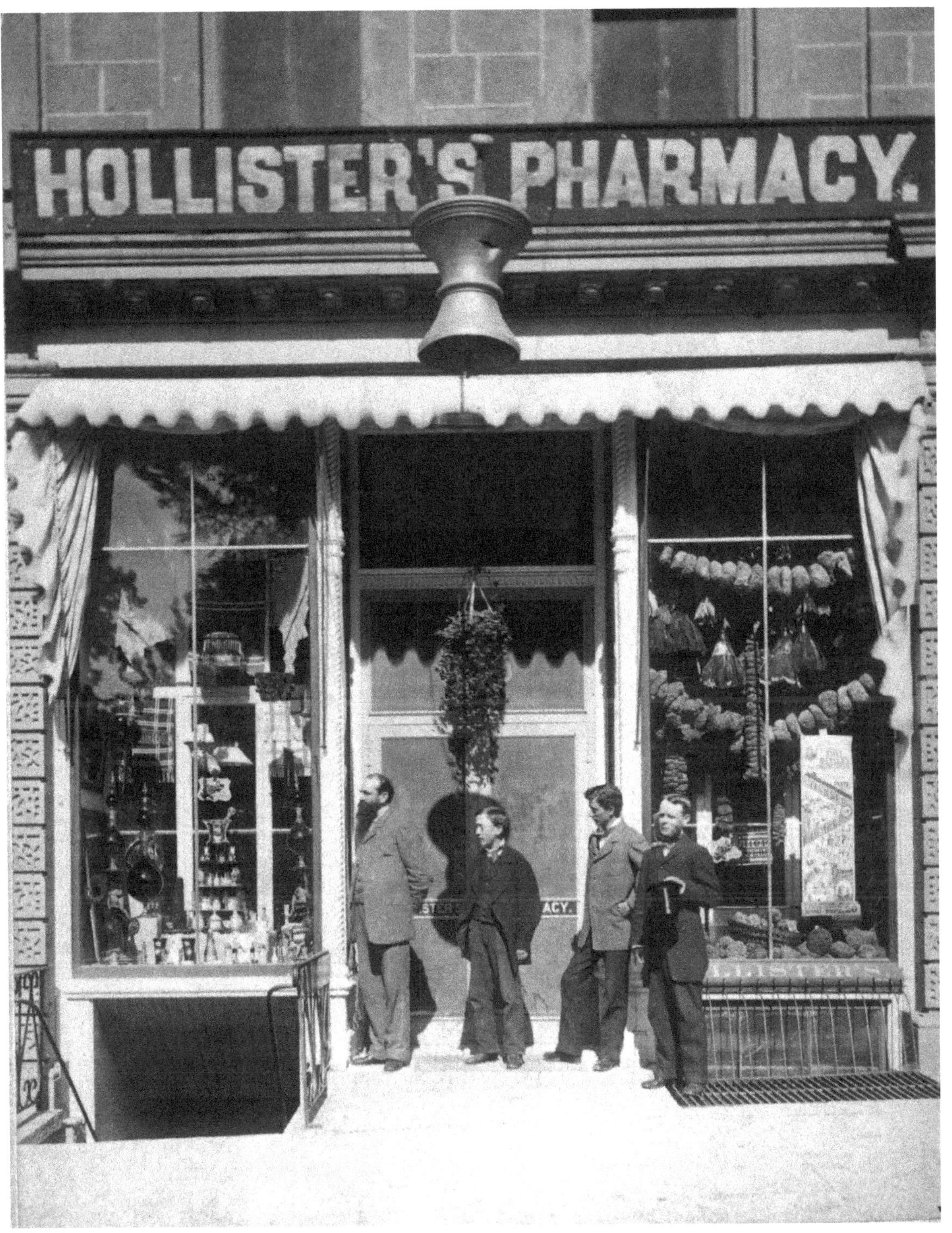

Albert H. Hollister (1843–1910), the man with the long beard, is shown in front of his pharmacy on 3 North Pinckney Street. The children are unidentified. Hollister first opened a pharmacy in 1876. Through his research in the Rocky Mountains on the medicinal properties of various herbs, he formulated a popular "Rocky Mountain Tea," advertised as a "tonic necessary for the maintenance of a clean, vigorous body." His will established the Hollister Pharmaceutical Library Fund for publishing pharmaceutico-historical publications, the only such fund in the United States devoted exclusively to that purpose.

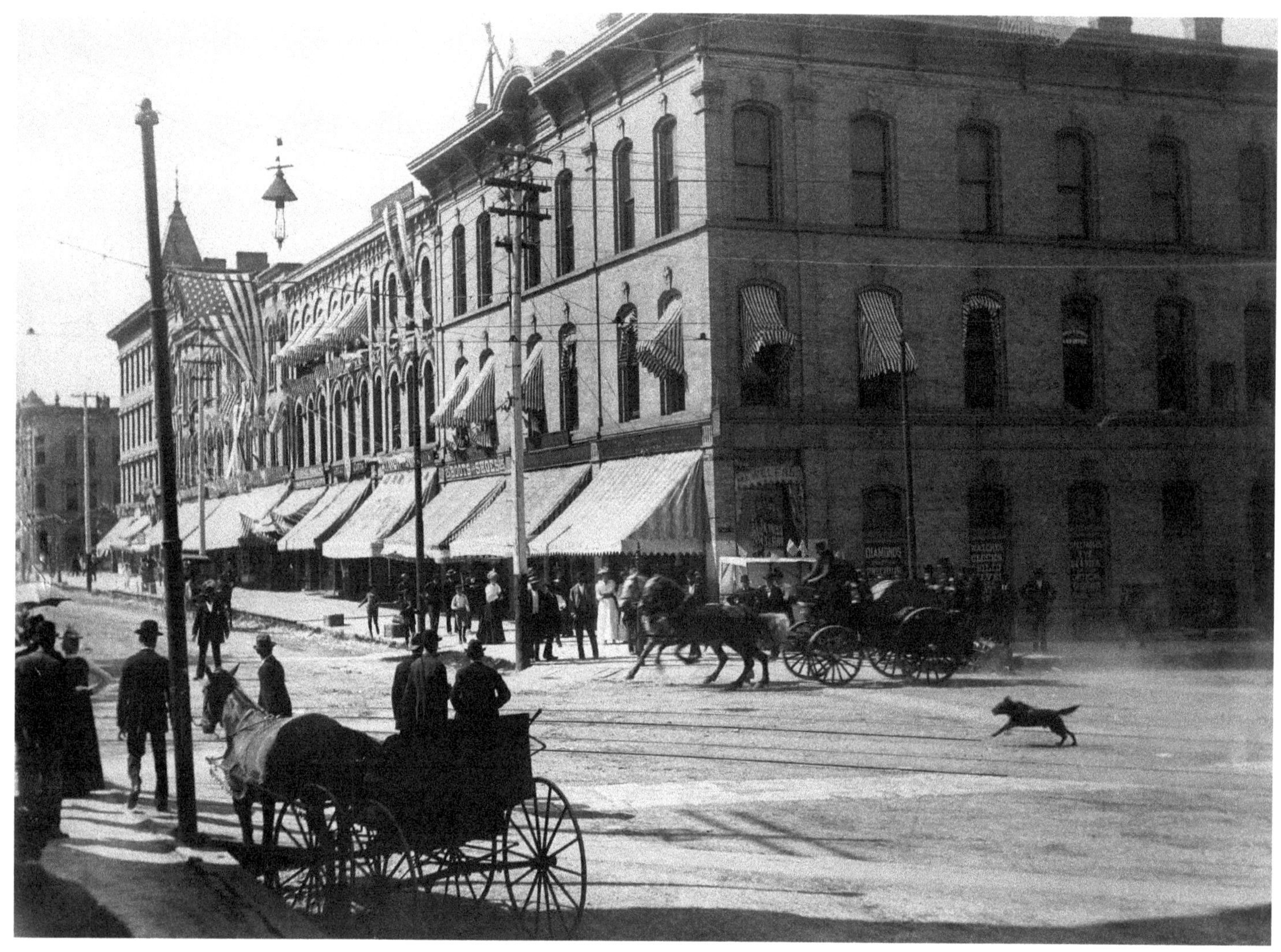

Amateur photographer William Oppel, a Madison grocer, took this rare action photo of nineteenth-century fire fighting. A hose wagon of the Madison fire department races around the corner of North Pinckney and East Main streets. Oppel was also an officer of Relief Company No. 2 (originally Fire Company No. 2).

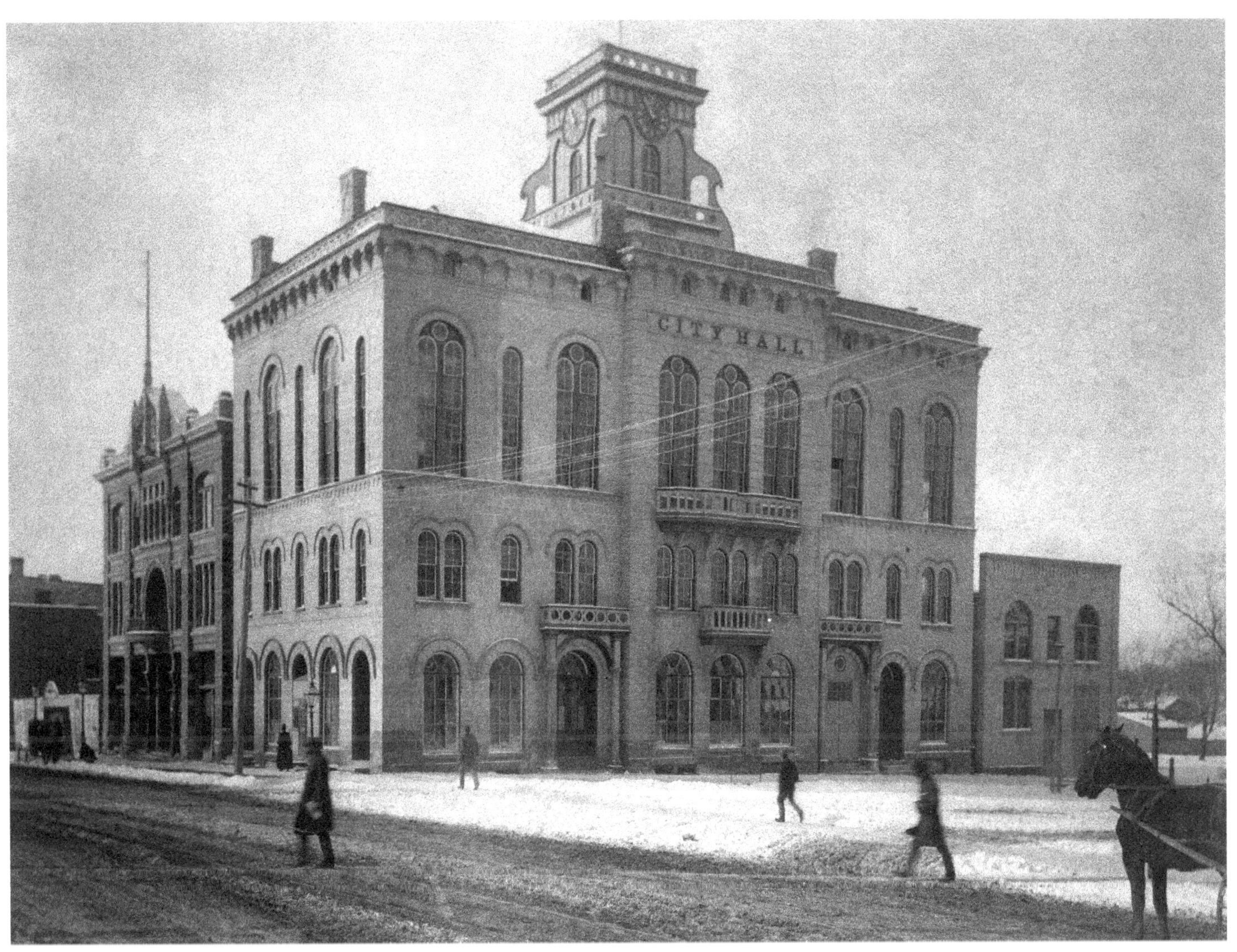

When the City Hall opened at the corner of Mifflin Street and Wisconsin Avenue in 1858, Mayor George B. Smith called it an "edifice which is an ornament to the city." The three-story building was designed by August Kutzboch, who with Samuel Donnel, also designed the second state Capitol in Madison. The third floor was a public auditorium. Behind it stands the Fuller Opera House on Mifflin Street, which opened in 1890. Both buildings were leveled in 1954 to make way for a Woolworth's.

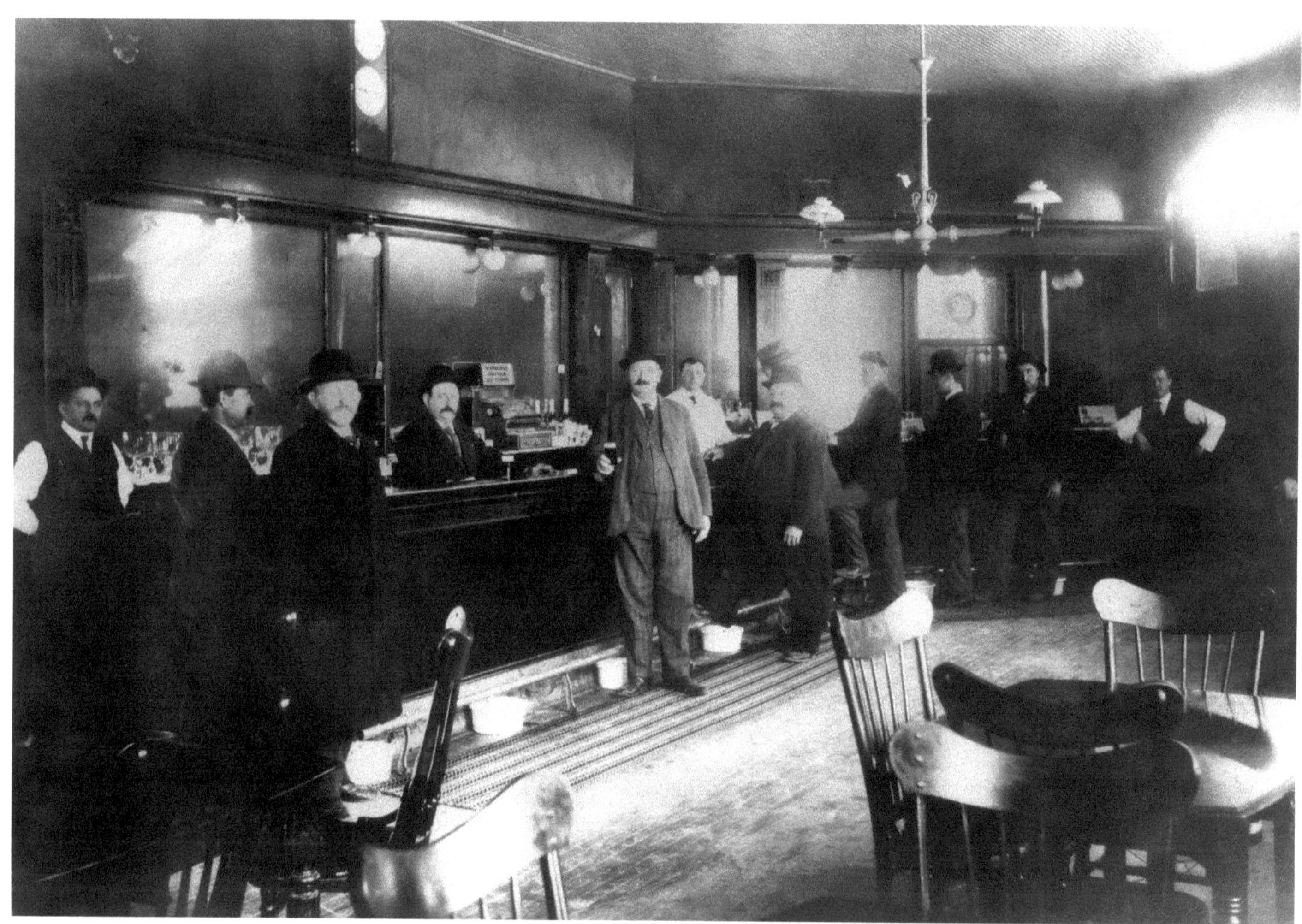

Only men are present in this photograph of the Hausmann Brewery Bar about 1895. The sign behind the bar reads "No intoxicating drinks sold to minors." The brewery opened in 1854. By the mid 1880s, Hausmann, located at the corner of State and West Gorham streets, was the largest brewery in Madison, producing nearly 6,000 barrels of beer a year. The saloon attached to the brewery was a favorite spot for Civil War soldiers, townspeople, legislators, university professors, and students. Lunch was free, and beer was 5 cents a glass. Before Prohibition, production had reached 1 million gallons a year. During a sub-zero blizzard on March 19, 1923, a blaze raced through the brewery wiping out the establishment that had served the city for nearly three-quarters of a century.

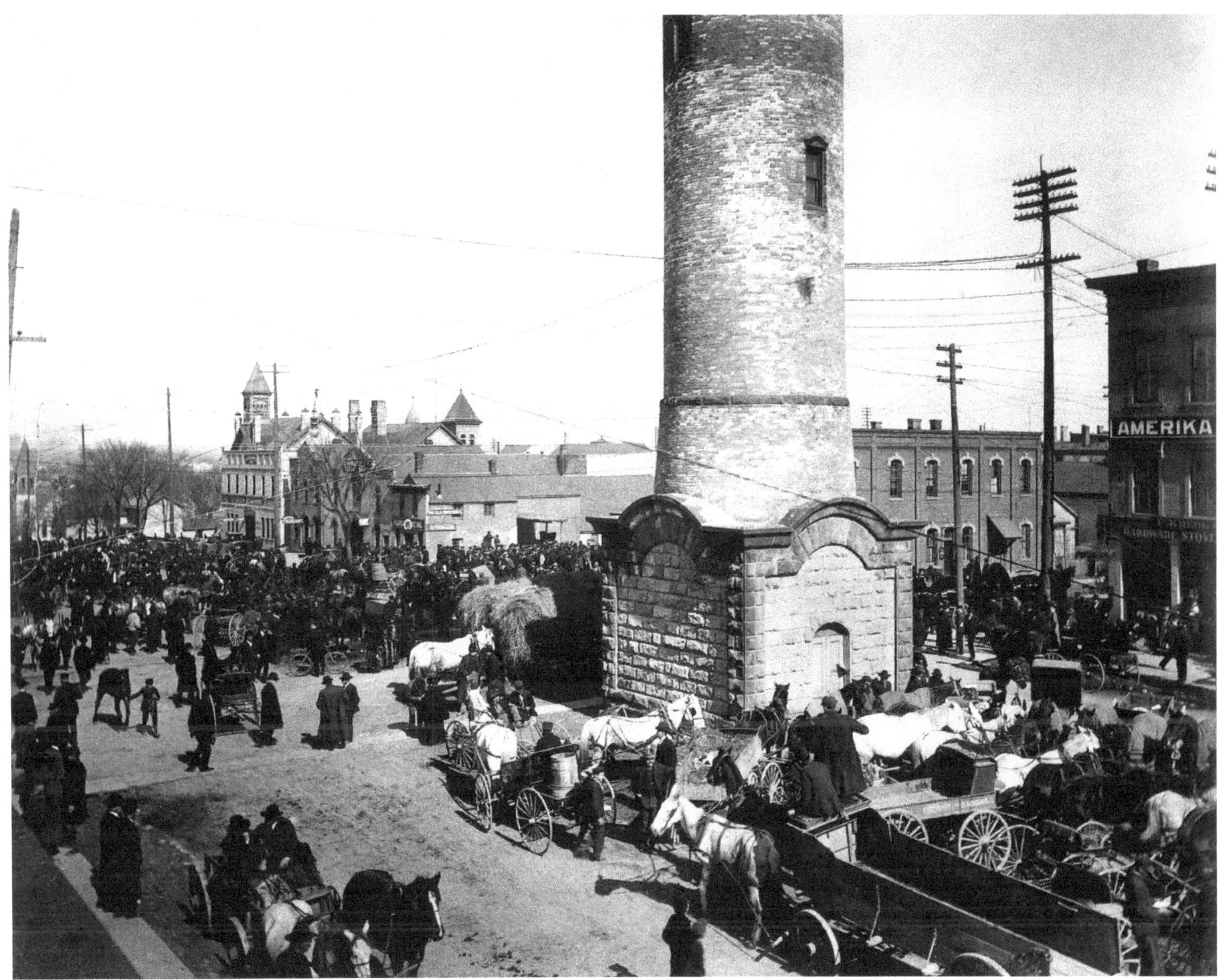

In 1889 the city built its first brick water tower. The following year, the Water Tower Horse Market opened on the first two blocks of East Washington Avenue, where a monthly horse market was held. In the background behind the 125-foot-tall tower stands the office of the prominent newspaper for Americans of Norwegian descent, the *Amerika.* In December 1920, the tower was dismantled.

The funeral for Governor Lucius Fairchild on May 26, 1896, is considered one of the most elaborate ever staged in Wisconsin history. Fairchild, who rose to the rank of colonel, had returned to Madison as a hero of the Civil War, particularly of the Battle of Gettysburg. After his body lay in state in the Capitol, Fairchild was buried at Forest Hill Cemetery.

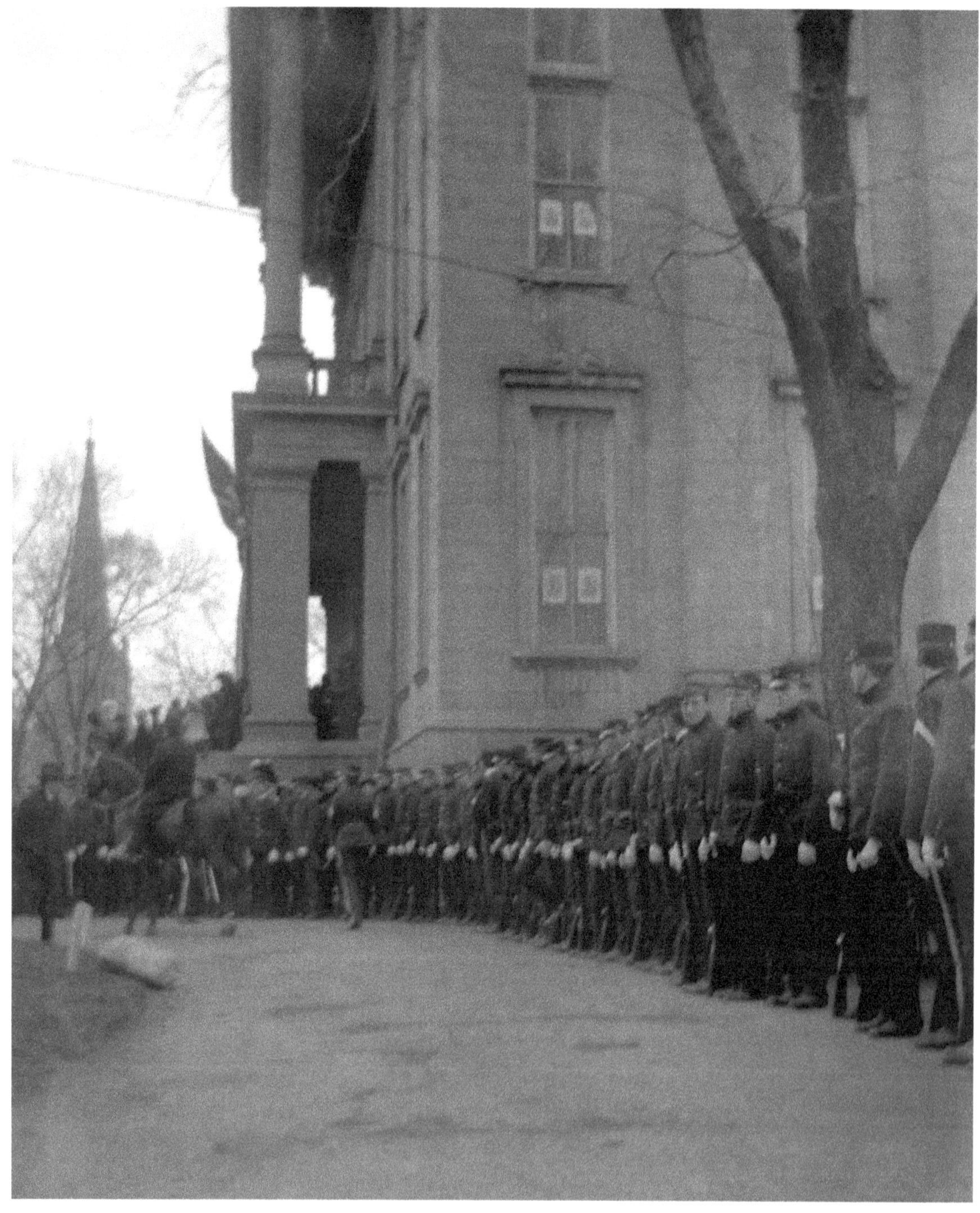

William A. Oppel ran a successful grocery store, seen here in 1896, at 116 East Main Street. His store prospered as the source of provisions for Ladies Hall (later Chadbourne Hall) and for fraternities and sororities at the University of Wisconsin.

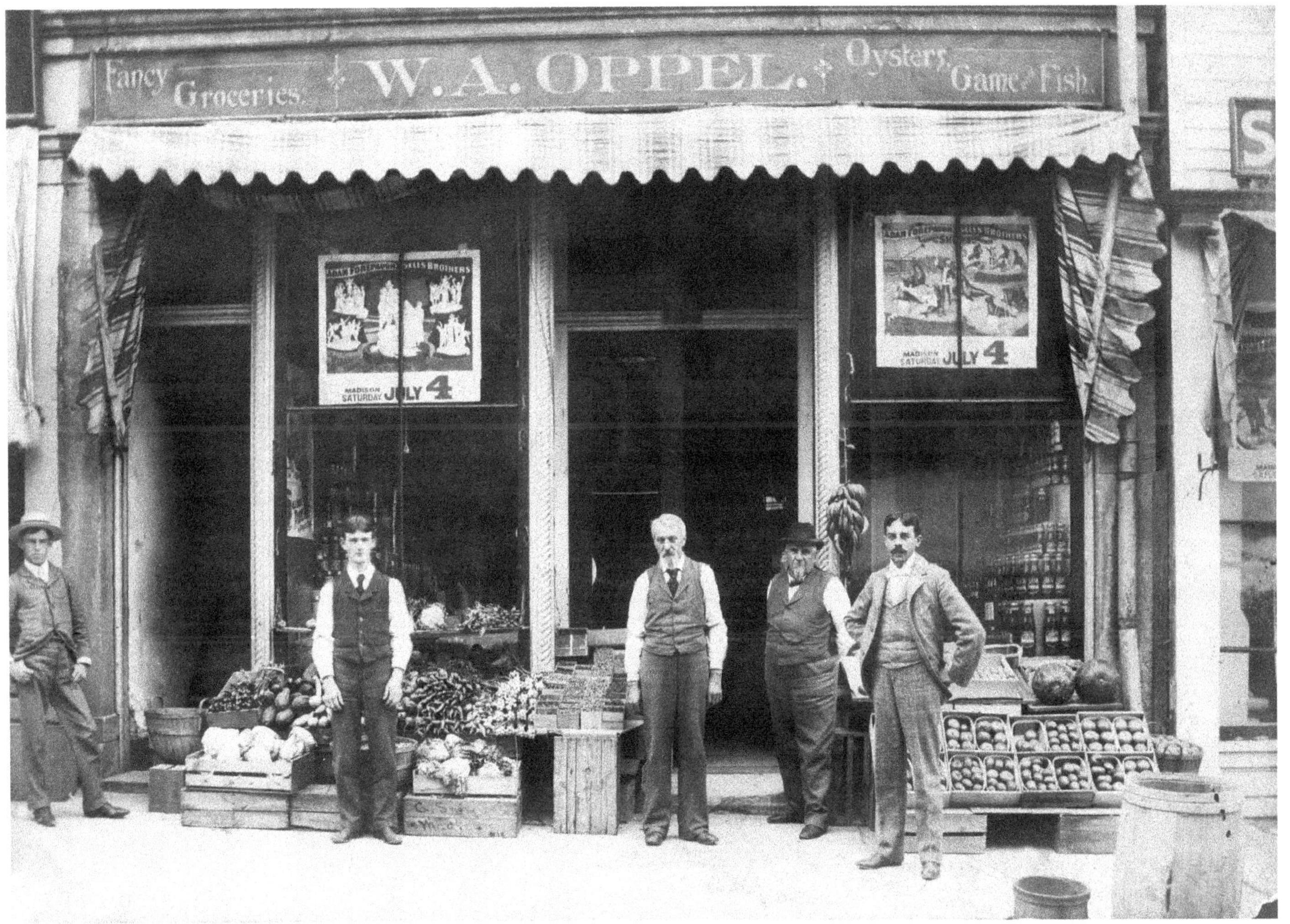

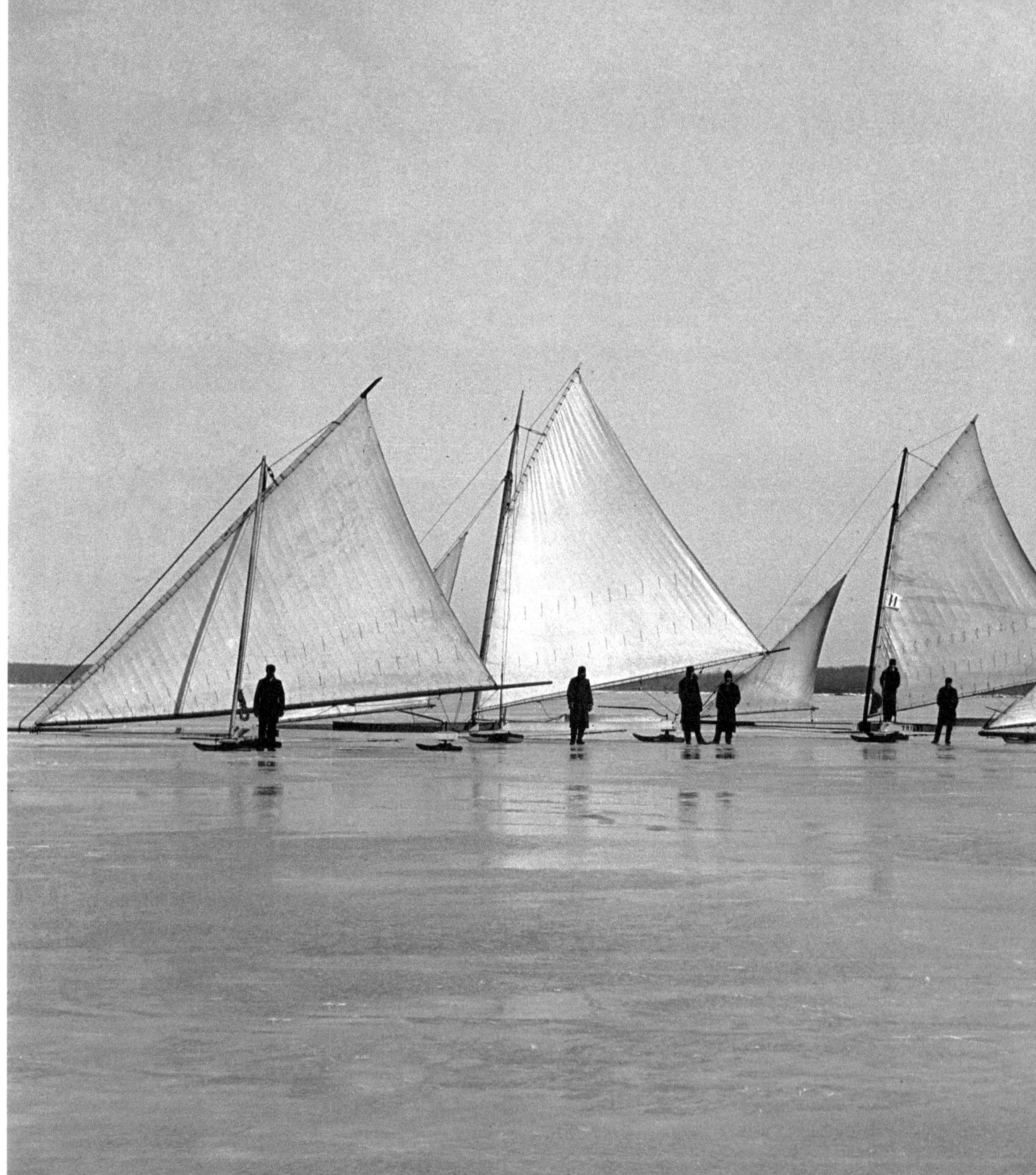
11

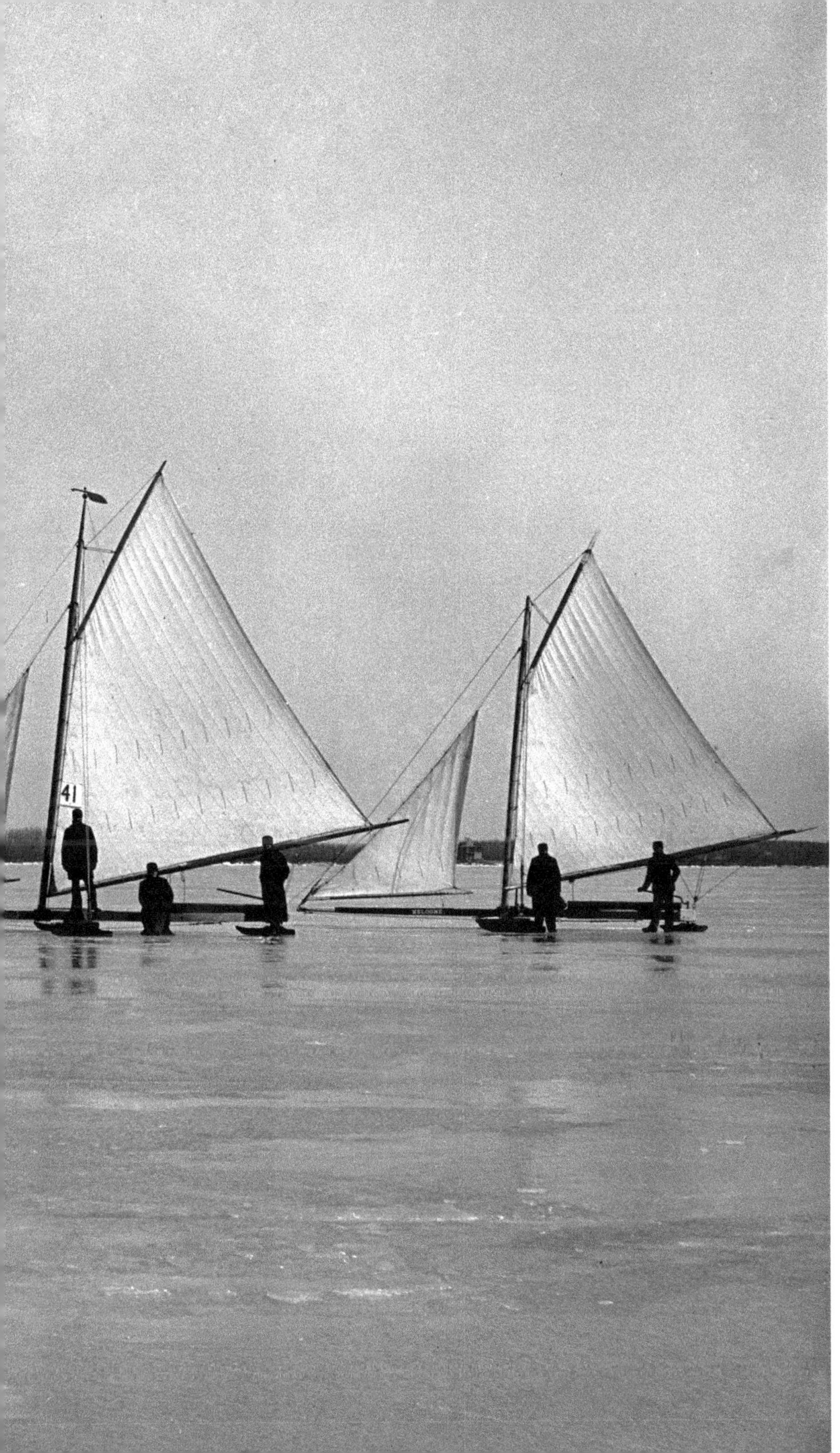

Madison has been one of the nation's centers of iceboating for more than a century. Iceboats on Lake Mendota are captured in this 1896 image. Iceboating began during the Civil War era in the upper Hudson and spread quickly to other cold weather venues. An 1878 *Harper's Weekly* included an engraving of iceboating in Madison. By 1900 more than 200 iceboaters were sailing lakes Mendota and Monona, with an intense rivalry among skippers on each lake.

This 1897 view looks north on Mifflin Street from the Carroll Street intersection on the Capitol Square.

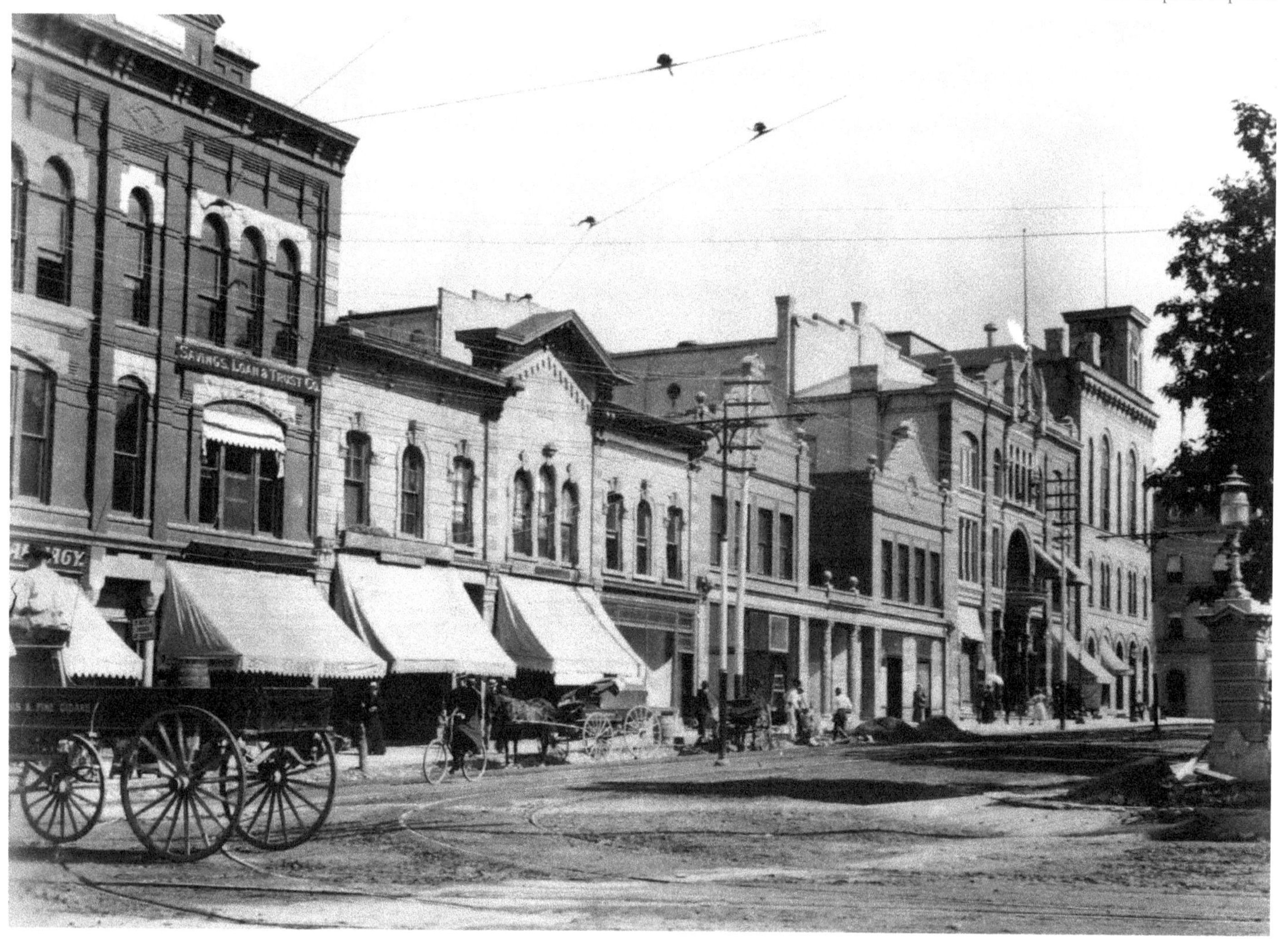

This image, from a group of cyanotype prints, documents the construction of the Wisconsin Historical Society building around 1899. A variation of the cyanotype process is used to create blueprints. The process became popular around 1900 to create a quick initial print, perhaps in a hotel room on location, before returning to a studio to make a final print.

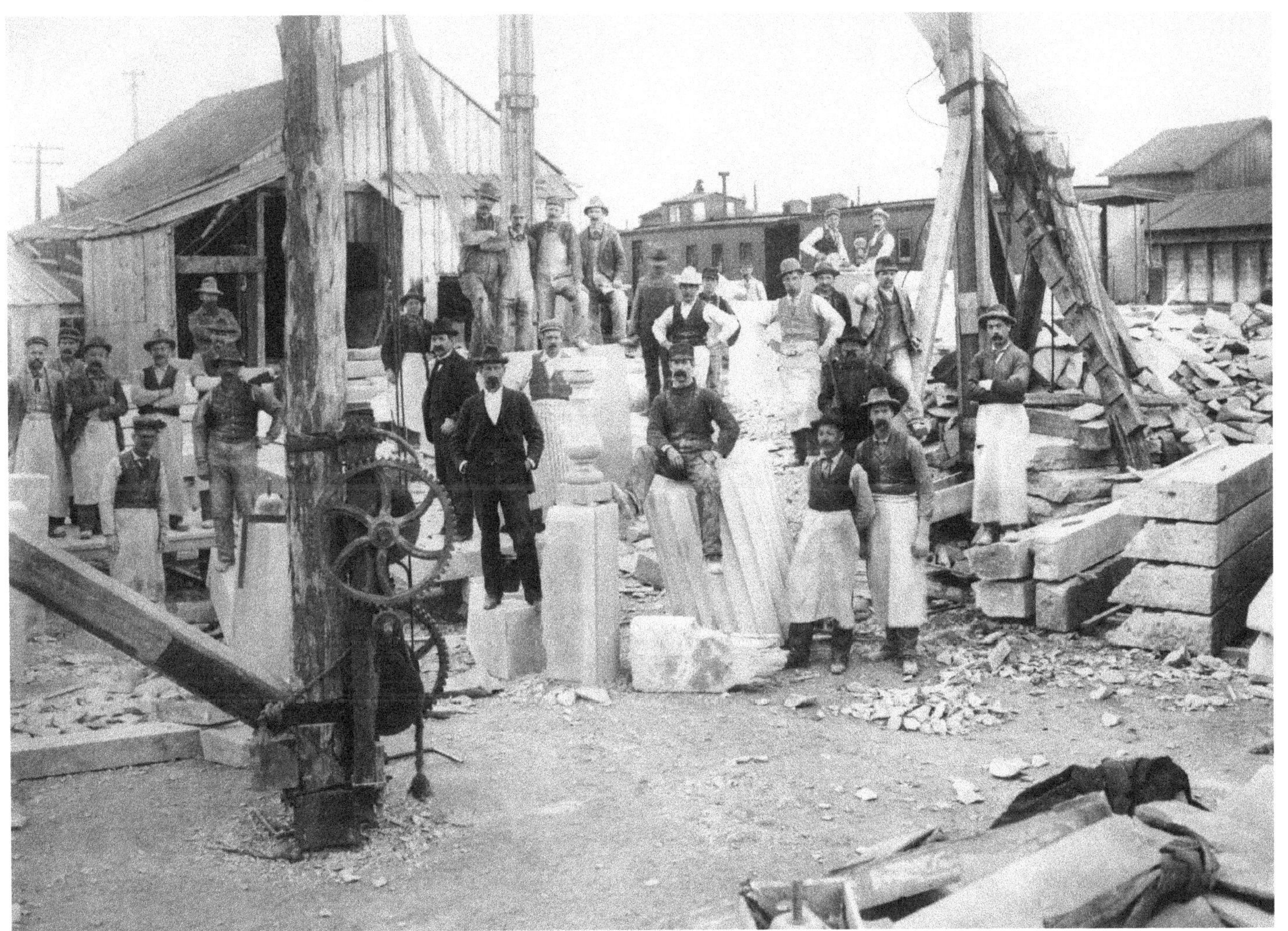

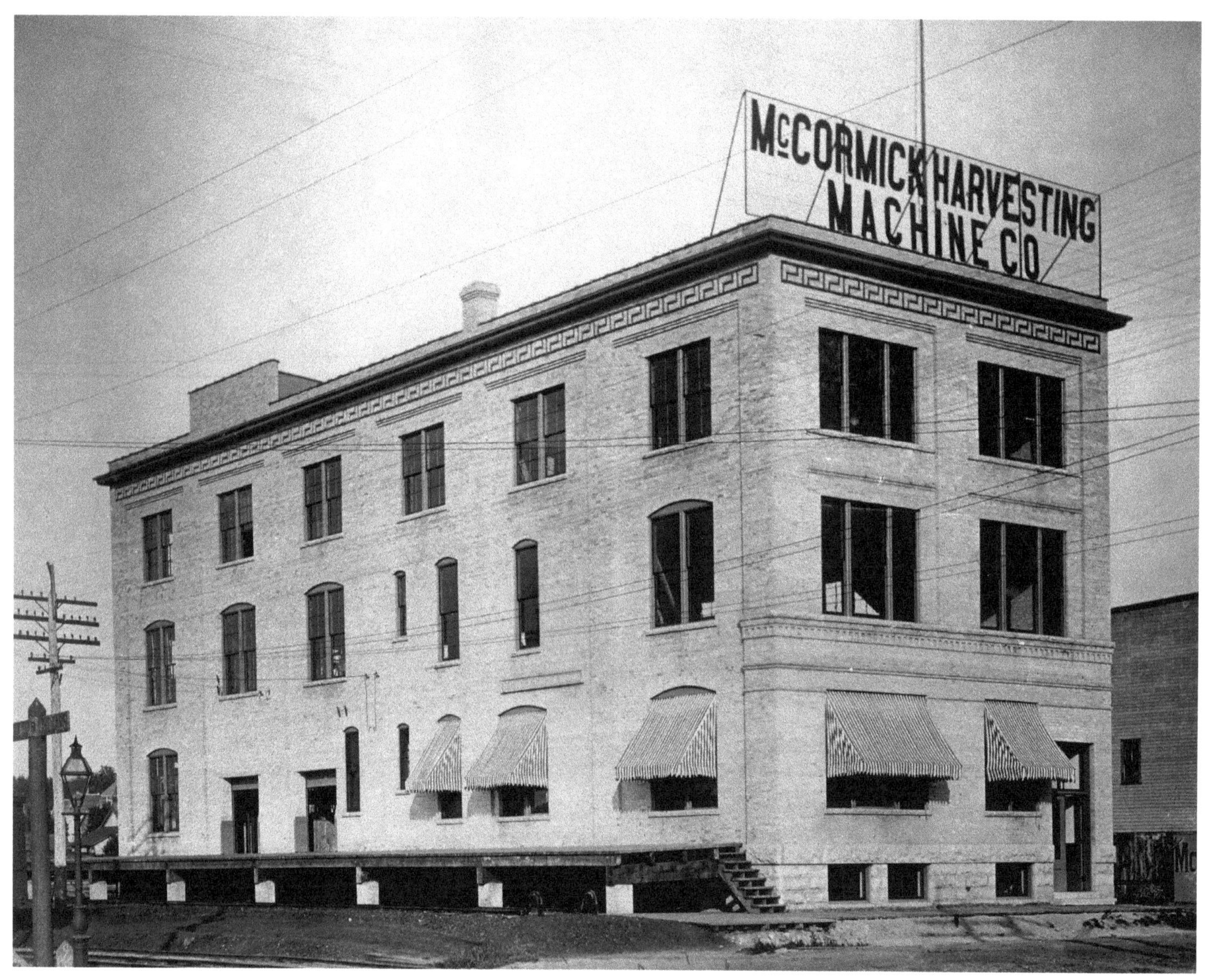

This photograph was taken about a year after the McCormick Dealership was built in 1898 next to the Madison and Watertown railroad tracks. The McCormick Harvesting Machine Company (1848–1902) later became the International Harvester Co. By the 1930s, as the nation's leading manufacturer of trucks, the Chicago-based IH had a sales network of about 11,000 dealers across the country.

Growing Ambitions
(1900–1919)

In the first decades of the new century, Madison saw dramatic growth that included construction of today's Capitol, a new home for the Madison Free Library, the new Madison High School (later renamed Central after East High School was built), and the opening of Madison General Hospital. It also saw the birth of the *Capital Times,* the city's second daily newspaper, the founding of the Henry Vilas Zoo, and the hiring of John Nolen, the future dean of urban planners, as Madison's park superintendent.

Although not embraced at the time, John Nolen's *Madison: A Model City* laid out ambitious plans for parklands, broad avenues, and a Grand Mall (now occupied by the Monona Terrace and Convention Center and other public buildings). Nevertheless, Thomas Brittingham, the richest man in the city, came forward with an $8,000 donation to create a twenty-seven-acre park. Echoes of Nolen's vision now resonate in community planning nearly a century later.

The city by this time was laced with railroads and streetcar lines. Automobiles and motorcycles also became common. These developments made extended neighborhoods, called "streetcar suburbs," such as University Heights, possible. Some of the expansion was doomed from the outset, however, by the waterways that give Madison its scenery—literally sinking the Lake Forest Land Company and its development on Lake Wingra, which has since become known as the Lost City.

The pattern of development in the city was profoundly affected by industrialist John Johnson's founding of Gisholt Manufacturing on East Washington Avenue, which operated well into the twentieth century and fed the Madison Compromise—"factories east, faculty west." Another Norwegian, Magnus Swenson, one of the founders of the College of Agriculture at the University of Wisconsin, used his patents as the basis for a new industry, founding the U.S. Sugar Company, also on the east side, in an area now part of the Olbrich Botanical Gardens.

Madison continued to be a venue for innovation. One of the nation's oldest radio stations began broadcasting during this time, starting in 1914 with engineering professor Edward Bennett on the University of Wisconsin campus and a license for 9XM. The station began with Morse code transmissions of weather forecasts, added experiments with music from phonograph records, and in 1919 aired the first documented clear radio transmission of human speech.

Citizens embraced the war effort during World War I, not only with marches and other shows of loyalty, but with political and economic action. Grain was needed to feed the troops, so prohibition became an act of patriotism. Madisonians voted to deny licenses to saloons in 1917, anticipating Prohibition by nearly three years.

At the end of the decade when workers were returning from the war, Madison, like many cities, faced labor unrest. As in earlier decades, the city moved into another time of anticipation and struggle over its future.

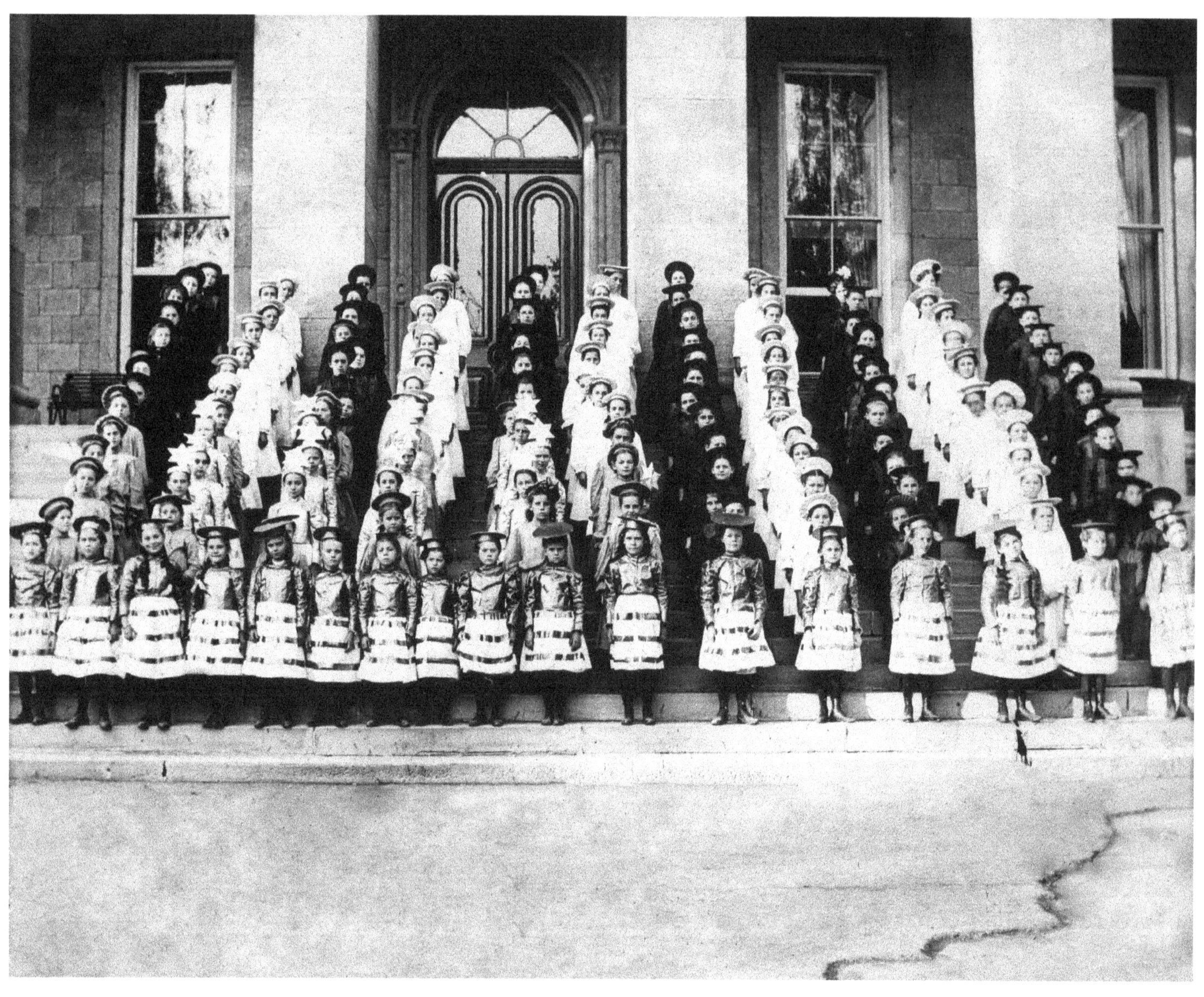

Students at the Kehl School of Dance create a "living flag" on the steps of the Capitol on July 4, 1900. The school, still in operation as a family business, was founded in 1898 by Frederick W. Kehl as Kehl's Dancing Academy at 309 West Johnson Street.

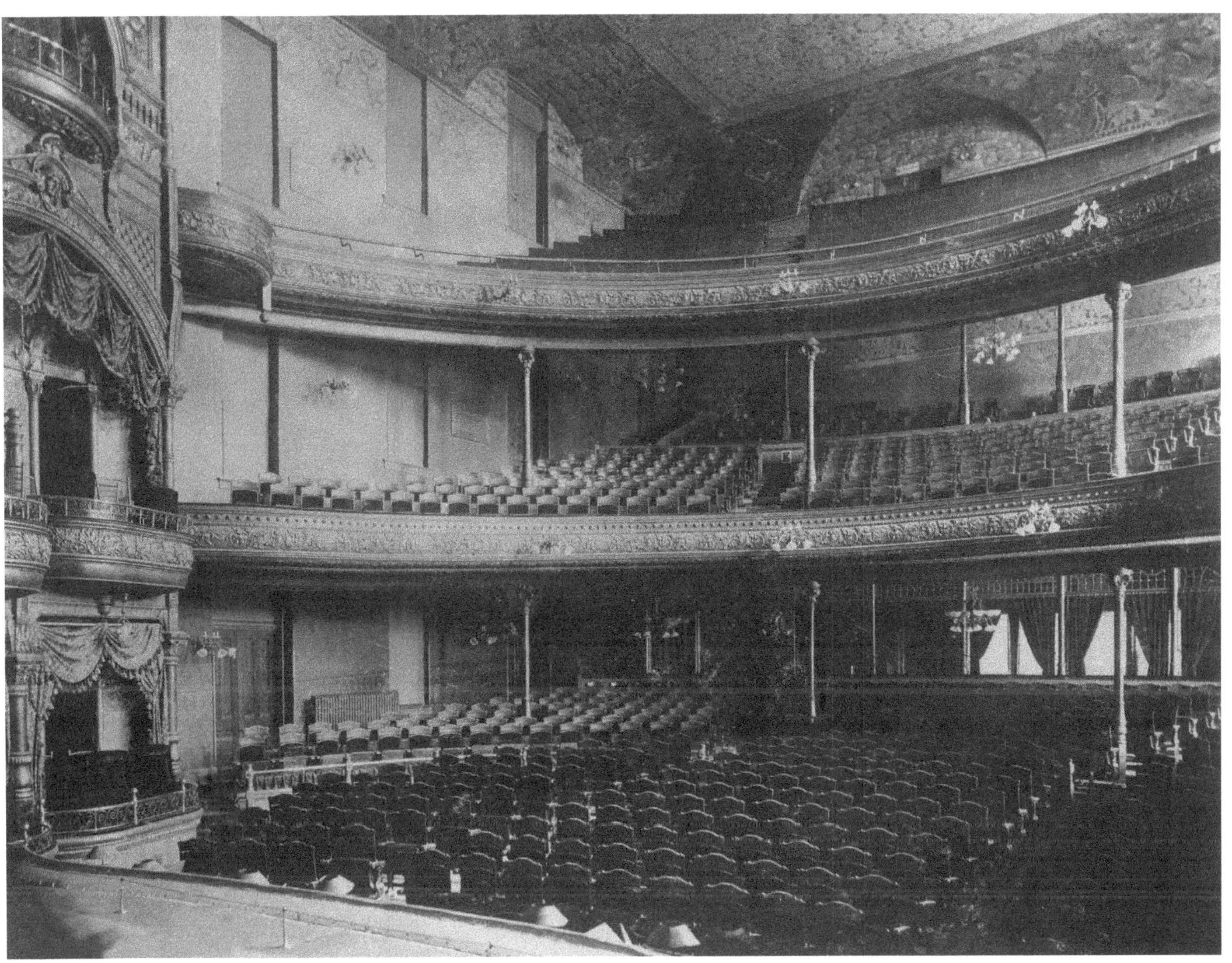

The highly successful Fuller Opera House, at 6-10 West Mifflin Street, at the turn of the century hosted two to three shows a week. The stage had five drop curtains and three trapdoors. The opera house seated 1,200 on the main floor and included a second-level balcony, a third-level gallery, and ten private boxes. It boasted parquet floors, gold gilt and amber walls, and 500 gas and electric lights. The exterior was finished in gray pressed brick and trimmed in putty-colored Bedford stone, with oiled oak doors and stained-glass windows. It was remodeled in 1921 as the Parkway Theater and movie house and was razed in 1954 for a Woolworth's.

Near the turn of the century, the Wisconsin Idea took shape in the minds of University of Wisconsin president Charles Van Hise and Governor Robert LaFollette. The concept added a third mission beyond teaching and research that extended the services of the university to serve the needs of Wisconsin citizens. Here a women's carpentry class about 1900 was part of that initiative through the university's extension programs.

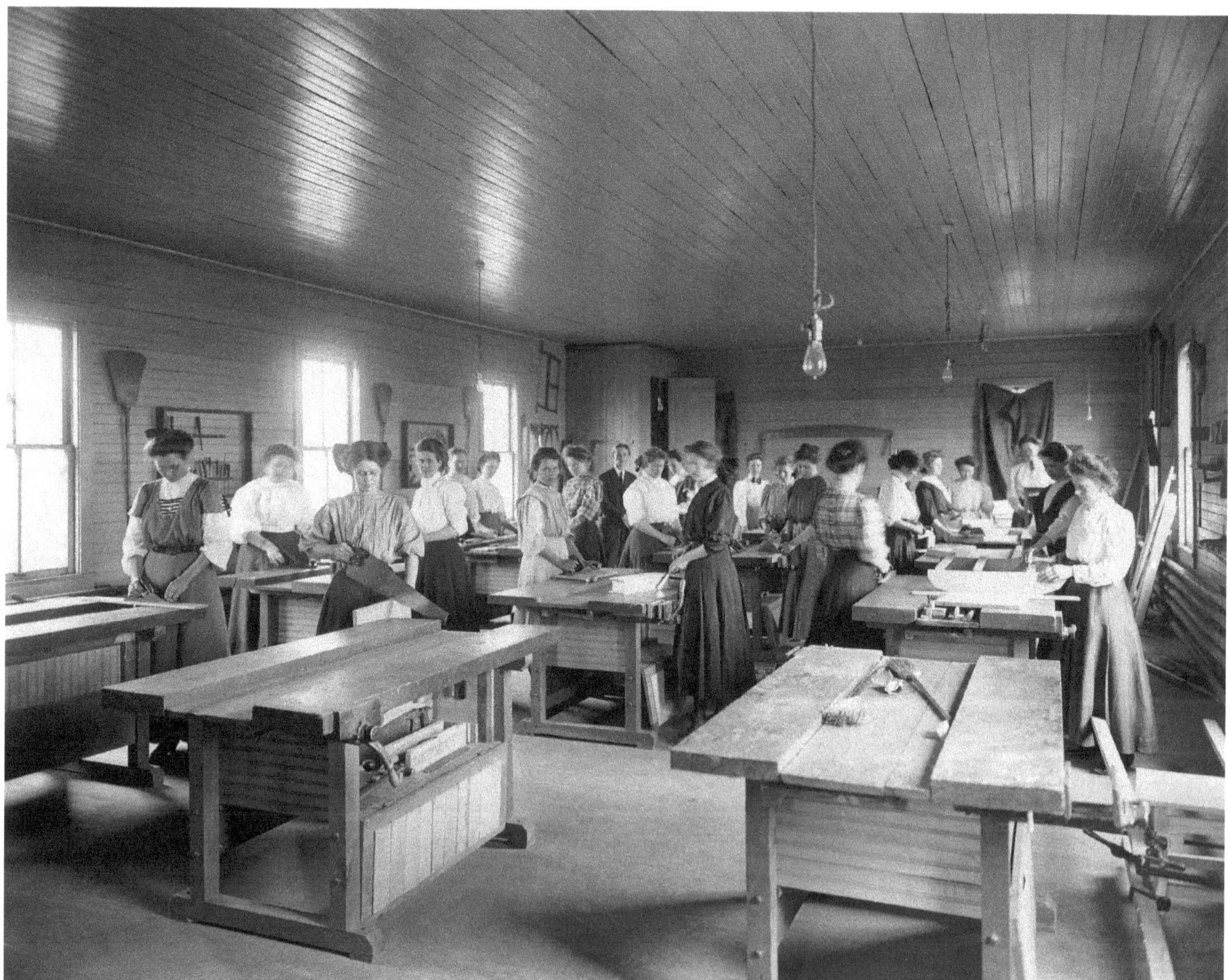

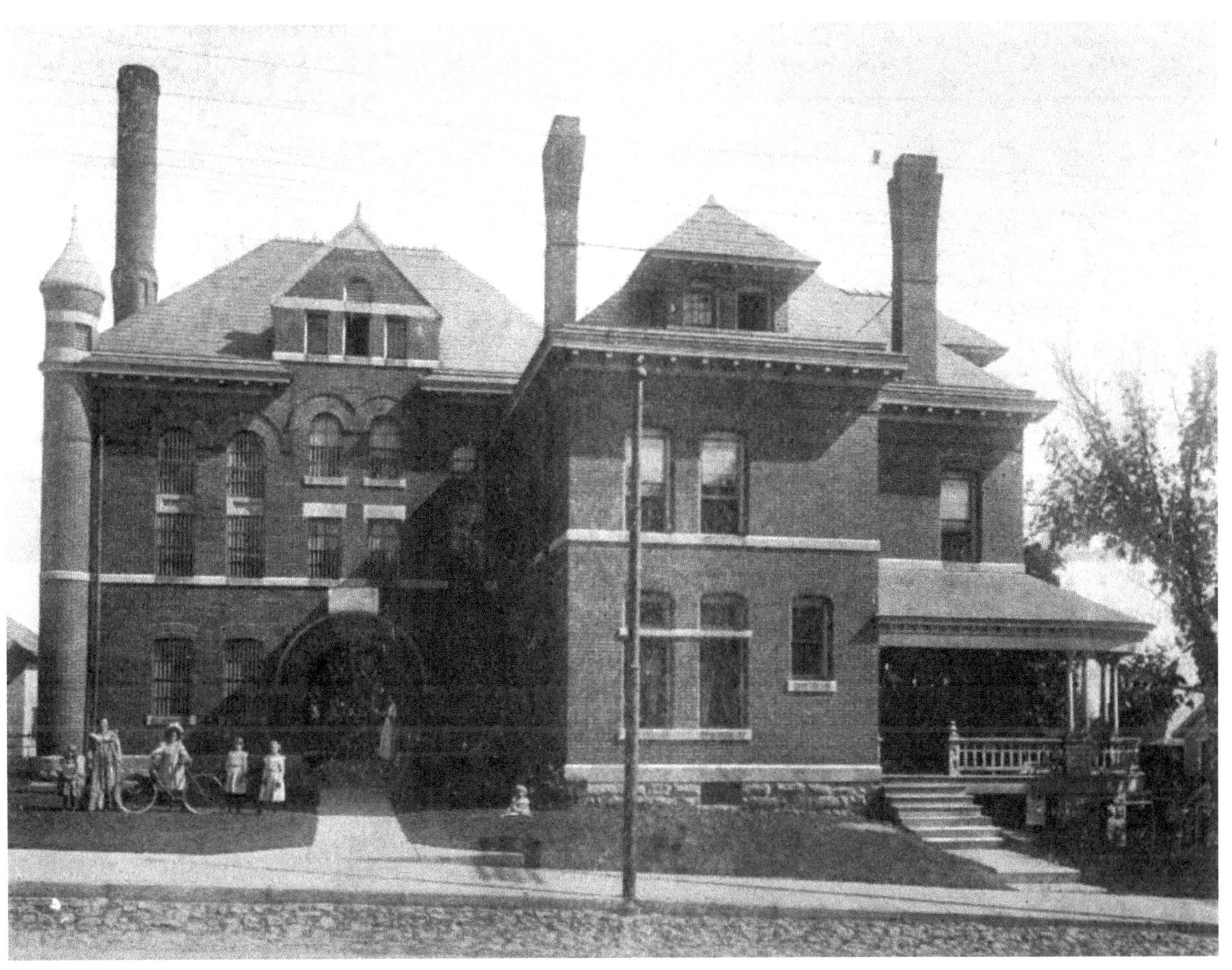

This photograph from around 1901 shows the Dane County Jail built on West Main Street in 1884-86. The sheriff's residence sits to the right. The courthouse and jail were leveled in 1958.

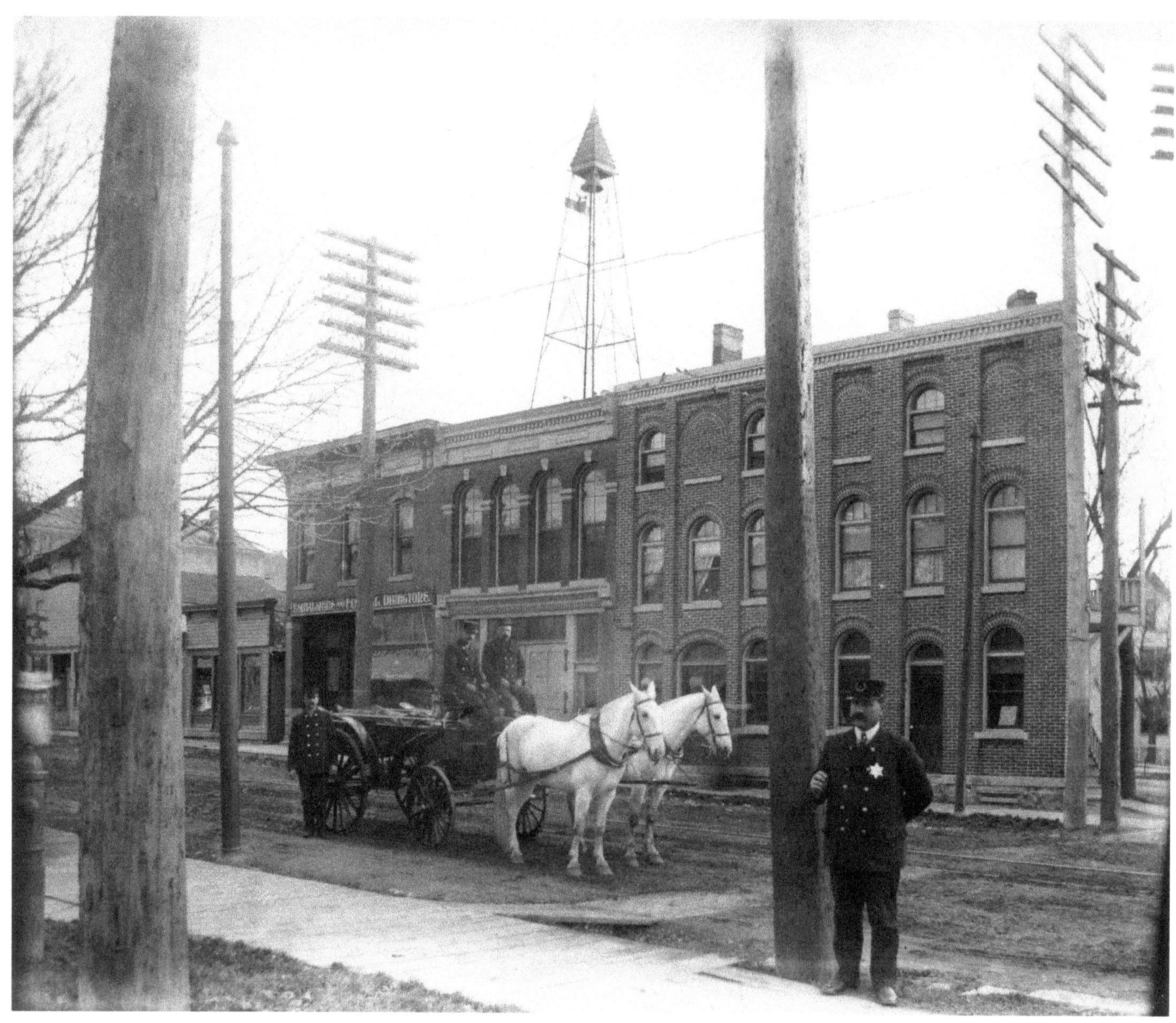

The city's first two fire engine houses were completed in spring 1857 at a cost, including lots, of $4,600. Shown here is Fire Station #2 (center building with bell tower) at 125 State Street, designed by Stephen V. Shipman. Madison Fire Company No. 2 was organized June 23, 1856, by German residents, who also considered it a business and social group. Volunteers were paid $12 a year to cover expenses related to their services. The city hired its first 16 full-time fire fighters around 1901, a year or so before this image was recorded. The building is still standing today, although greatly altered.

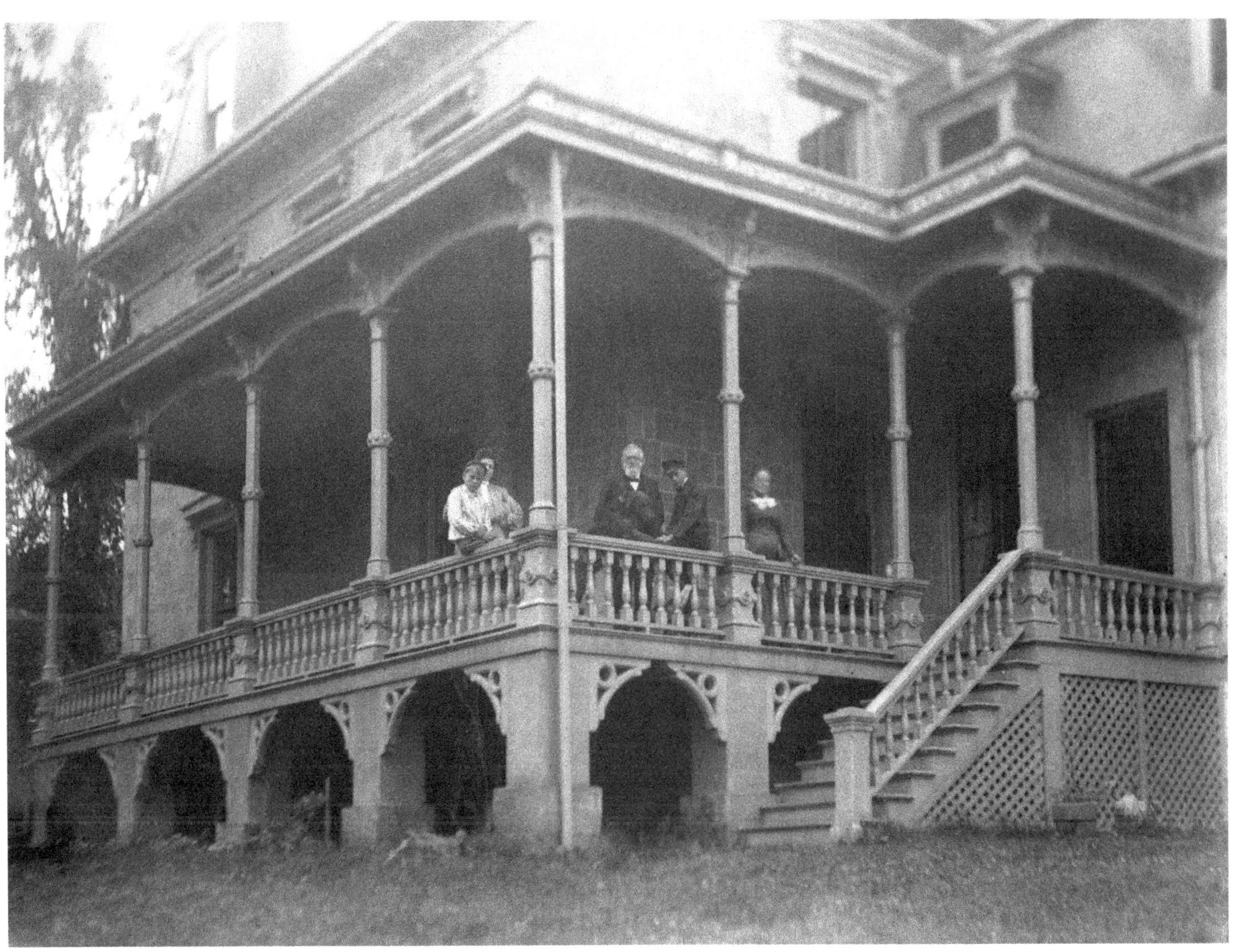

The Storer residence at 104 East Gilman Street is shown here around 1903. G. L. Storer (standing, at center) was a key figure in the creation of the First Unitarian Society of Madison in 1878. At that time Jenkin Lloyd Jones, the uncle of Frank Lloyd Wright, conducted services for the group.

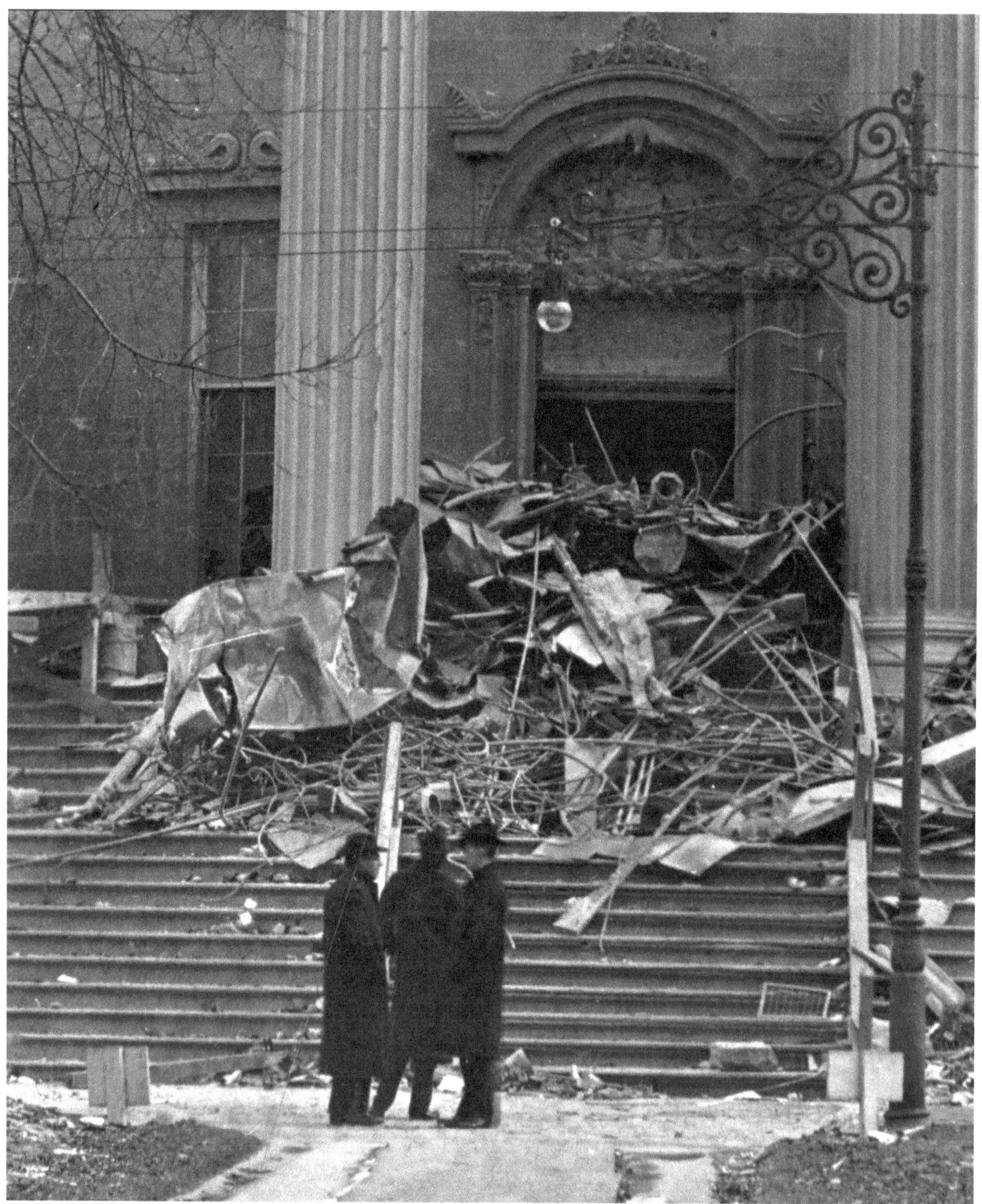

Only a few known photographs exist showing the ornamentation on the west entrance to the Capitol. The seal is visible in this 1904 image of the damage caused by the February 26-27 Capitol fire. The alto relievo (high relief) seal was added in 1862, panned by the *Wisconsin State Journal* as "squalid rather than ornamental."

In 1905, construction crews built a double streetcar track around the Capitol Square. This view shows work on North Pinckney Street. Following a national trend, horse-drawn and mule-drawn streetcars were replaced with electric streetcar lines in 1892. By 1896, the city had twenty electric streetcars. This led to the development of "streetcar suburbs," such as University Heights. In 1919, the Oscar Mayer Company paid for a line extension to carry workers to its east-side plant. Madison's streetcar system began to decline in the 1920s, the final blow coming from an ice storm on February 13, 1935. Buses, becoming popular, took over in the emergency. One month later the last electric lines were taken down.

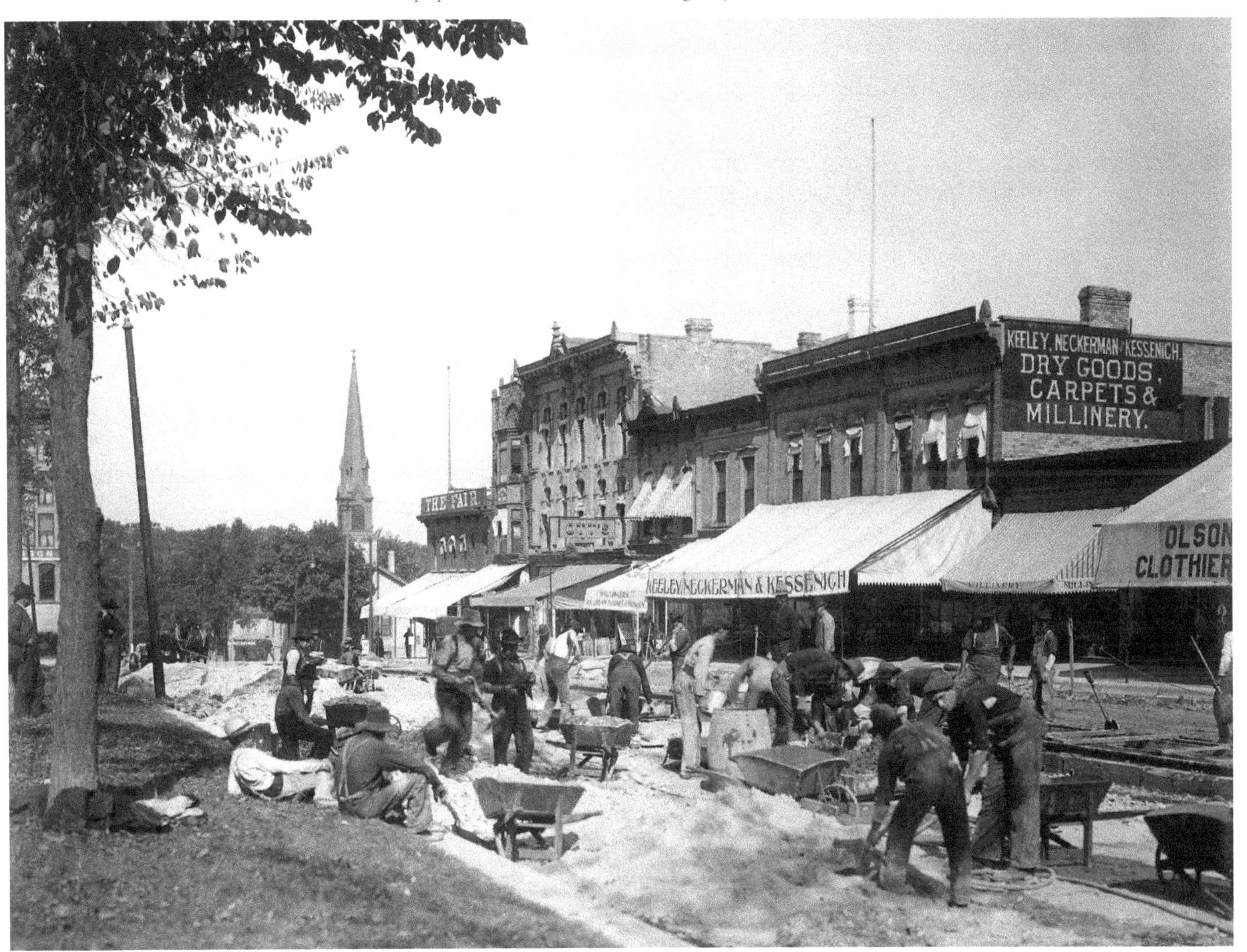

Children play on a makeshift diving board around 1905 at what became Brittingham Park on (Lake) Monona Bay. That summer the *Wisconsin State Journal* demanded bath houses for Madison. "Boys are swimming on Lake Monona at the foot of Hamilton Street without bathing suits. They come out of the water and race up and down the railroad tracks. They 'dismantle' on the railroad bridges and jump in the water when passenger trains pass. On Lake Mendota a grown-up man enjoys a daily plunge without a suit." That same year lumber baron Thomas E. Brittingham, Madison's richest man at the time, came forward with an initial $8,000 donation to purchase land for a twenty-seven-acre park.

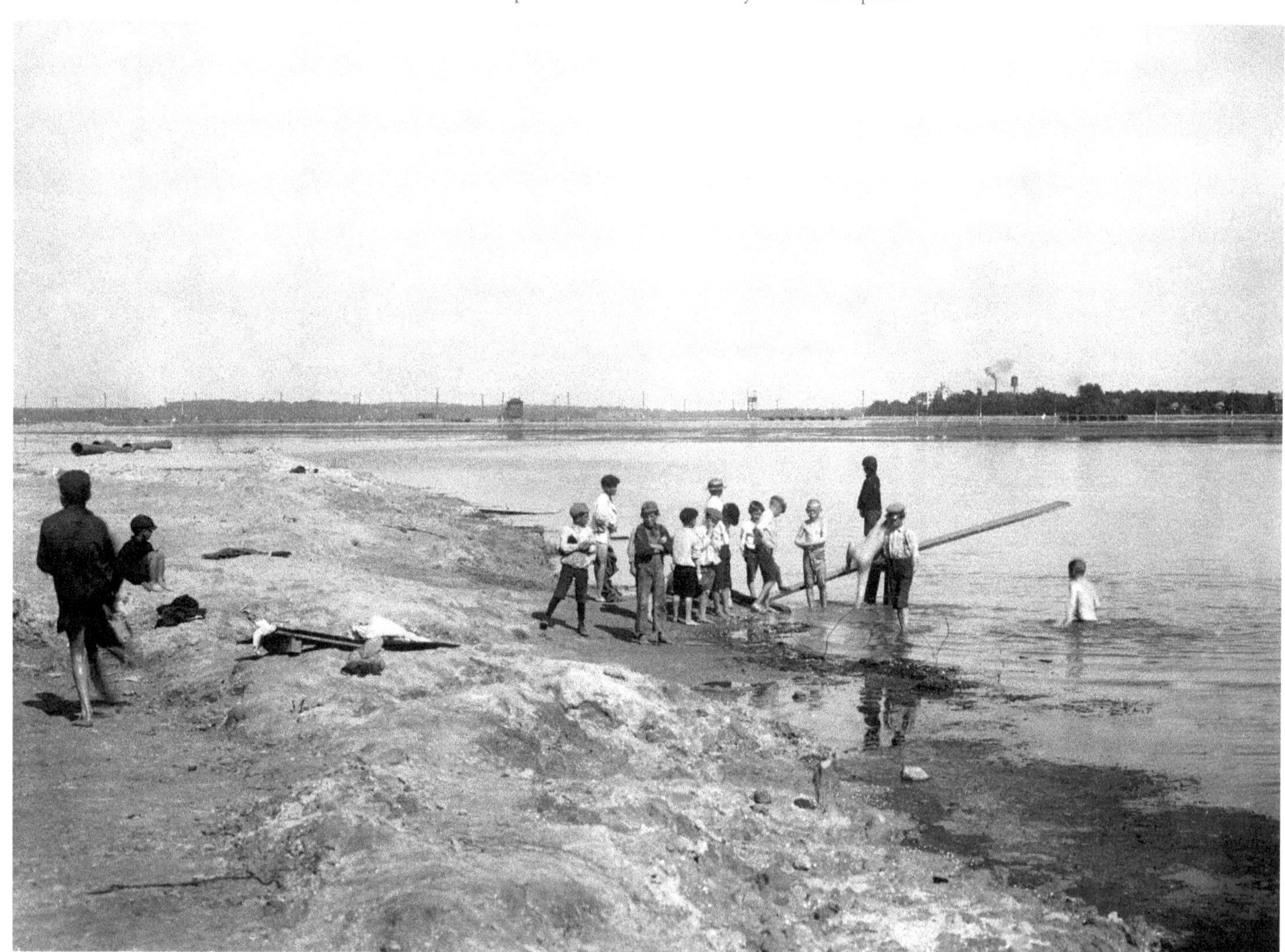

This 1905 image shows the interior of Sumner's Drug Store, a fixture in downtown Madison at 15 South Pinckney Street. The store was founded fifty years before in 1855. From left to right are George "Jud" Stone, Edwin Sumner, Bert B. Collyer, and a fourth man unidentified.

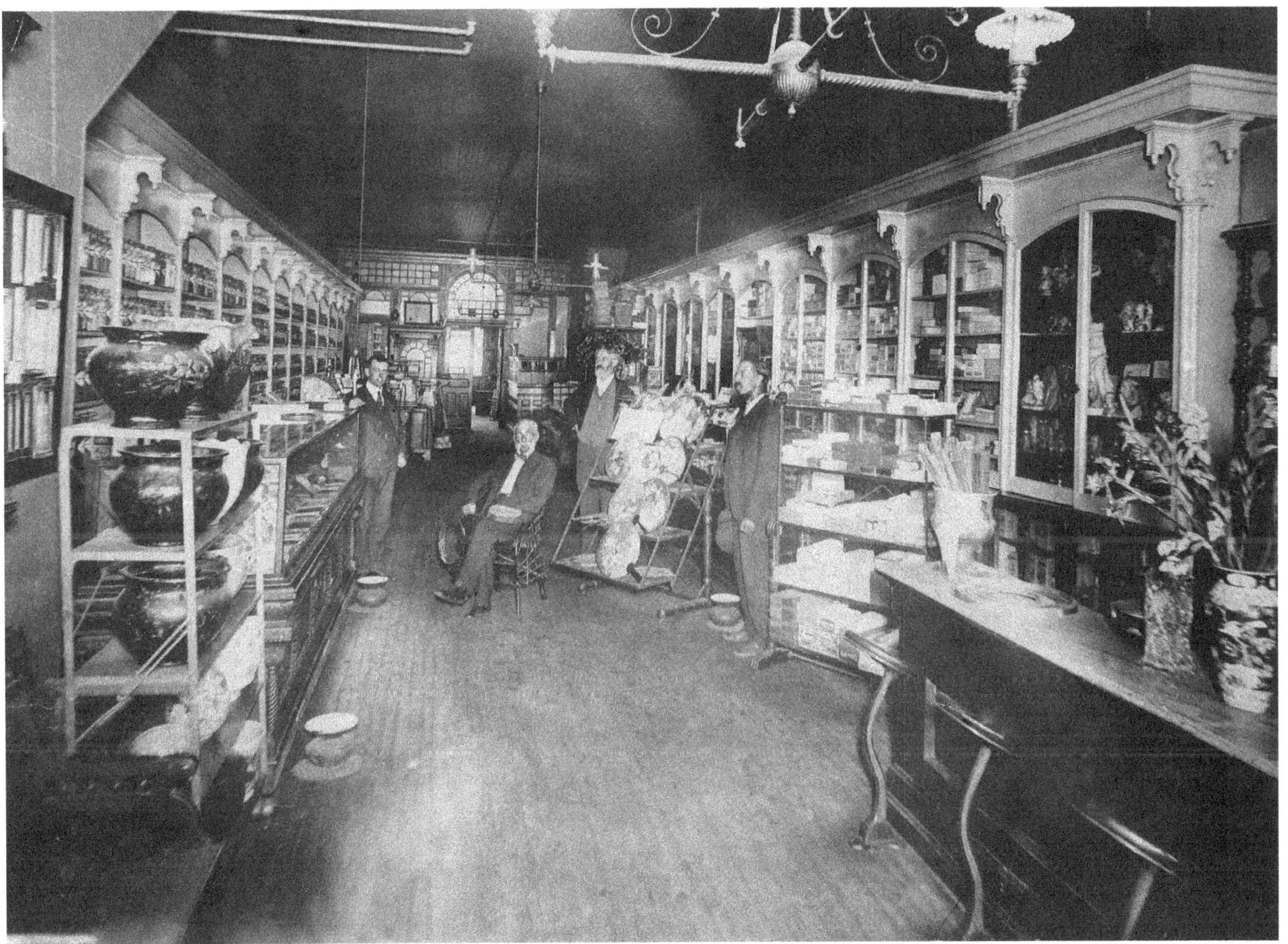

The Fred Schenk Grocery Store, as seen here around 1907 at the corner of Atwood Avenue and Winnebago Street. The area later became known simply as Schenk's Corners. The store also carried housewares, cigars, clothing, and general merchandise, and hosted Madison's first branch library. A librarian visited twice a week with new books to refresh the small collection of fifty to one hundred fifty books.

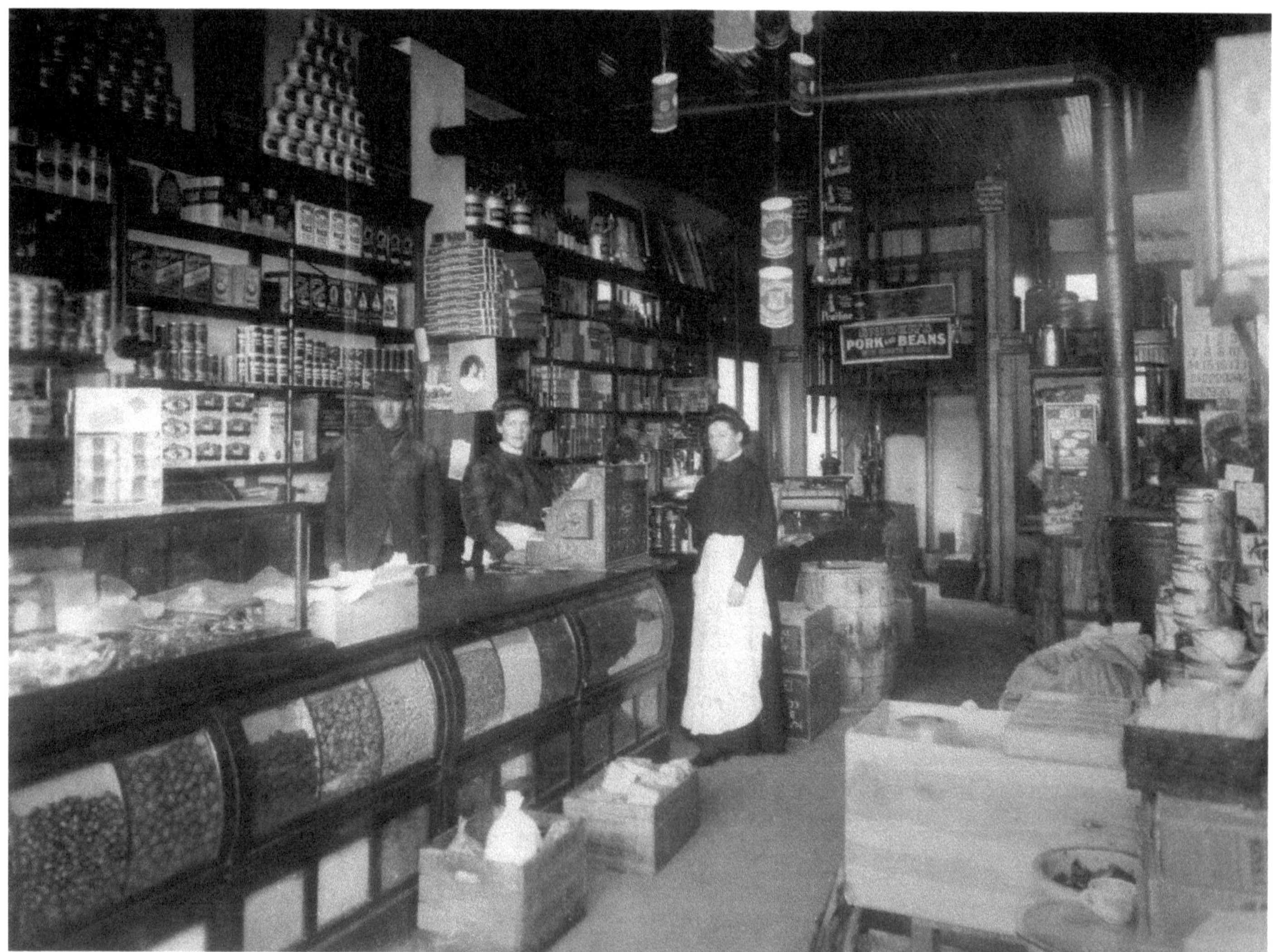

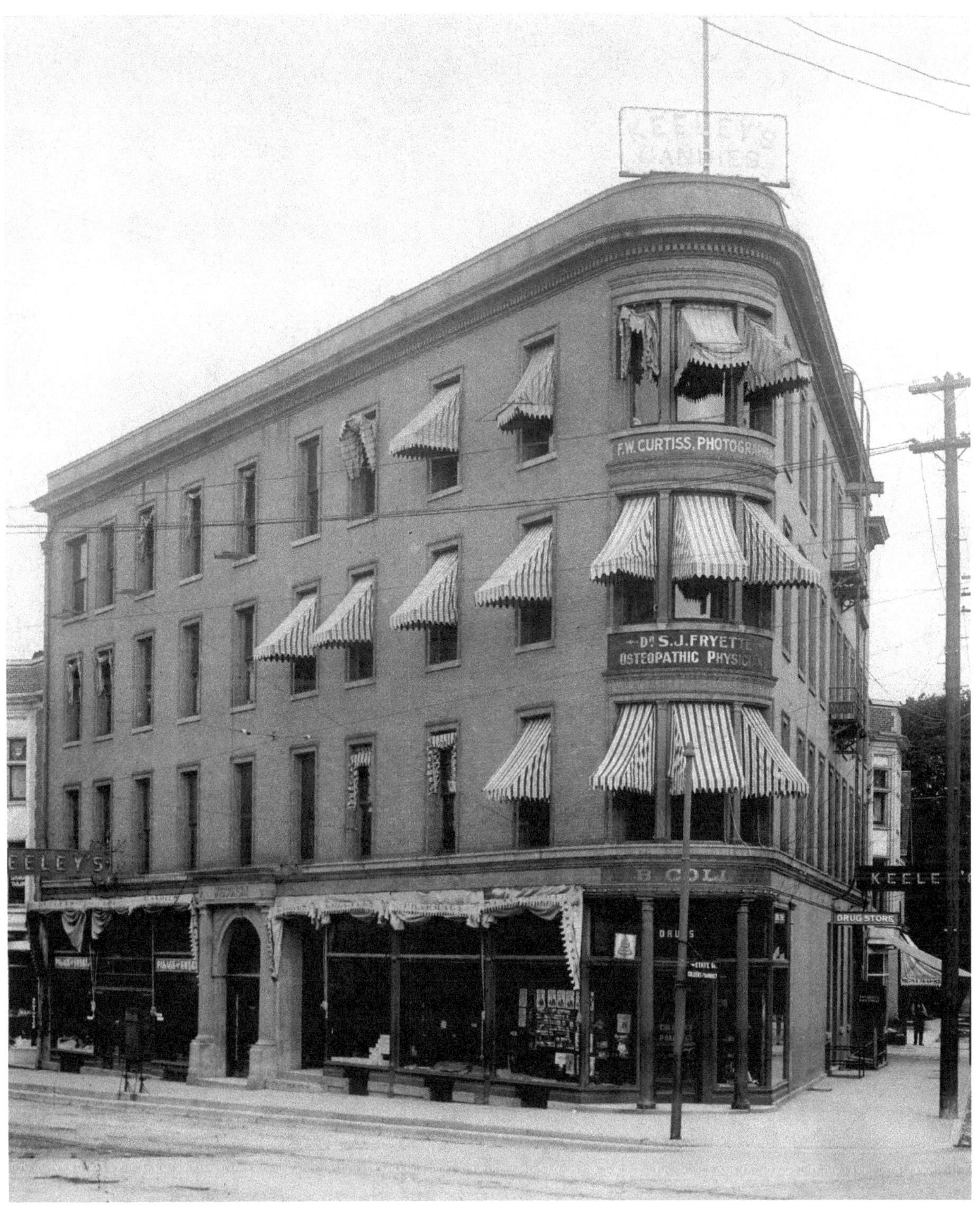

Shown here in 1907, the Wisconsin Building was constructed around 1901. At the junction of State and Carroll streets, the building faced the Capitol and housed Collyer's Drug Store, and later Commercial State Bank. Other businesses in the building included Keeley's Palace of Sweets, osteopath S. J. Fryette, and photographer F. W. Curtiss. Current occupants include the Madison Children's Museum and Lindsay, Stone & Briggs advertising agency.

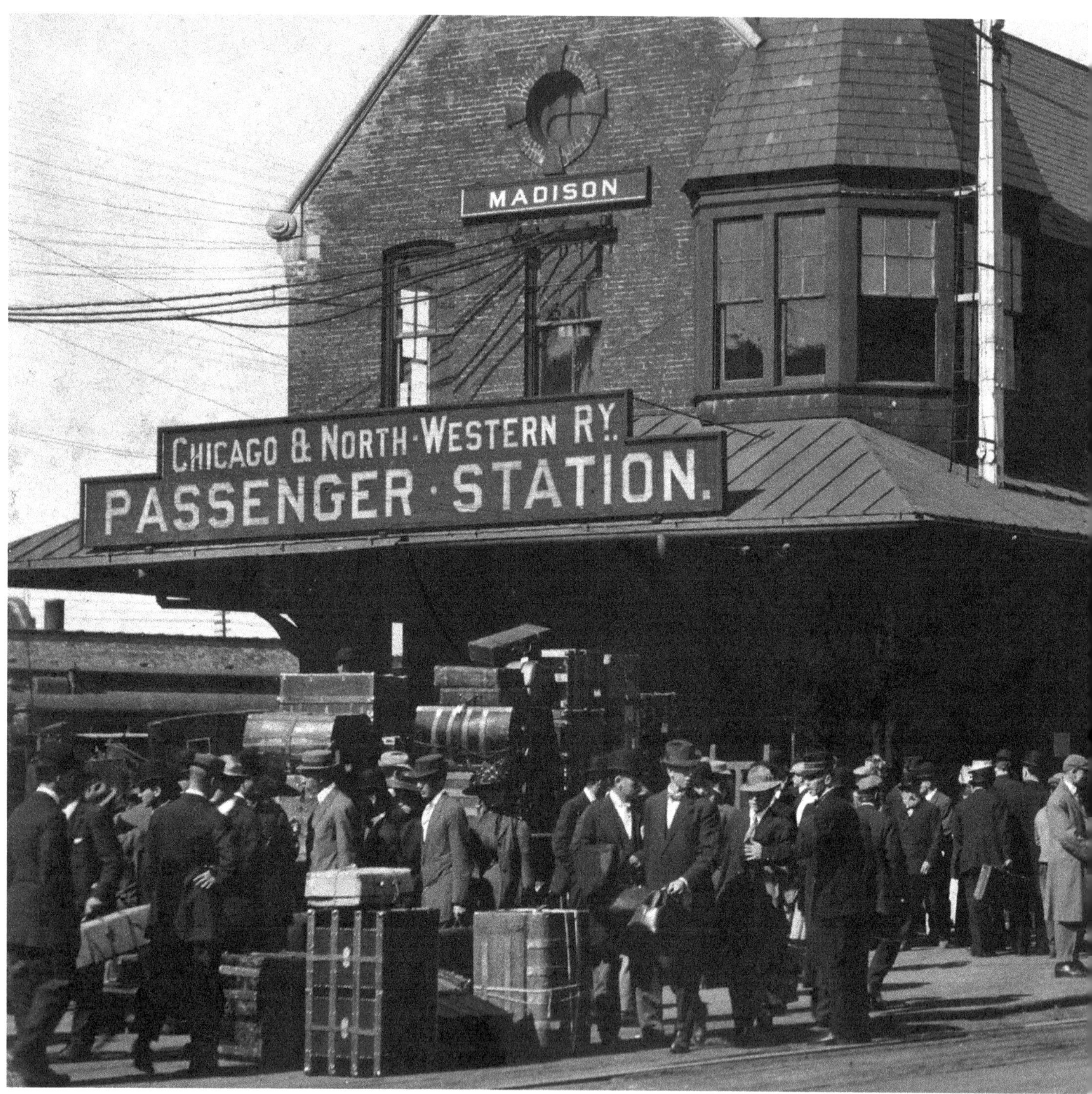
MADISON
CHICAGO & NORTH-WESTERN RY.
PASSENGER·STATION.

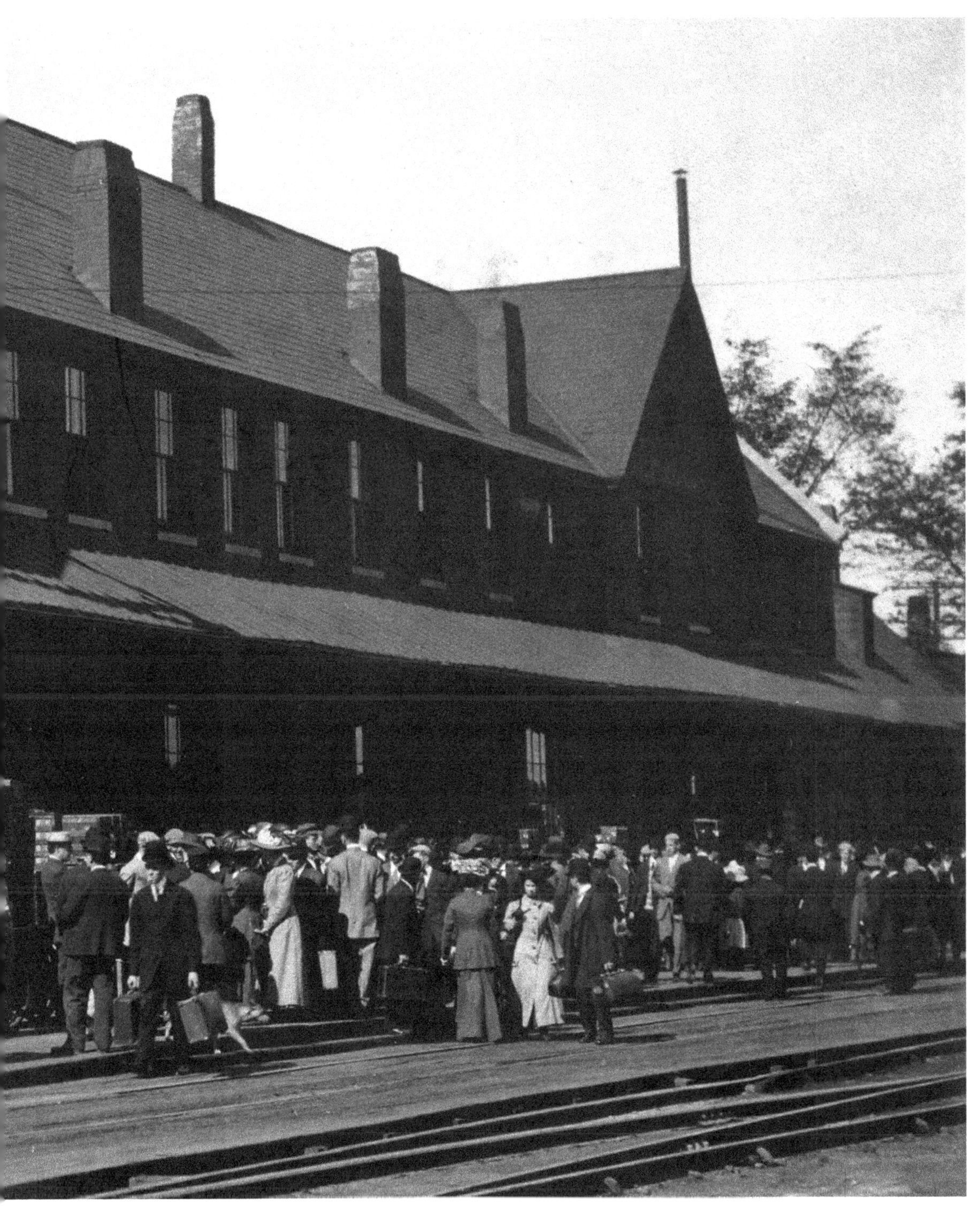

In 1909, the Chicago and North Western Railroad station is crowded with people waiting on the platform. Chicago and North Western was considered the largest of the Midwestern railroads of the time, reaching its apogee in 1910. The left-handed operation of the C&NW set it apart from other railroads in the United States. The most likely explanation is that the stations, oriented for inbound traffic, were arbitrarily placed all on one side of the tracks when the line was a single track. When a second track was laid into Chicago, the depots would have had to be rebuilt or moved, so the outbound track ended up on the left, allowing inbound passengers to wait in the warm depot. This depot still stands at the corner of West Washington Avenue and Bedford Street.

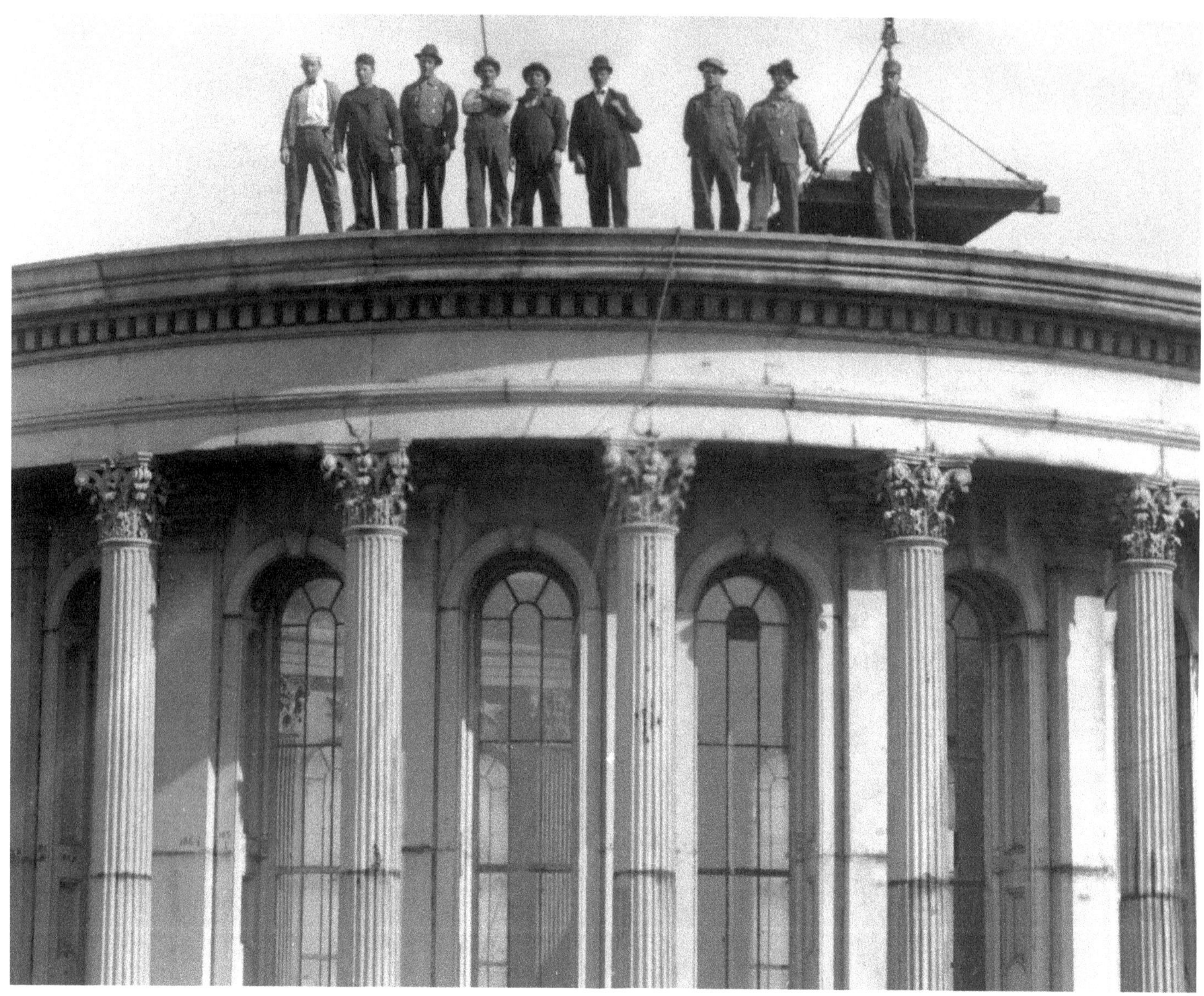

Workmen in 1909 methodically disassemble the dome during the demolition of the third Capitol (the second in Madison). The stones of the dome were numbered and stored on the University of Wisconsin campus for reassembly on Bascom Hall. When that idea was rejected, the dome was sold for scrap. Architectural details can be seen through the windows, such as the Corinthian pillars and the plaster stars between each. It was reported in 1890 that the dome interior was painted to represent the night sky.

In this 1914 image, East Washington Avenue is crowded with people and horse-drawn vehicles. One of the main thoroughfares in the city, it was laid out by Leonard J. Farwell, a future Wisconsin governor. Farwell purchased most of the east side in 1847. He also drained the marshes between the Capitol and the Yahara River. In 1903 the city council asked the Madison Park and Pleasure Drive Association to draw up a plan for beautifying East Washington Avenue. The plan, created by John Olin, called for a boulevard from Butler to Baldwin streets with twenty-four-foot-wide roads on each side.

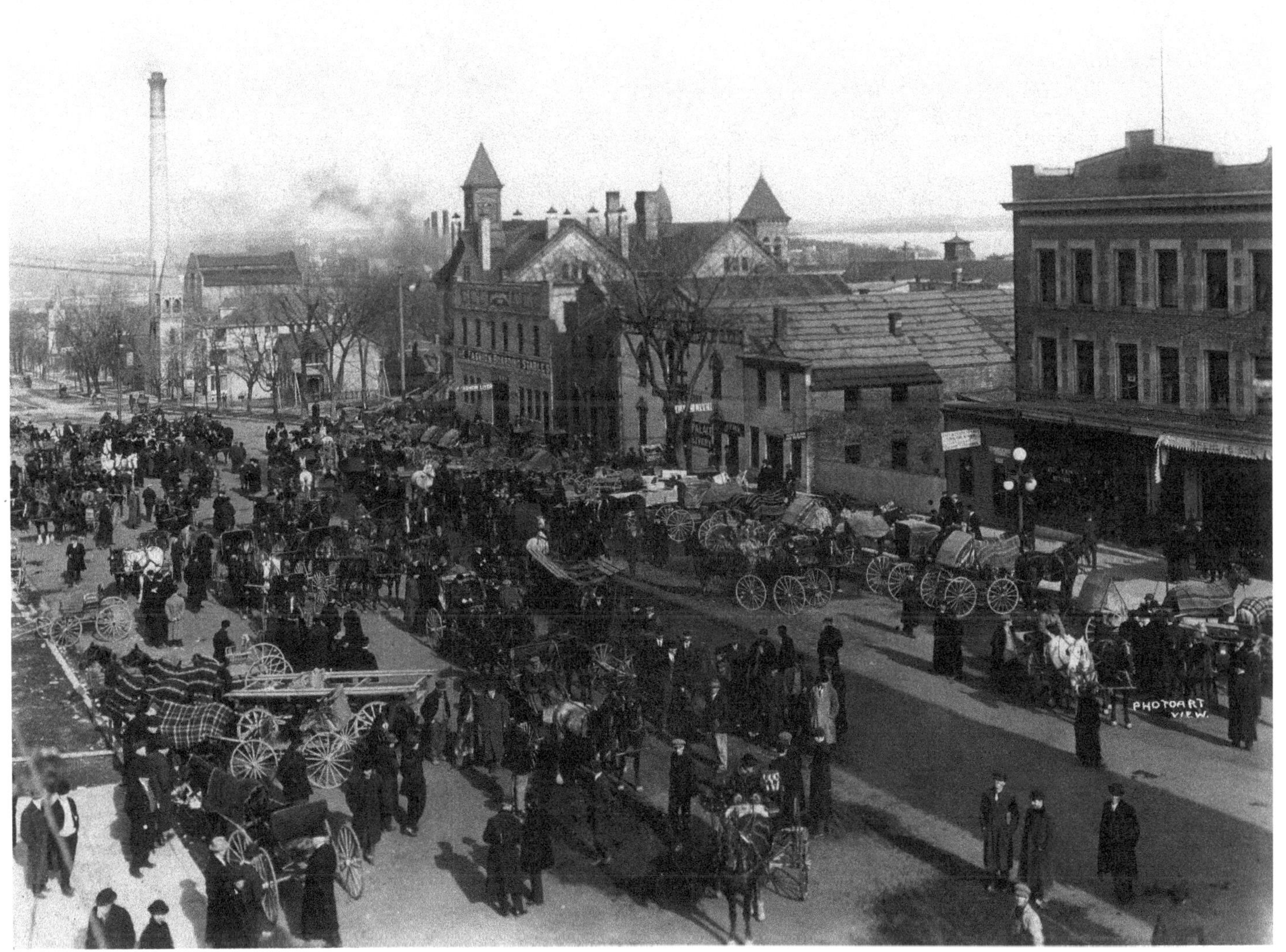

This open trolley car in 1910 ran on the Fair Oaks line. Here it idles near the Forest Hill Cemetery, one of the first U.S. National Cemeteries in Wisconsin. The motorman is Jack Schwenn; the conductor is Charlie Cramer. The route ran from a barn on Fair Oaks Avenue to Winnebago Street to Jenifer, up King Street to the Capitol Square, then down State Street to Park Street. It went over to University Avenue, traveled west and turned on Breese Terrace down to Monroe Street, then right on Harrison to Regent Street, ending at what is now the Forest Hill Cemetery gate house.

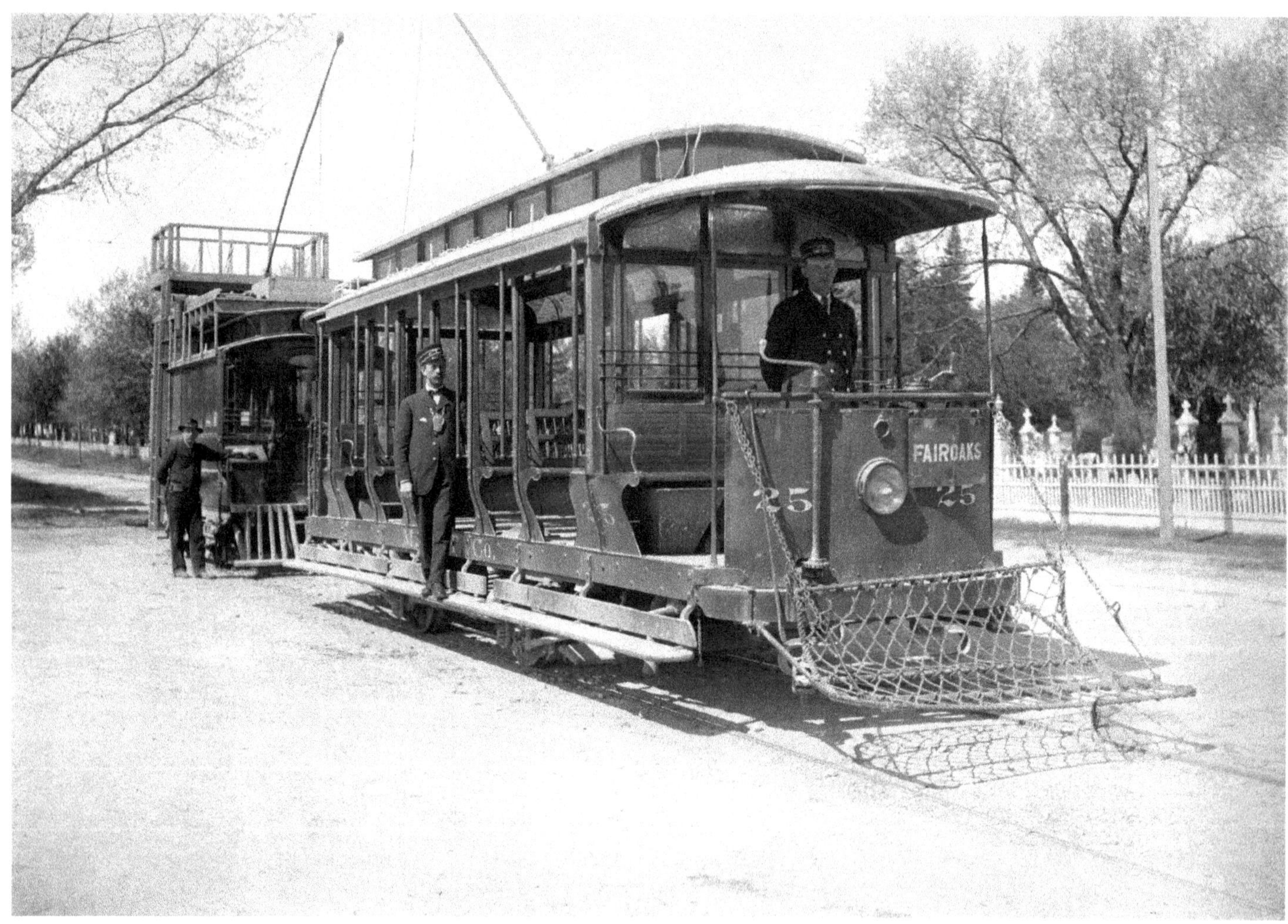

The Old Marketplace Neighborhood on the near northeast side of Madison, shown here in 1910, ran from Blount to Livingston streets between Dayton and Mifflin streets.

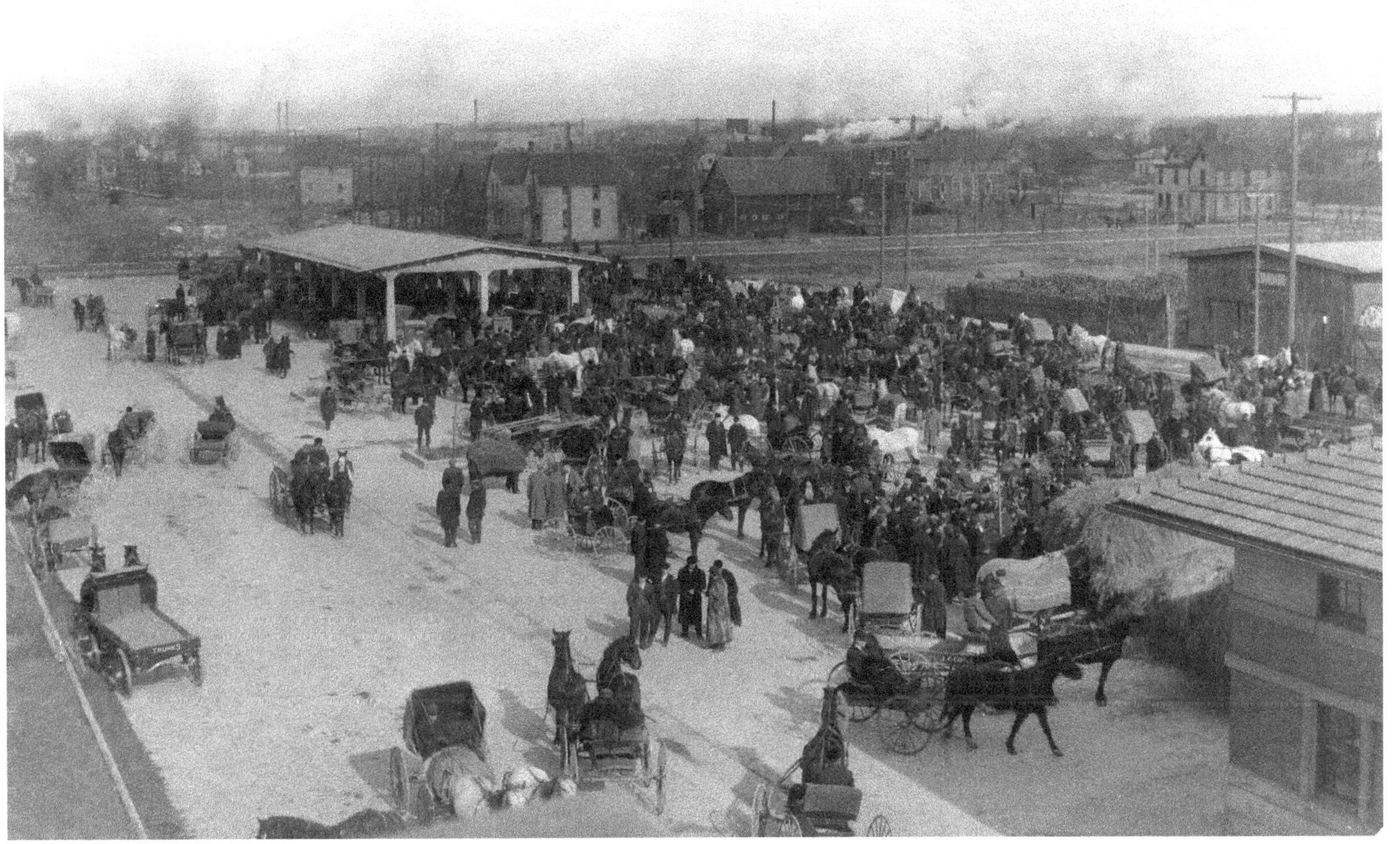

Men on motorcycles line up in front of Harry McDaniel's Motorcycle and Bike Shop on State Street in 1912. Harley-Davidson is one of Wisconsin's and America's signature brands. It got its start in a tiny garage in Milwaukee in 1901. By 1903 childhood friends William Harley and Arthur Davidson had built a motorized bicycle and a recognizable motorcycle the following year. By 1920, Harley-Davidson had grown into the largest motorcycle manufacturer in the world.

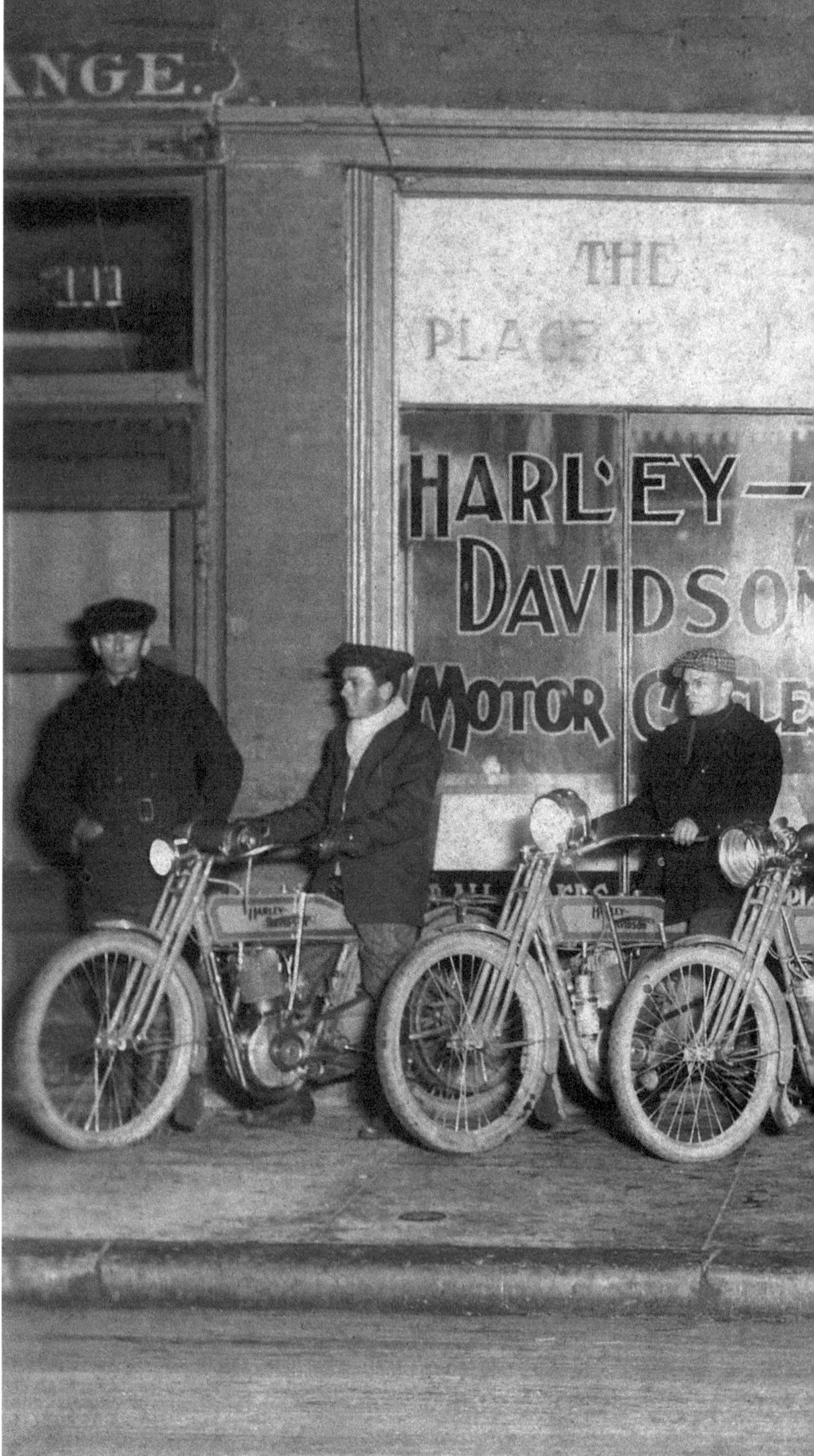

BICYCLES
IVER JOHNSON

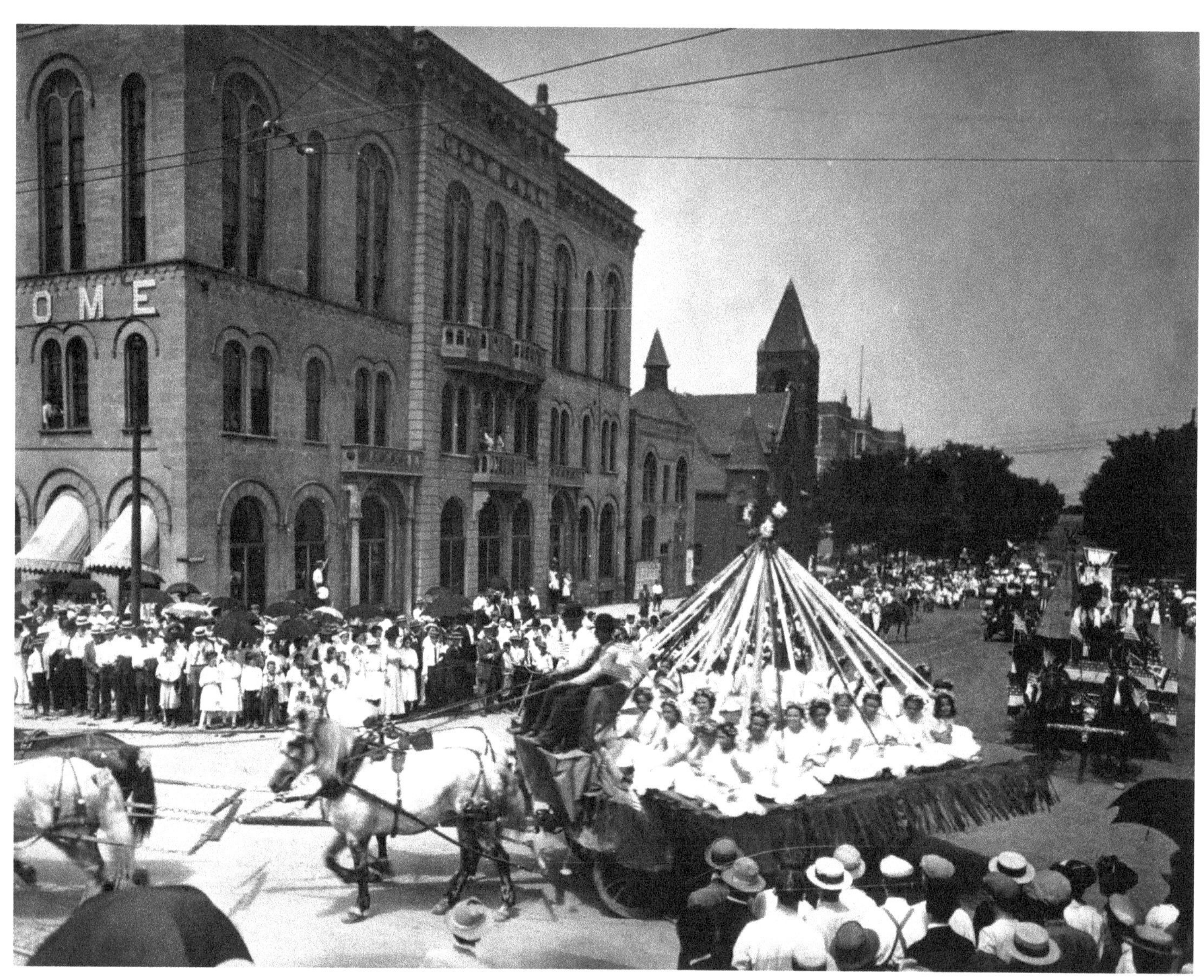

A 1910 parade, probably Memorial Day, rounds the Capitol Square featuring a horse-drawn May Pole with dancers from the Kehl School of Dance.

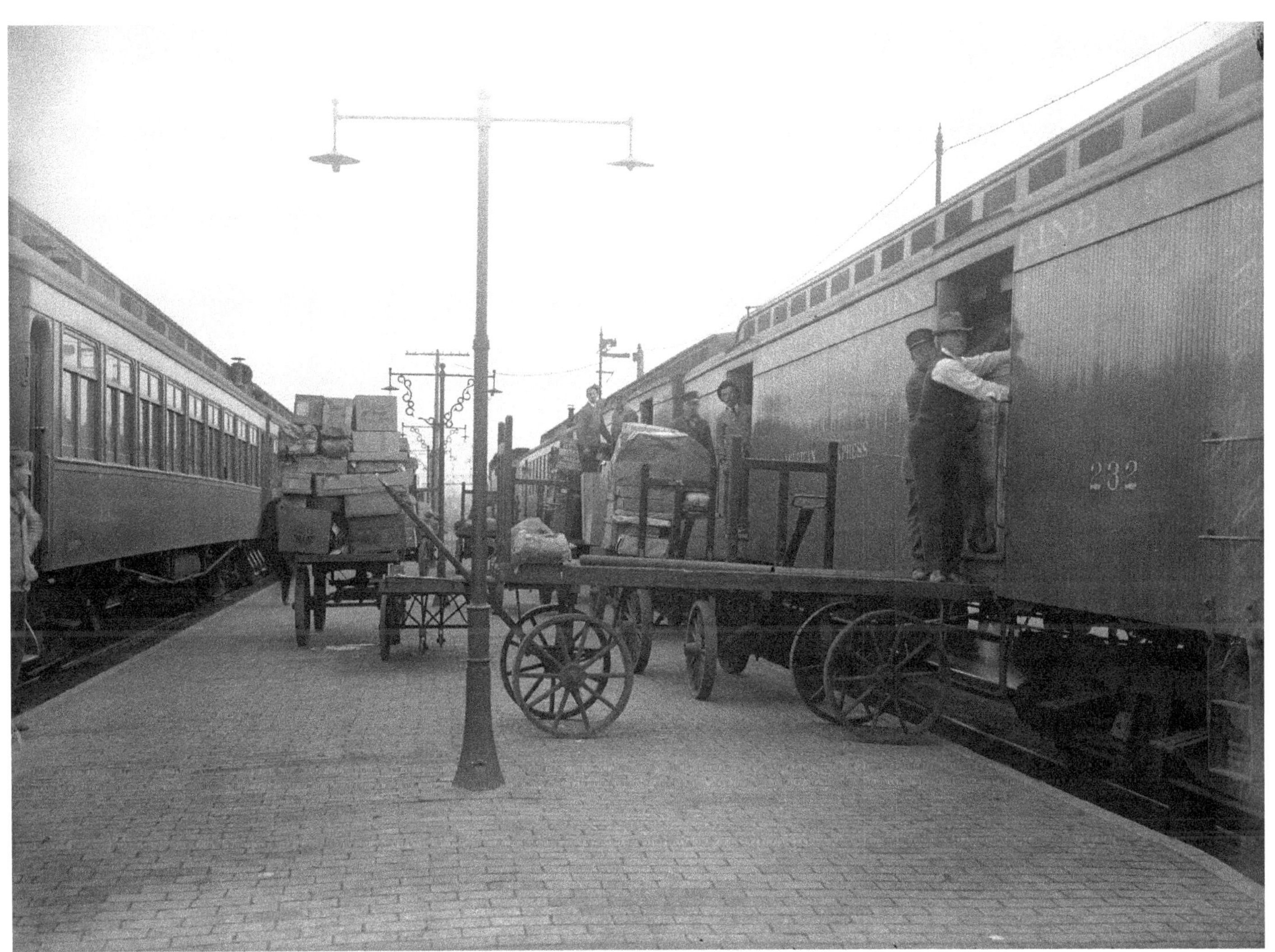

As in most cities of the time, trains crisscrossed Madison. At one time, the city had six railroad stations. Here freight is unloaded from a Chicago, Milwaukee, St. Paul, and Minneapolis train, probably at the west Madison depot at 640 West Washington Avenue.

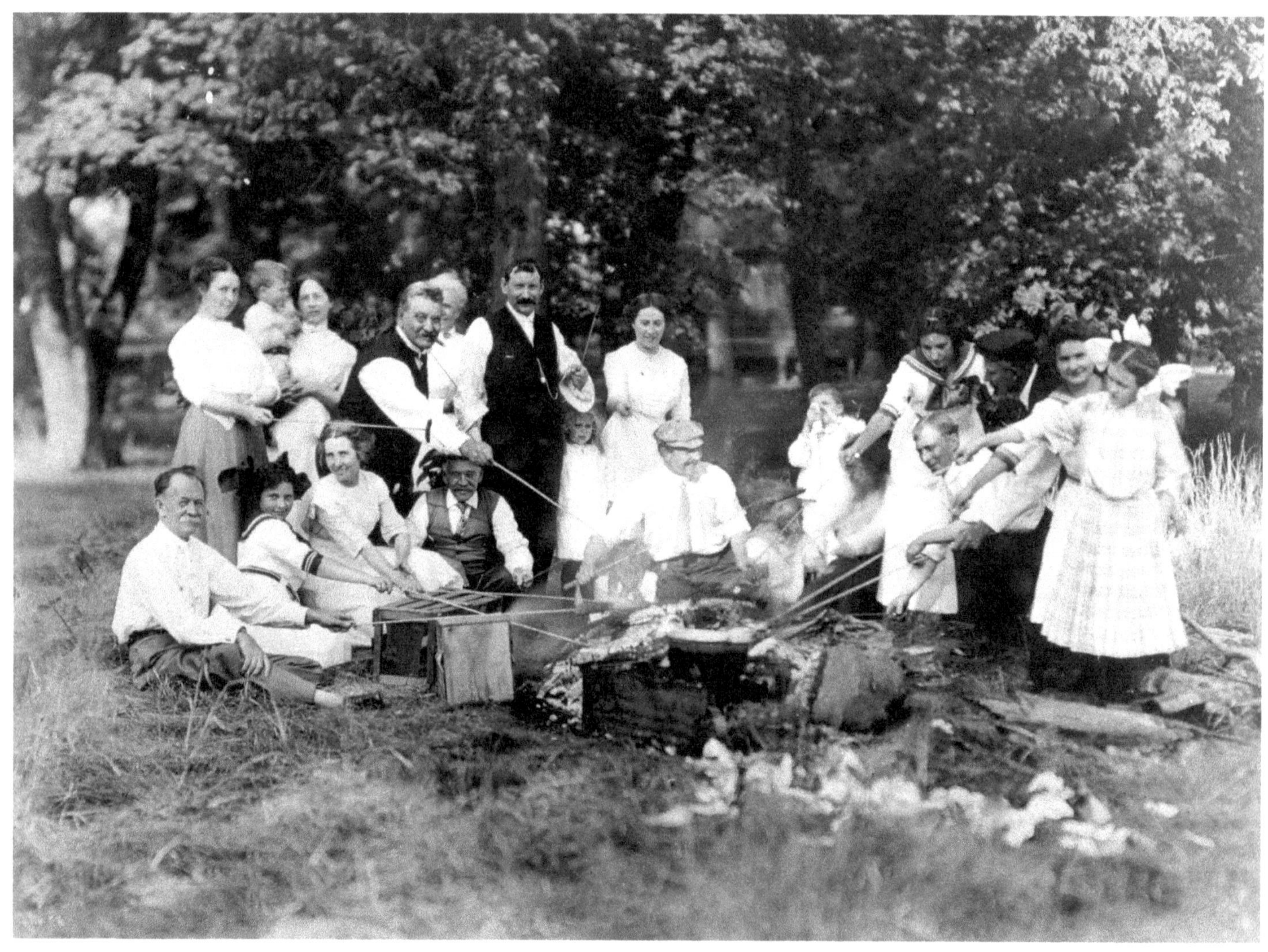

The Benedict Goldenberger family enjoys a wurst roast about 1912. Goldenberger was a cooper and vinegar maker, possibly on Murray Street.

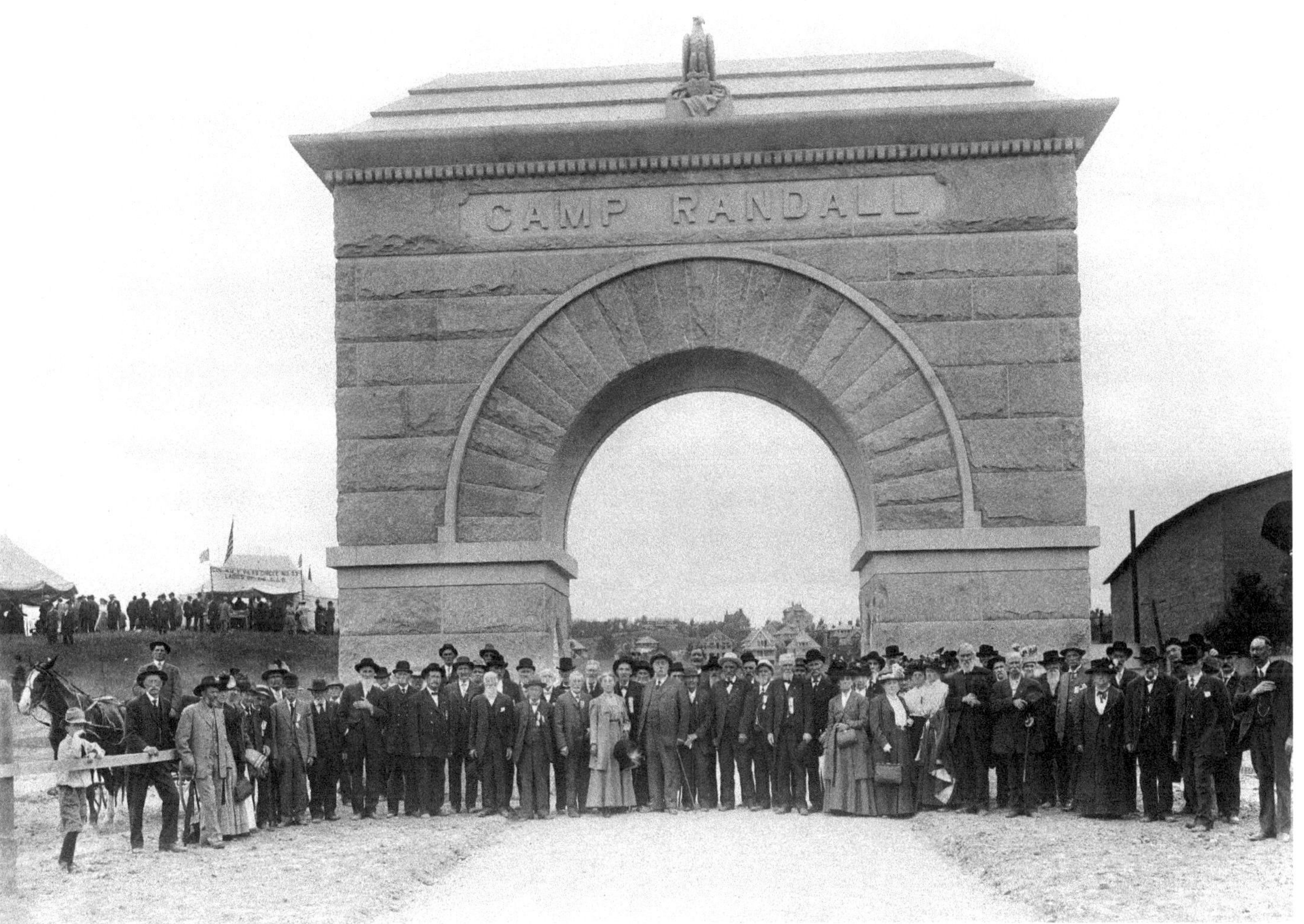

A group of people pose in front of the Camp Randall Memorial Arch during its dedication in 1912. Camp Randall, the name now associated with the stadium that hosts championship football at the University of Wisconsin-Madison, was originally the training ground for Civil War recruits. At the outbreak of the Civil War, Major Horace A. Tenney started preparing the fairground near the university to receive Wisconsin troops, with plans for a barracks, prison yard, guard house, officers quarters, stables, and general hospital. His orders came from Governor Alexander Randall, in whose honor the camp was named. More than 70,000 men traveled from around the state to train there.

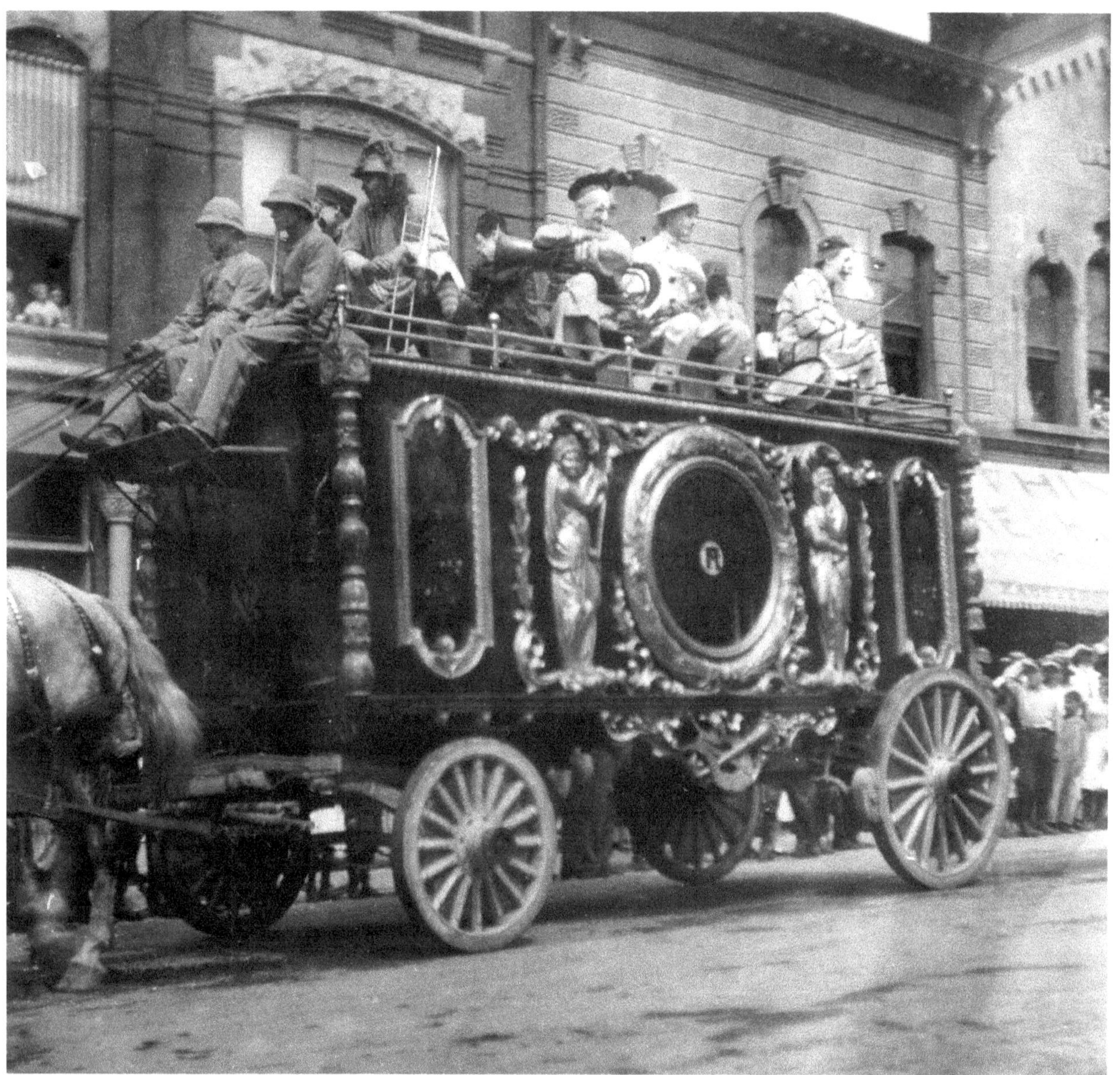

A horse-drawn Ringling Circus wagon with clowns riding on top is part of a 1910 parade in downtown Madison. Three years before, the Ringling Brothers of Baraboo, Wisconsin, had just purchased their largest competitor—Barnum & Bailey Circus, the Greatest Show on Earth. They toured both shows independently for twelve years before wartime labor shortages forced them to merge the shows in 1919. The result required 100 double-length railroad cars and 1,200 employees, making it the largest traveling amusement enterprise up to that time. Children in town could get free tickets in exchange for helping to water the elephants.

Madison was an ice mecca, providing abundant supplies from its lakes for transport by rail to customers. In this 1912 photograph, men are harvesting ice at Conklin & Son Coal and Ice on Lake Mendota. *U*-shaped tools split the partly sawed blocks from the ice, and pike poles are used to slide the blocks to the conveyor. The steel frame of the new Capitol is just visible to the right of the icehouse.

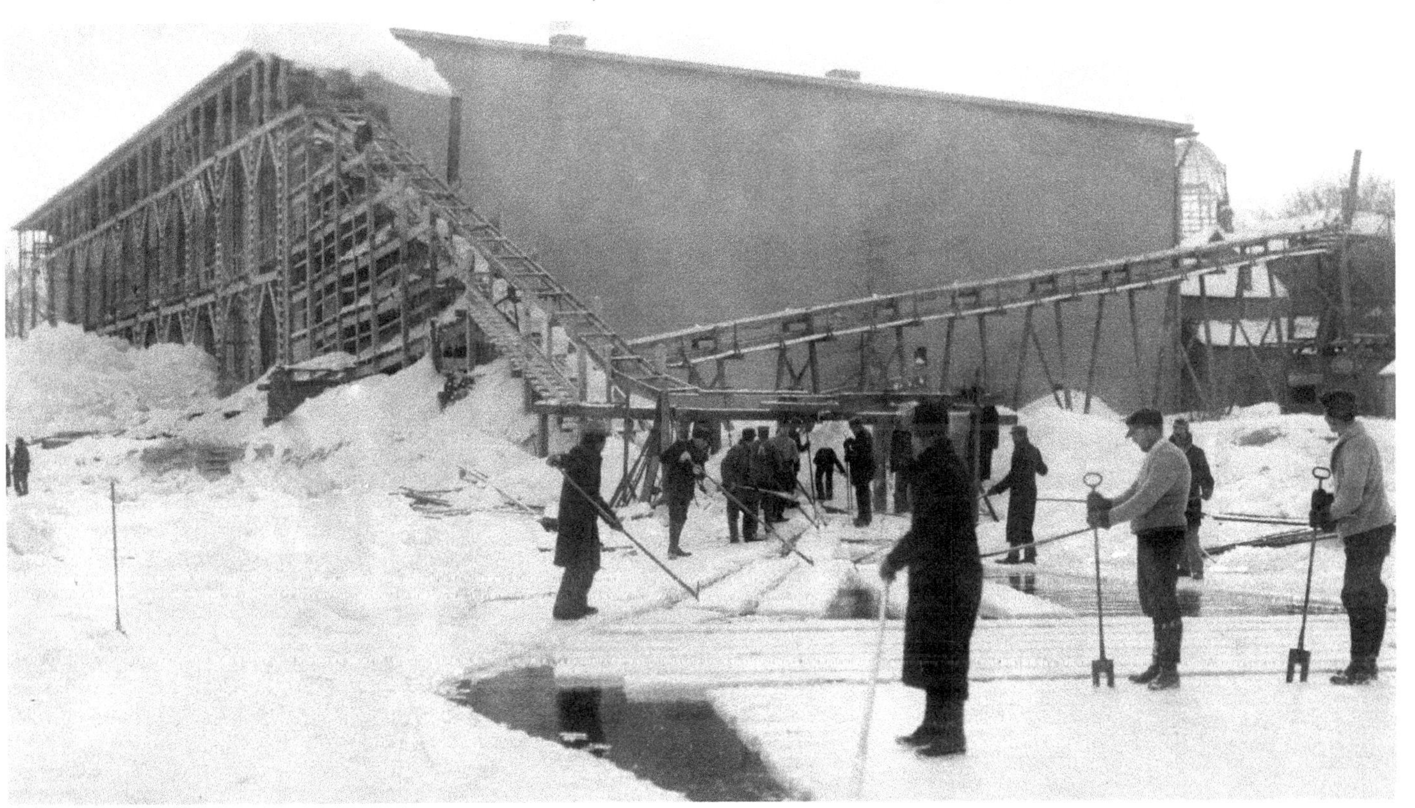

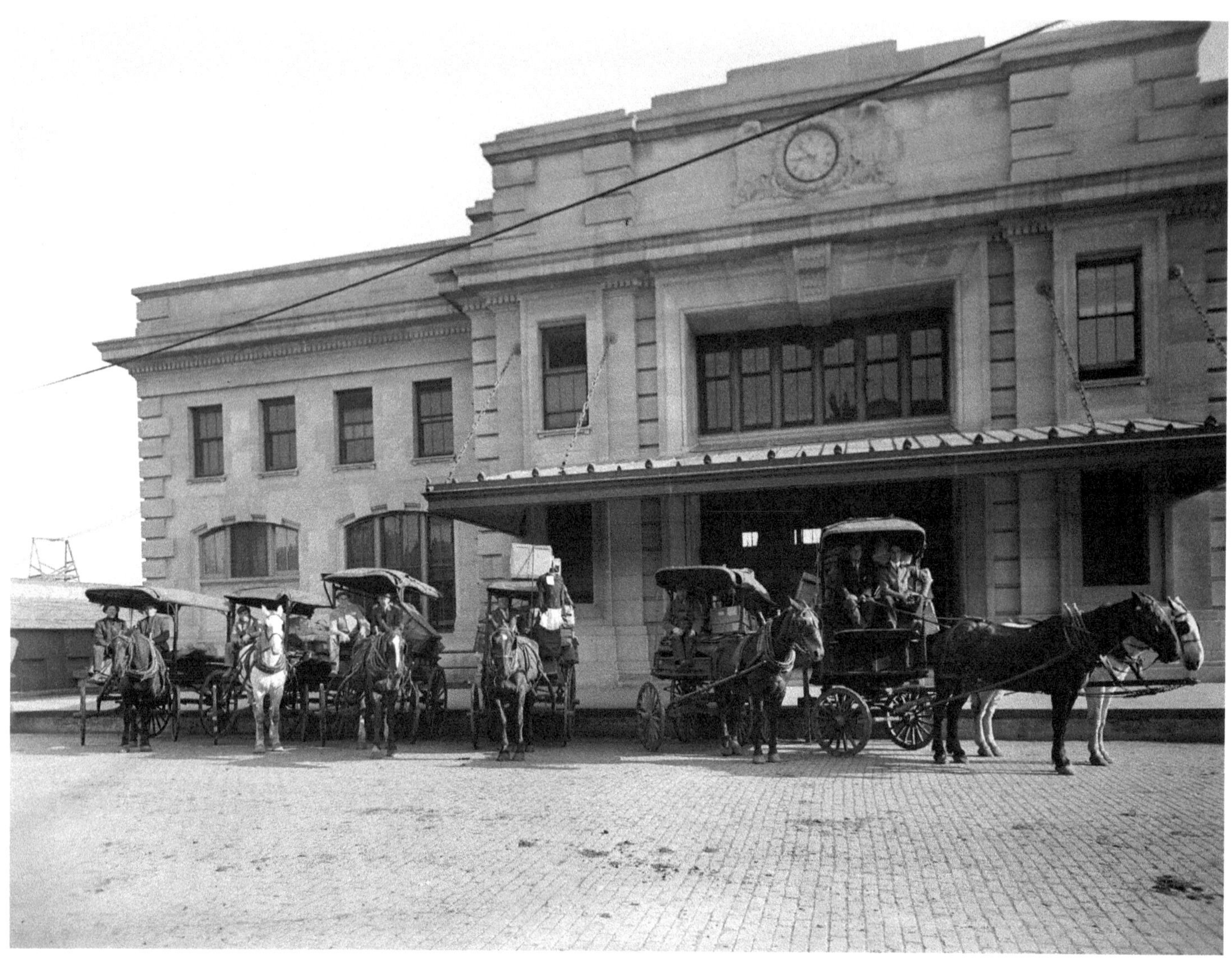

Horse-drawn American Express wagons wait in front of the Chicago & Northwestern Railway depot at Blair and East Wilson streets in 1913. The building now houses Madison Gas & Electric. Fifteen years before, on January 25, 1898, at 9:50 A.M., the boiler of passenger engine 249 exploded in the C&NW roundhouse a few blocks east of the passenger depot, killing three people and injuring five others.

In July 1914, workers begin raising the three-ton *Wisconsin* statue that sits atop the dome of the state Capitol (the fourth State Capitol, the third in Madison). The gilded bronze statue covered in 23.5-carat gold leaf was created by Daniel Chester French, who is best known for the gigantic seated figure of Abraham Lincoln in the Lincoln Memorial in Washington, D.C. The Capitol statue includes a badger and clusters of grapes on top of Wisconsin's head, and an orb in her left hand.

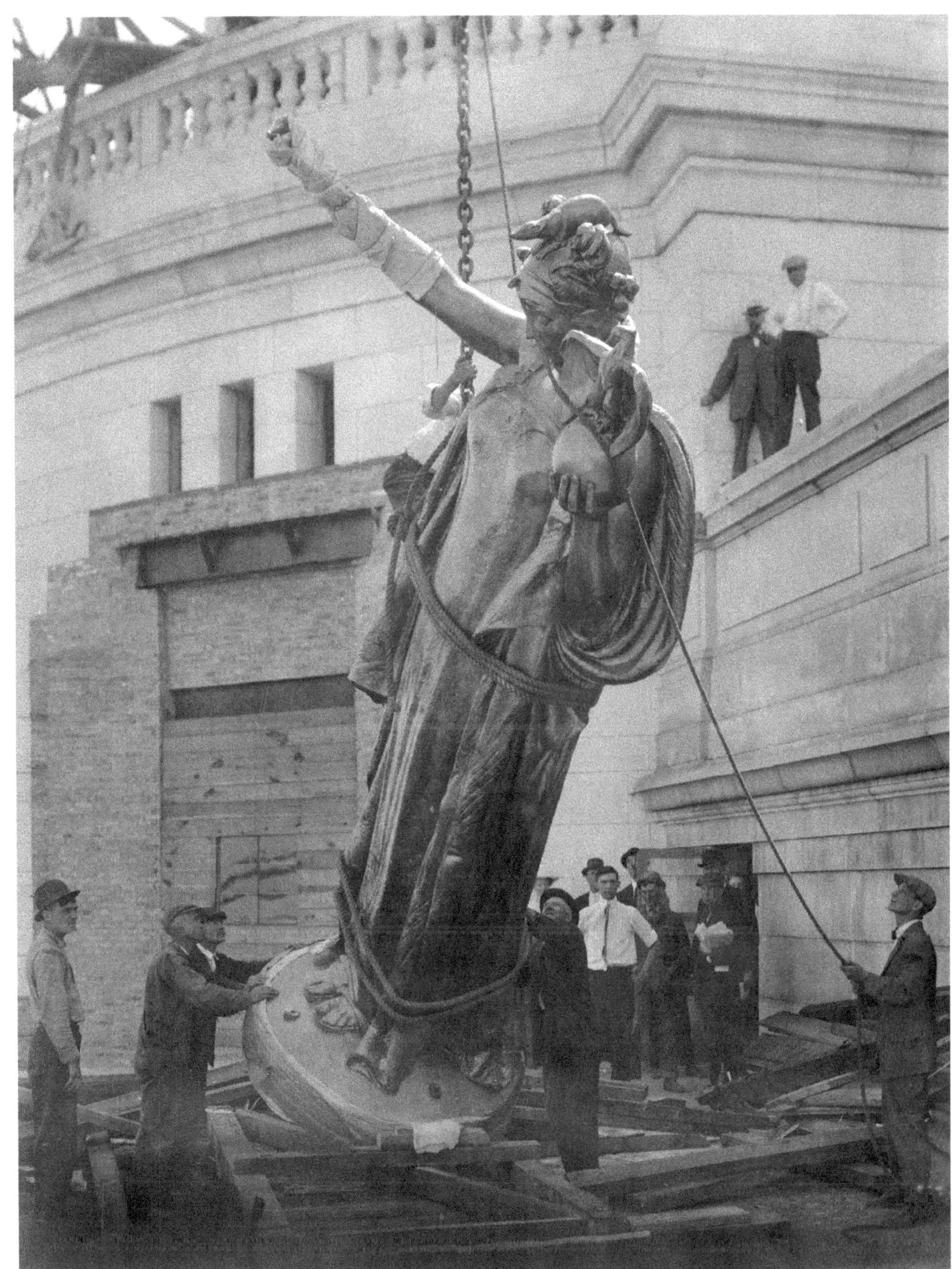

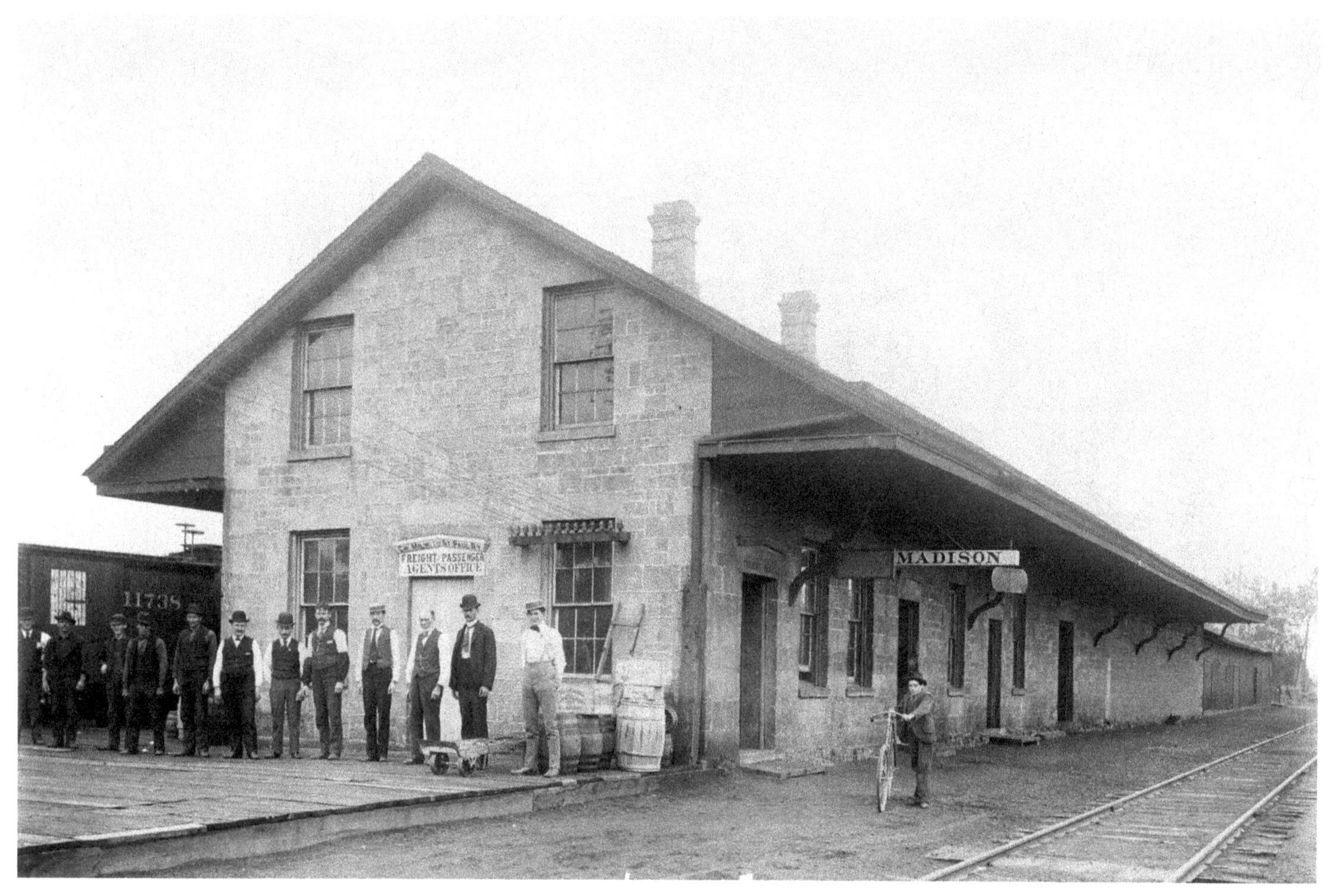

The Madison freight depot of the Chicago, Milwaukee, and St. Paul Railway around 1915. Throughout the railway era, competition for freight was intense. P. Hinrichs, agent for the railroad, stands second from right in a black suit and hat.

On March 31, 1917, men march down State Street from the Capitol in what was described by the *Wisconsin State Journal* as a "monster Loyalty Day Parade." The parade, held during the build-up in the week before President Woodrow Wilson asked Congress for a declaration of war to enter World War I, drew thousands. At 3:00 P.M. the Loyalty Parade marched from Wisconsin Avenue, down Mifflin to Pinckney, picked up a second group of marchers at East Washington Avenue, then moved on to Main, Carroll, State, Park, University Avenue, University Drive, and ended at the Stock Pavilion for a 4:00 P.M. rally.

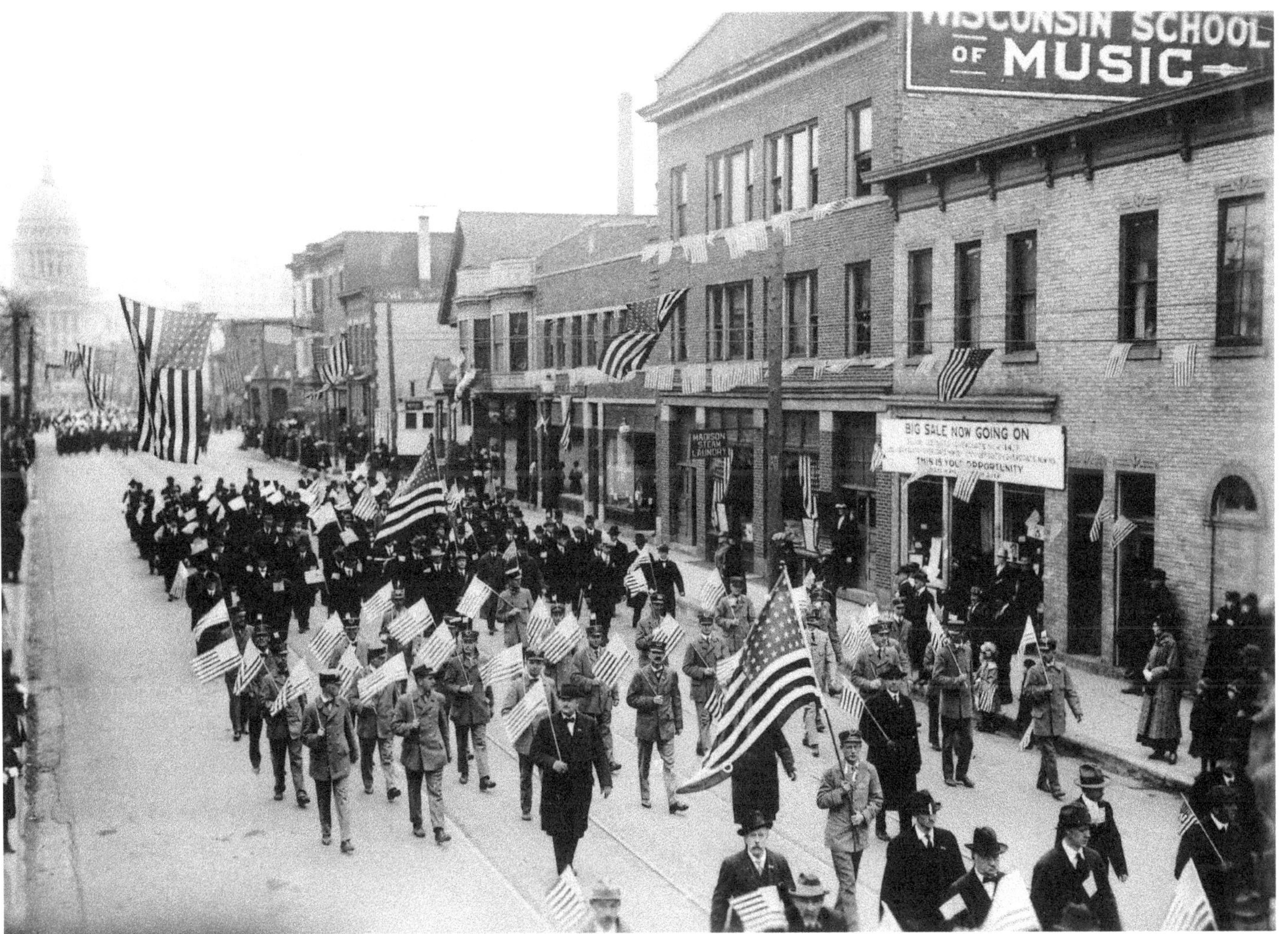

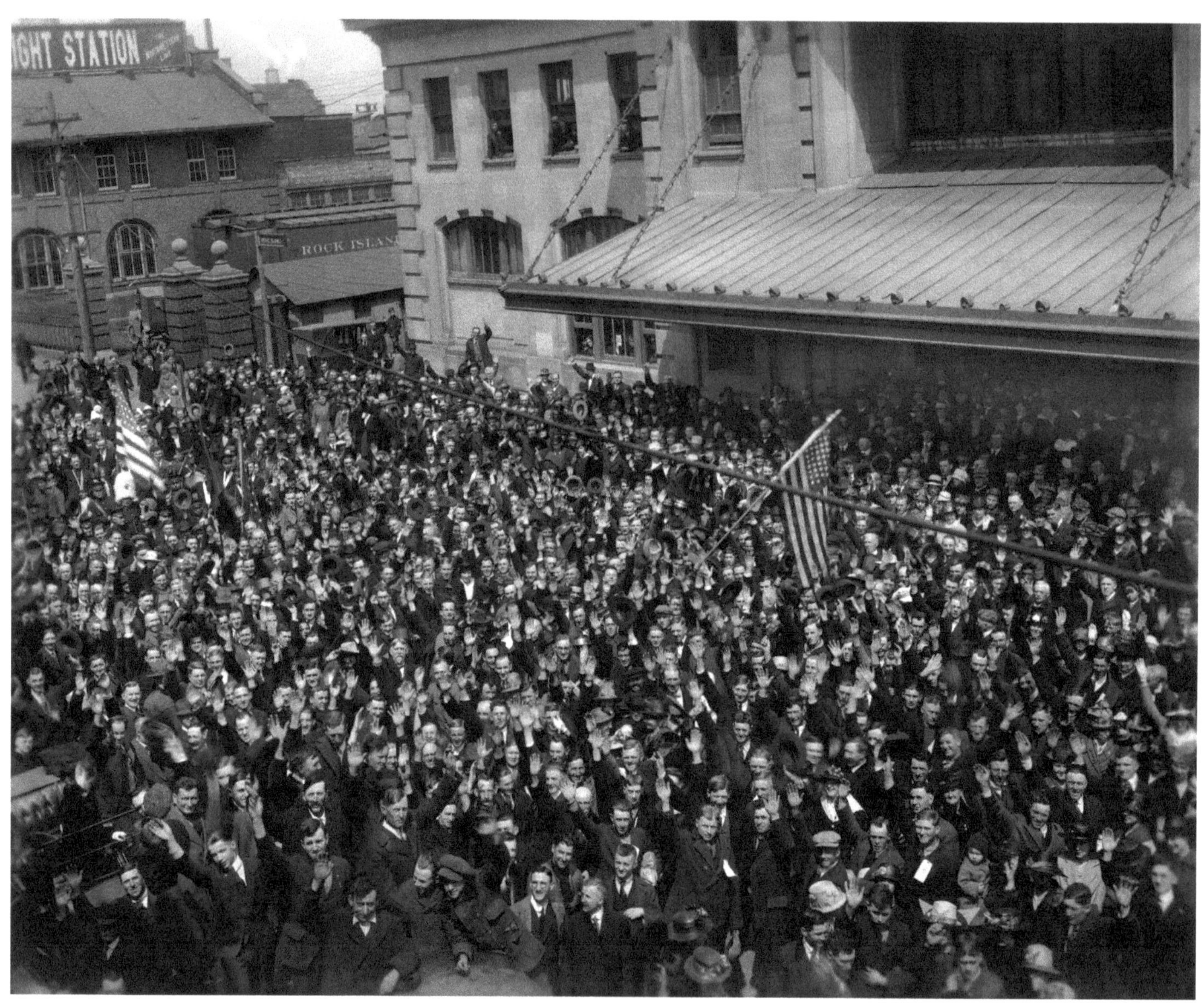

On May 25, 1918, a year after the United States entered World War I and Congress passed the Selective Service Act, these draftees collect at the Chicago Northwestern Railroad station on East Wilson and Blair streets. They were on their way to basic training and then France. Nearly 3,000 Madison men eventually joined the war effort.

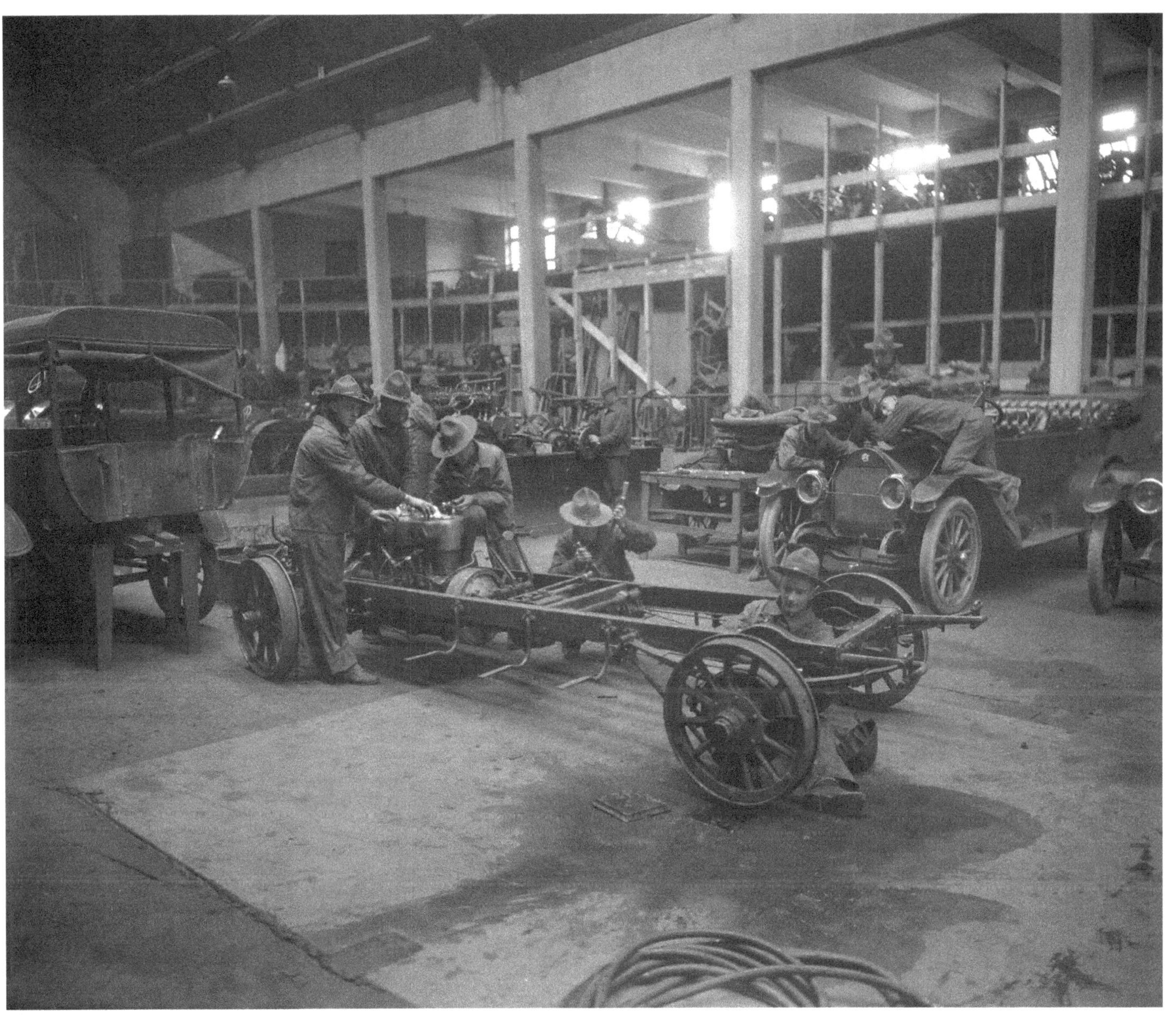

This 1918 photograph shows University of Wisconsin cadets learning about repair and maintenance of automobiles and trucks during World War I.

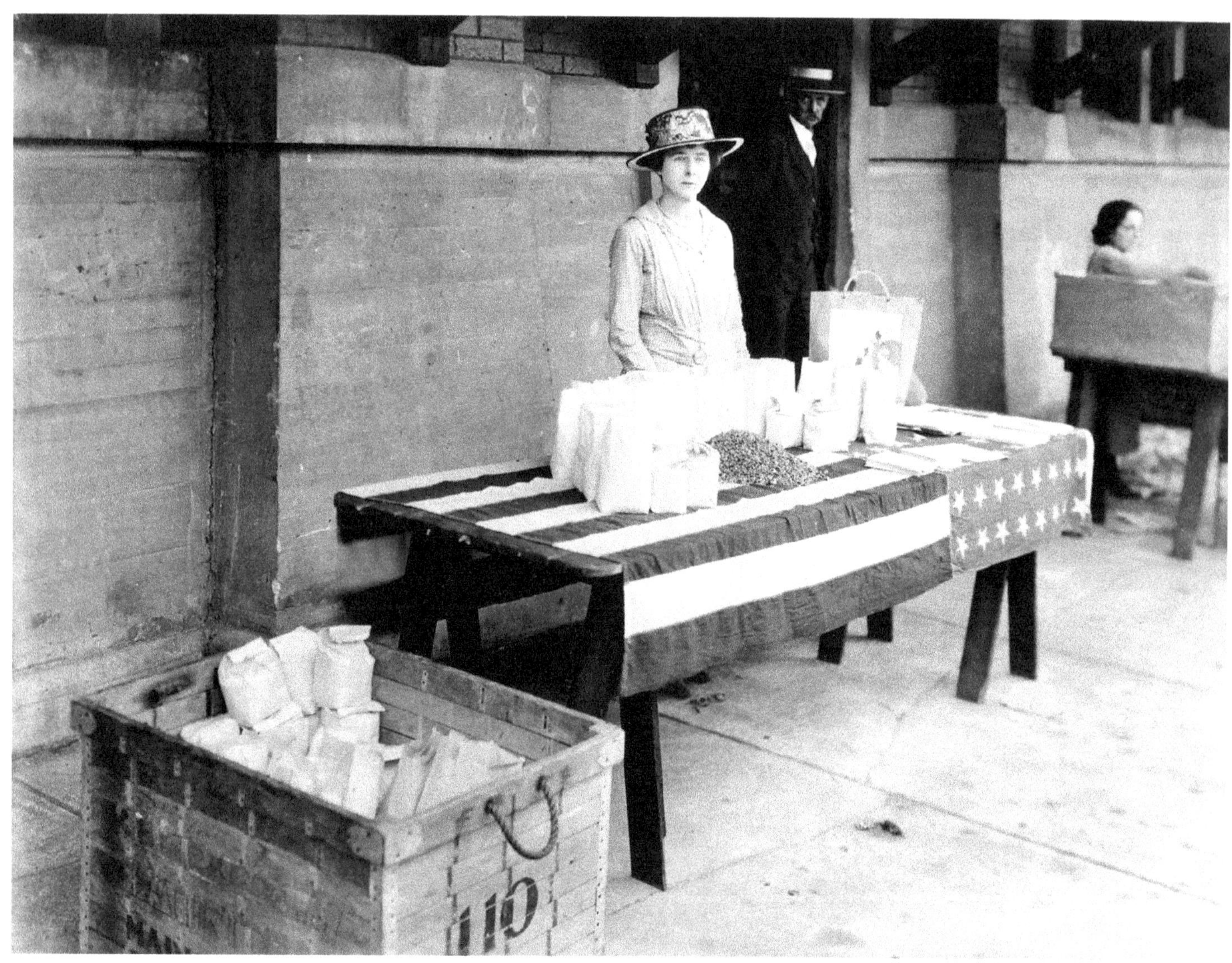

In 1918, a member of the Dane County Council of Defense Food Board sells dried corn at the farmer's market. Women's organizations sold wheat substitutes during World War I to comply with food conservation measures. More than 3,000 pounds were sold in Madison in 1918. The controls were introduced through the federal Lever Act, also known as the Food and Fuel Control Act, in 1917, which was managed by the Food Administration headed by Herbert Hoover. As part of the effort, Americans embraced wheatless Mondays, meatless Tuesdays, and porkless Saturdays.

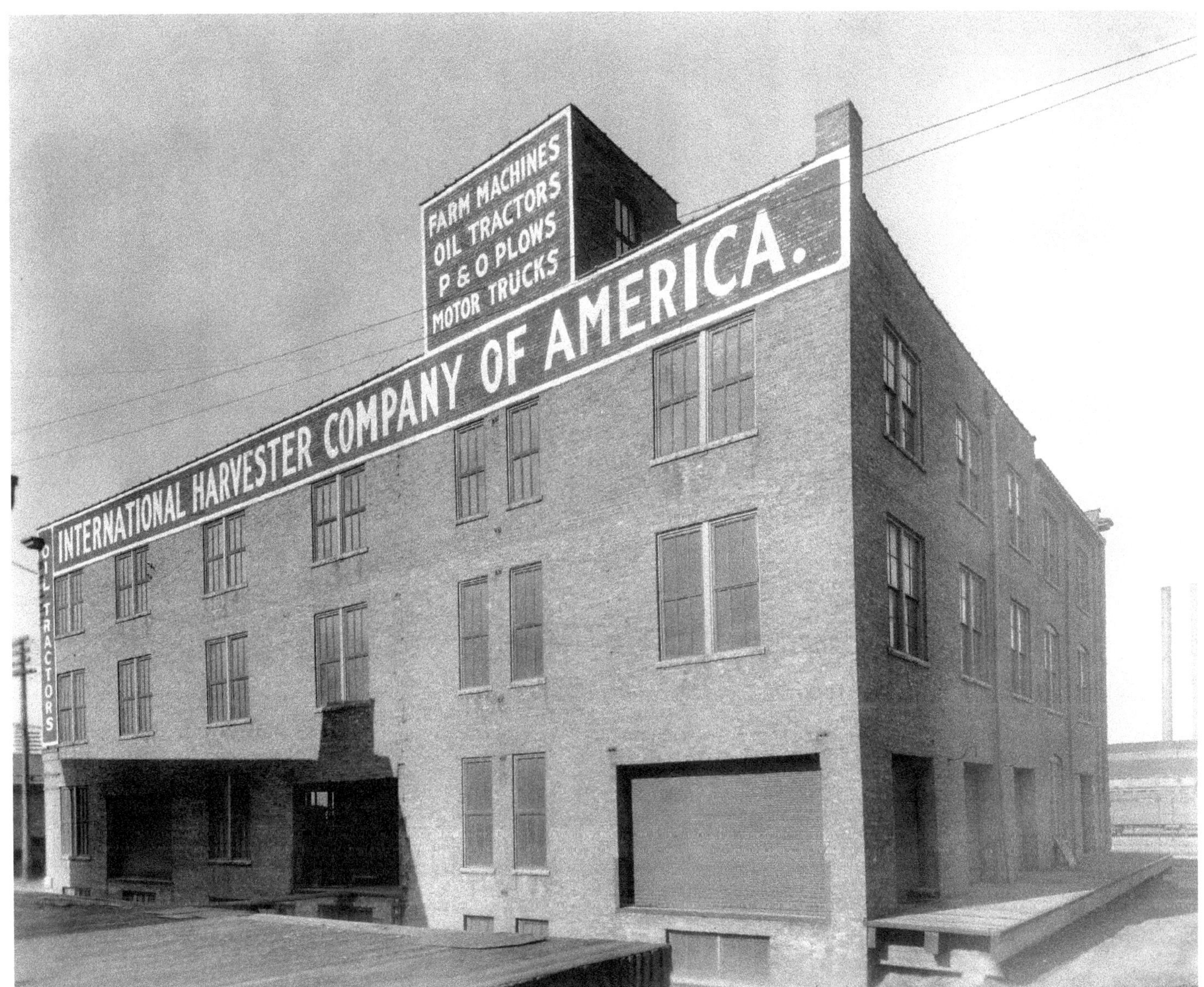

This photograph from October 25, 1919, shows the International Harvester branch building in Madison. This image with its advertisement for "farm machines, oil tractors, P & O plows, motor trucks" is from the massive combined McCormick-International Harvester collection, the largest single collection held by the Wisconsin Historical Society archives. In addition to hundreds of thousands of images dating from the 1840s through the 1980s, the collection includes more than 12 million manuscript pages and 300 films.

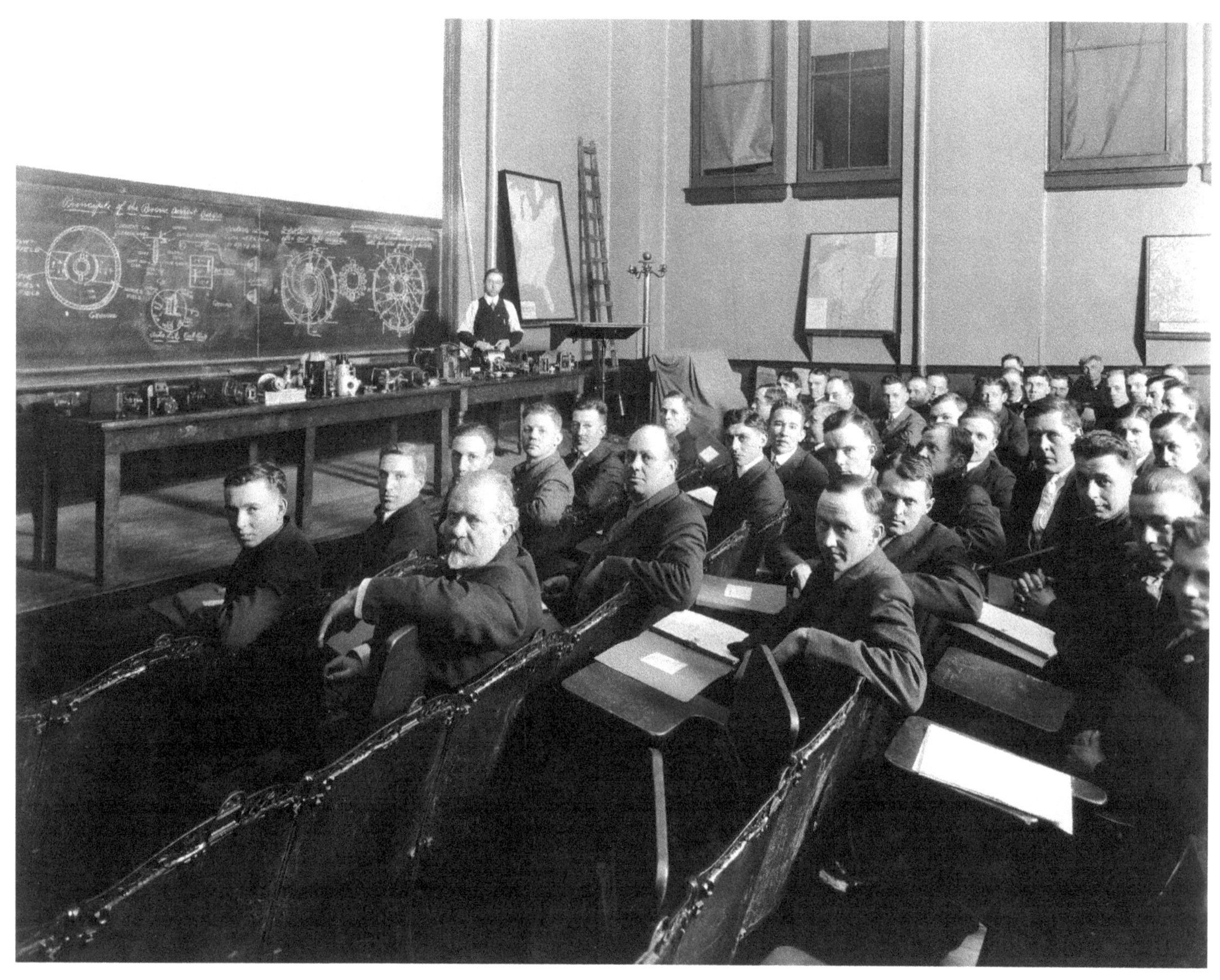

Men are attending what appears to be a University of Wisconsin Extension engineering class under Professor Consoliner, around 1919.

Peacetime Conflict

(1920–1939)

Like the rest of the nation, as if unable to find a middle, Madison faced extremes during the 1920s in politics, religion, and business.

Prohibition was in full swing, yet the sale of liquor in the Bush neighborhood thrived. In politics, the Progressive tradition, both in the state and in the city, had become a political standard around which many rallied when Senator Robert "Fighting Bob" La Follette ran for president in 1924.

In fearsome counterpoint, the Ku Klux Klan made a brief appearance in Madison in the early 1920s. The Klan, declaring itself the defender of Americanism, held marches down main thoroughfares, even forming a student group on the University of Wisconsin campus. Meanwhile, antimilitarism and the fight against mandatory ROTC on the university campus was a popular cause.

New technologies in communications and transportation changed the fabric of daily life. Although more mobile, informed, and connected than in any other era, citizens here and elsewhere settled into isolationism.

Everywhere one looked, contradictions took center stage. Darwinism did battle with Fundamentalism. The poor suffered while the market went bullish. And in the marketplace, demand did not match supply.

The unprecedented economic boom seemed destined to go on forever, until an Indian Summer day in 1929—Black Thursday—brought it crashing down and marked the start of the Great Depression.

In spite of this great hardship, Madison movie houses were filled; automobiles fostered the growth of food stands, drive-ins, and family restaurants; and Madison opened an airport. The growth of the arts saw wide access to photography and the rise of photojournalism. The 35mm camera was invented in 1924, and flashbulbs replaced dangerous flashpowder in 1930.

Madisonians pictured in this era—candid images of the hard-working, the loyal, the religious, and the funny, as well as the famous—are people who seem remarkably poised for standing on a stage that seemed to be moving.

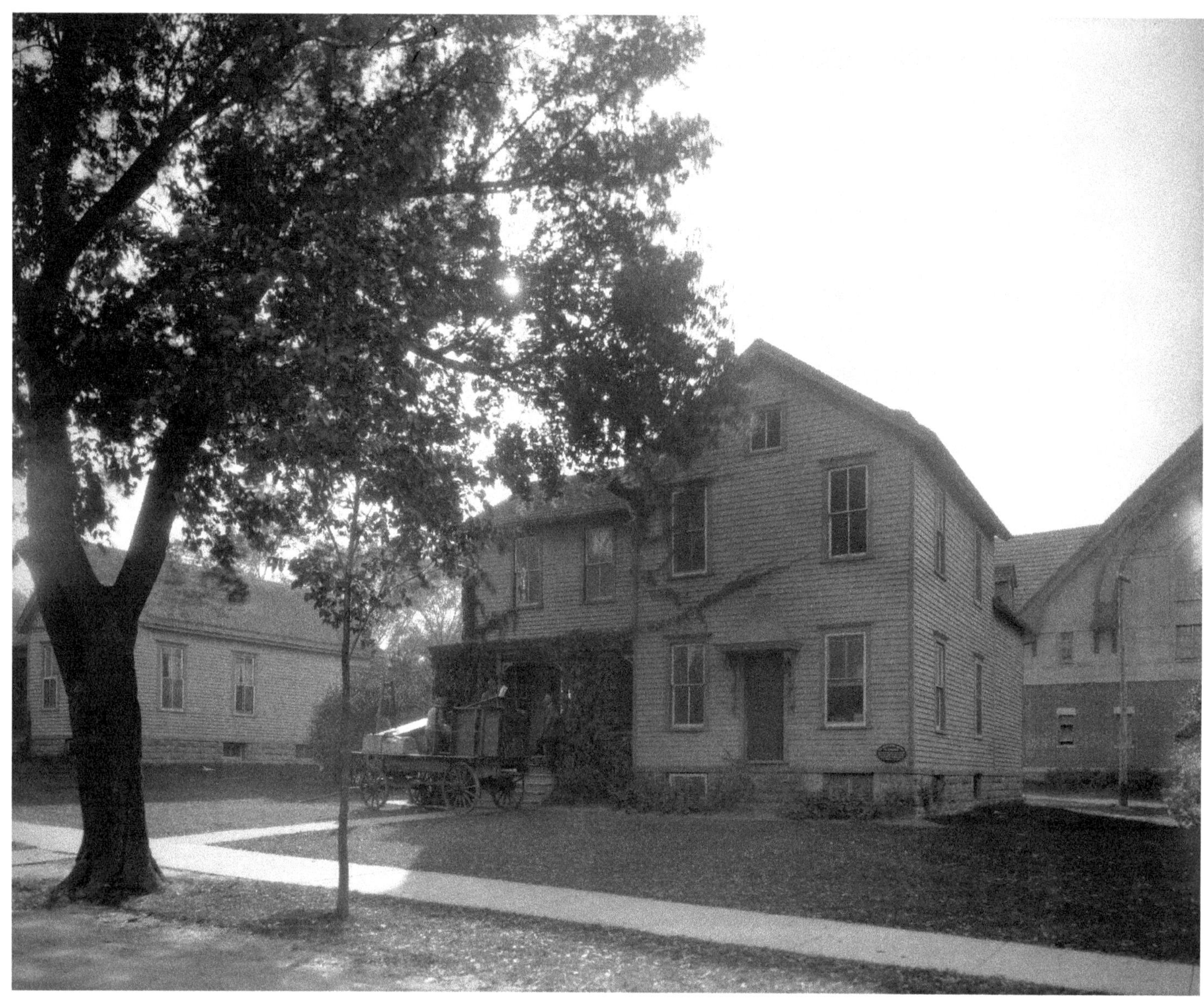

This 1920 image shows the building that was used for the first dairy school at the University of Wisconsin. The program, which began in 1890, was the first in the United States and the world, and was significant in moving farmers from wheat production to dairying. Stephen Babcock, who established it, developed the first test for the butterfat content of milk. This simple test enabled cheese makers to give farmers a fair price for their milk. It also permitted high-quality butter and cheese to be manufactured consistently.

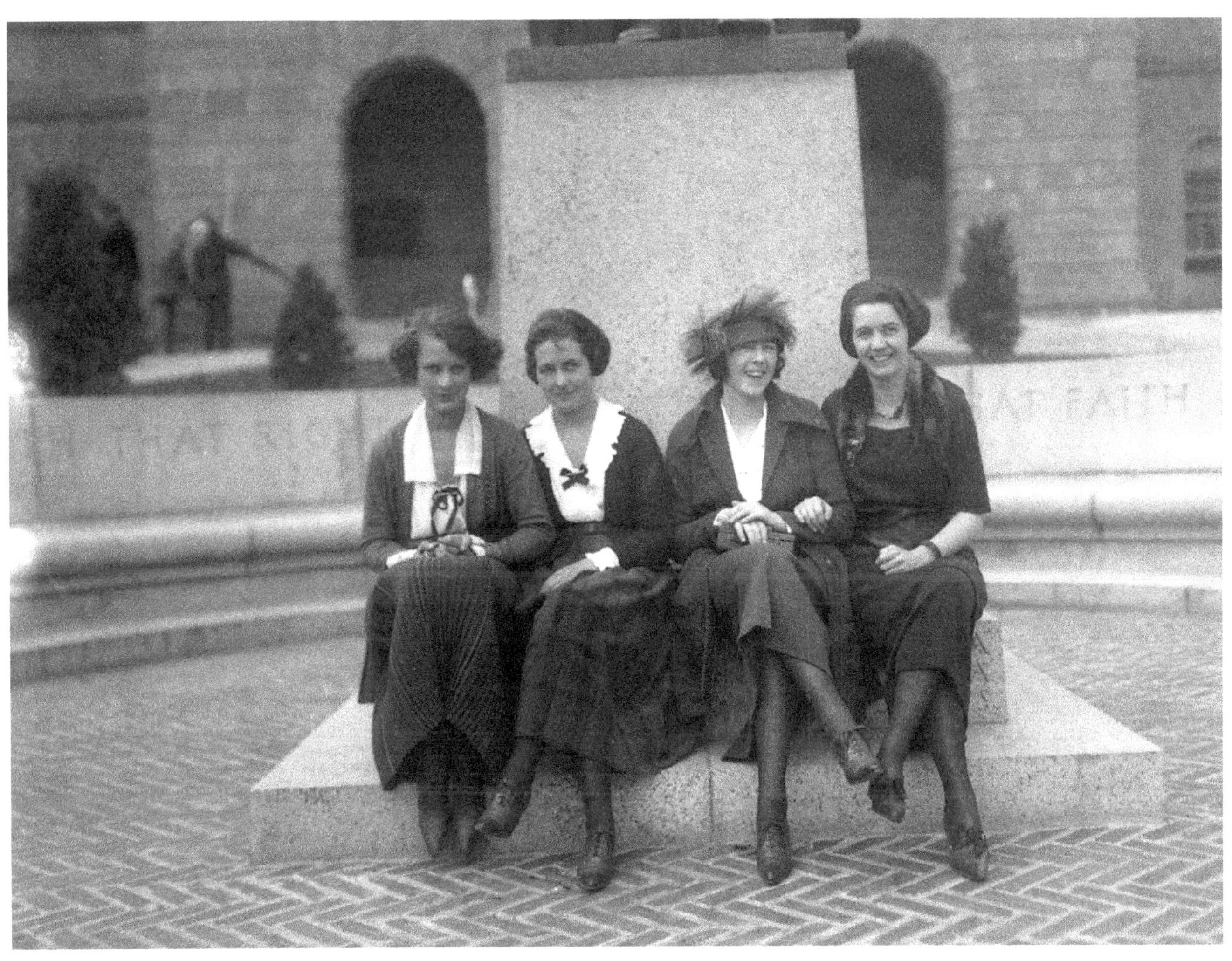

University of Wisconsin coeds sit at the base of the Lincoln statue on Bascom Hill in 1920. The university began admitting women ten years after it was founded in 1848, far in advance of many other universities in the nation.

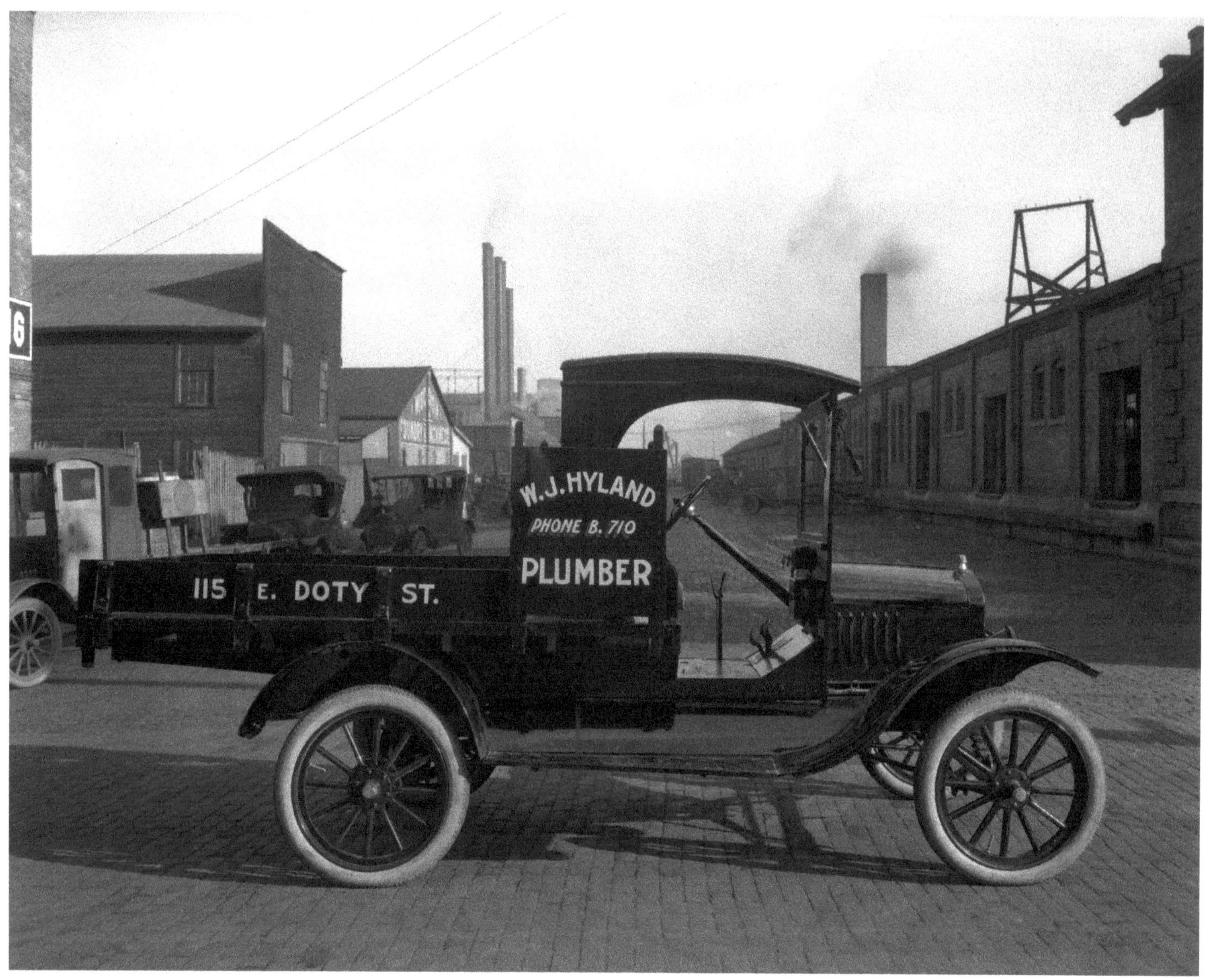

This is the Ford truck owned by W. J. Hyland Plumbing, 115 E. Doty Street, around 1920. About this time the company installed a new plumbing system at the *Wisconsin State Journal* offices, which had recently expanded. The inking system on the presses was also installed by Hyland.

Two women stand in front of the United States Sugar Company factory at 3244 Atwood Avenue, just north of Olbrich Park. The development of the processing plant parallels the rise and fall of the sugar beet industry in the Midwest and the United States. Magnus Swenson, a member of the staff of the College of Agriculture at the University of Wisconsin, held a number of patents on sugar processing inventions. He and a group of investors opened the factory at 7:00 A.M., October 22, 1906. The plant operated until May 1924. In May 1929, James Russell Garver purchased the building for general storage and to sell dairy and poultry feeds. In 1997 the Olbrich Botanical Society acquired the property and gave it to the city of Madison for the future expansion of the Olbrich Botanical Gardens, possibly for community and art studio space.

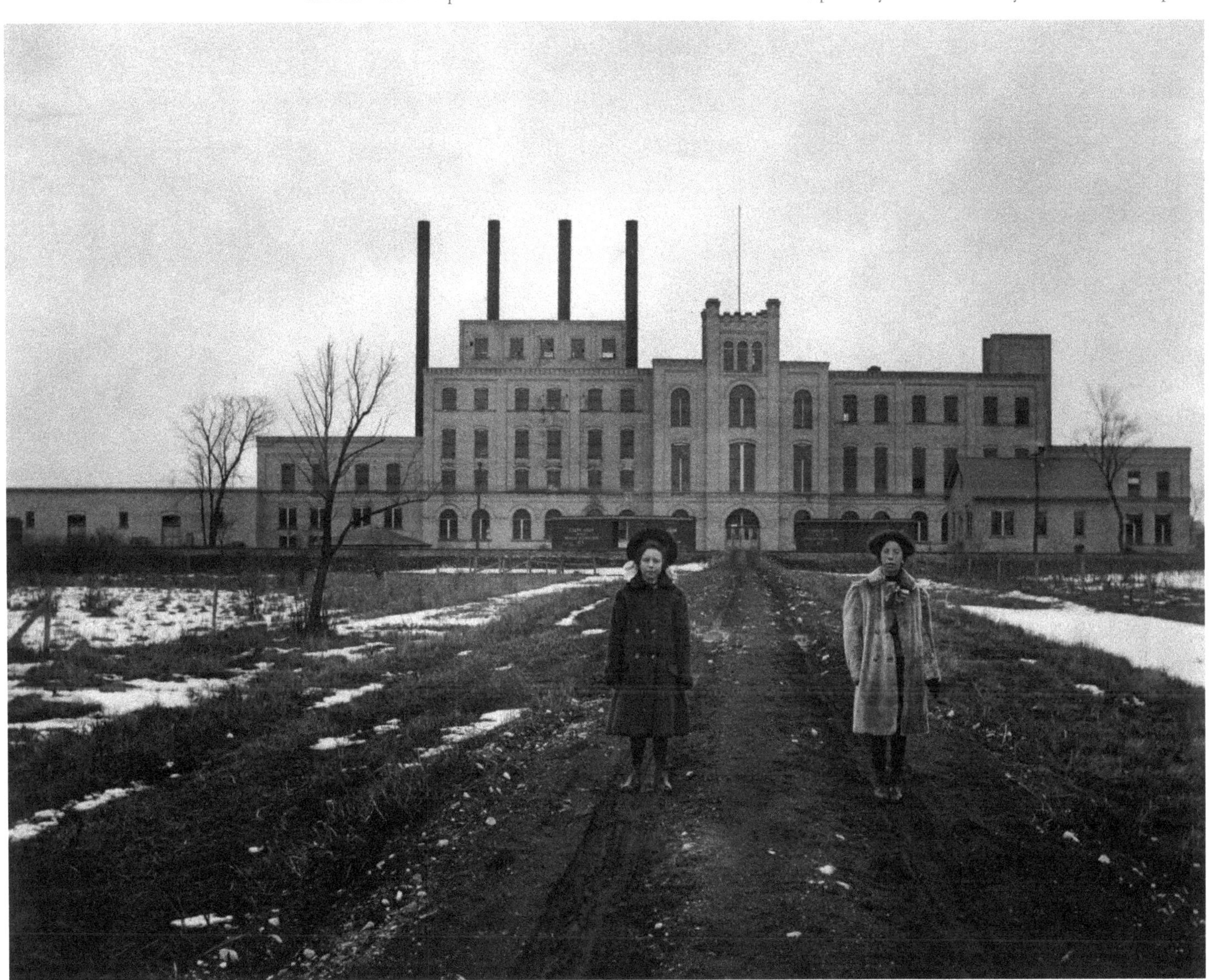

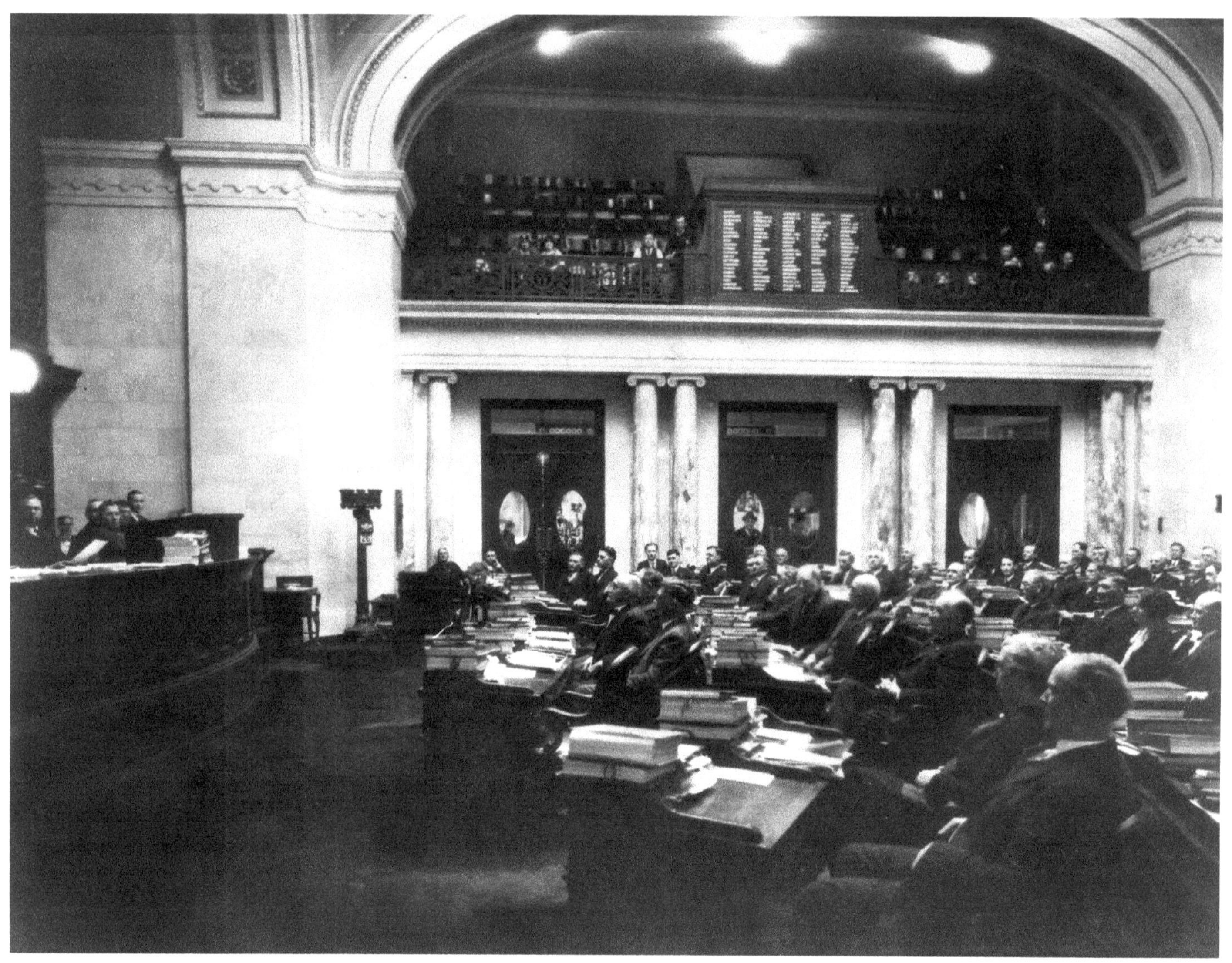

This view shows the House Chamber in the Wisconsin State Capitol in 1925. A significant piece of legislation in this year made Wisconsin the first state to require doctors and other professionals treating the sick to complete training in the basic sciences of anatomy, physiology, pathology, and diagnosis.

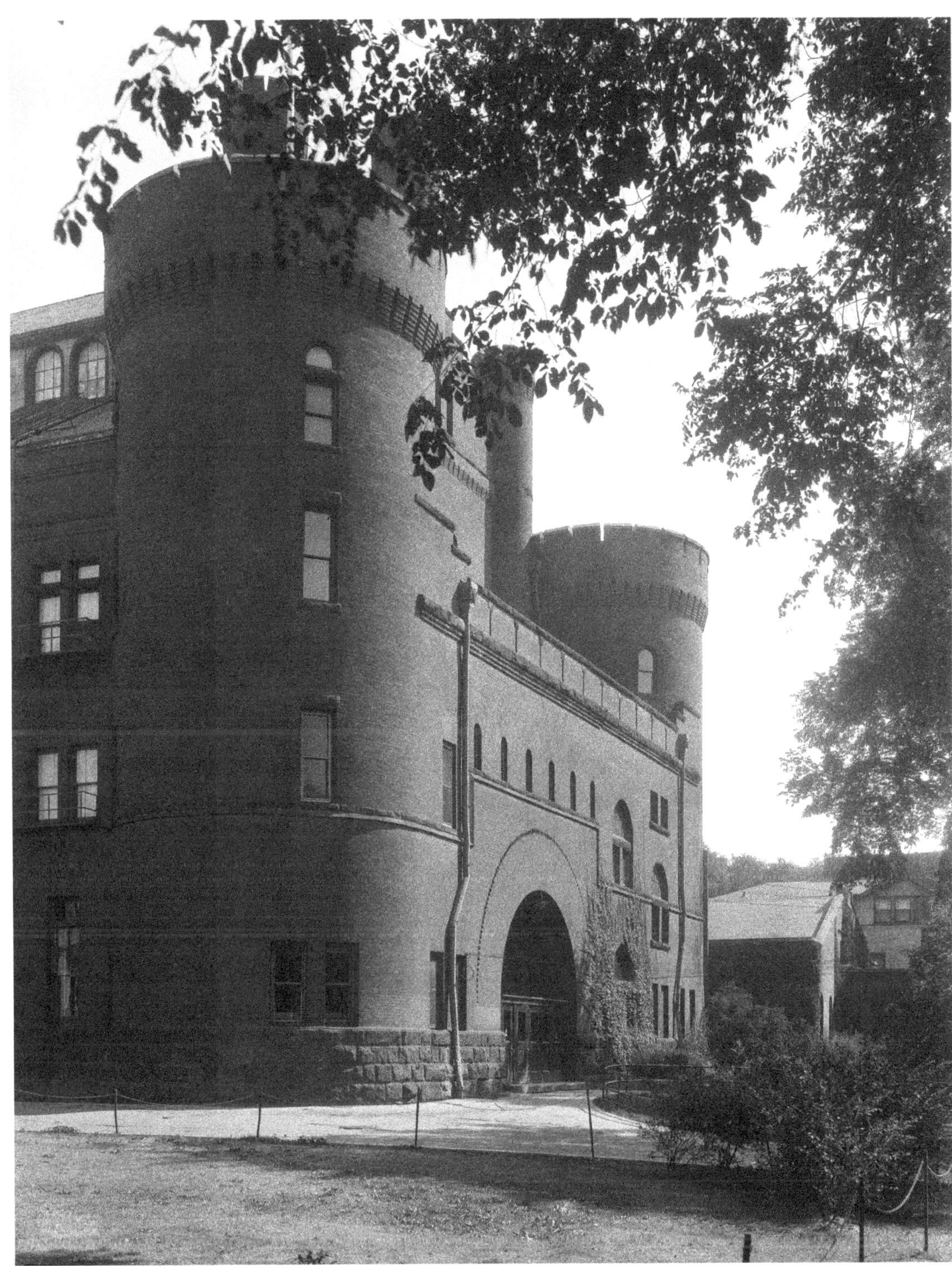

This 1926 photograph shows the Romanesque Revival–style Red Gym, previously called the Armory, at the University of Wisconsin. Designed by Conover and Porter, its cornerstone was laid on June 20, 1893, and the Armory was opened in May 1894 to house military drills and gymnastic exercises. Its design featured stepped gables, turrets and towers with battlements, and broad arched entryways on the south and west facades. The Armory was the venue in 1904 for the state convention when Robert M. La Follette's Progressives won control of the Wisconsin Republican Party. The occasion holds national significance in the history of the Progressive movement as the "gymnasium convention."

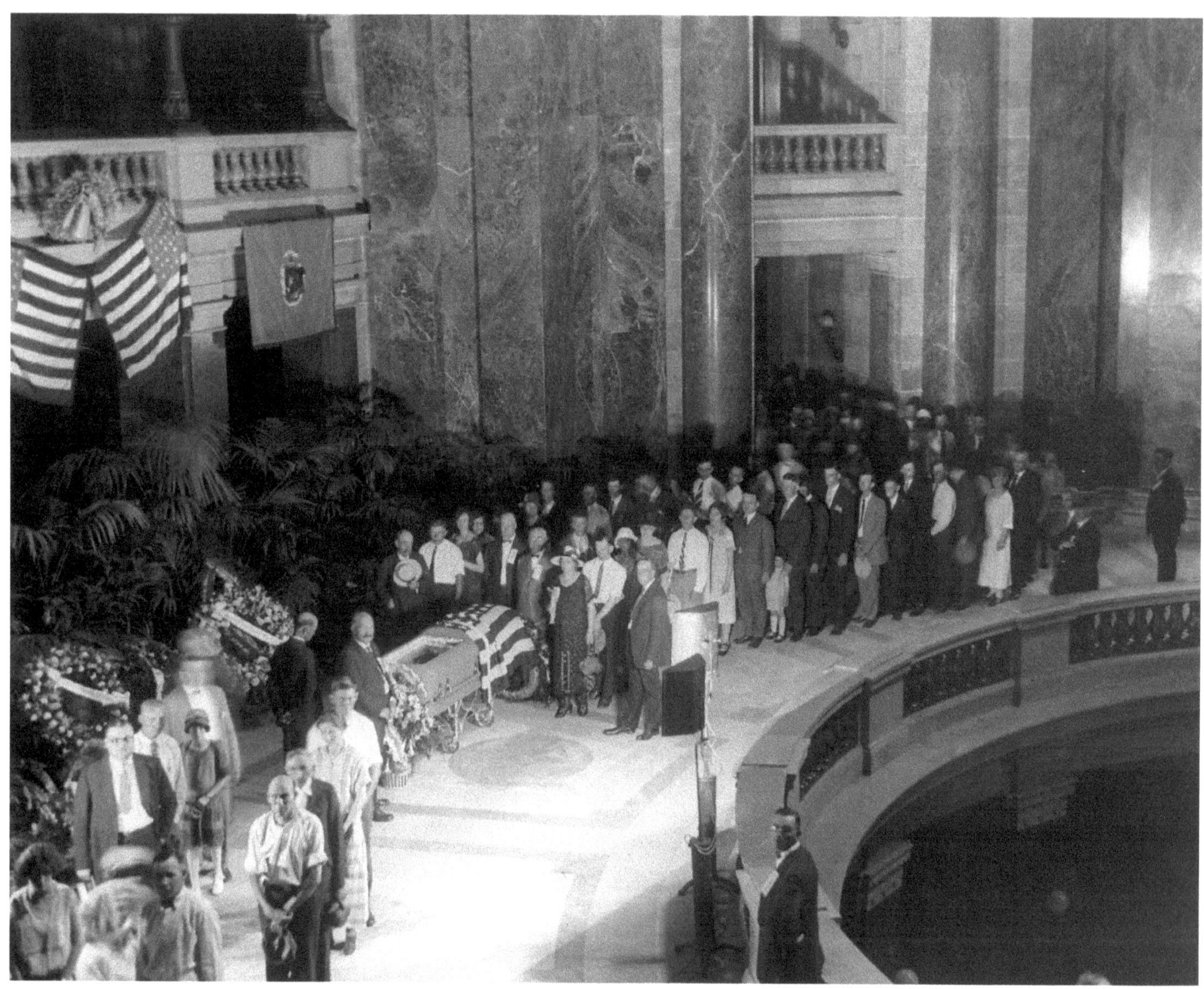

Robert M. La Follette lies in state in the Wisconsin Capitol rotunda on June 21, 1925. Although affiliated with the Republican Party, La Follette remained staunchly independent and frequently clashed with party leaders, earning him the epithet "Fighting Bob." Born in Primrose, Wisconsin, he graduated from the University of Wisconsin in 1879, and was elected a district attorney the following year. In 1884, he was elected to the House of Representatives, where he served three terms. He served as governor from 1900 to 1906, when he returned to Washington to serve three terms in the Senate. In 1909, he founded *La Follette's Weekly Magazine* (later called *The Progressive* and still published monthly in Madison). In 1924, he ran for president on the Progressive Party ticket, earning approximately one-sixth of the popular vote.

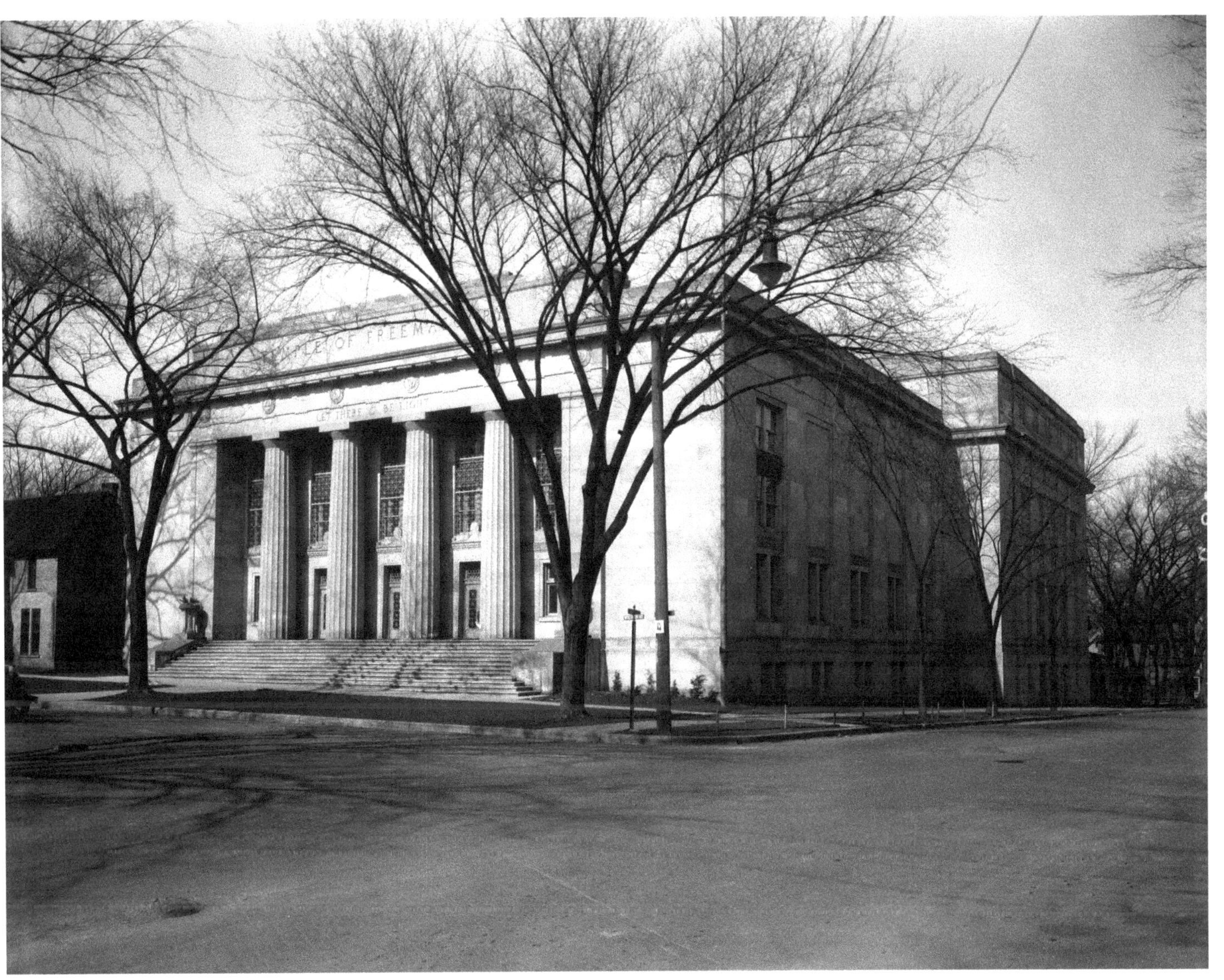

The Masonic Temple, at 301 Wisconsin Avenue, shown here April 15, 1926, was constructed in spring 1923 for $500,000. It featured thirty-foot columns of Bedford stone and included a 1500-seat auditorium that was also used as a musical venue. It was designed by the Madison architectural firm Law, Law, and Potter. One of the partners, James Law, later served as Madison's mayor (1933-43), promoting the building of a lakeshore drive, an area now known as Law Park.

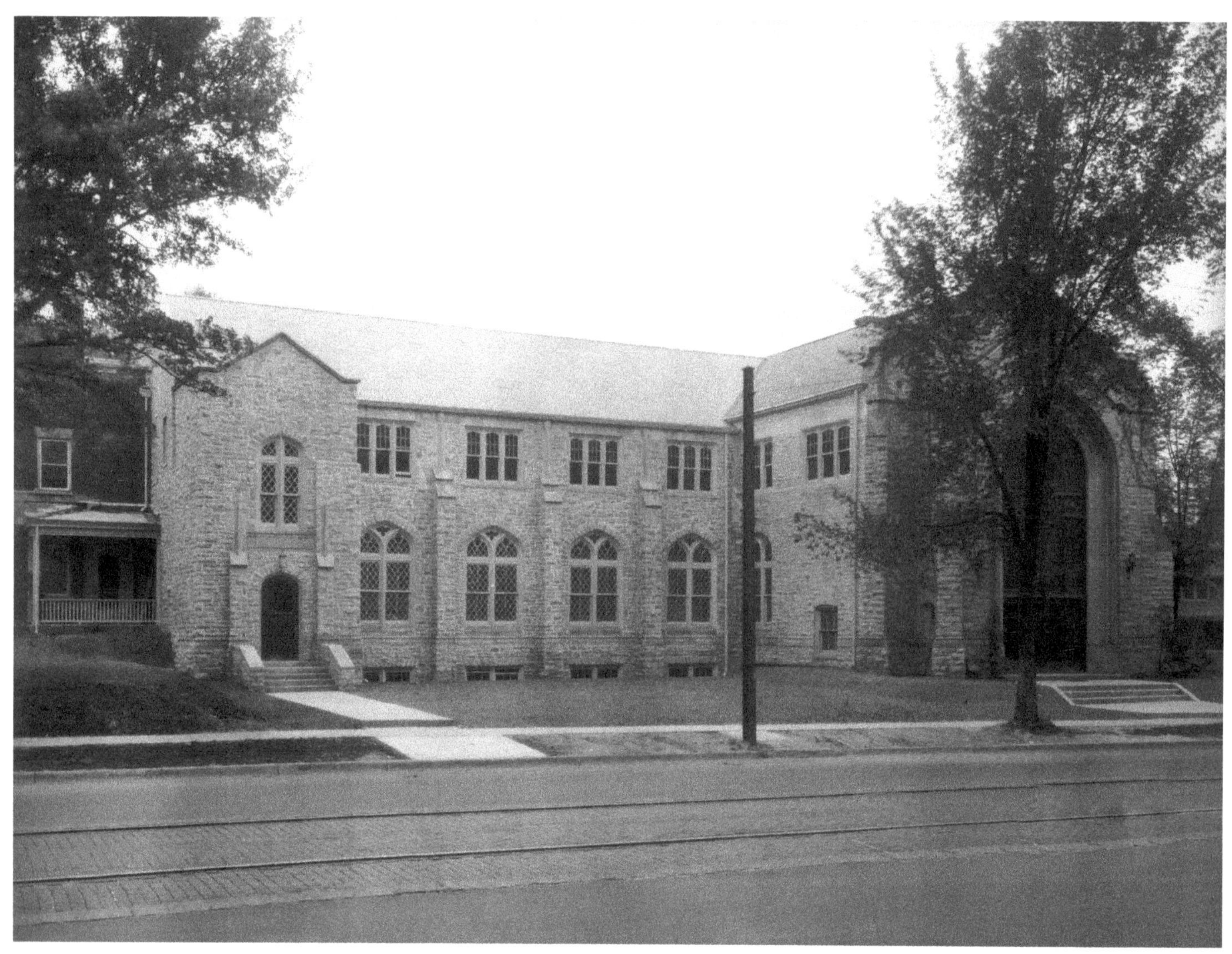

In 1928, a wing of one of Madison's oldest landmark homes was torn down to make way for an addition to the Methodist church at 1127 University Avenue, shown here in 1926. The red brick mansion was built in 1851 by Abel Brooks, a "forty-niner" who returned to Madison after making his fortune in the California gold rush and for whom Brooks Street is named.

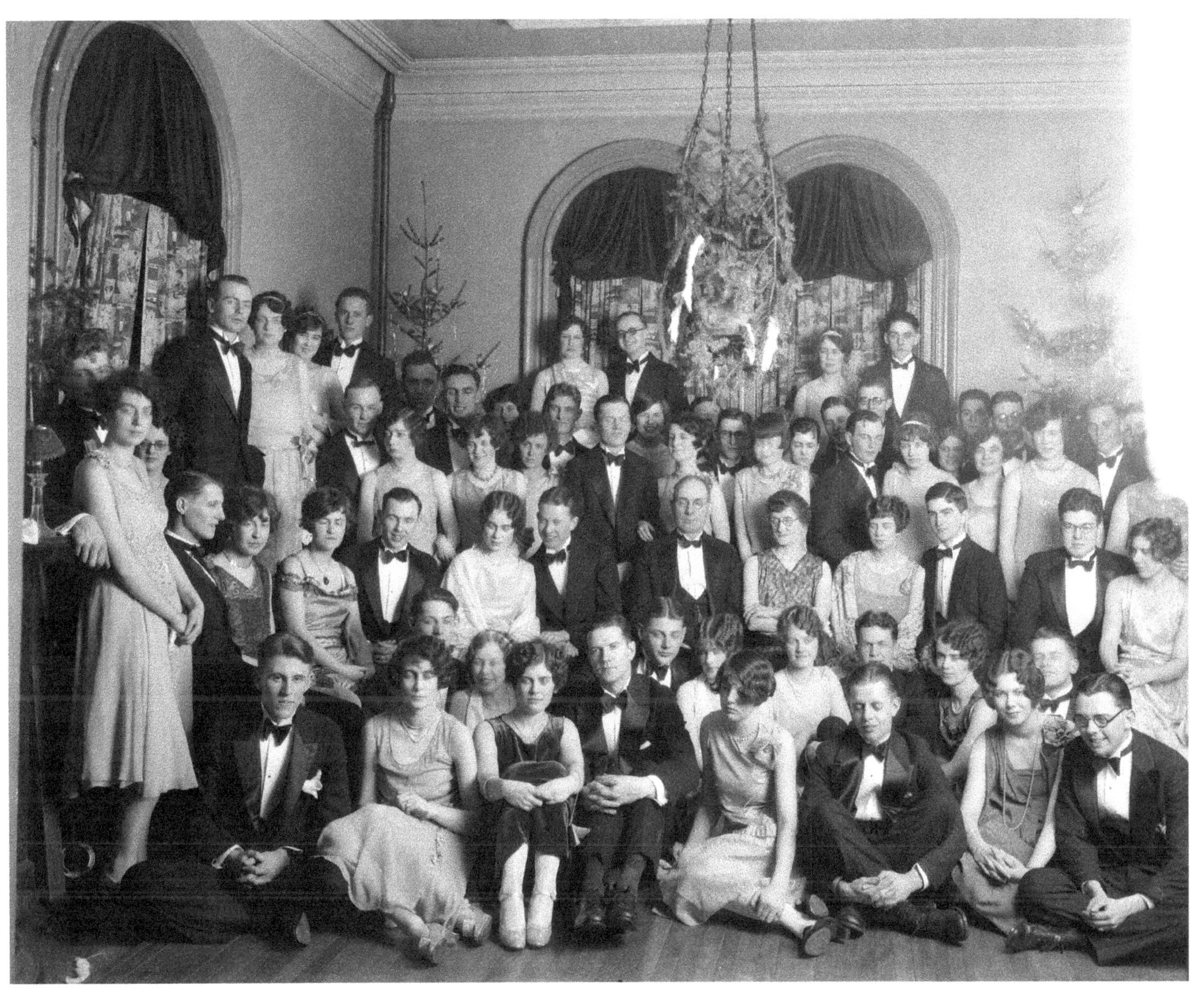

This group portrait was taken at the Alpha Kappa Lambda fraternity Christmas party in 1926.

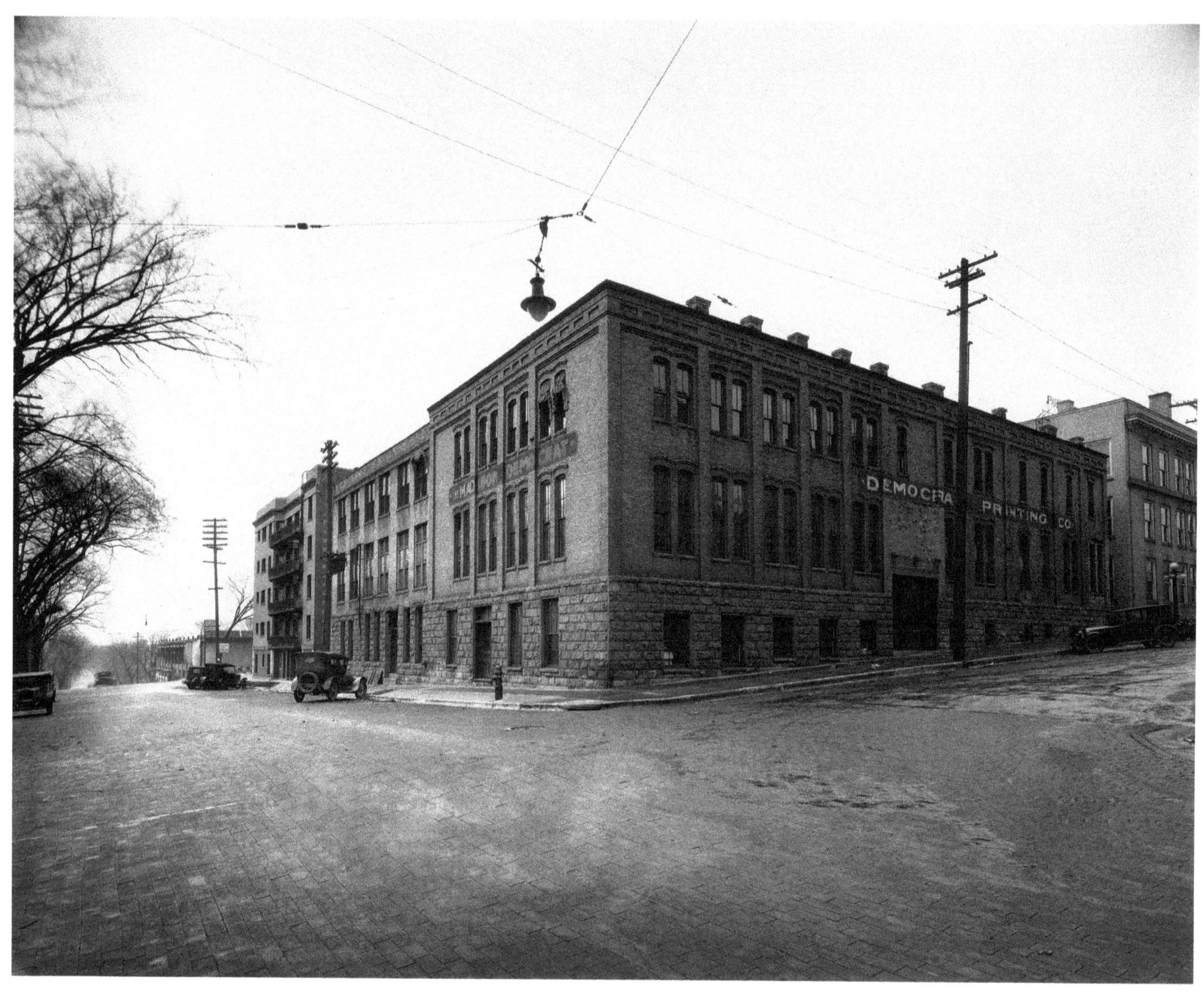

The Democrat Printing Company, known at one time as the "official" state printer and publisher of the *Madison Democrat,* is shown here at the corner of Carroll and Doty streets in 1927. The company, founded in 1860 and incorporated in 1890, became known as Webcrafters in 1965, one of the early entrants to offset printing. Another corporate descendant began as the four-person library department of the Democrat Printing Company in 1905, which Norman Bassett took over and named Demco Library Supplies in 1925.

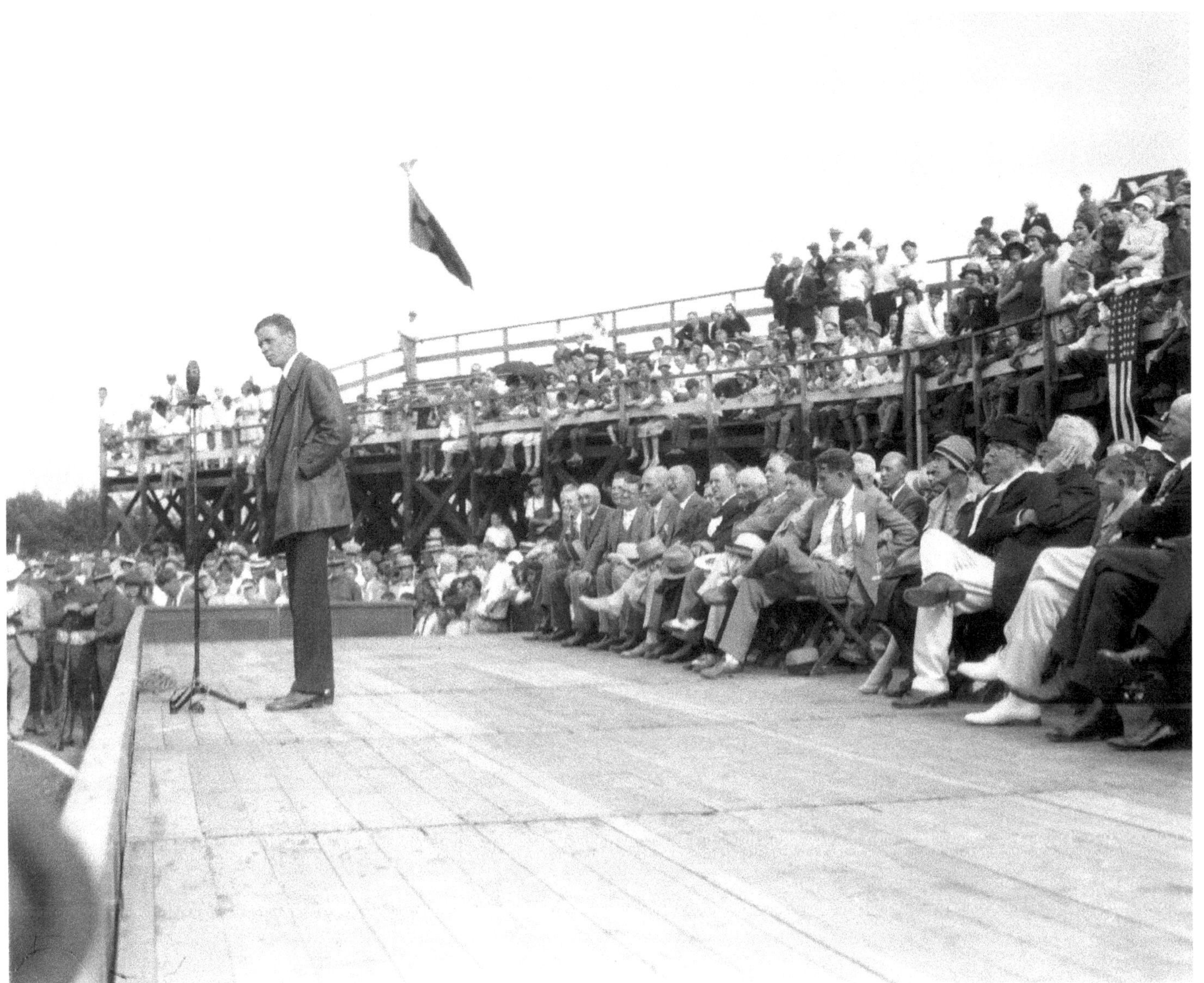

Charles Lindbergh, a former University of Wisconsin engineering student (1920-22) who completed the first solo flight across the Atlantic Ocean in 1927, speaks to a crowd of 40,000 at Camp Randall Stadium on August 22, 1927. He received an honorary degree from UW in 1928.

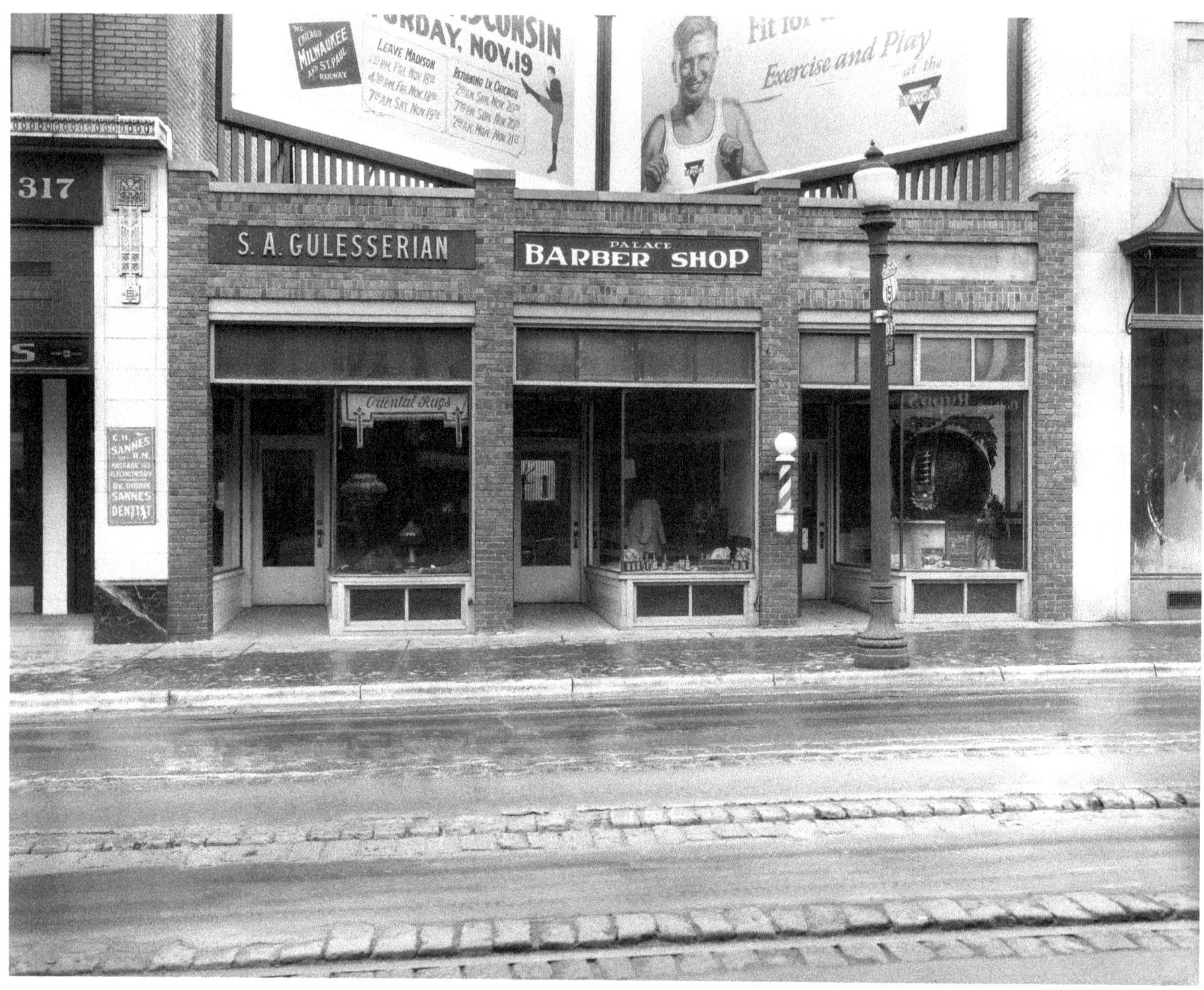

The Madison Oriental Rug Company, at 316 State Street, shown here in 1927, was owned by Solomon Gulesserian. The Palace Barber Shop is next door. Still in operation with a third generation, Gulesserian Oriental Rugs is now at 8 South Breese Terrace.

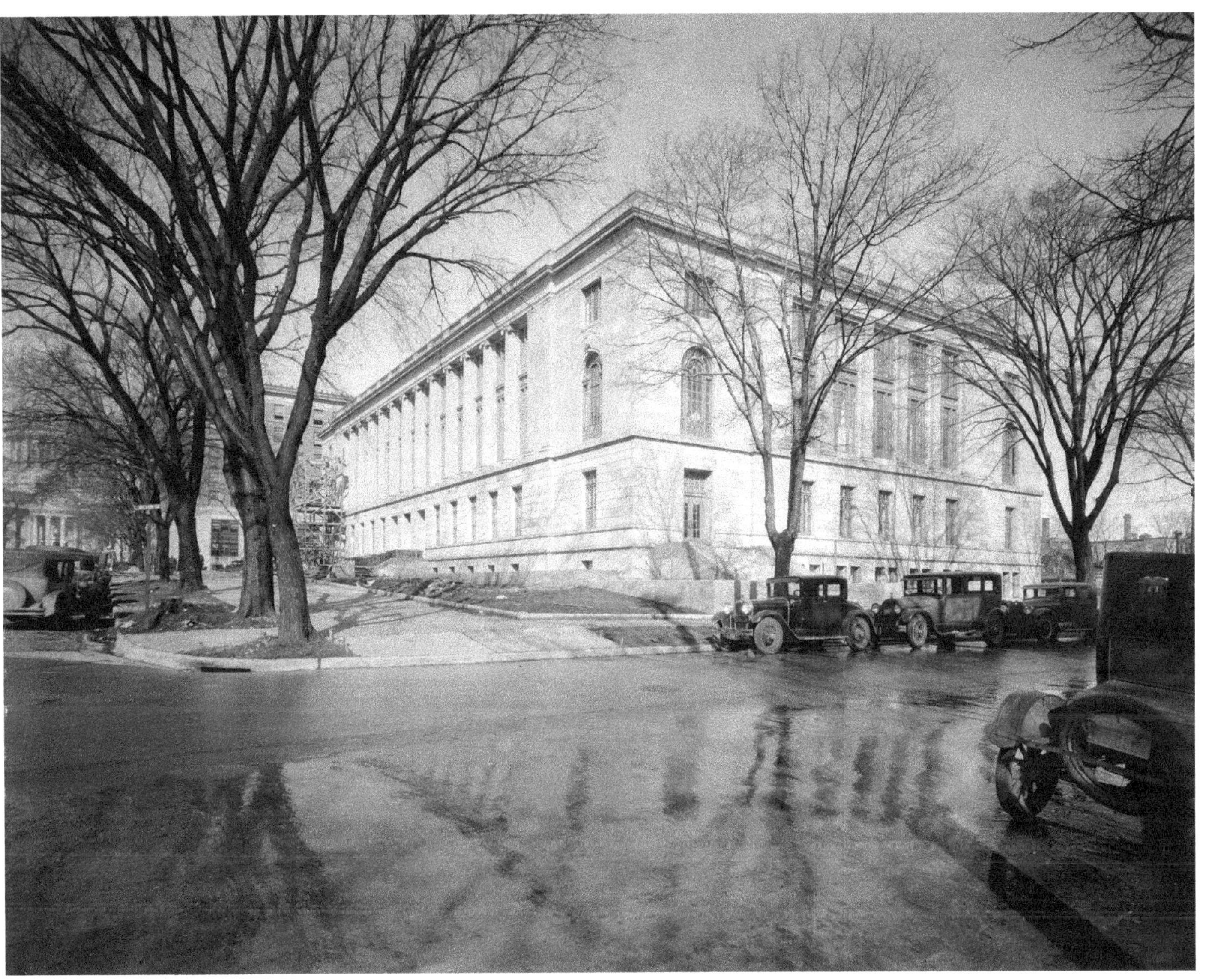

The U.S. Post Office and Federal Courthouse was under construction in this April 1927 photo, ninety years after the city's first post office was established in Eben Peck's store, a log cabin on South Butler Street. The view looks north from Wilson Street toward the nearly completed front and south sides of the building on 215 Monona Avenue, now Martin Luther King Jr. Boulevard. The building replaced an 1871 post office building across the Capitol Square at the corner of Wisconsin and Mifflin streets, which was razed in 1929 to make way for the Manchester building.

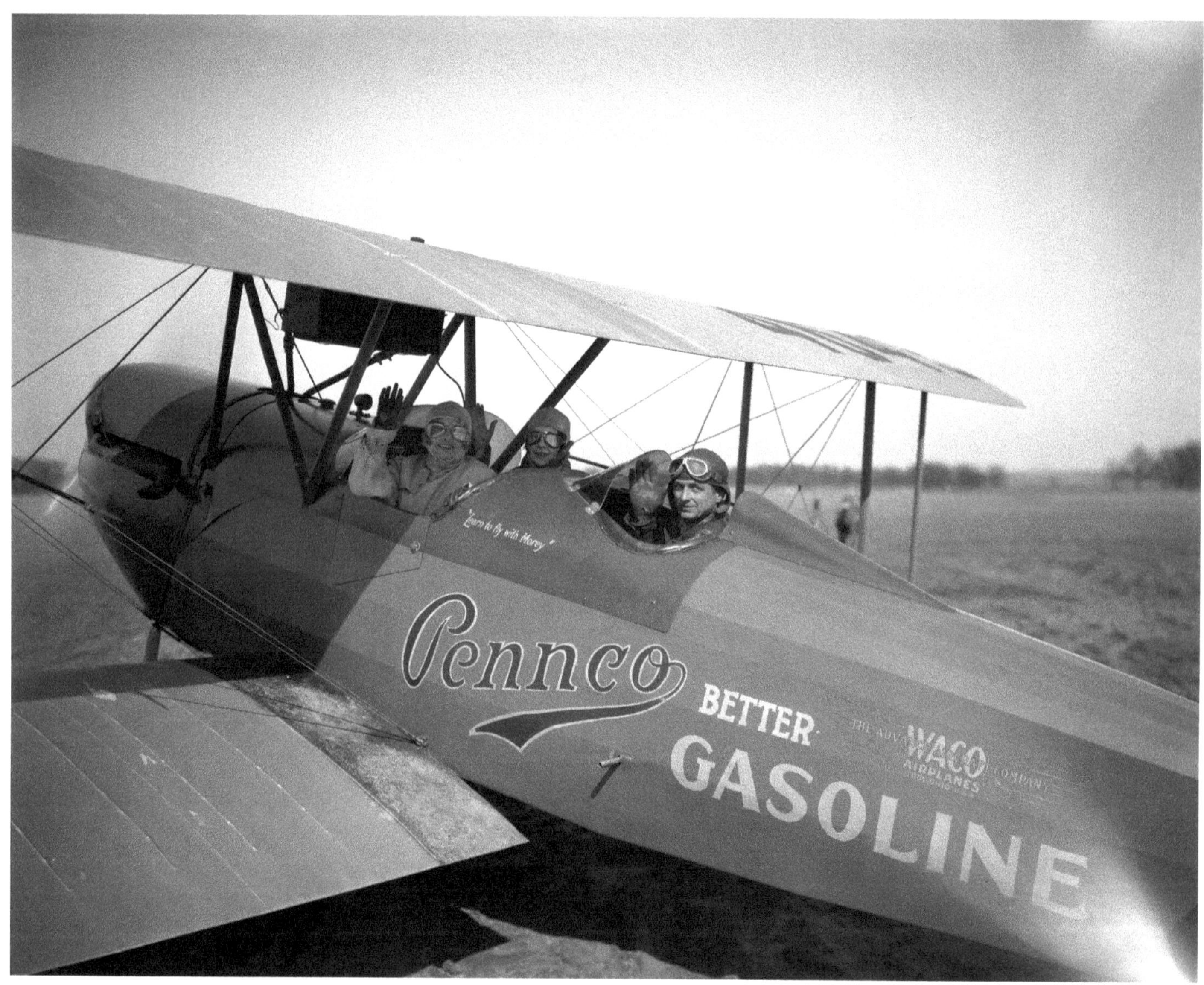

Howard Morey at the controls of an airplane that advertised Pennco Oil, his distributorship of Waco airplanes, and his flying school—diverse operations typical of commercial airline operations when this photograph was taken in 1928. Because of the oil company support, Morey's airport was first known as Pennco Field and later Royal Airport in an unsuccessful partnership with Royal Transit Co. to establish a commuter airline between Madison and Chicago. Morey lost his hangar and his airplane in a fire in 1932 on the property south of Lake Monona, so he returned to barnstorming and charter work. In 1938 he became the manager of the new Madison Municipal Airport.

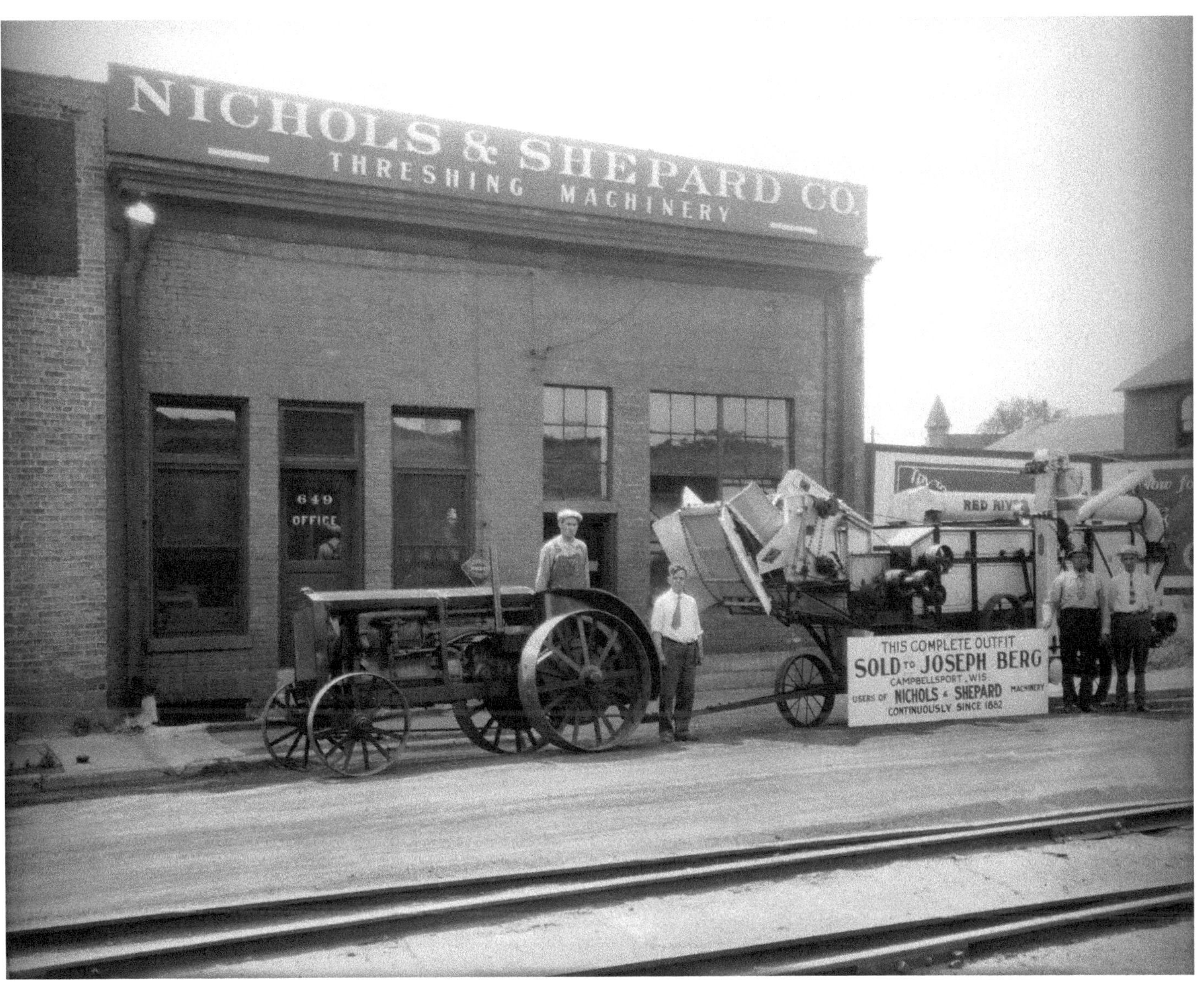

Shown here in 1928 is the Nichols-Shepard Company store, located at 649 East Mifflin Street, with a tractor and threshing machine. The sign, in acknowledgment of a loyal forty-six-year customer, reads in part, "This complete outfit sold to Joseph Berg, Campbellsport, Wis."

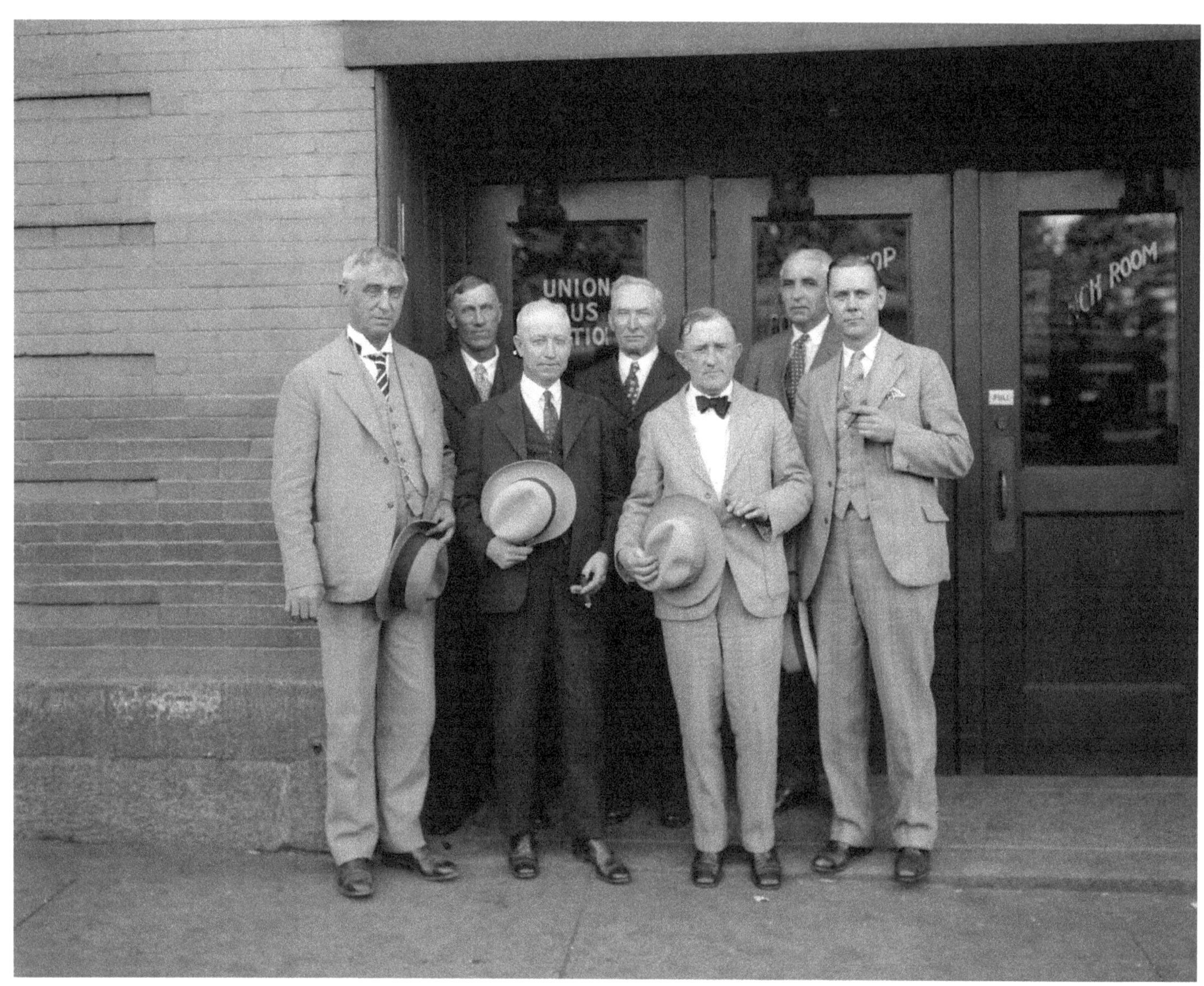

On October 9, 1928, members of the Progressive Republican Alfred E. Smith For President Club pose in front of the Park Hotel, at 22 South Carroll Street. From left to right are Dr. Adolf Gunderson, George A. Nelson, Fred A. Bachman, John E. Cashman, Dr. W. C. Sullivan, Hugo Meuhrske, and Col. Frank W. Kuehl.

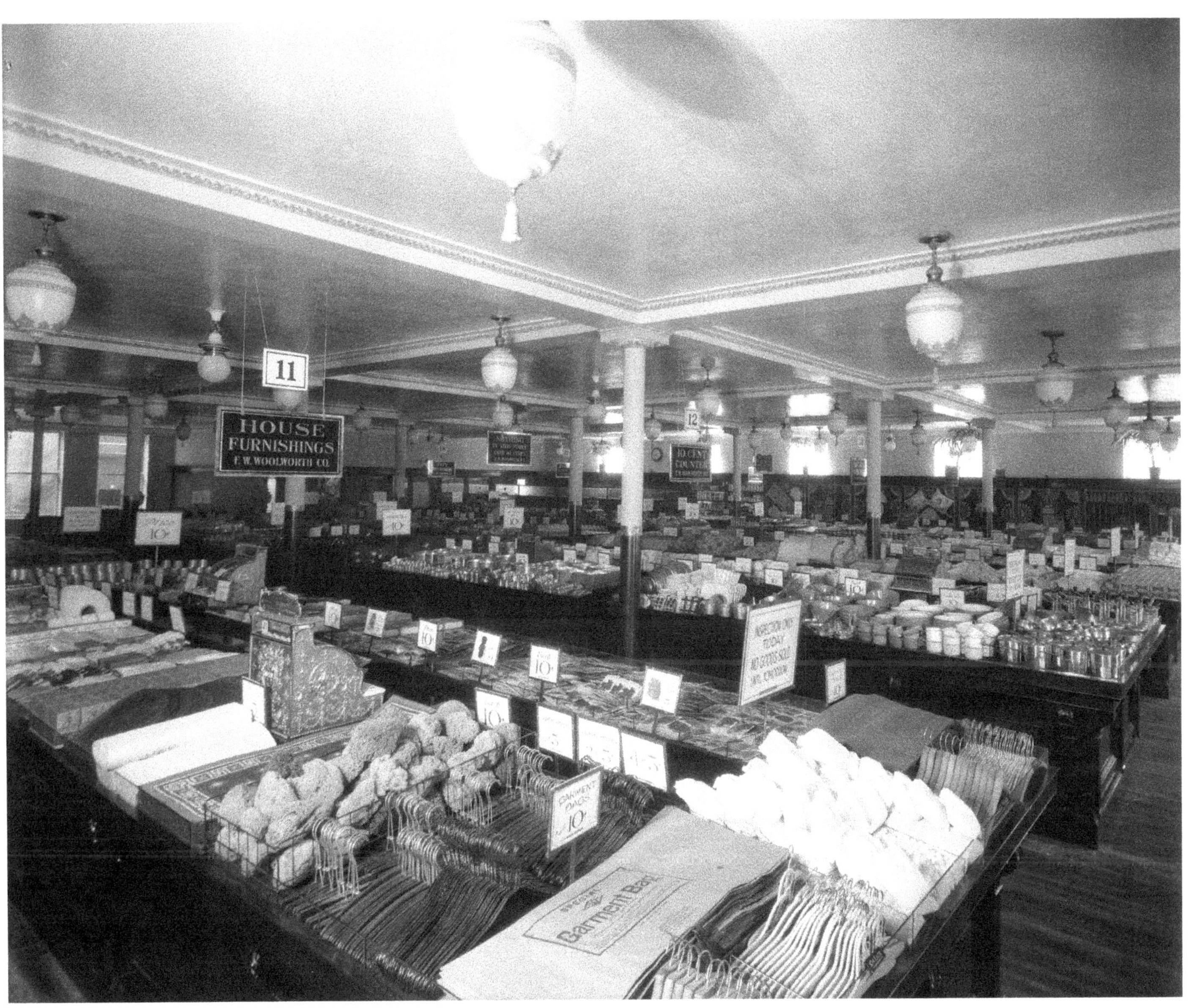

Woolworth's Variety Store, shown here in 1928, was located at 1 East Main Street. The national chain celebrated its fiftieth birthday the following year, just months before the stock market crash. By 1929 most stores were selling 15-cent lines to supplement their 5-cent and 10-cent lines.

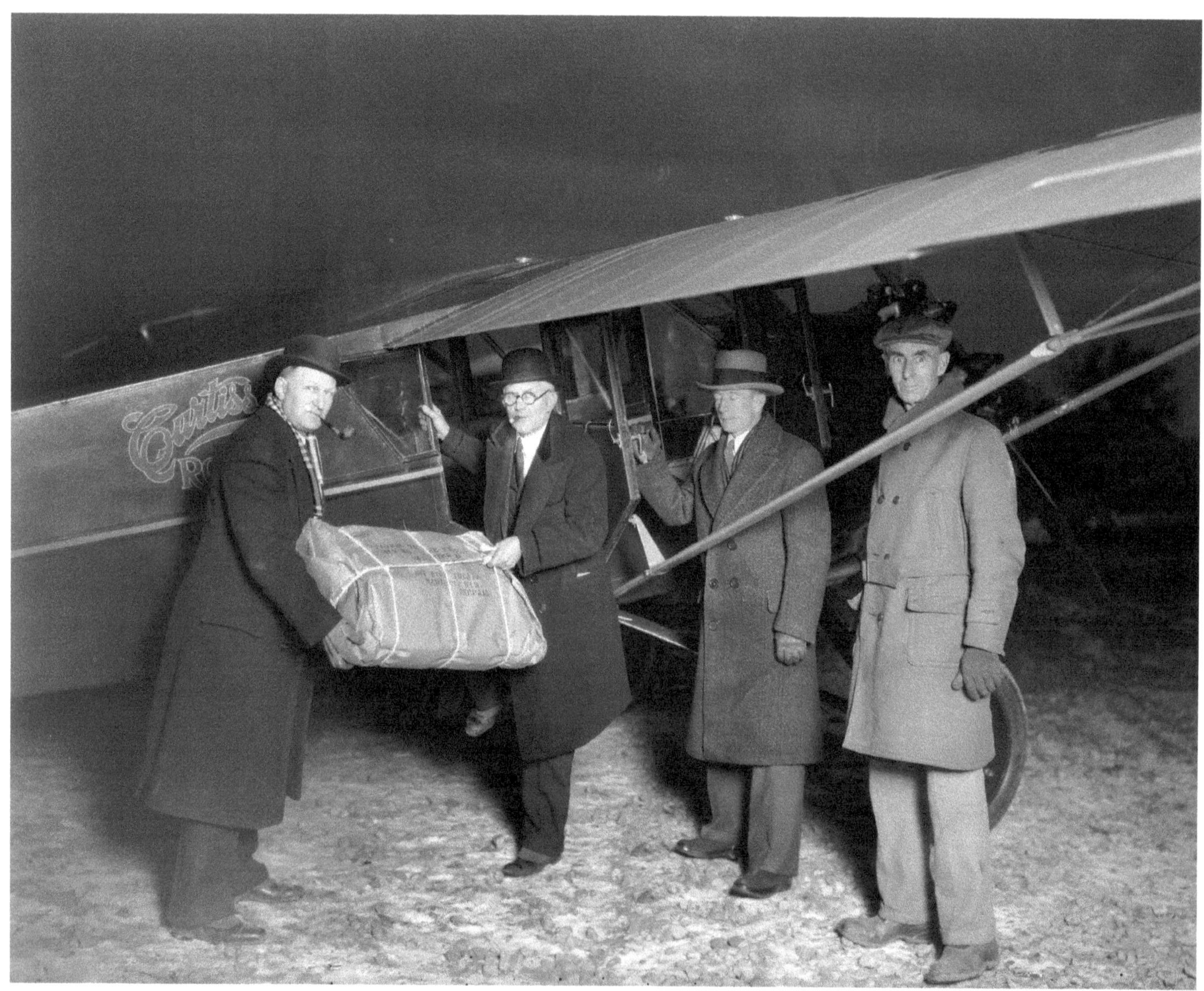

Four men stand beside a Curtiss airplane in December 1929 to receive a parcel flown in from the National Theatre Supply Company for the Eastwood Theatre, now known as the Barrymore. The Eastwood was the first theater in Madison built exclusively to show the new "talkies" motion pictures and was the only leading theater outside the downtown area until the 1960s.

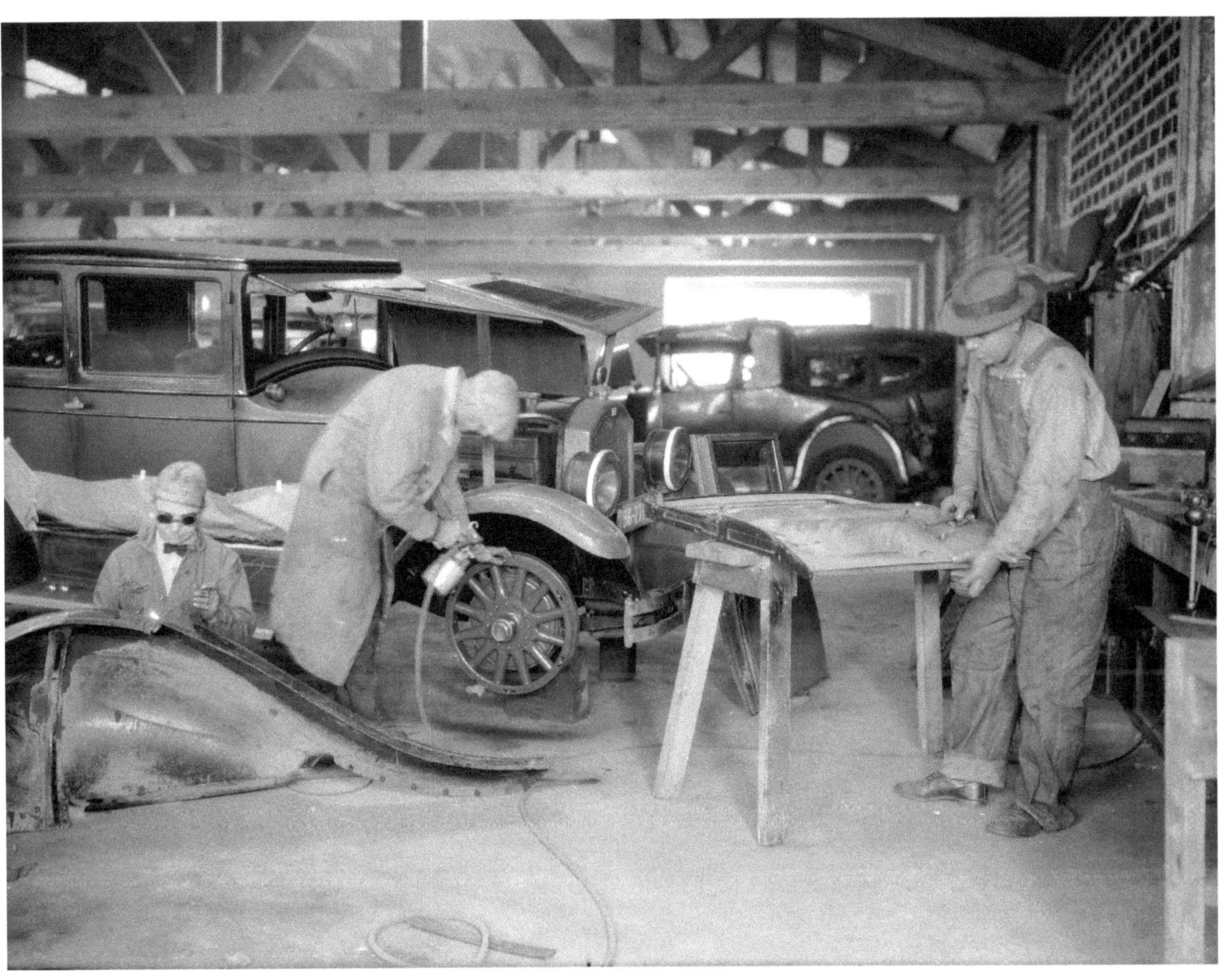

Three mechanics work on an automobile in the Capital Buick Body Shop, at 750 East Washington Avenue, in 1929.

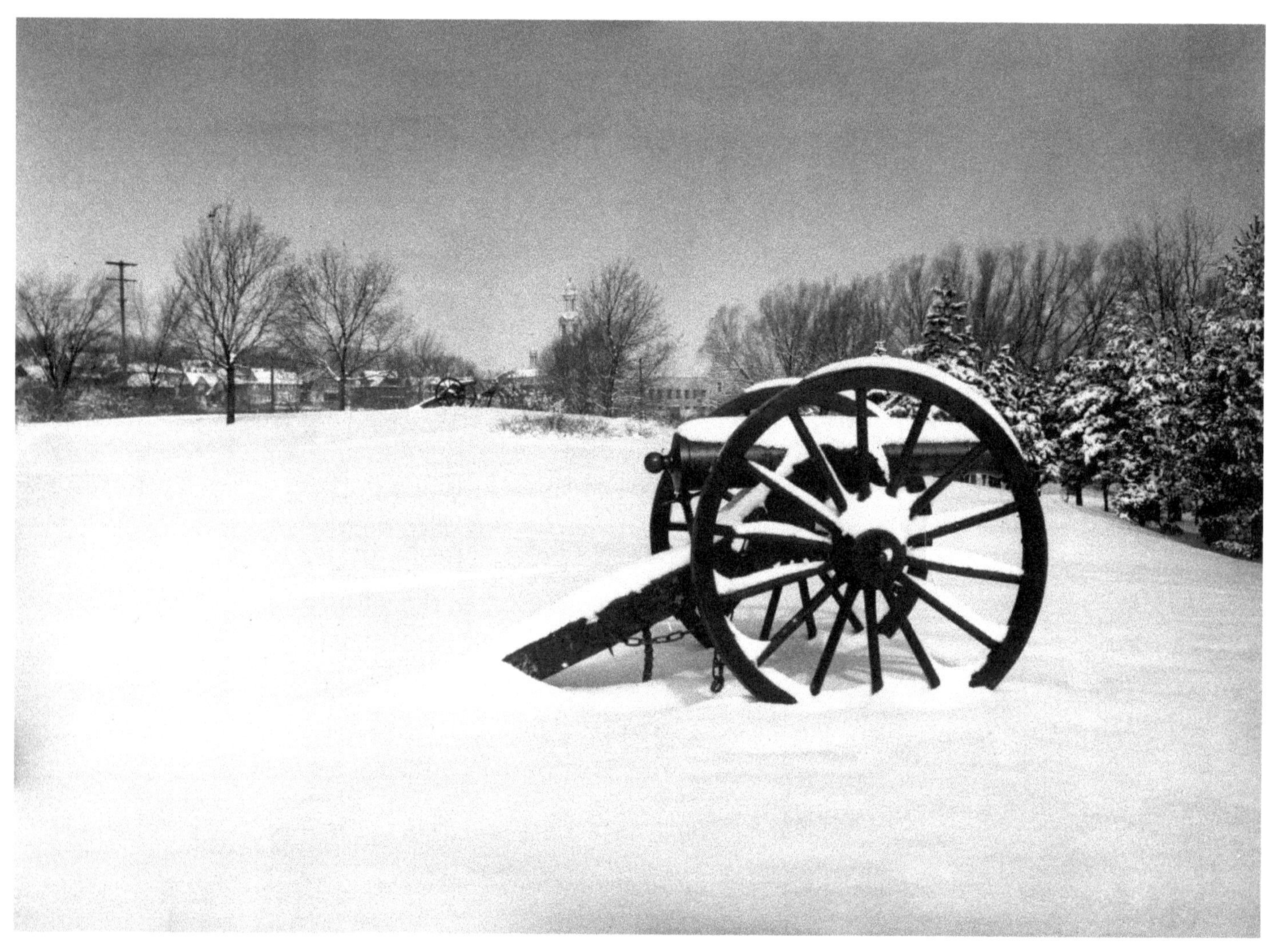

A Civil War cannon, partly covered with snow, stands at Camp Randall stadium in 1929. During World War I, the camp was reopened briefly to accommodate troops for drilling.

Central High School band members pose in their uniforms with their instruments in front of the Masonic Temple on Wisconsin Avenue across from the school in 1929. The history of Madison's first high school goes back to 1854, when the school board authorized Damon Kilgore to rent the basement of the Methodist church, which later became the location of the Belmont Hotel, for "advanced education." Attendance expanded rapidly, such that classes became scattered in buildings around central Madison during the late 1800s. The high school building was constructed in 1909 between Carroll Street and Wisconsin Avenue. The school closed in 1969 and remodeling was completed as the Madison Area Technical College's central campus. An entry arch on Wisconsin Avenue remains as a historic landmark.

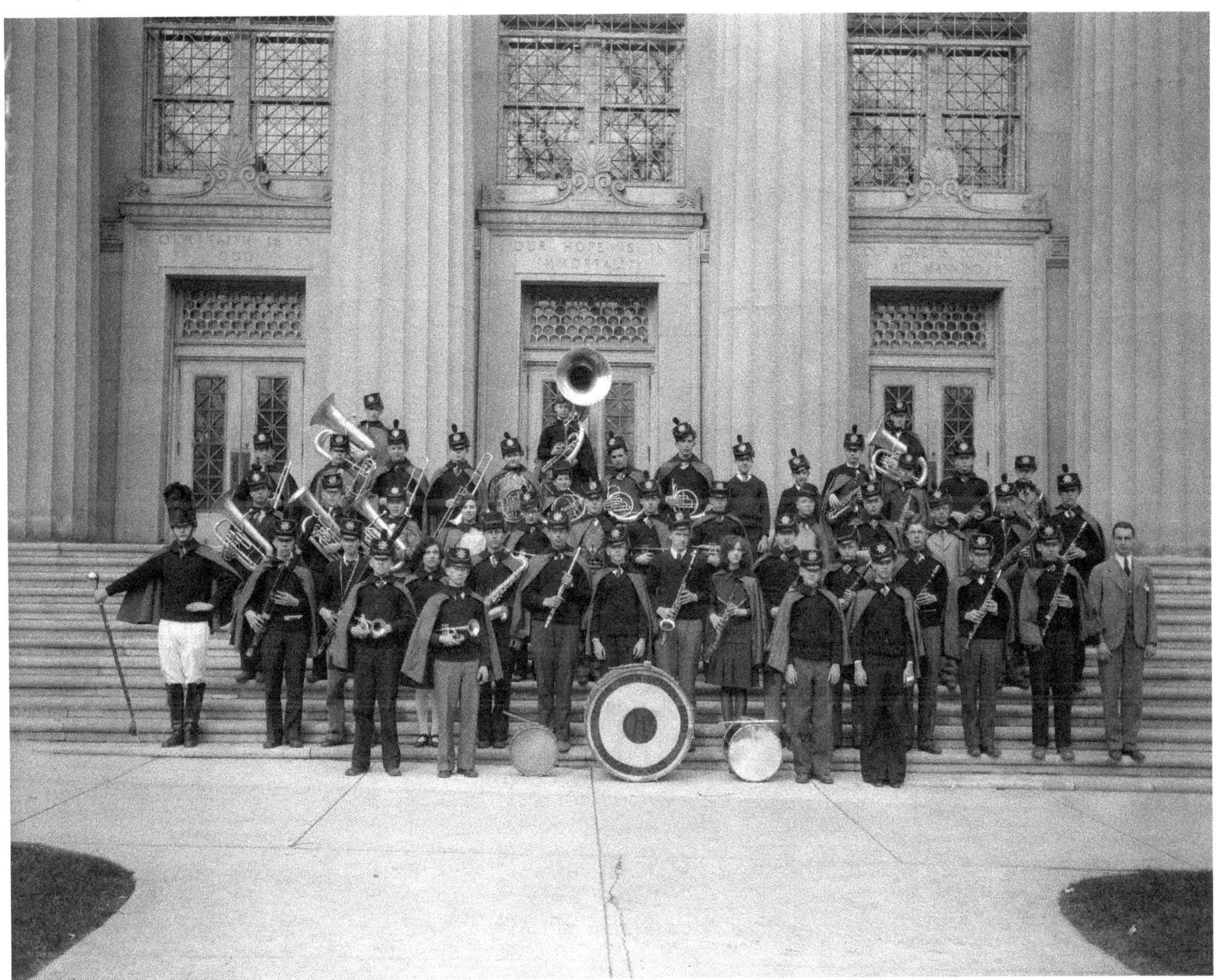

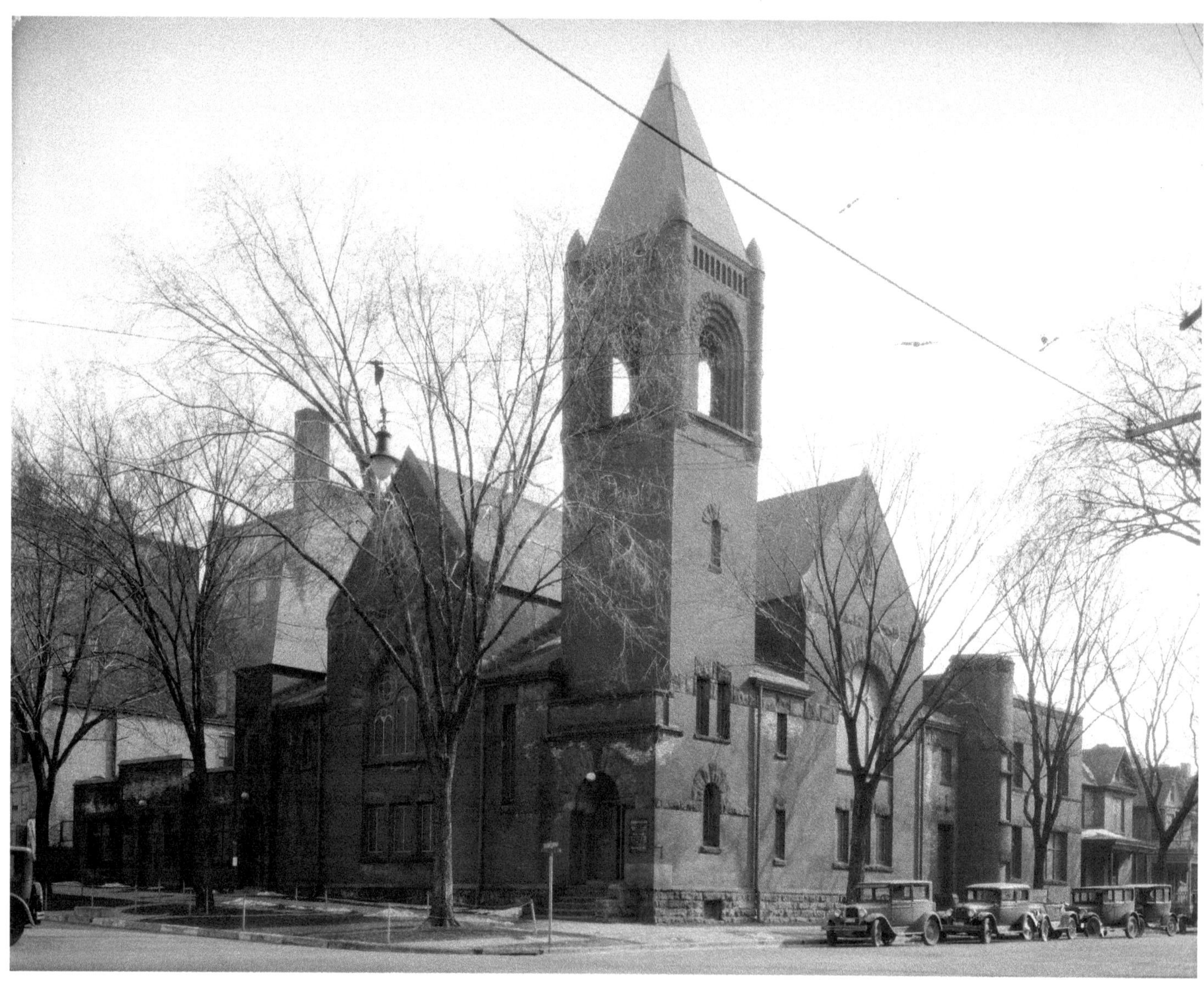

Christ Presbyterian Church at 124 Wisconsin Avenue is shown here in 1929. The building was constructed in 1914 after a fire destroyed a smaller building. The congregation was founded in 1851.

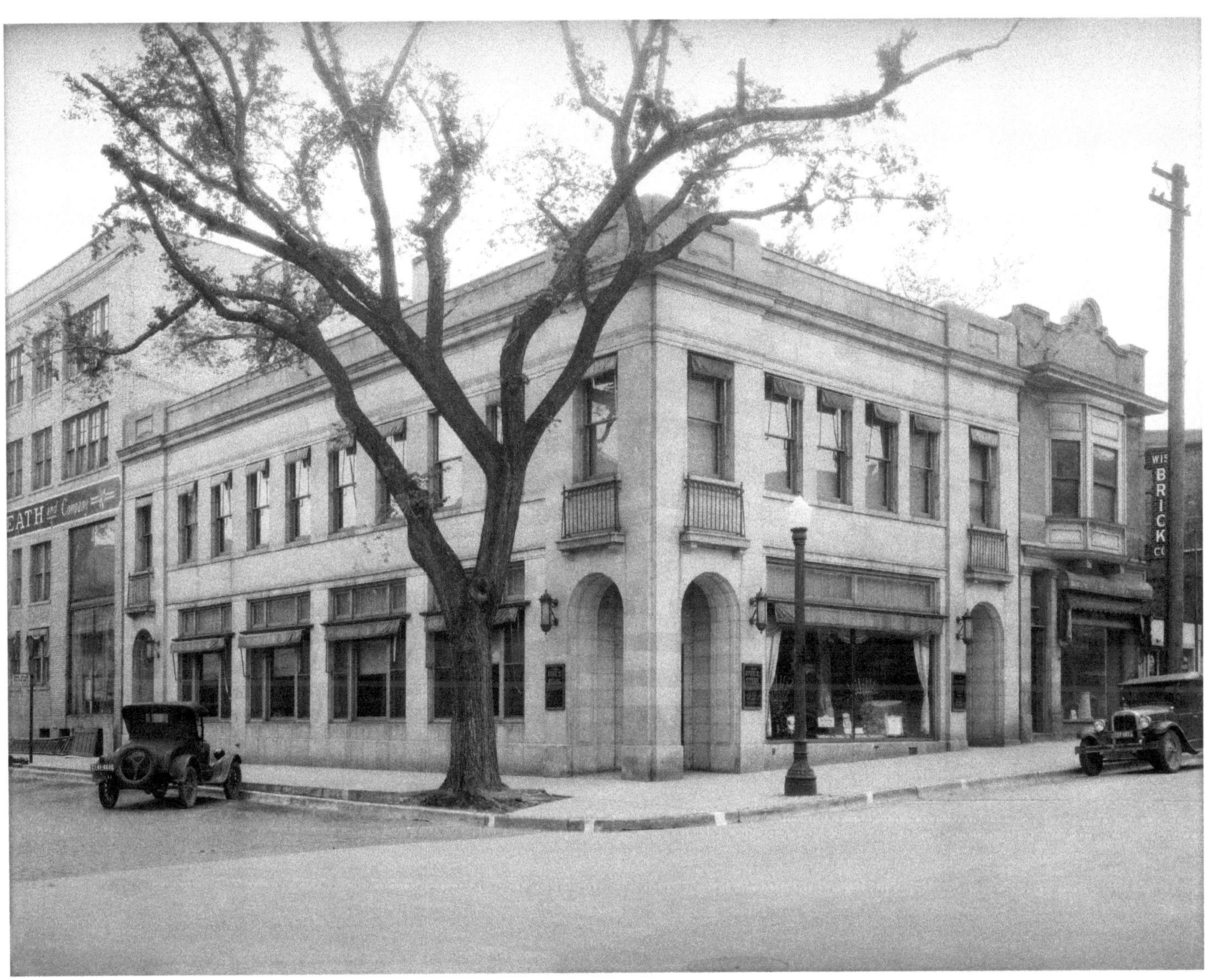

The Paul E. Stark Company at 124 West Mifflin Street and the Northwestern Mutual Insurance Company at 122 West Mifflin are shown in their new building, constructed just a few years before this photo was taken in 1929. The real estate company had been in operation since 1912. By 1925, sales had exceeded $1.5 million. The company has since entered its fourth generation.

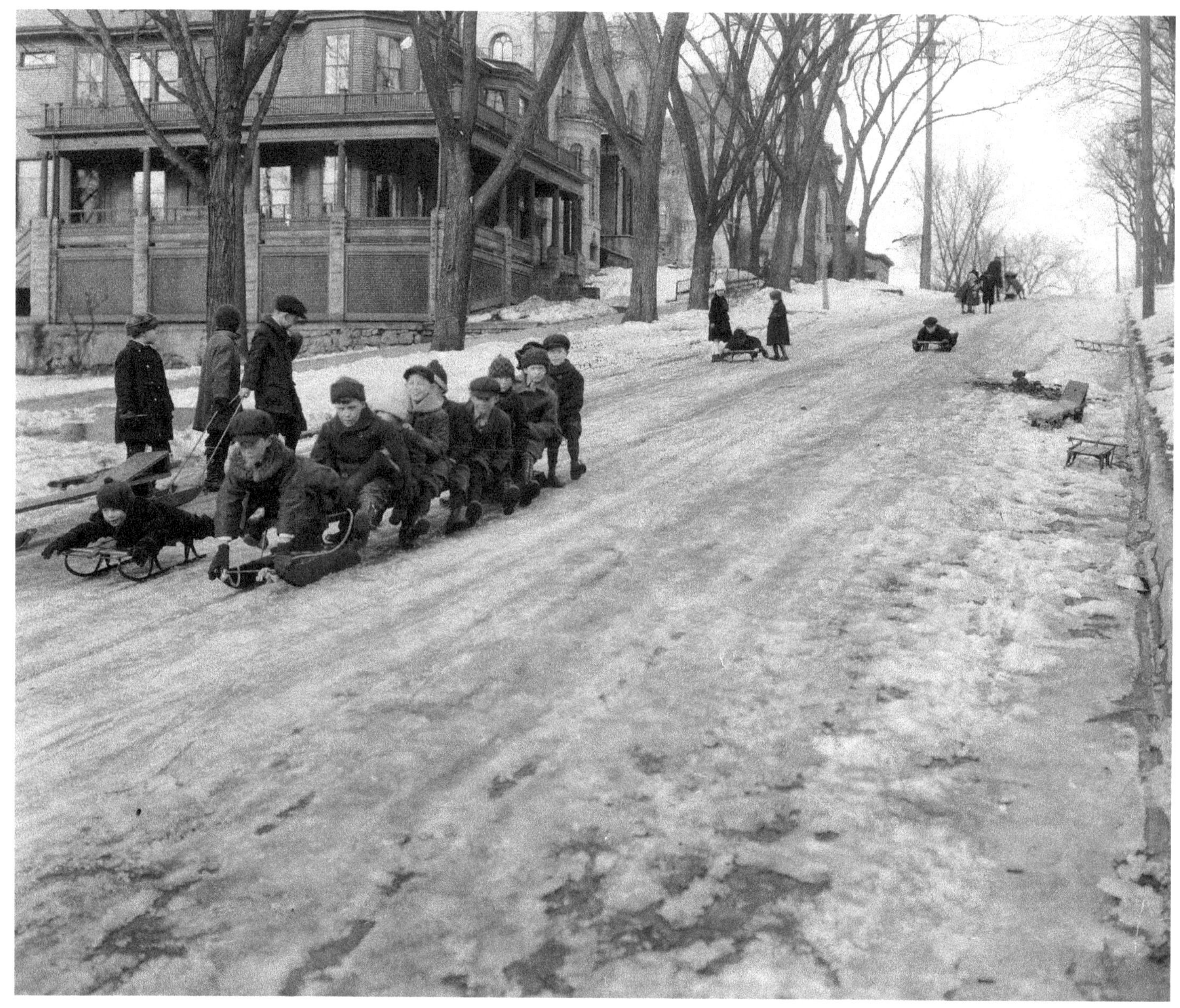

Children sled down North Pinckney Street in this mid-1920s image from the Frank L. Custer Local History Research Files of the Wisconsin Historical Society. Custer (1912–2000), a Central High School graduate and respected Madison historian, was a longtime columnist for the *Capital Times,* writing the newspaper column "Looking Backward."

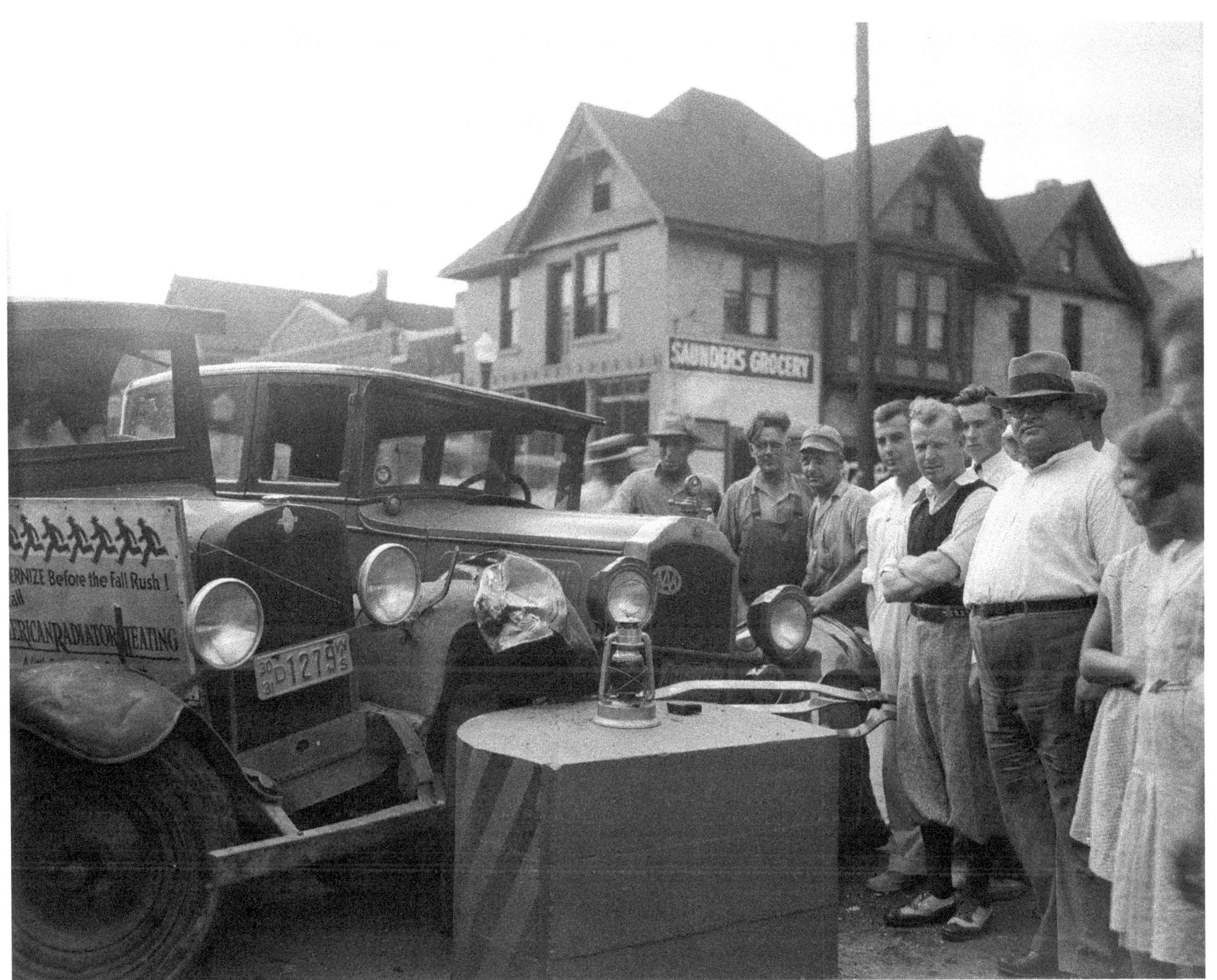

An auto accident between a Hooper truck and a Willys-Knight automobile at University Avenue and Murray Street attracts a crowd in 1930. The Willys-Knight was an upscale automobile produced between 1914 and 1933. The company was absorbed into Kaiser Jeep and later American Motors.

The Capitol Theater at 209 State Street advertises Amos 'n' Andy in October 1930 in *Check and Double Check*. The theater is flanked by the Lurosé women's clothing store and the Kaybee clothing store. The Capitol Theater has since been restored as part of the Overture Center for the Arts, a $205 million endeavor funded with a gift from W. Jerome Frautschi to the city of Madison.

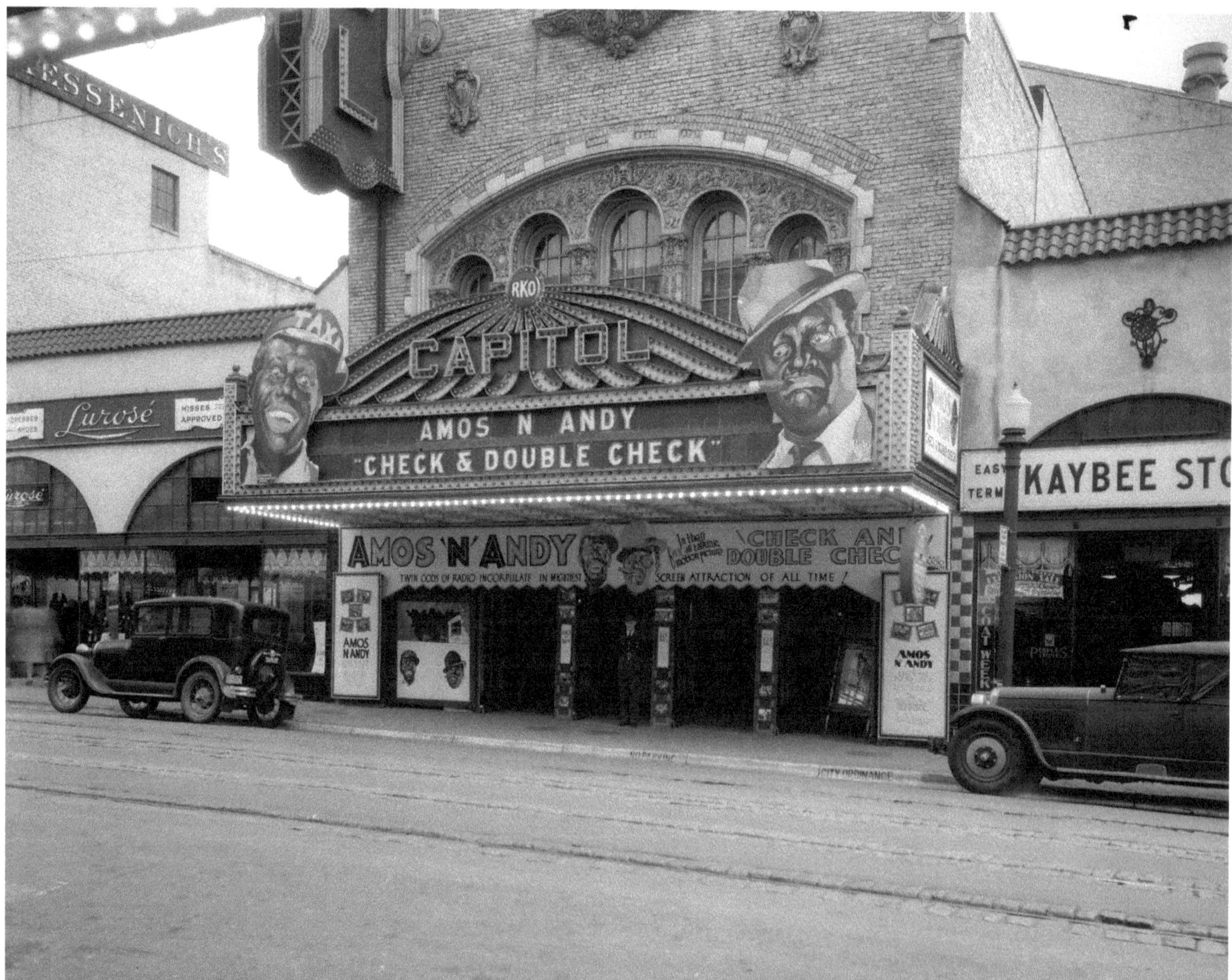

Bock Oil Burner company employees work in the machine shop in 1930, one year after it opened. The company, still in operation, is at 110 South Dickinson Street and continues to manufacture water heaters and storage tanks.

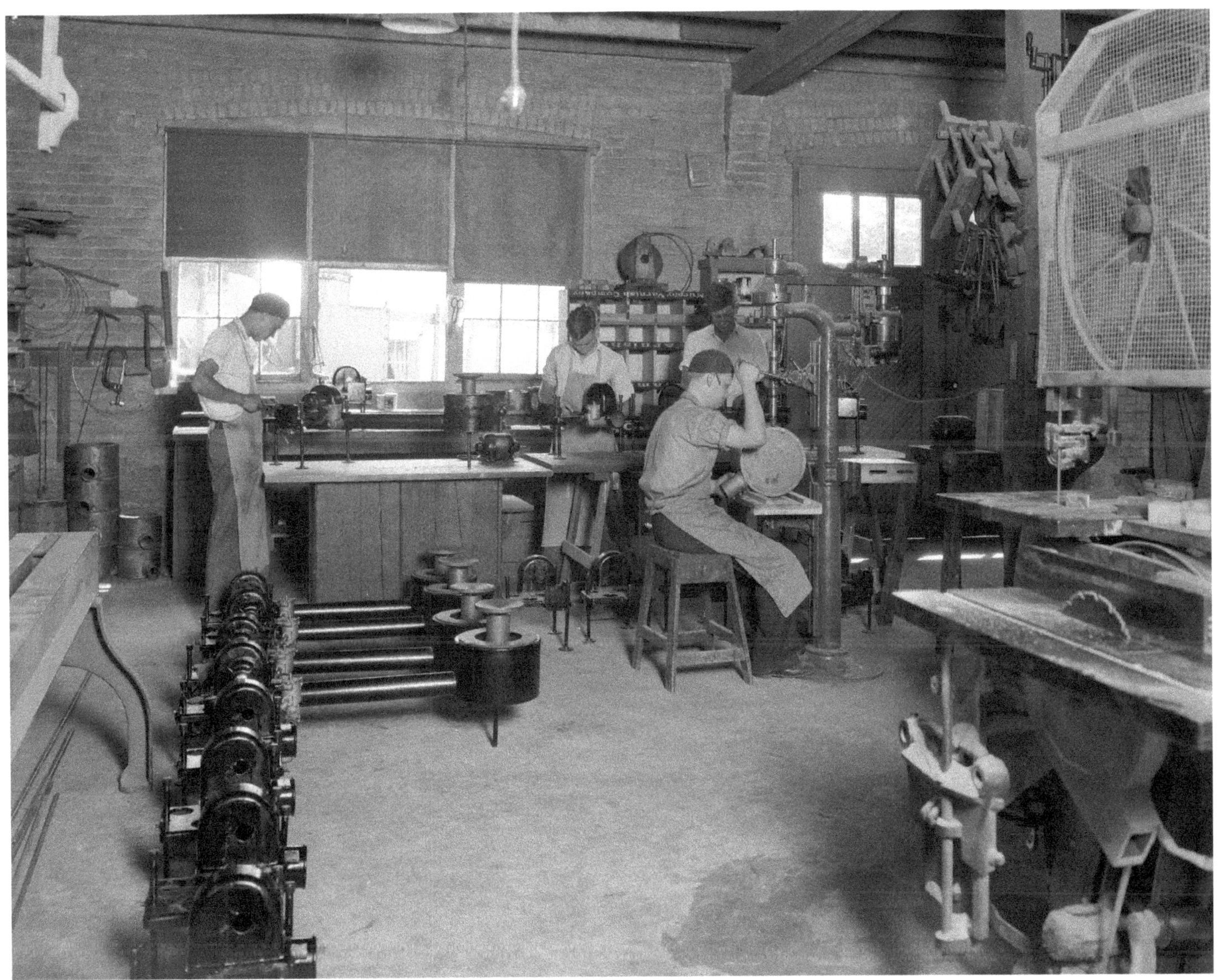

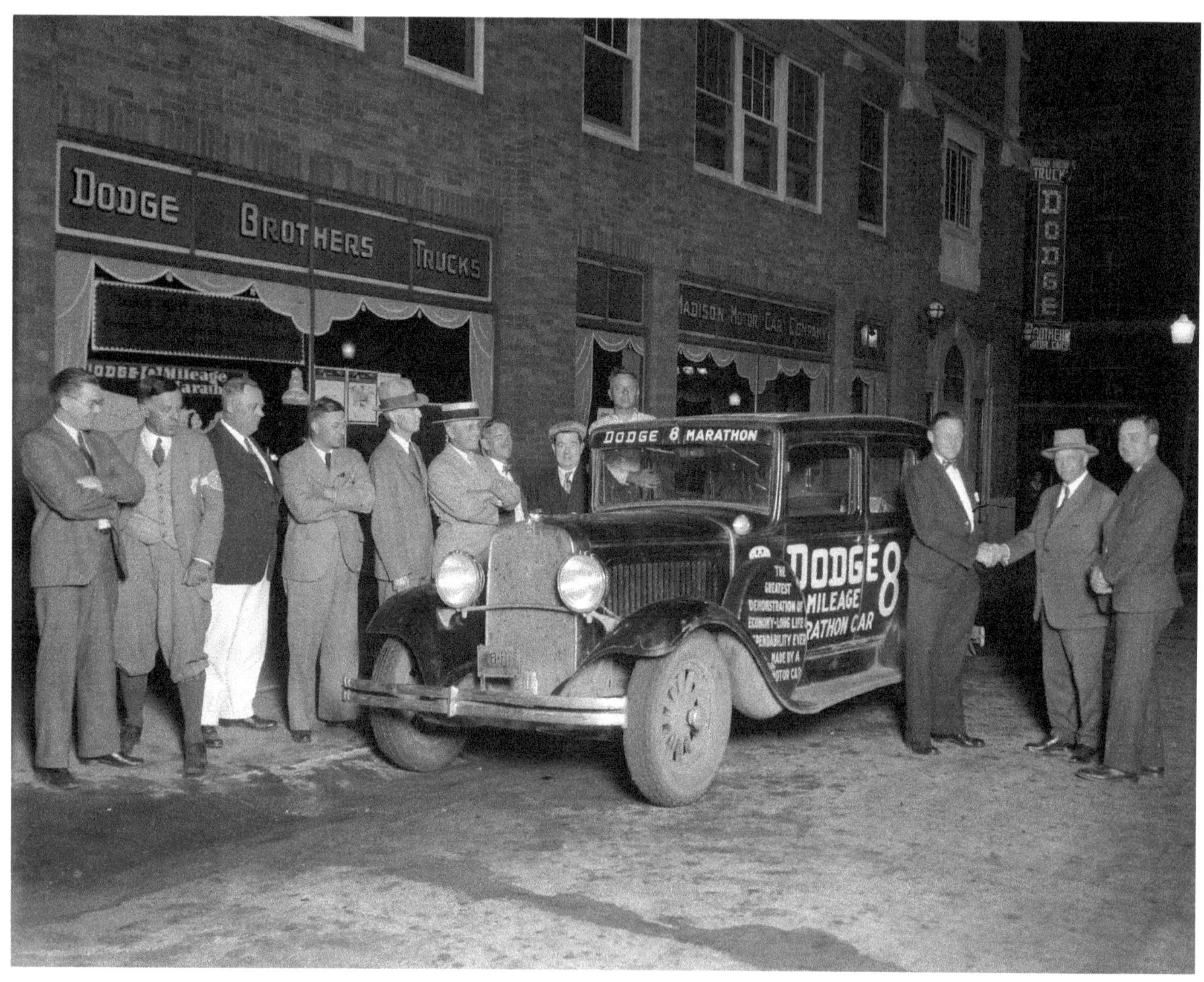

Shown here in 1930 is the Dodge 8 Mileage Marathon Car in front of Dodge Brothers Trucks and Madison Motor Car Company. The mounted spare tire proclaims, "The greatest demonstration of economy-long life-dependability ever made by a motor car." The building at 322 West Johnson is now occupied by Angelic Brewing Company.

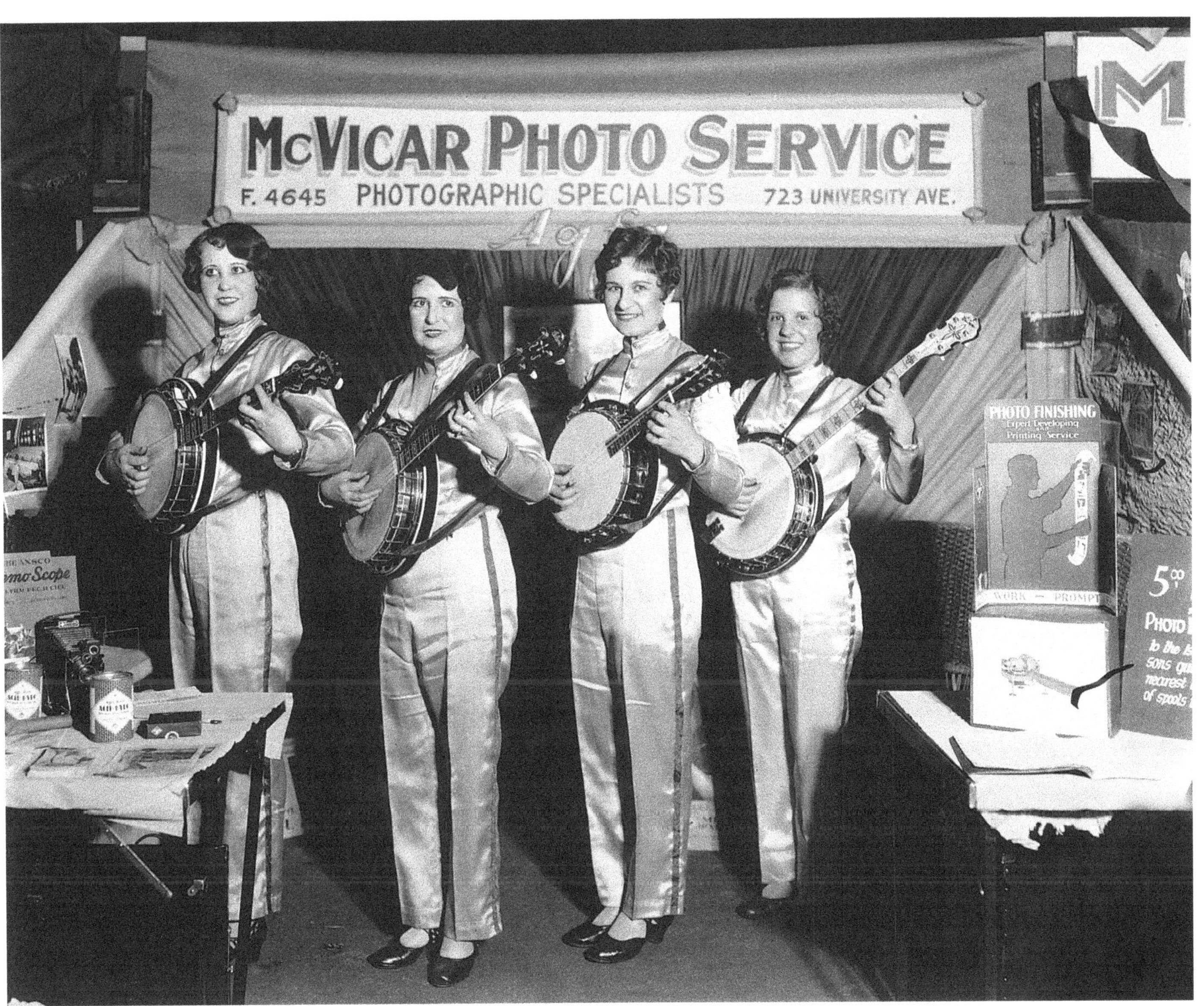

The 1930 fall festival of the East Side Businessman's Association included these four women playing banjos in the McVicar Photo Service booth. The club, which has been in existence since the early 1920s, has been located on Lake Monona at 3735 Monona Drive since 1954.

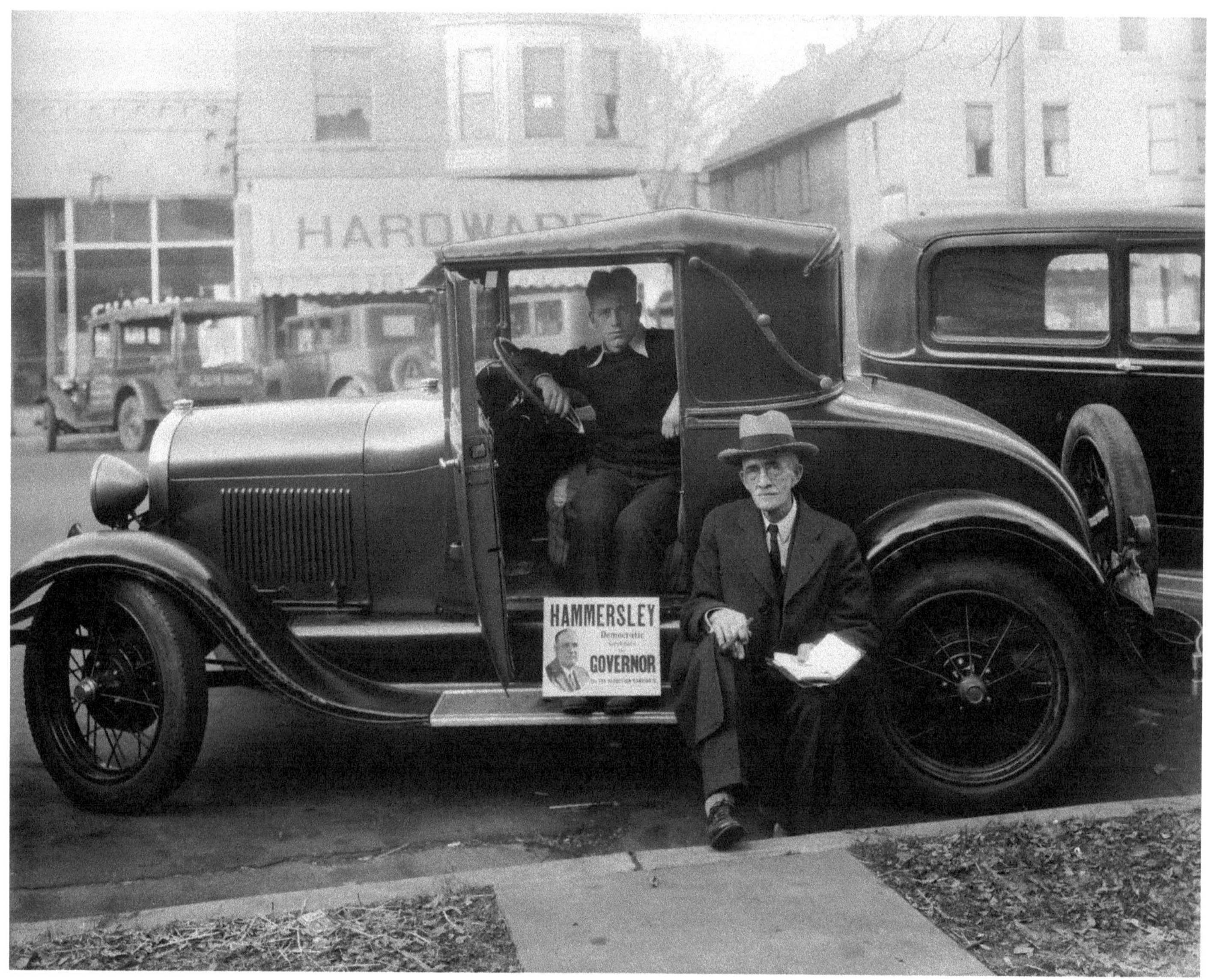

On November 3, 1930, Harold Cranefield, who earned his law degree the year before (seated behind the steering wheel), and another man pose with a campaign sign in support of Democrat Charles Hammersley for Governor of Wisconsin. Hammersley lost to Republican Philip La Follette, son of Robert. Cranefield spent the next thirty years working in connection with labor law and civil and political liberties.

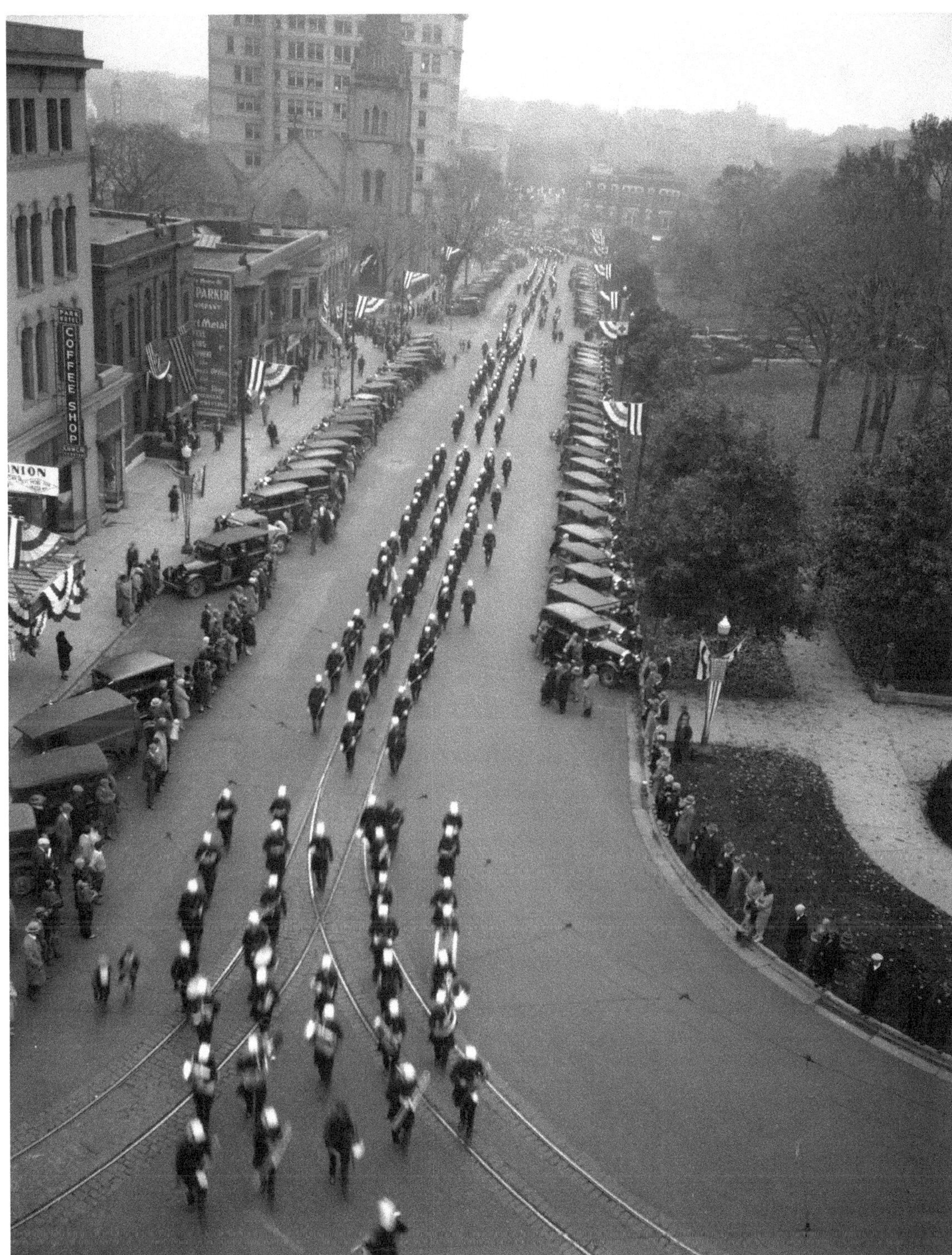

The Knights Templar parade south on Carroll Street during the Wisconsin Commandery convention, October 14, 1930. The Commandery represents the Military Order of the Loyal Legion of the United States, which originally included nearly 12,000 Civil War officers.

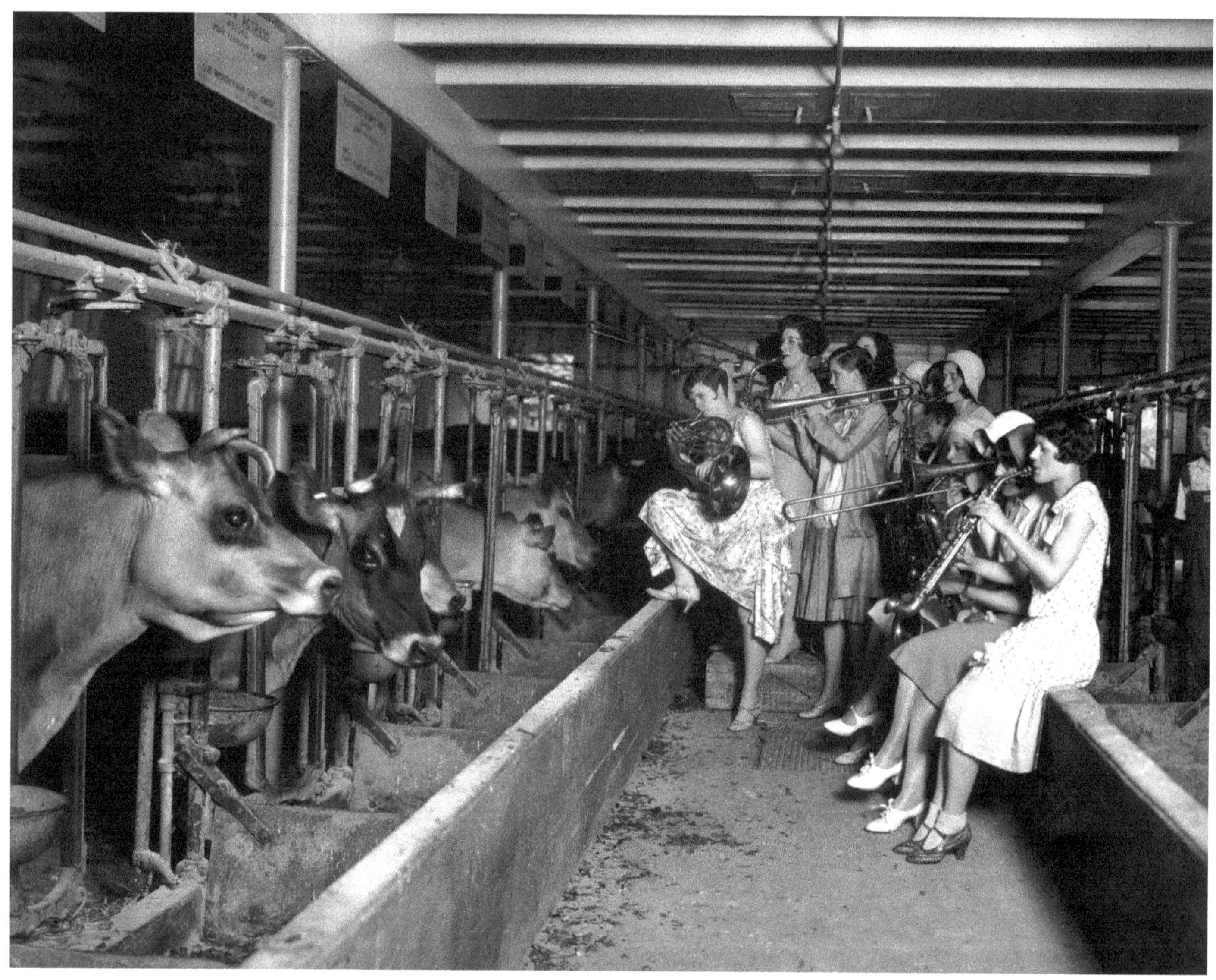

In 1930 the Ingenues, an all-girl band and vaudeville act, serenaded cows in the University of Wisconsin dairy barn. They were participating in an experiment to learn whether cows would give more milk after hearing soothing strains of music. The Ingenues are said to have been one of the models for the band that figured prominently in the 1959 Marilyn Monroe comedy *Some Like It Hot.*

A stunt car at the Dane County Fair in summer 1930 advertises the RKO film *Dixiana*. The fair began in 1850 when the Dane County Agricultural Society was founded. The first fair was held that year on a site near the Yahara River in Madison.

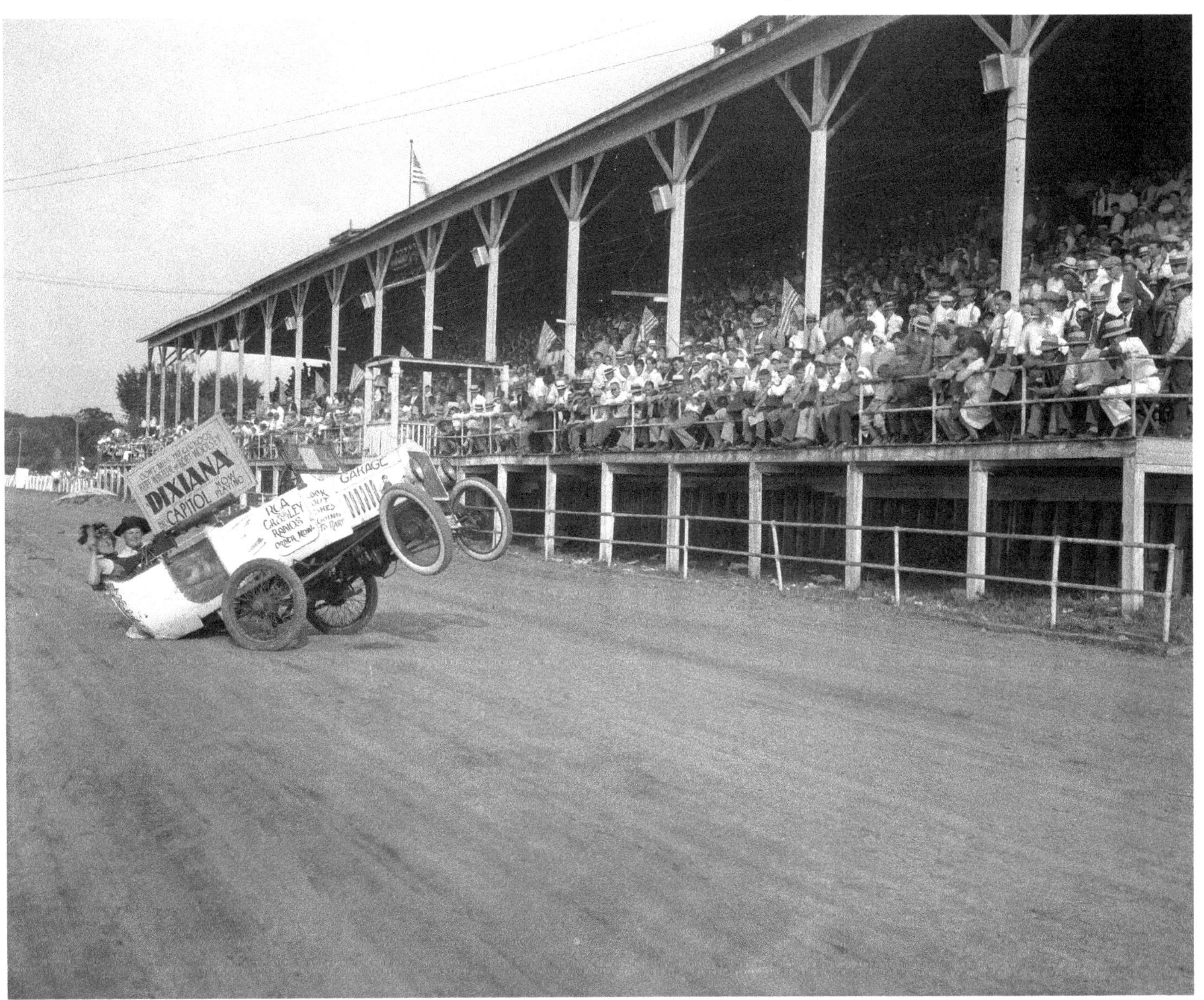

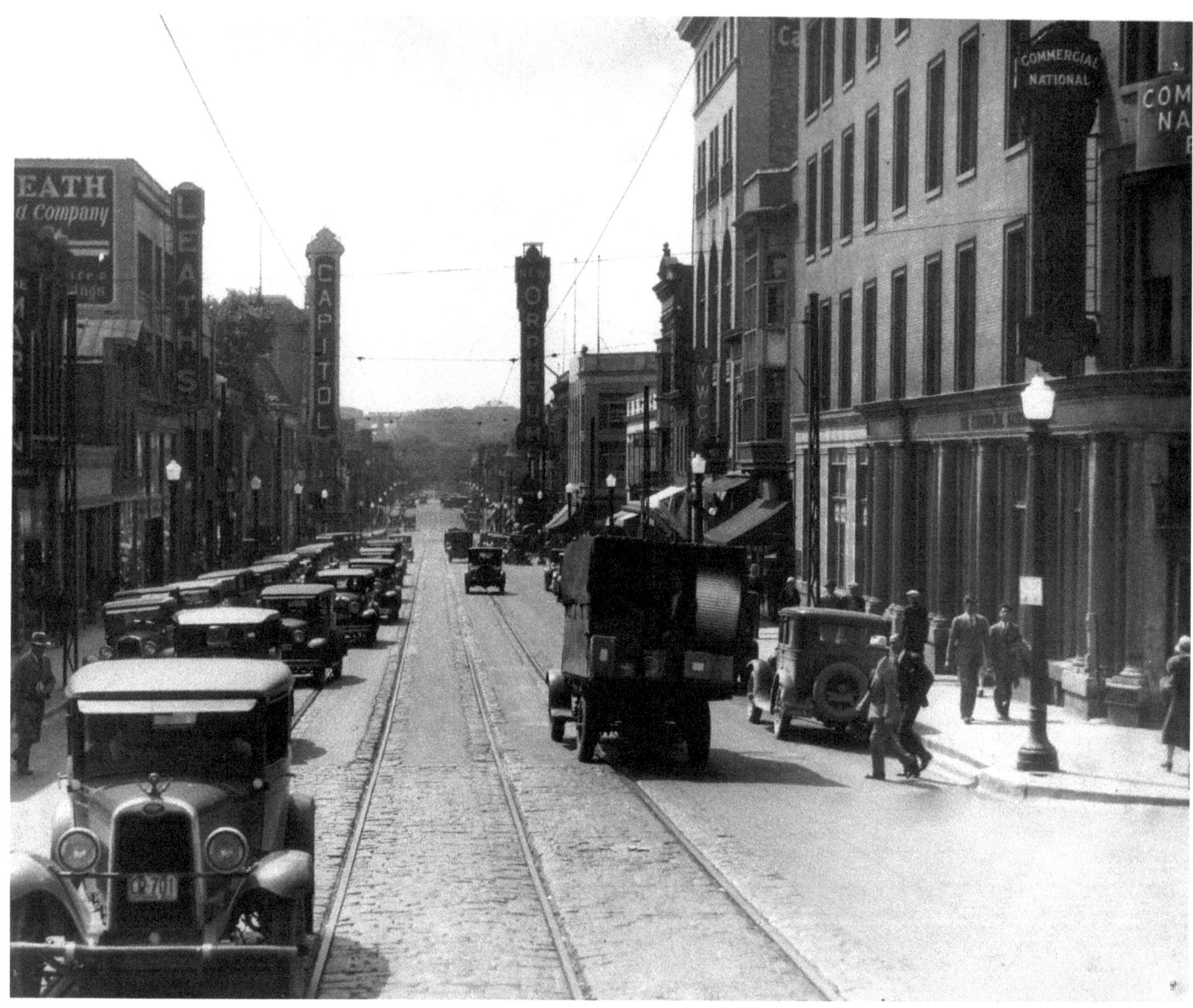

Heavy automobile traffic, delivery trucks, and pedestrians scurry along State Street in this view from around 1930. The street, running from the Capitol to the university campus, was turned into a pedestrian mall in the 1970s.

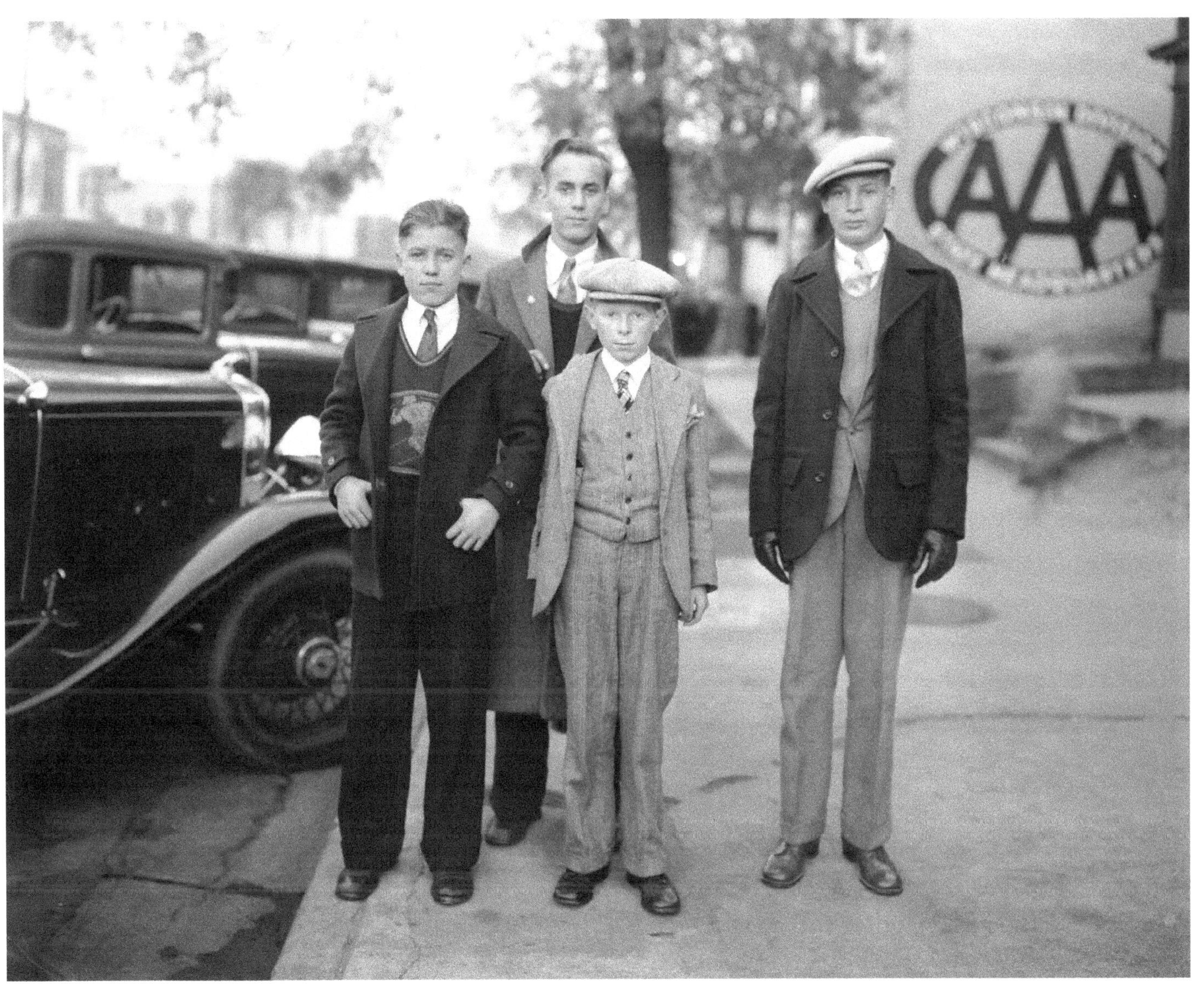

The Champion Wisconsin Cattle Judging Team in October 1931 was made up of these four boys. Starting in the mid nineteenth century, dairying had emerged as the most feasible alternative to wheat, which up to that time had been the focus of Wisconsin agriculture. The number of dairy cows increased rapidly, so that by 1899, more than 90 percent of Wisconsin farms raised dairy cows. By 1915, Wisconsin had become the leading dairy state in the nation.

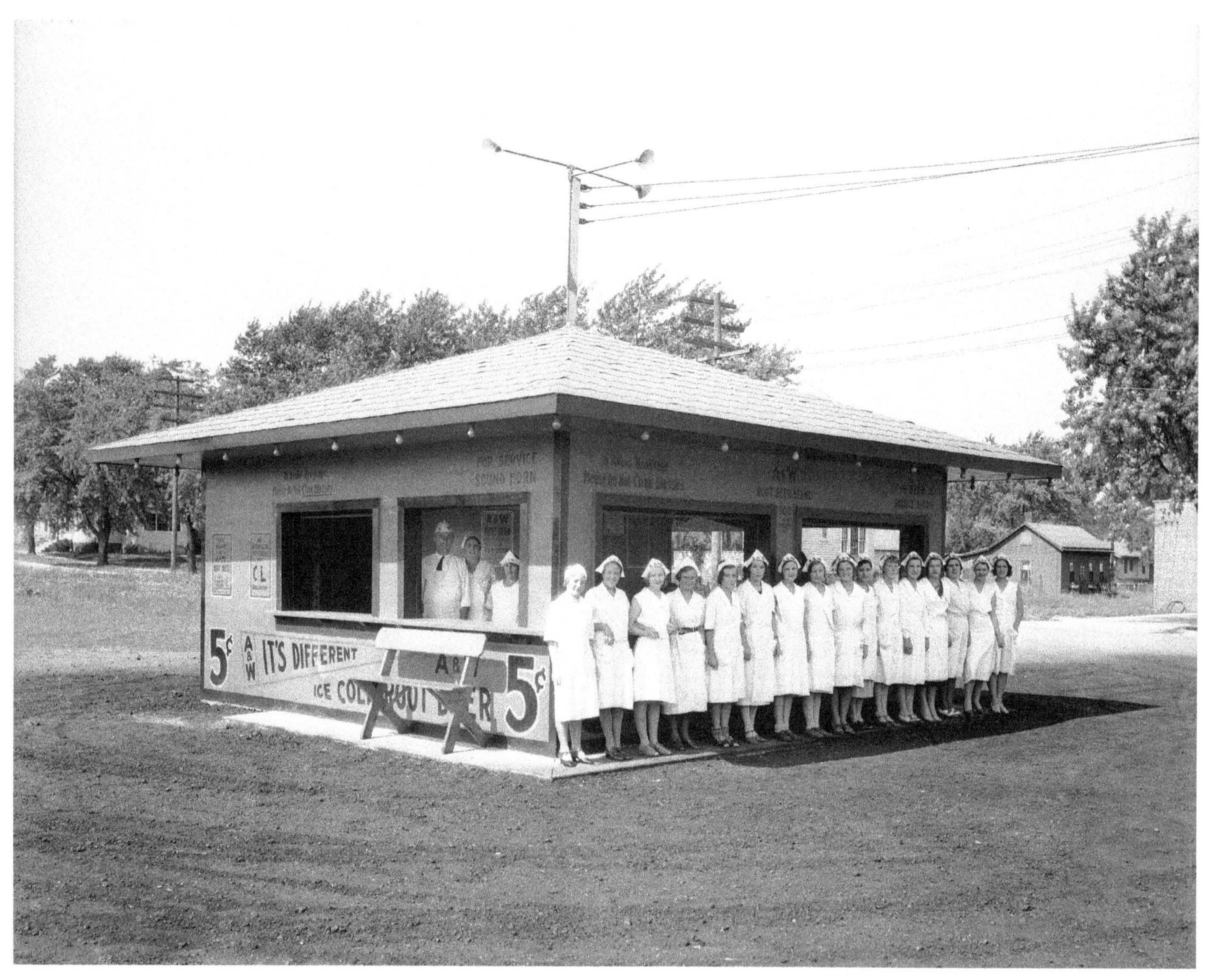

Employees in uniform pose in front of the A&W Rootbeer stand at 900 South Park Street in 1931. At the time of this photo, the California company was twelve years old and had nearly 170 franchise outlets throughout the West and Midwest.

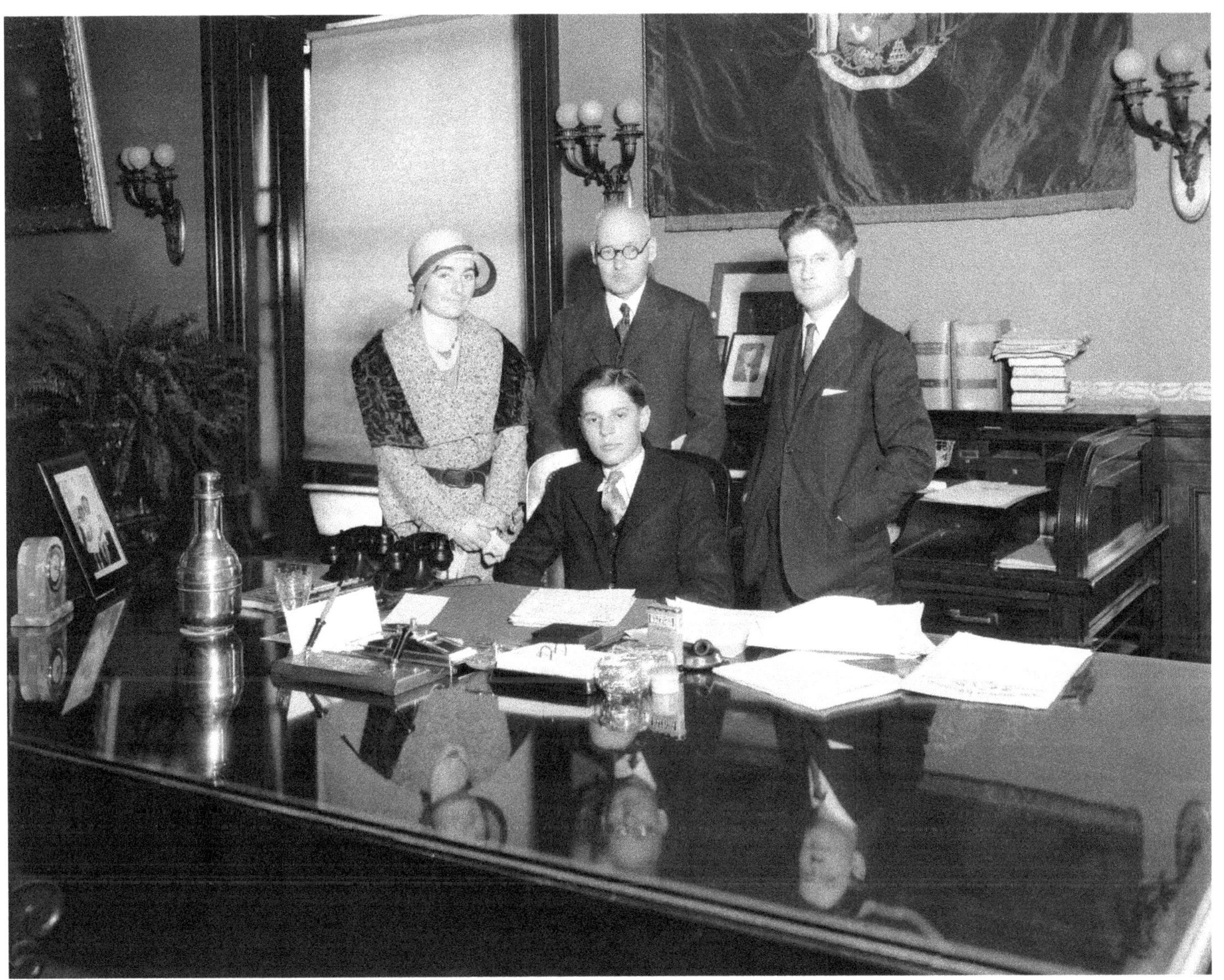

Blanche McCarthy, president of the Wisconsin Teachers' Association; John Callahan, state superintendent of public instruction; and Governor Philip F. La Follette stand behind Appleton High School student Norman Clapp, seated in the governor's chair, March 18, 1931. Clapp represented Wisconsin in the around-the-world telephone conversation held in conjunction with International Good Will Day.

The Chicago-based Oscar Mayer company purchased a small meat-packing plant in Madison in 1919 and moved their headquarters to the city in 1955. In 1931, Oscar Mayer Diamond trucks advertise "Meats of Good Taste." The Mayers became one of the first meat packers to brand their products, a significant part of their success. At first, they used the name "Edelweiss" and later other brand names like "Moose" (for baker's lard and heavier bacon), "Approved Brand," and "Meats of Good Taste." In 1929, the brand name of Oscar Mayer was first printed on packages. By the early 1960s, the company had about 8,000 workers nationwide.

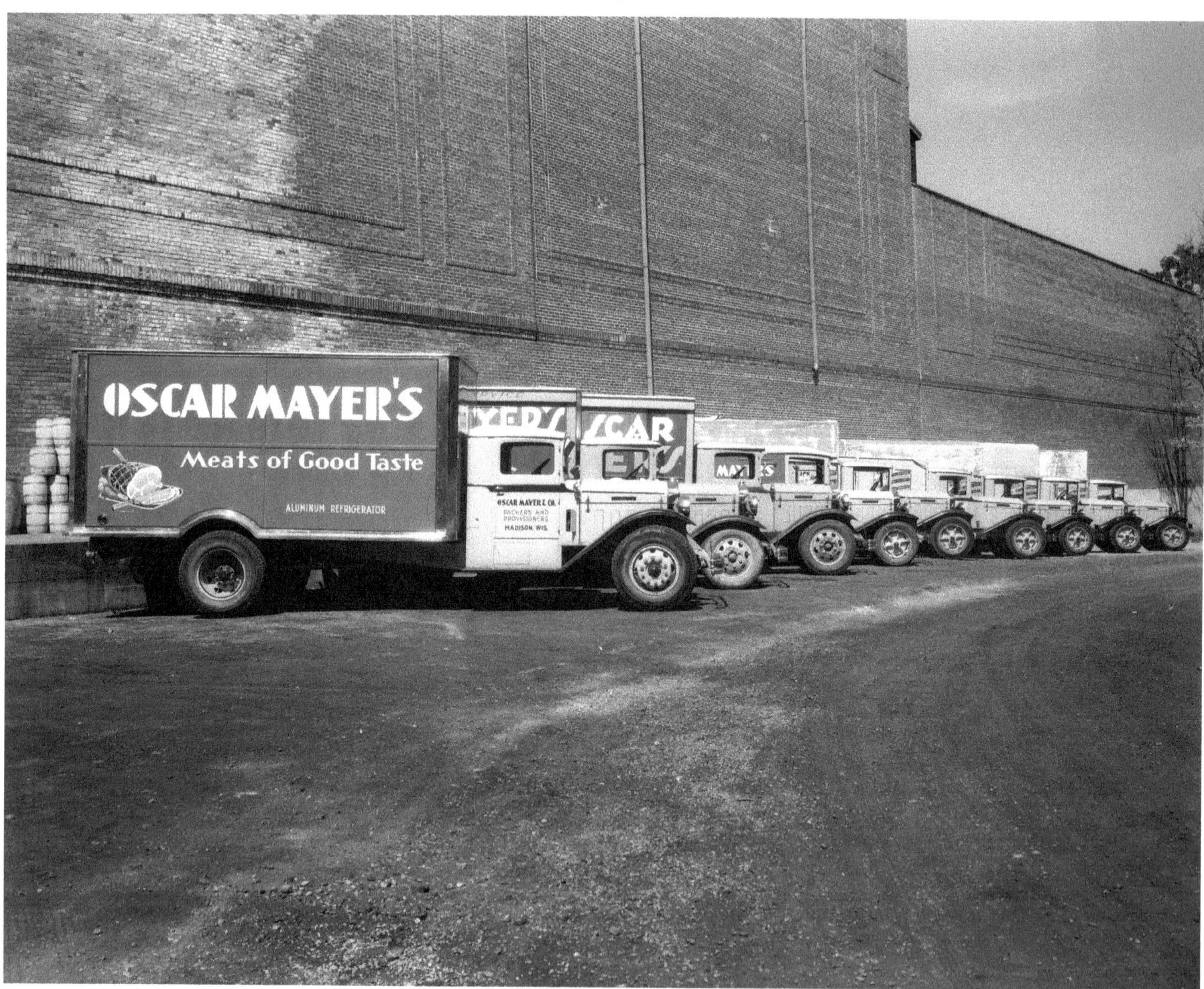

A young woman demonstrates her championship cow-milking skills as she milks a Holstein cow in October 1931 at the Dane County Fairgrounds. The fairgrounds occupy about 250 acres at the present Alliant Energy Center location.

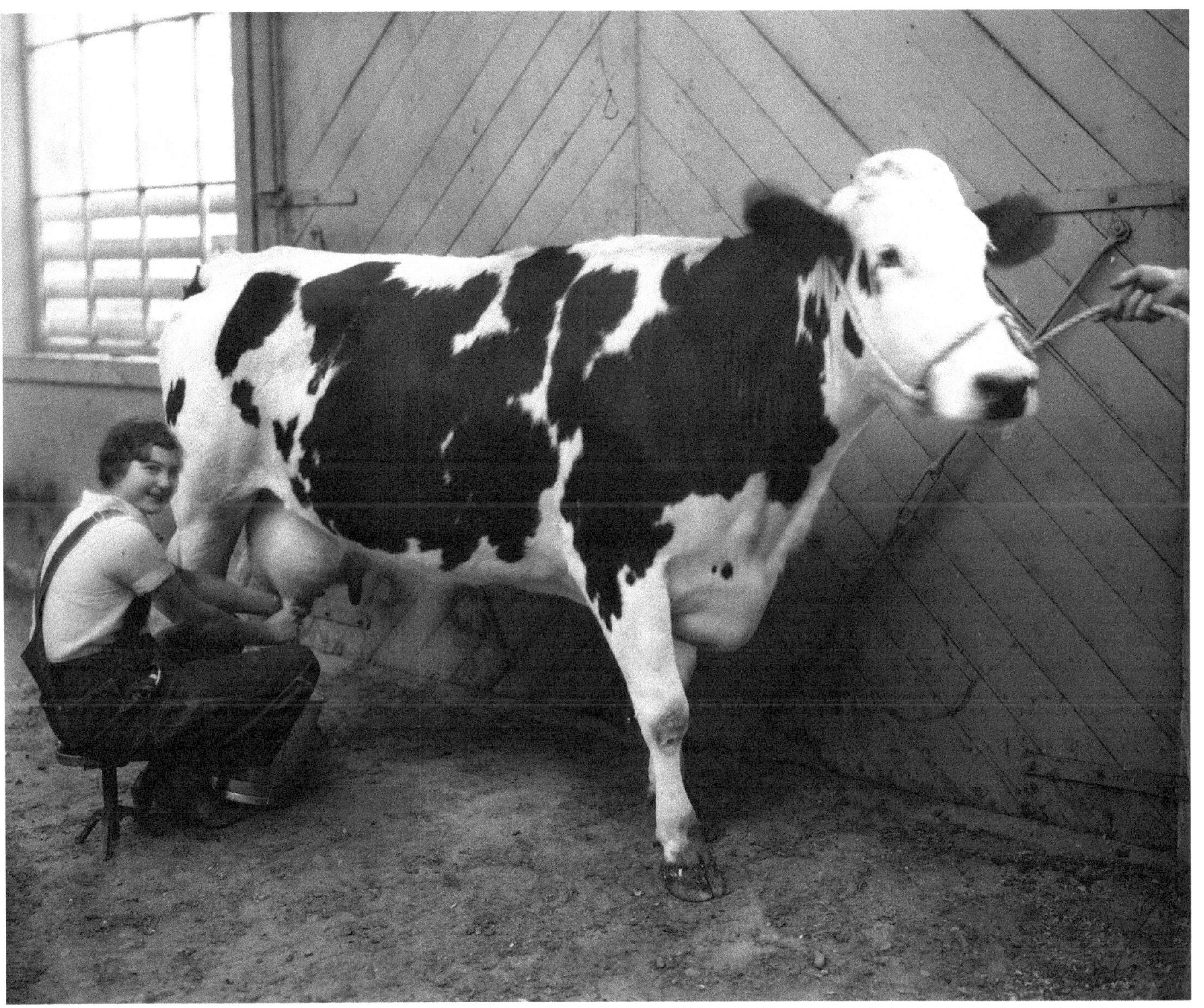

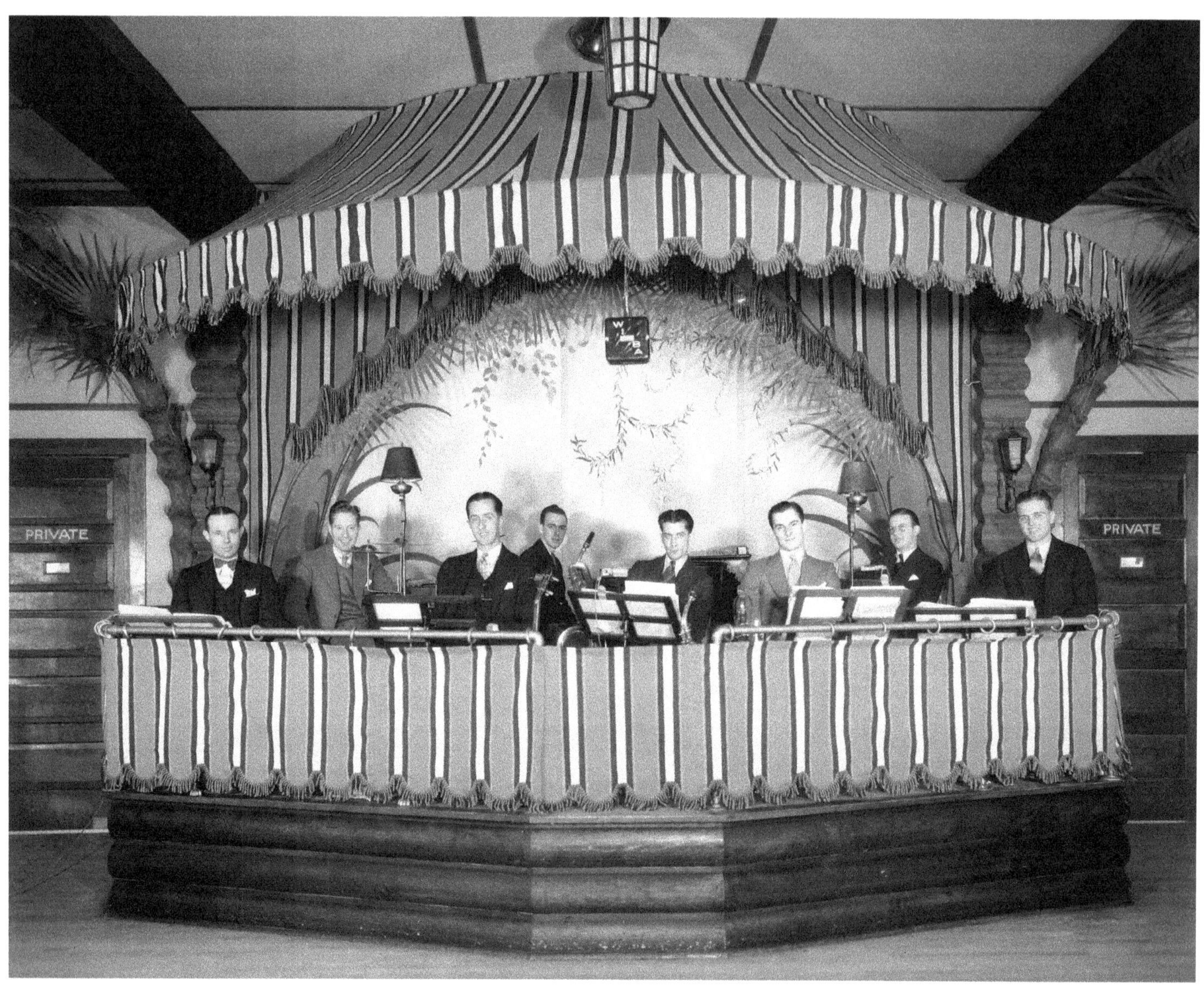

The musicians of the Chanticleer Orchestra pose in the bandstand with their instruments and sheet music at a performance on March 25, 1931.

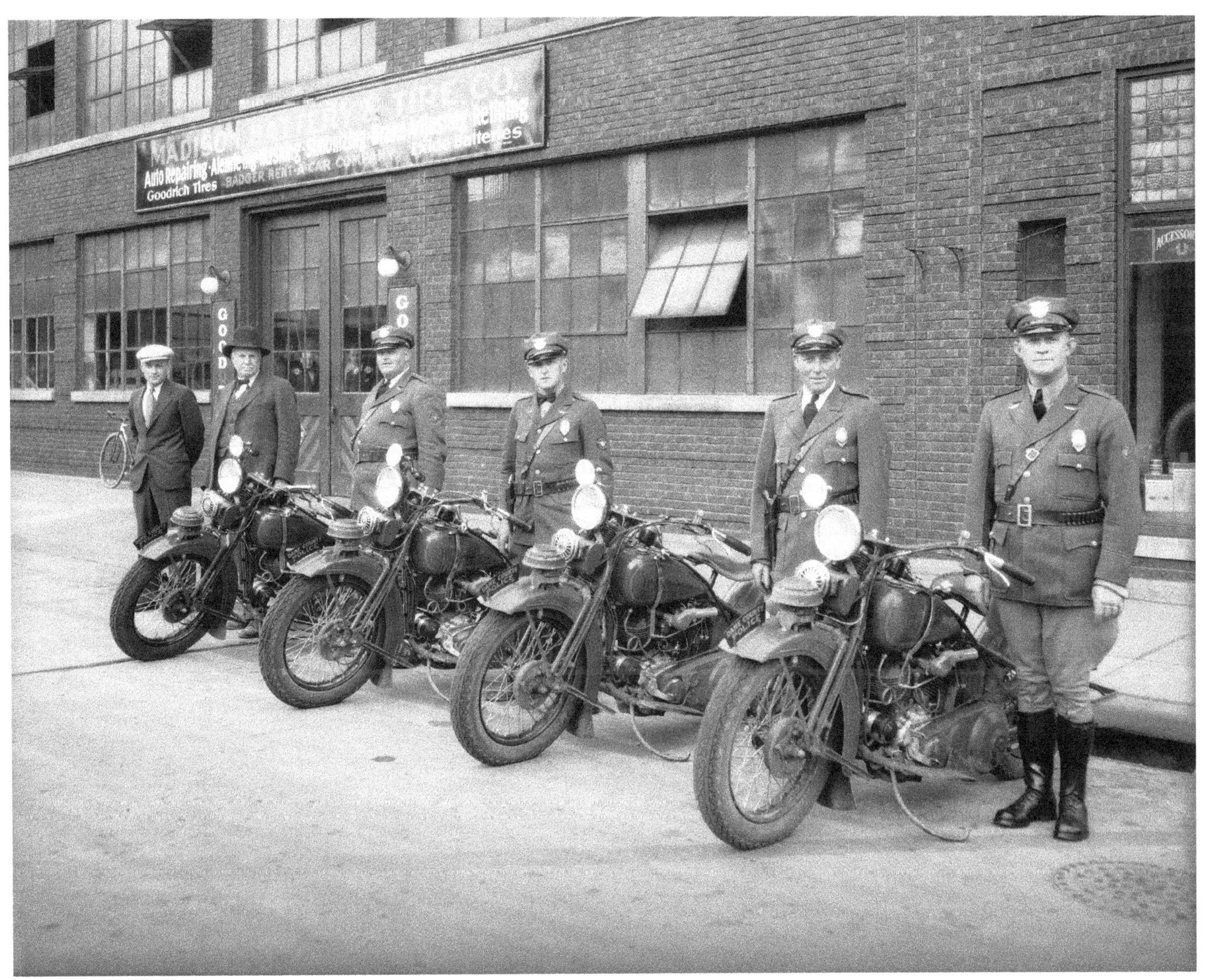

Dane County motor policemen are shown with four Harley-Davidson motorcycles in front of Madison Battery & Tire, at 250 State Street, in 1931.

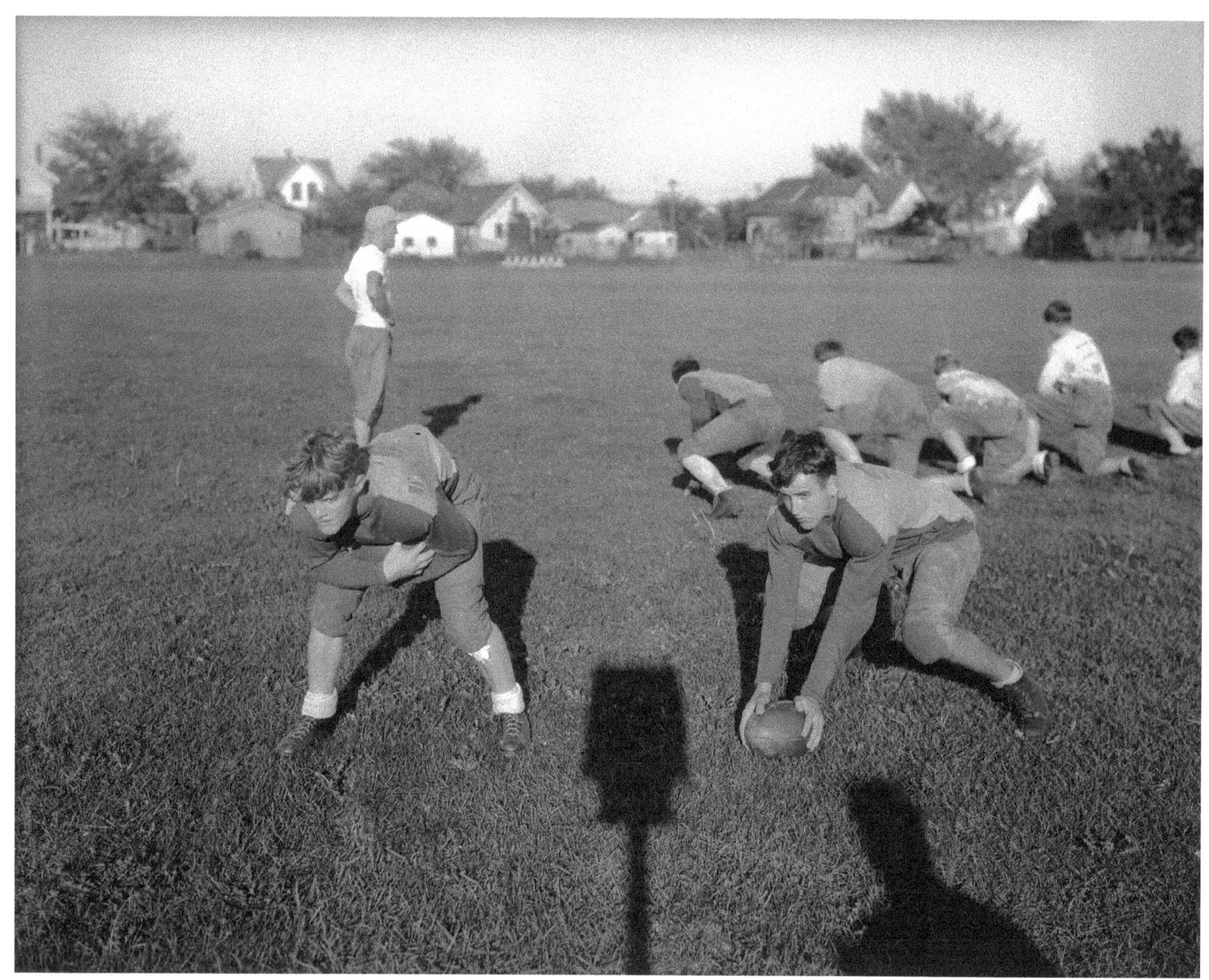

East High School football players practice in 1931. Madison's second high school opened on East Washington Avenue in 1922 and was designed by Frank Riley, one of Madison's most prolific architects during the first half of the twentieth century. Other familiar designs by Riley include the Yost-Kessenich Department Store, now part of the facade of the Overture Center; the Madison Club; and the governor's mansion.

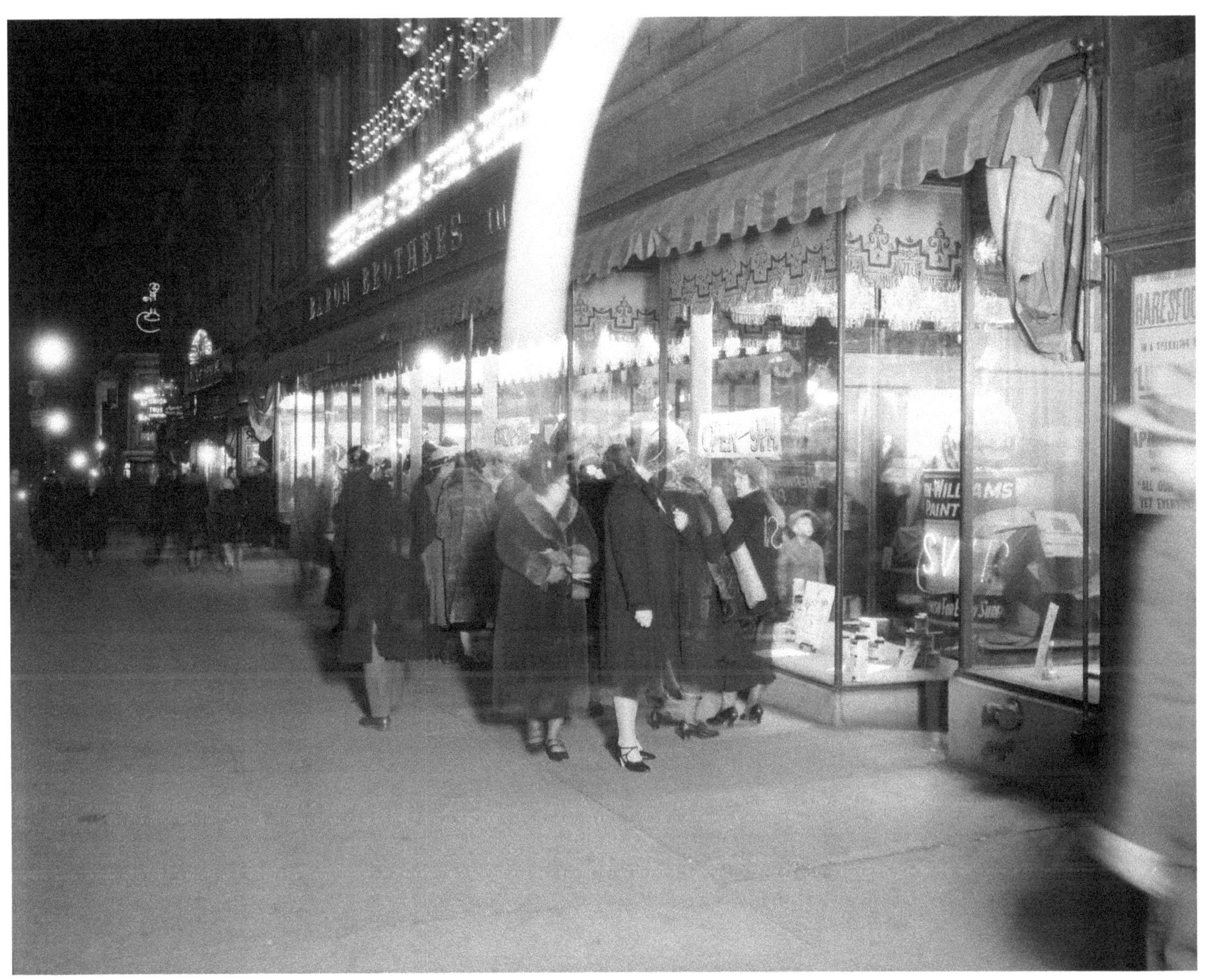

Women pause at a display window on a Saturday night in April 1932. On display is Sherwin-Williams paint at Baron Brothers Department Store, 12-18 W. Mifflin Street.

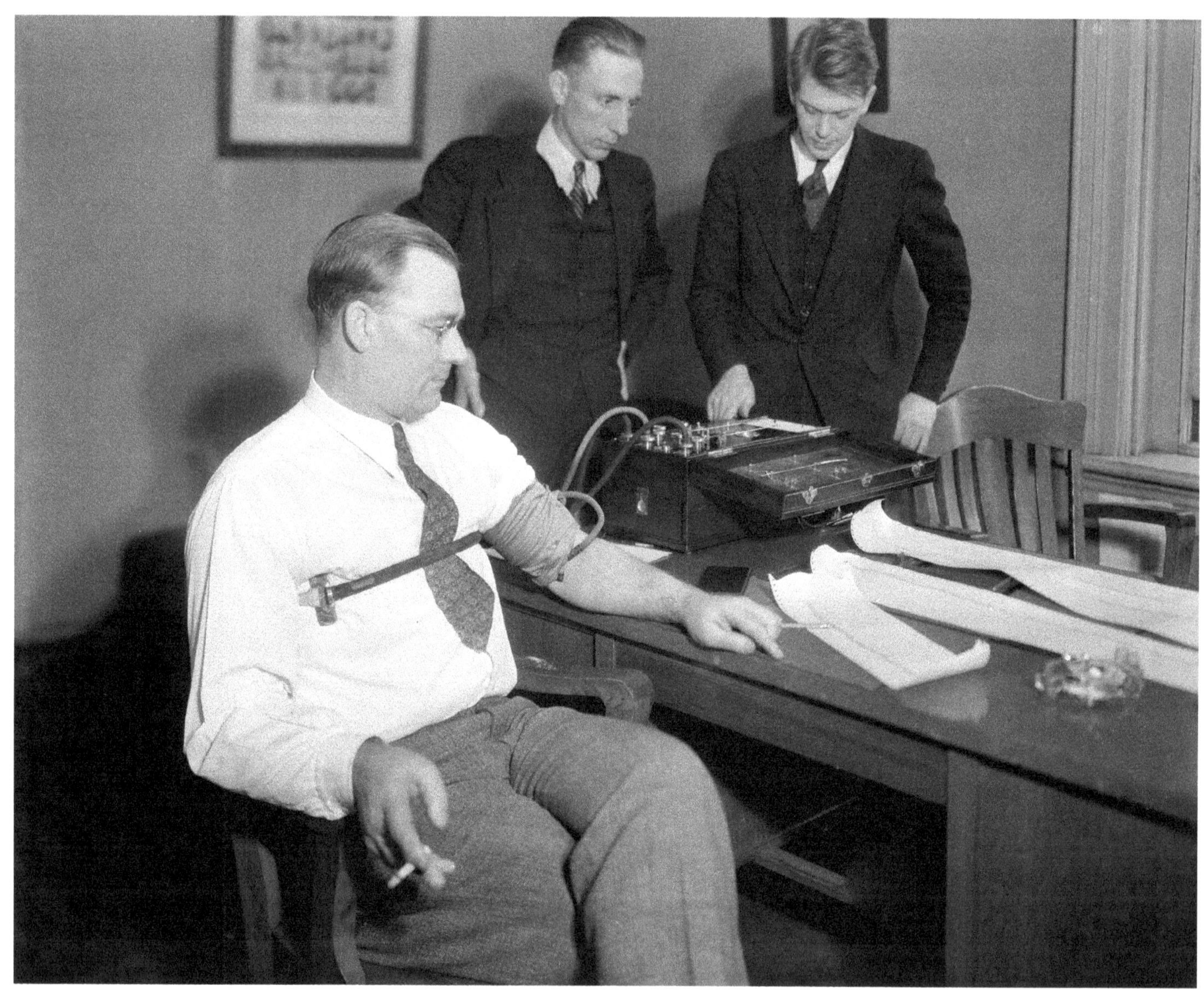

Technicians administer a lie detector test in December 1931 at District Attorney Fred Risser's office to be used in the James Corcoran poisoning case. Risser's son became a long-serving state legislator.

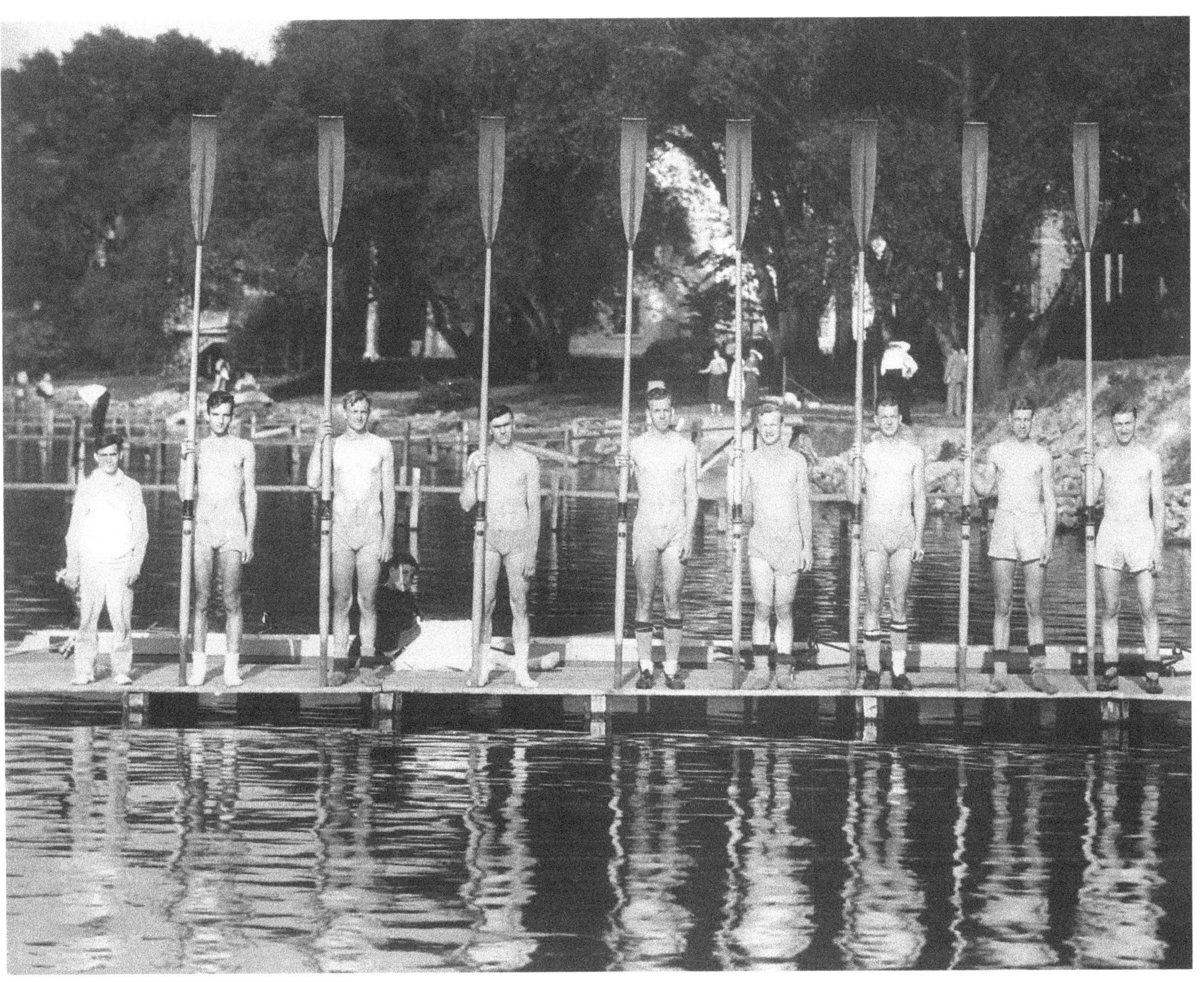

In May 1931, the University of Wisconsin rowing team poses with their long oars on a pier on Lake Mendota. The coxswain, the man who steers the boat and coordinates the rhythm of the rowers, stands at far left. Rowing was the first UW intramural sport in 1874, and Wisconsin rowers participated in every U.S. men's and women's Olympic rowing squad from 1968 through 2000.

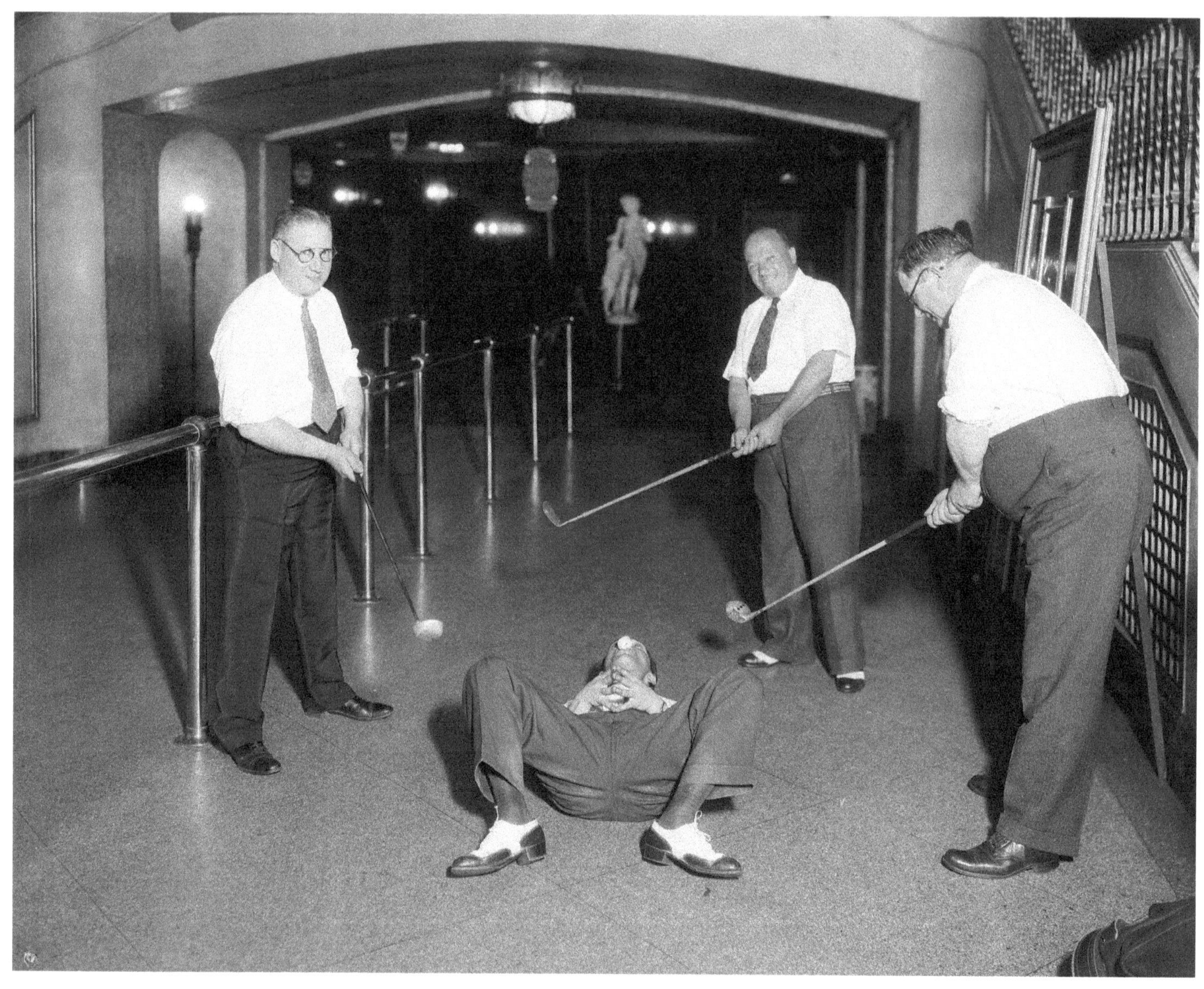

A 1932 promotional shot for the Fanchon & Marco show, a clever franchising show that sent performing "units" all over the country. Men enact a golf stunt trying to hit a golf ball off a man's nose while he lies on the floor of the Orpheum Theater, at 216 State Street.

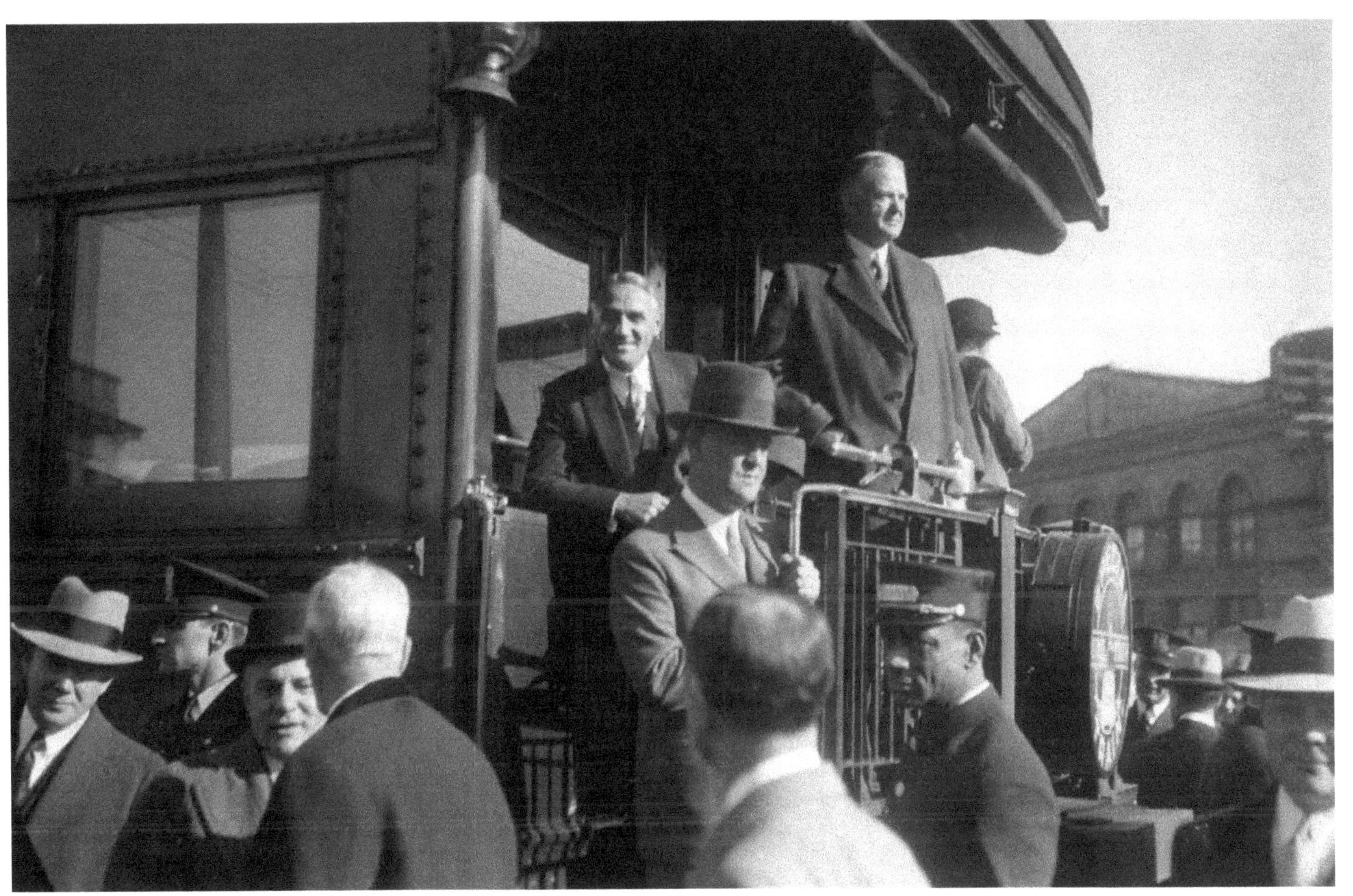

Wisconsin governor Walter Jodok Kohler (on the train, at left) stands beside President Herbert Hoover for a joint whistle-stop campaign visit in Madison in November 1932. Kohler, an industrialist (of the Kohler Company) and Republican politician, served as Wisconsin governor from 1929 to 1931, but like Hoover, was defeated in the 1932 general election.

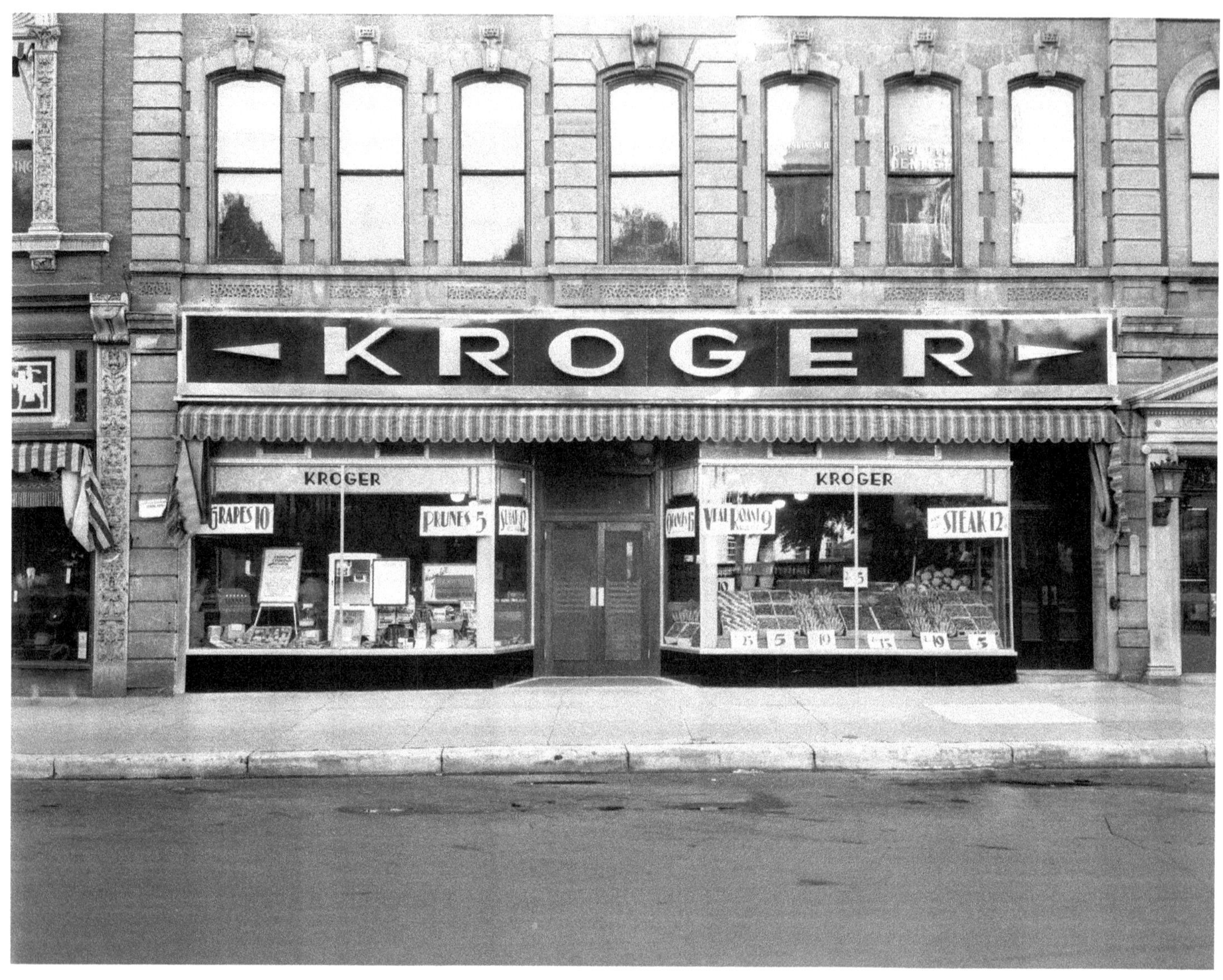

The Kroger Grocery Store enjoyed a prime location in 1932 at 3-5 North Pinckney Street. The store had a black vitrolite front and chromium trim with matching art deco letters.

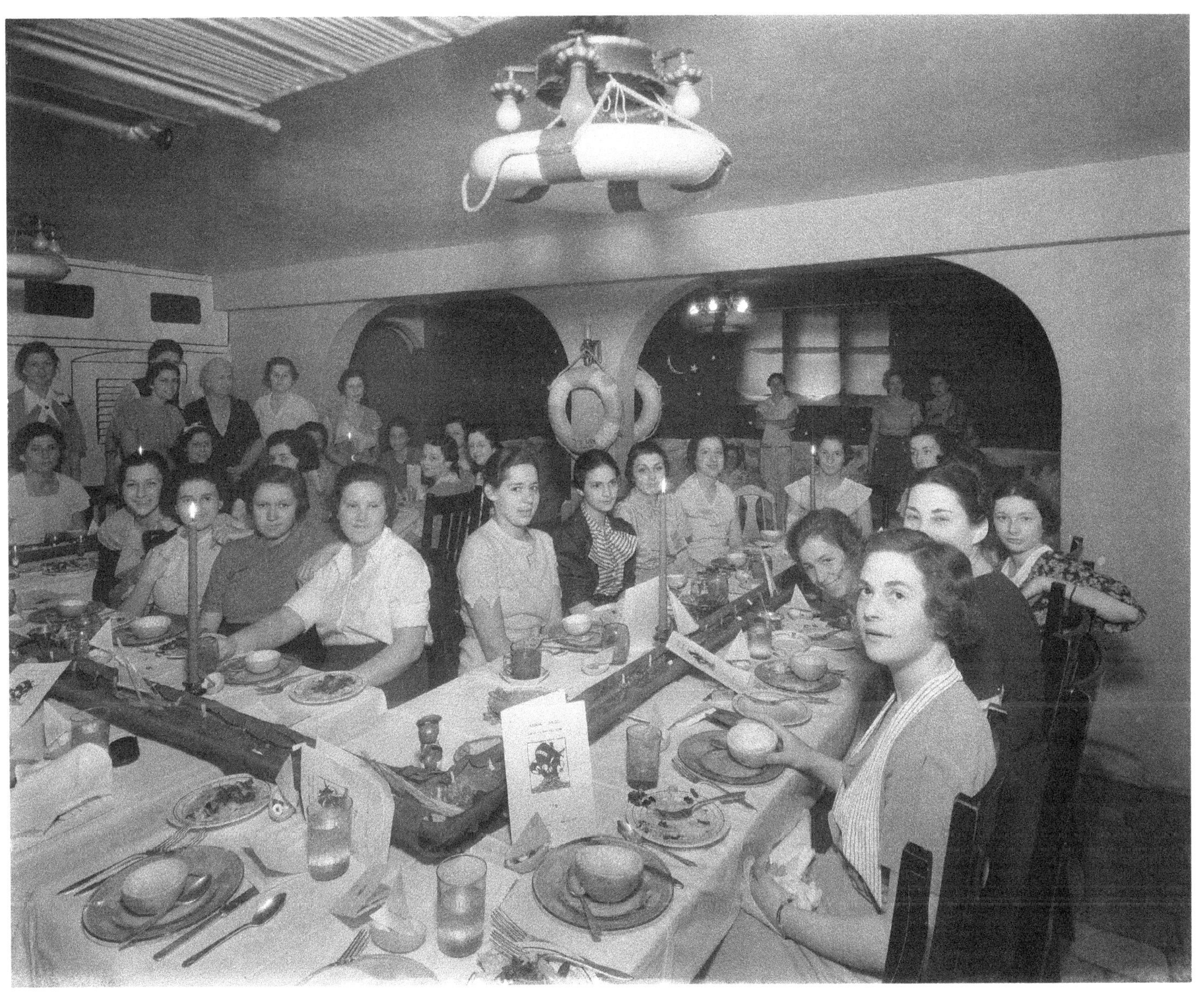

Alpha Epsilon Phi sorority women pose for a group portrait at 135 Langdon Street in May 1933. The event, decorated with a marine theme, was an informal finishing dinner to help the senior group celebrate the end of the school year.

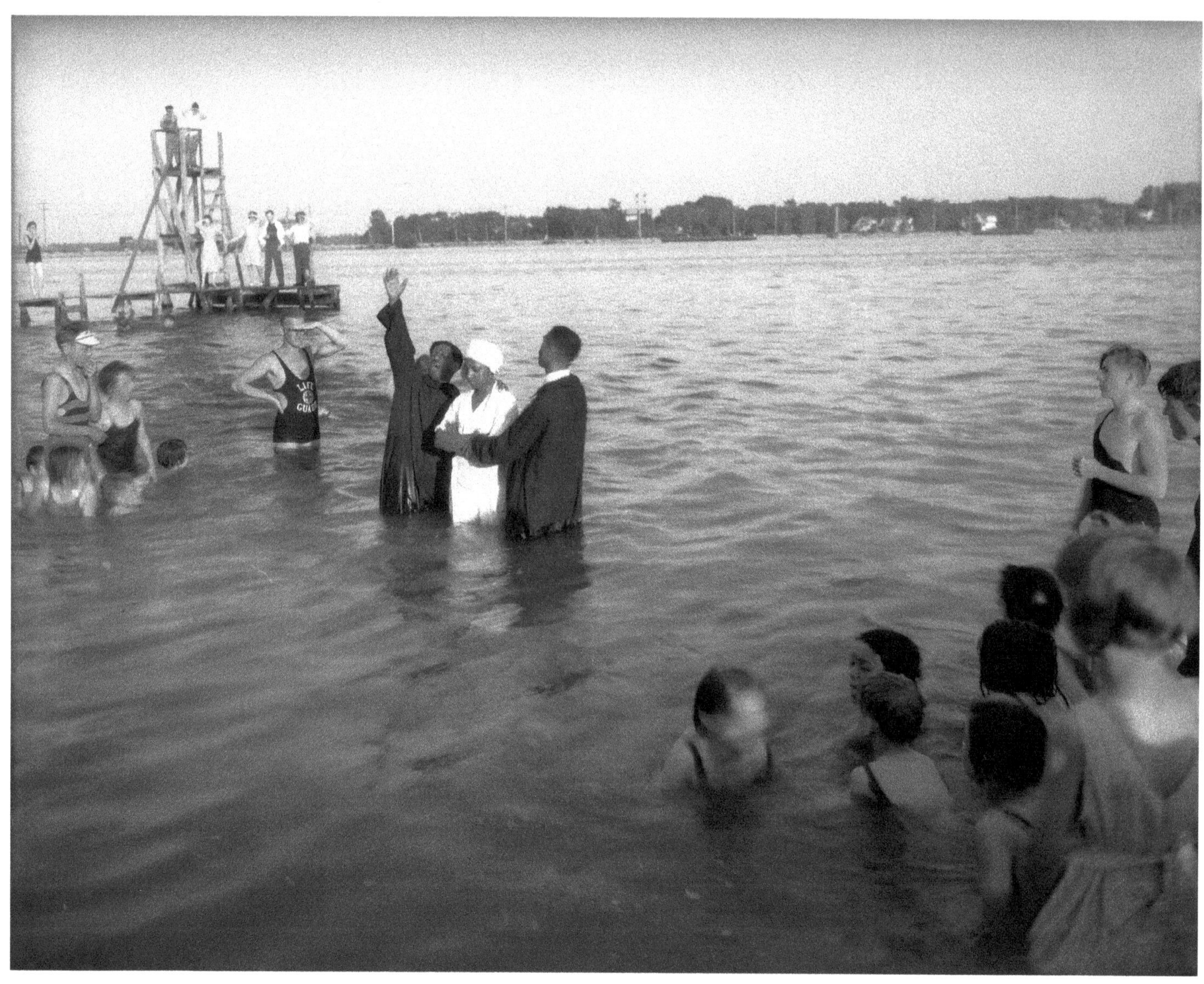

In June 1933, Lulu Elroy, at center in white robe, is about to be baptized in Lake Monona by Evangelist W. P. Butler, hand upraised, and Joseph Washington, pastor of Mt. Zion Baptist Church, with swimmers and a lifeguard observing.

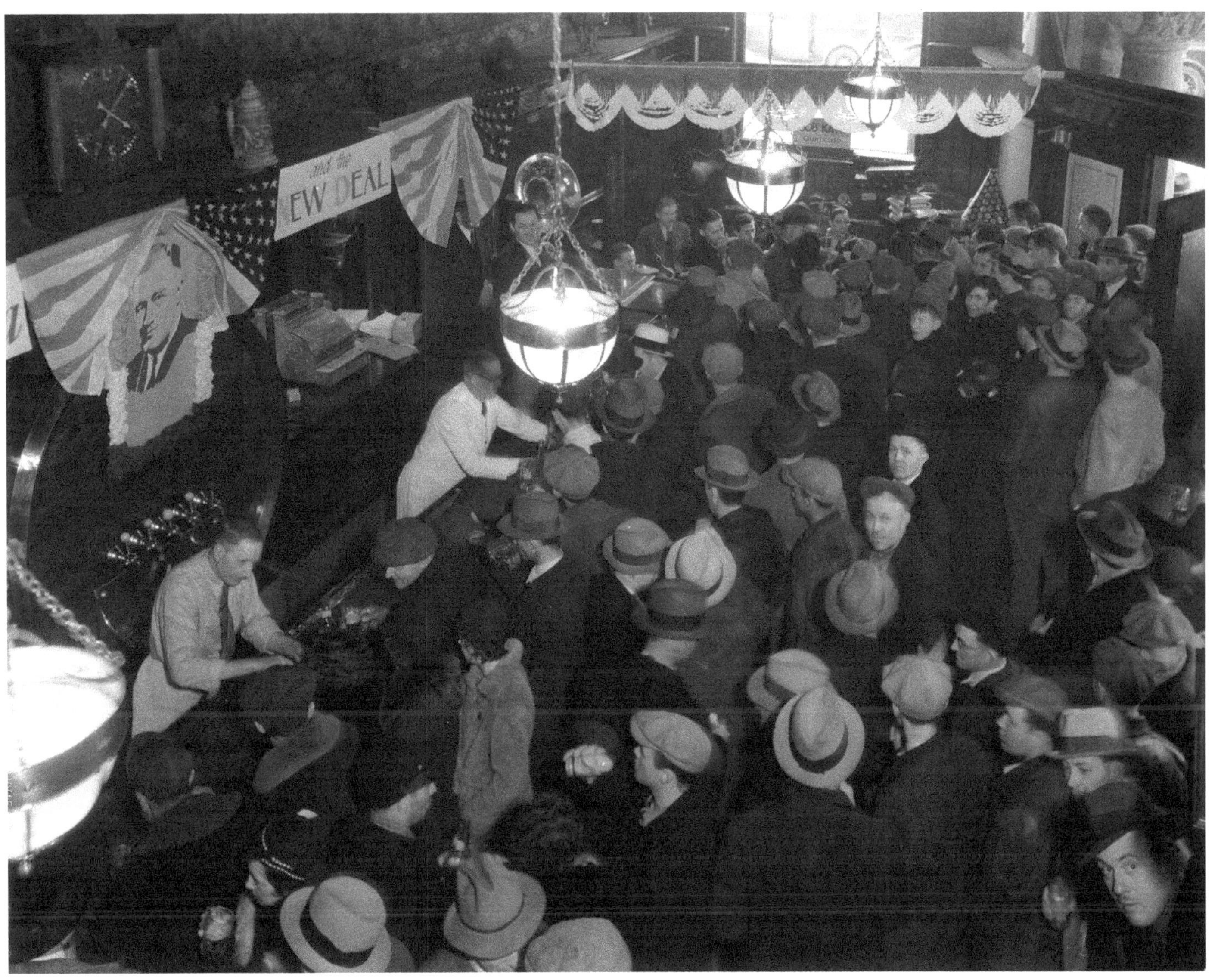

On April 7, 1933, an overflow crowd celebrating the end of Prohibition packs the bar at the Fauerbach Brewing Company, 651 Williamson Street. This date marked the end of prohibition for beer; prohibition ended for all alcohol the following December.

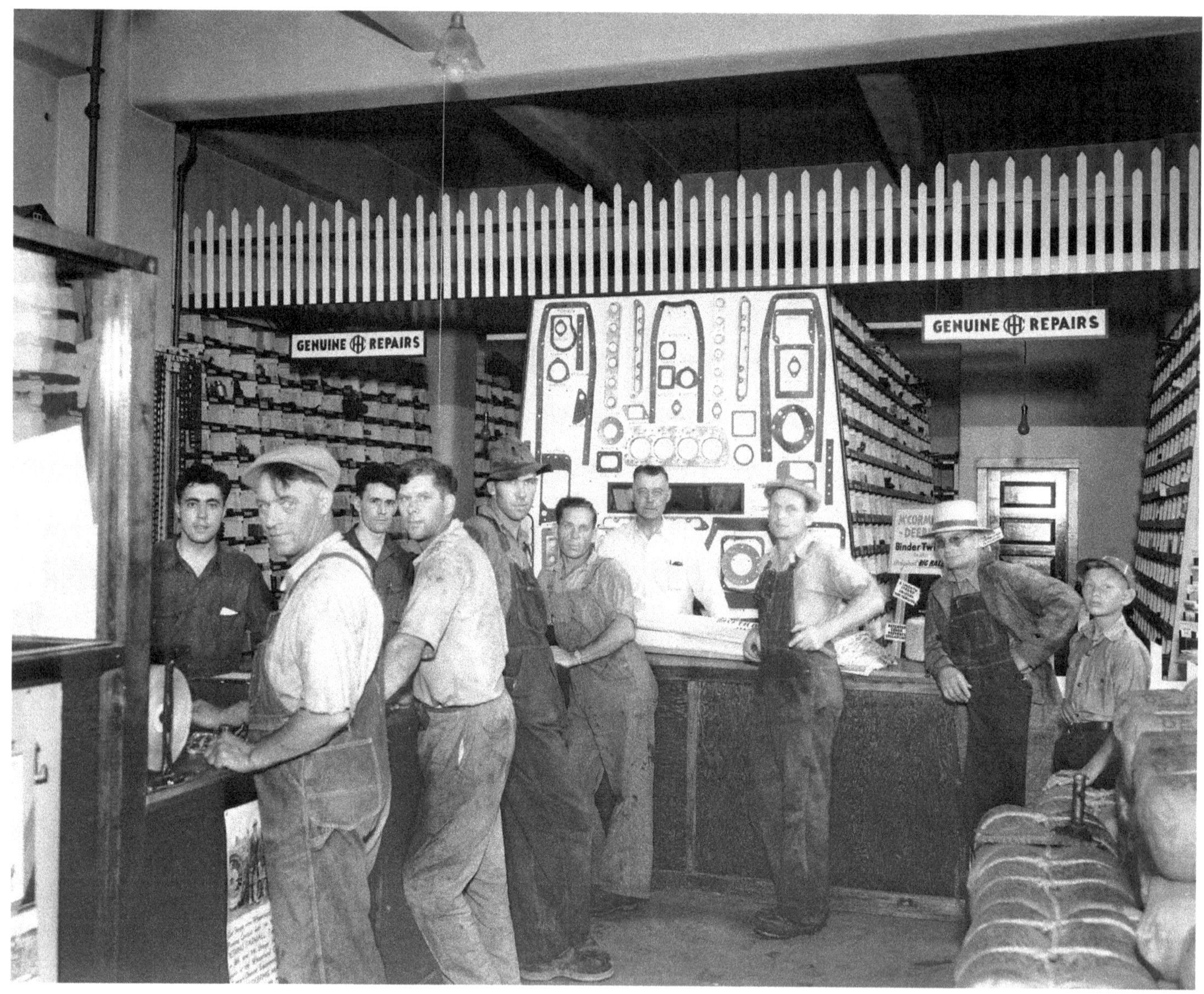

Customers visit the Niglis Implement Store at 724 Williamson Street in summer 1935. Three employees are working behind the counter.

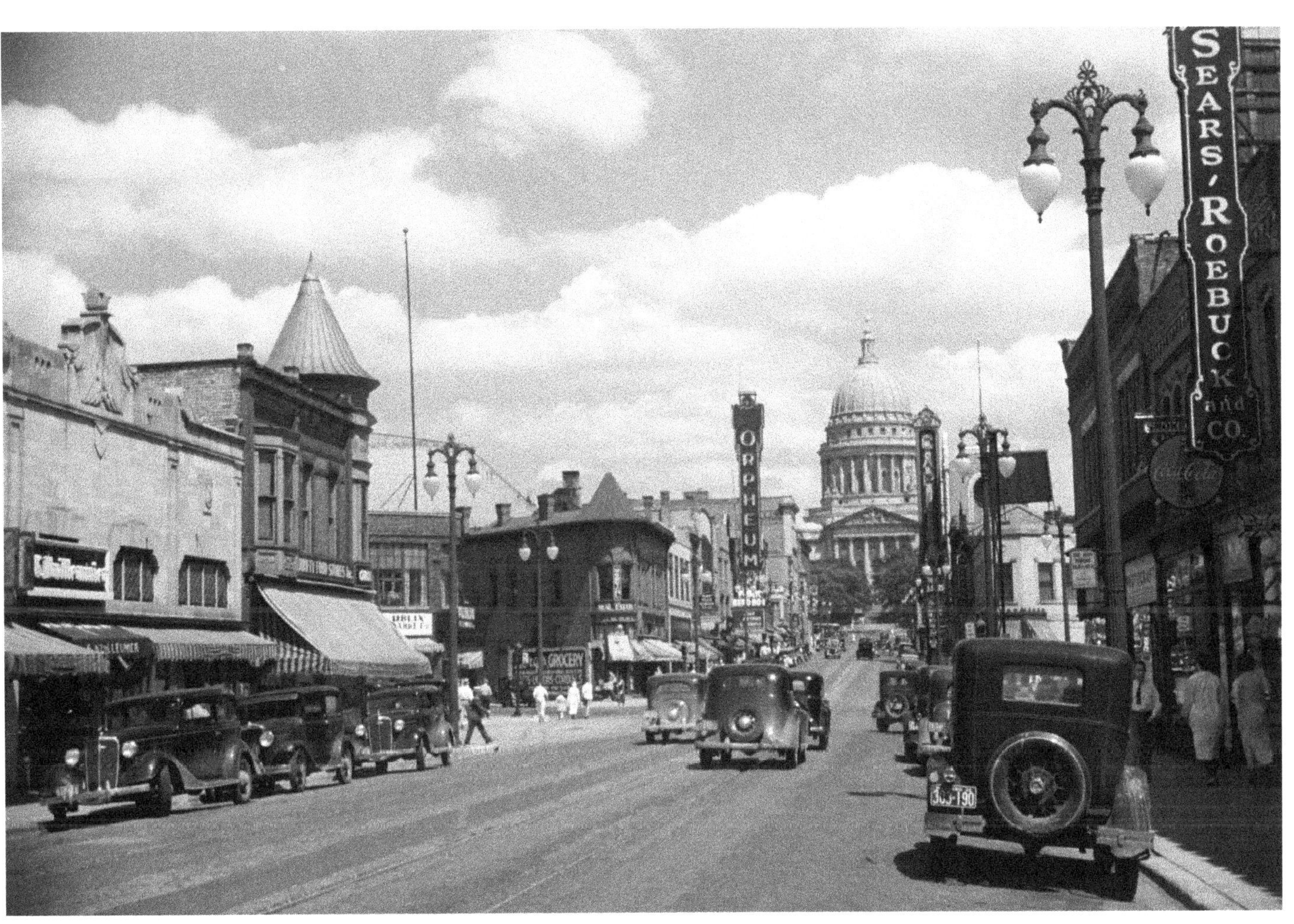

This view looking toward the Capitol from the 200 and 300 blocks of State Street was recorded in 1935. A Sears-Roebuck store was located just down the street from the Orpheum Theater.

During a stop in Madison on October 15, 1935, baseball great Babe Ruth signs autographs for clamoring fans while standing in a dressing gown in the doorway of a train.

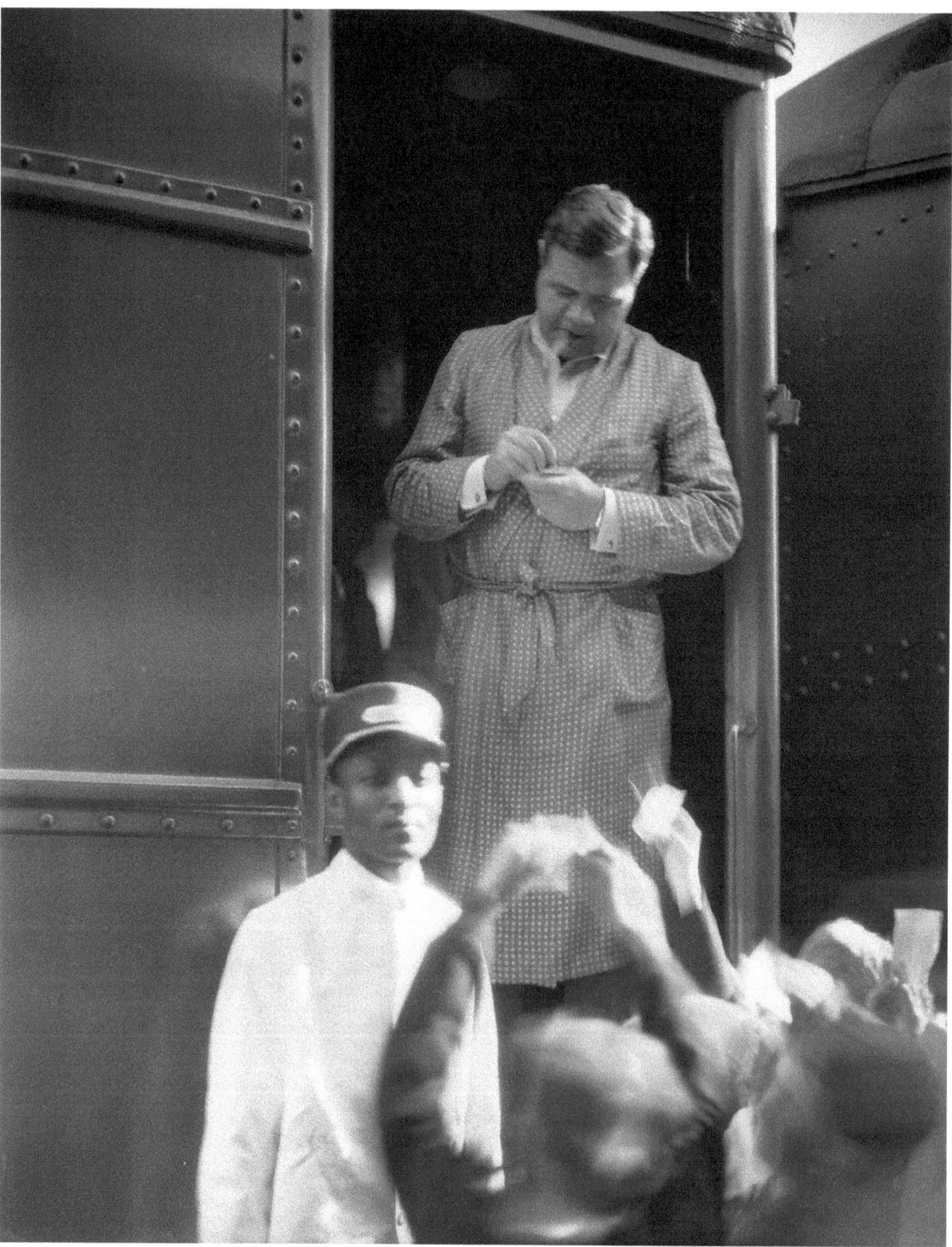

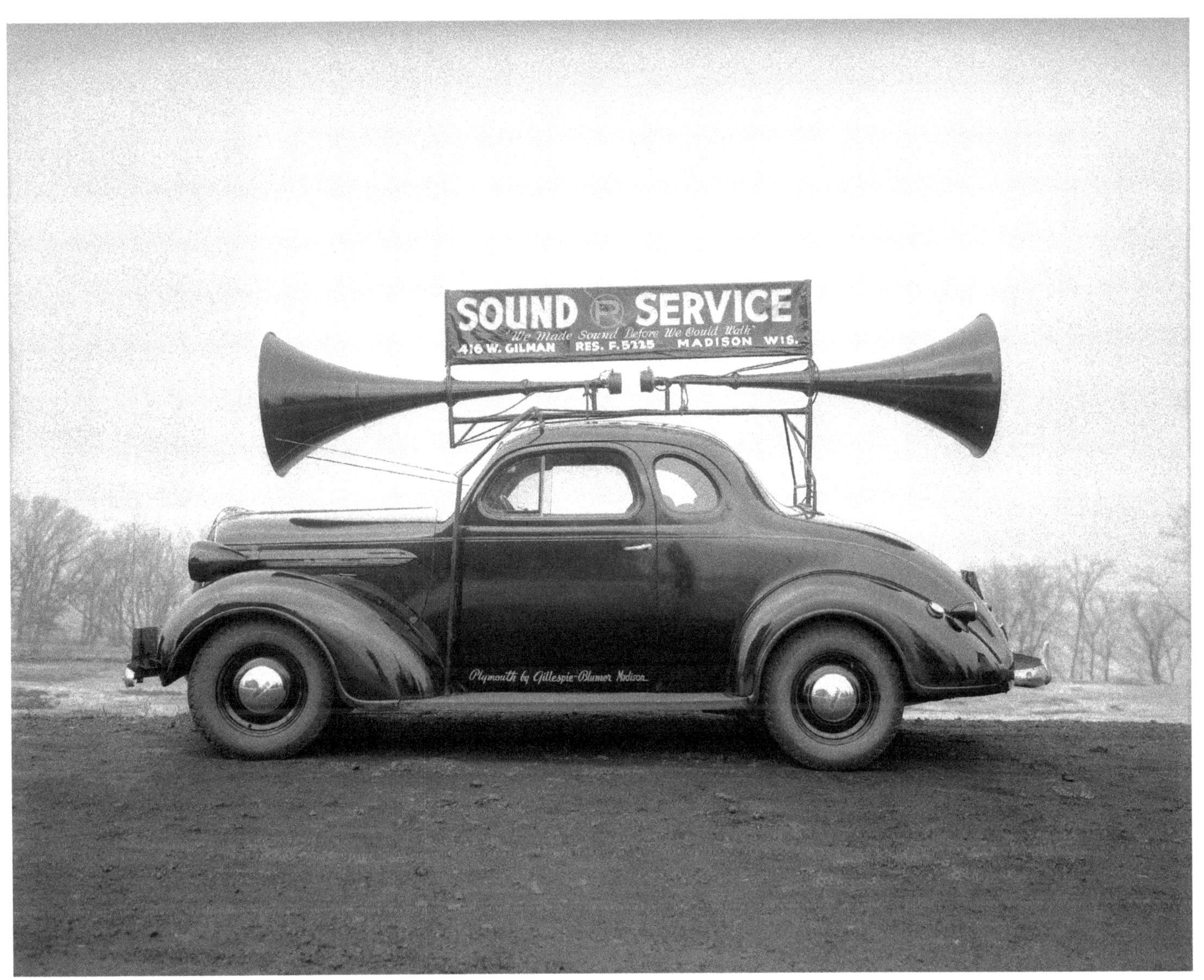

This Plymouth, from Gillespie Blumer of Madison, was the John P. Reed's Sound Service car in 1937. The automobile sports two loudspeaker horns and a sign on top.

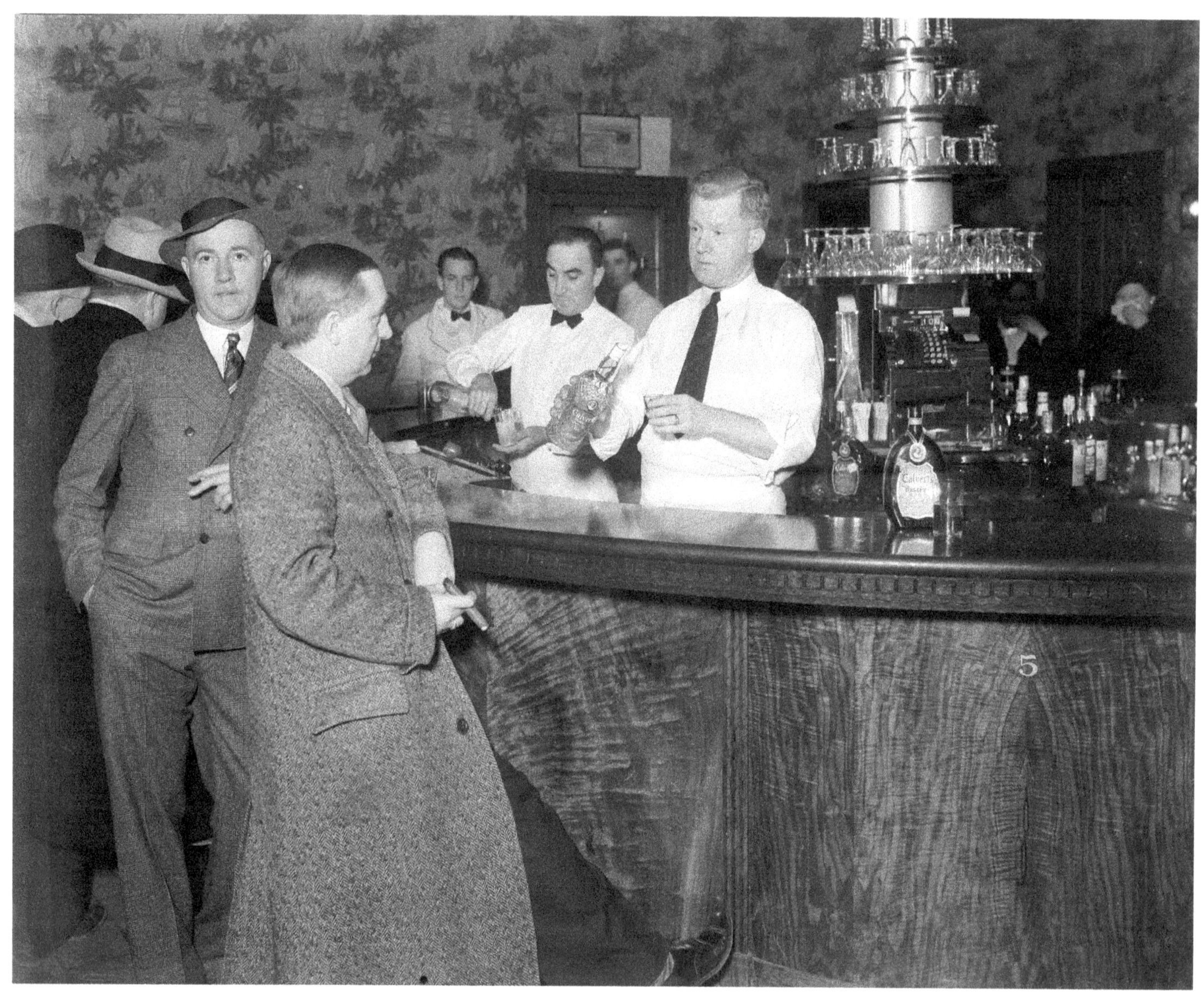

Two bartenders pour drinks for customers at the Circular Bar of the Park Hotel on the Capitol Square in 1937.

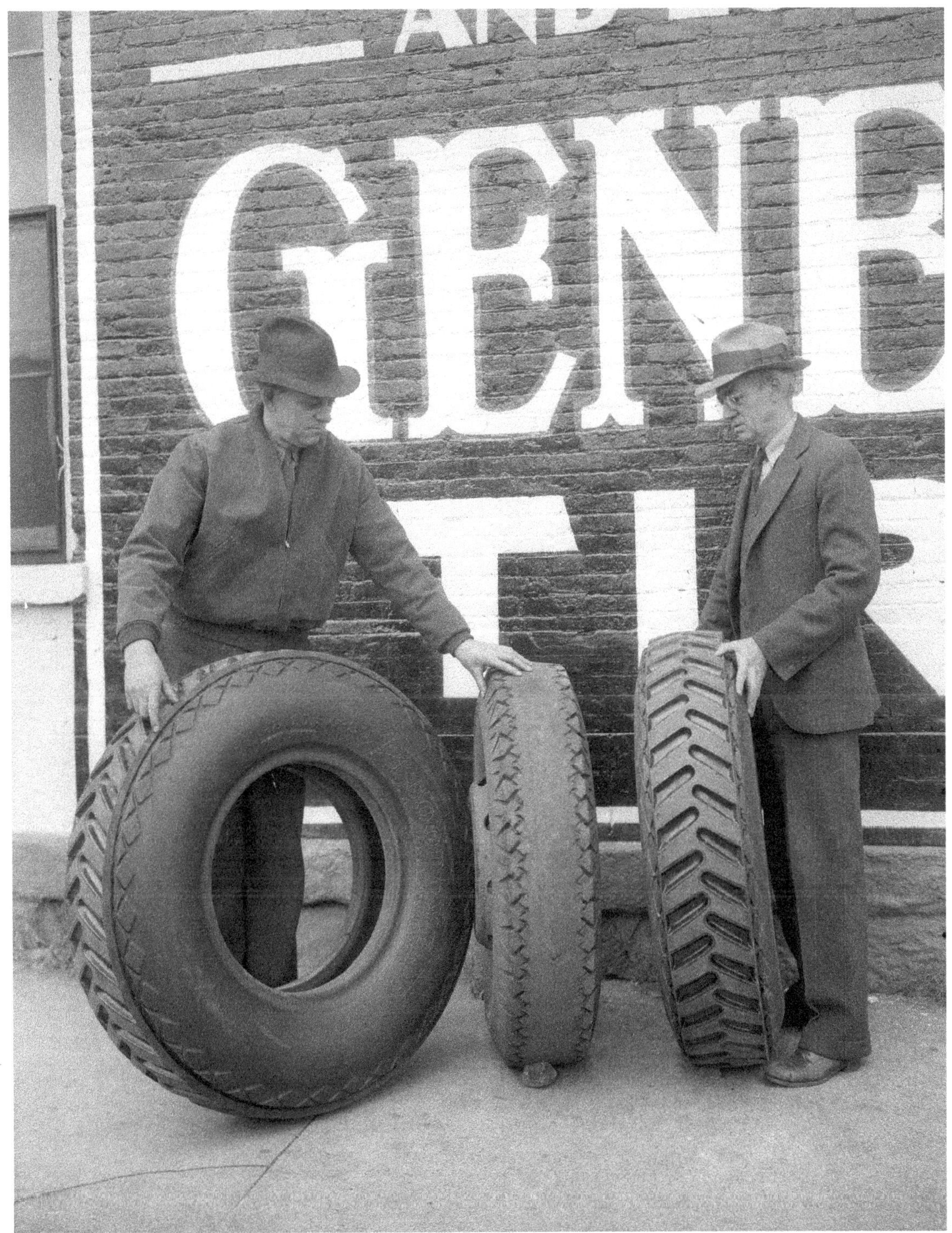

Two men compare a retreaded General truck tire against a worn-out tire at a Diamond gas station in 1937. The photograph was taken for Monona Tire, once located at 128 South Pinckney Street.

Four men pose next to an Iron Country Liquor Co. truck parked in front of the Capitol in 1937. Cream of Kentucky bourbon, advertised on the side of the truck, was first produced in 1923.

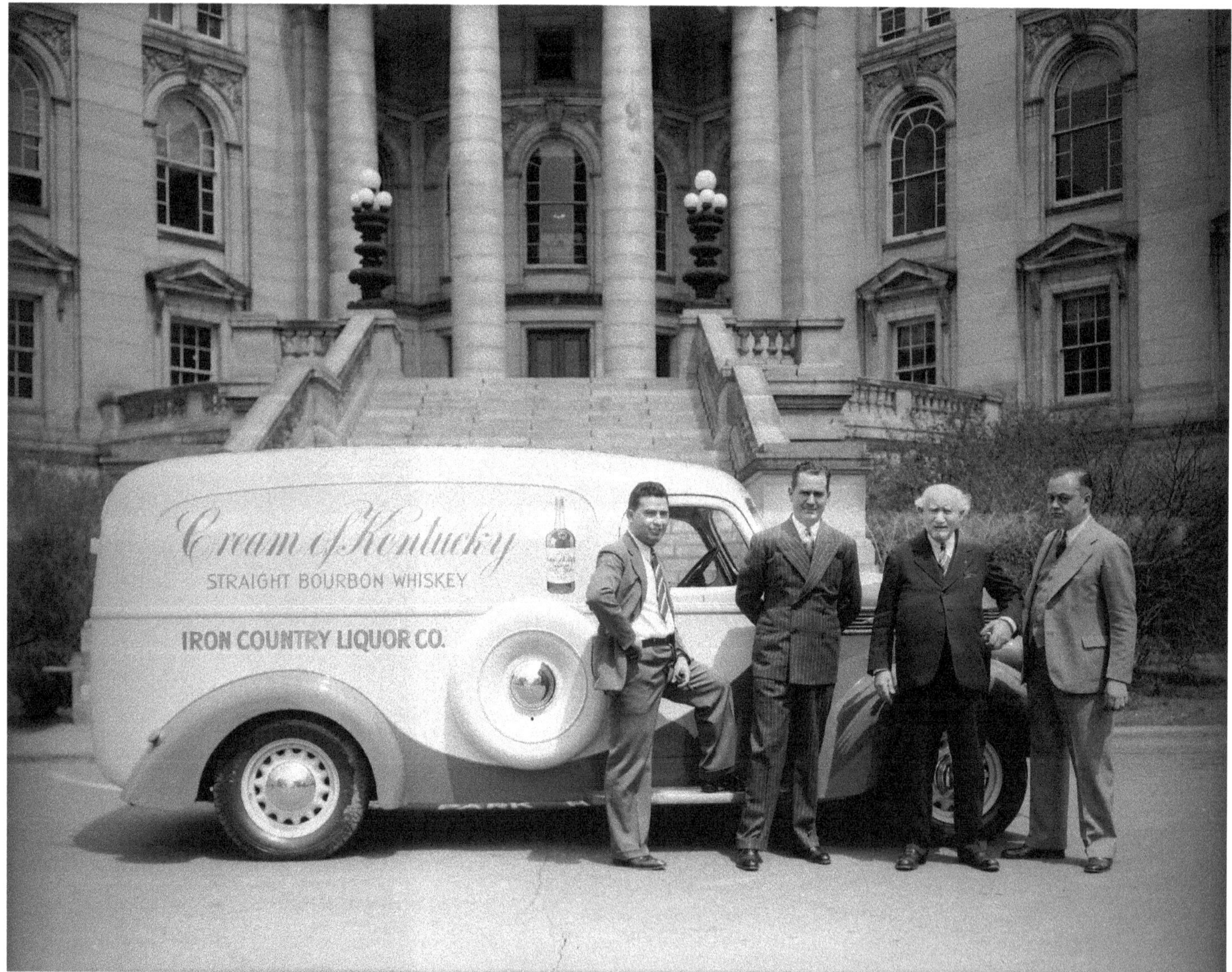

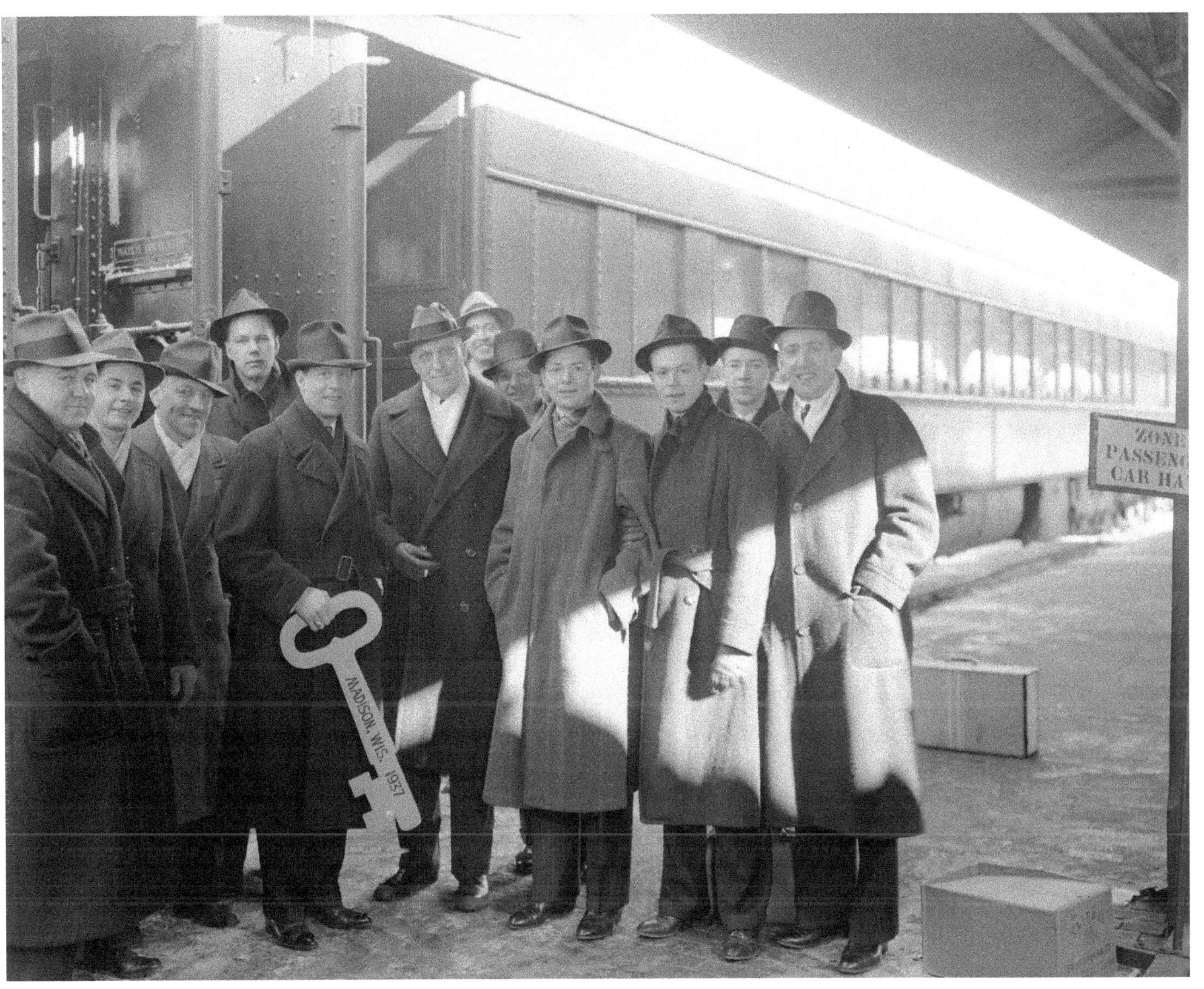

Crooner Rudy Vallee holds the key to the city of Madison in 1937. He is accompanied by eleven members of Sigma Alpha Epsilon fraternity in front of a Chicago and North Western railroad passenger car. In addition to singing, Vallee hosted "The Fleischmann Hour," nationally known as the Rudy Vallee Hour—the first-ever radio talk show, which ran from 1929 through 1939.

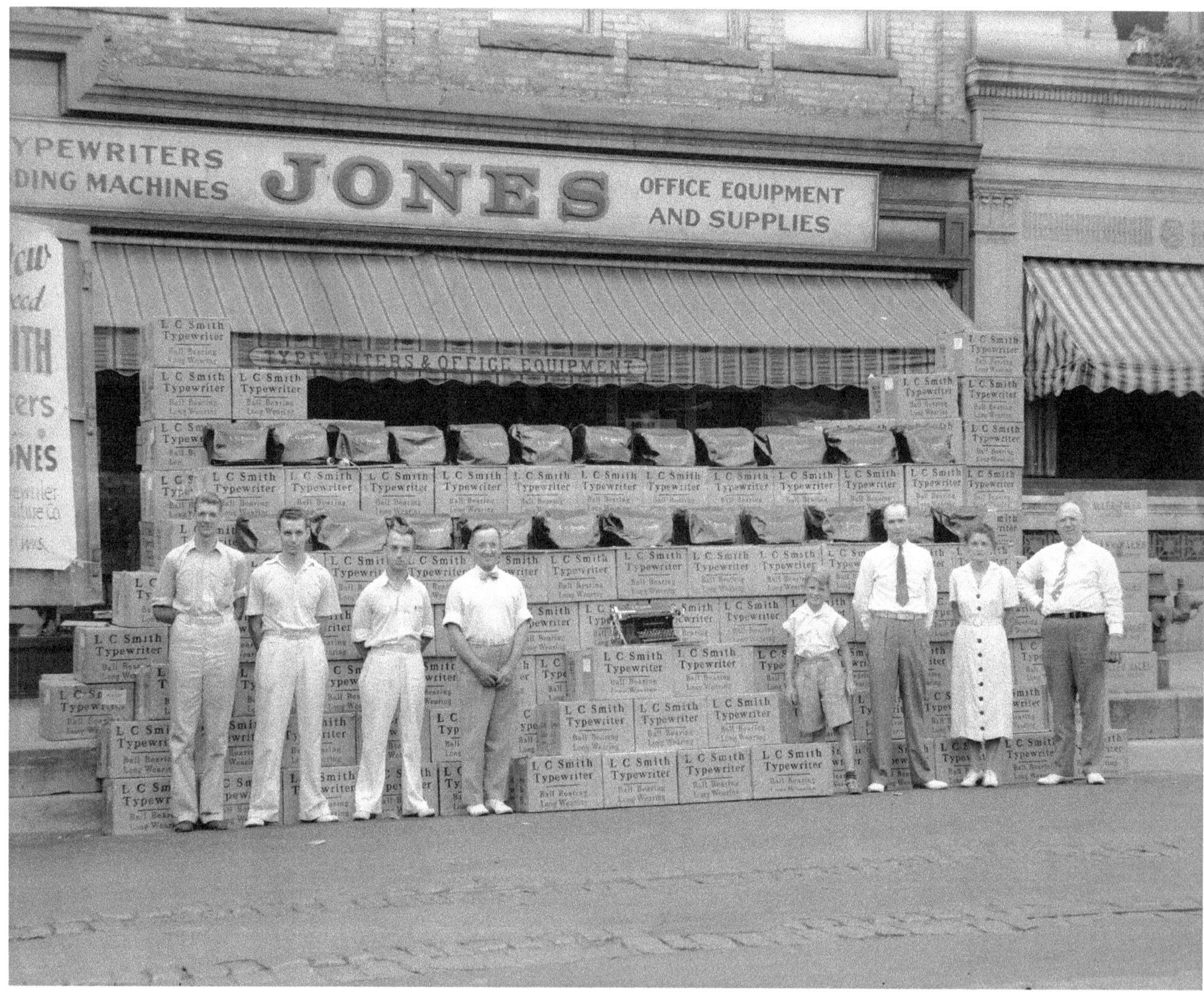

One child and seven adults stand in front of a display of Smith typewriter boxes in front of Jones Typewriter in 1937. The store, located at 506 State Street, was less than a block from its prime competitor, Stemp Typewriter at 533 State. The competitors continued to coexist for decades.

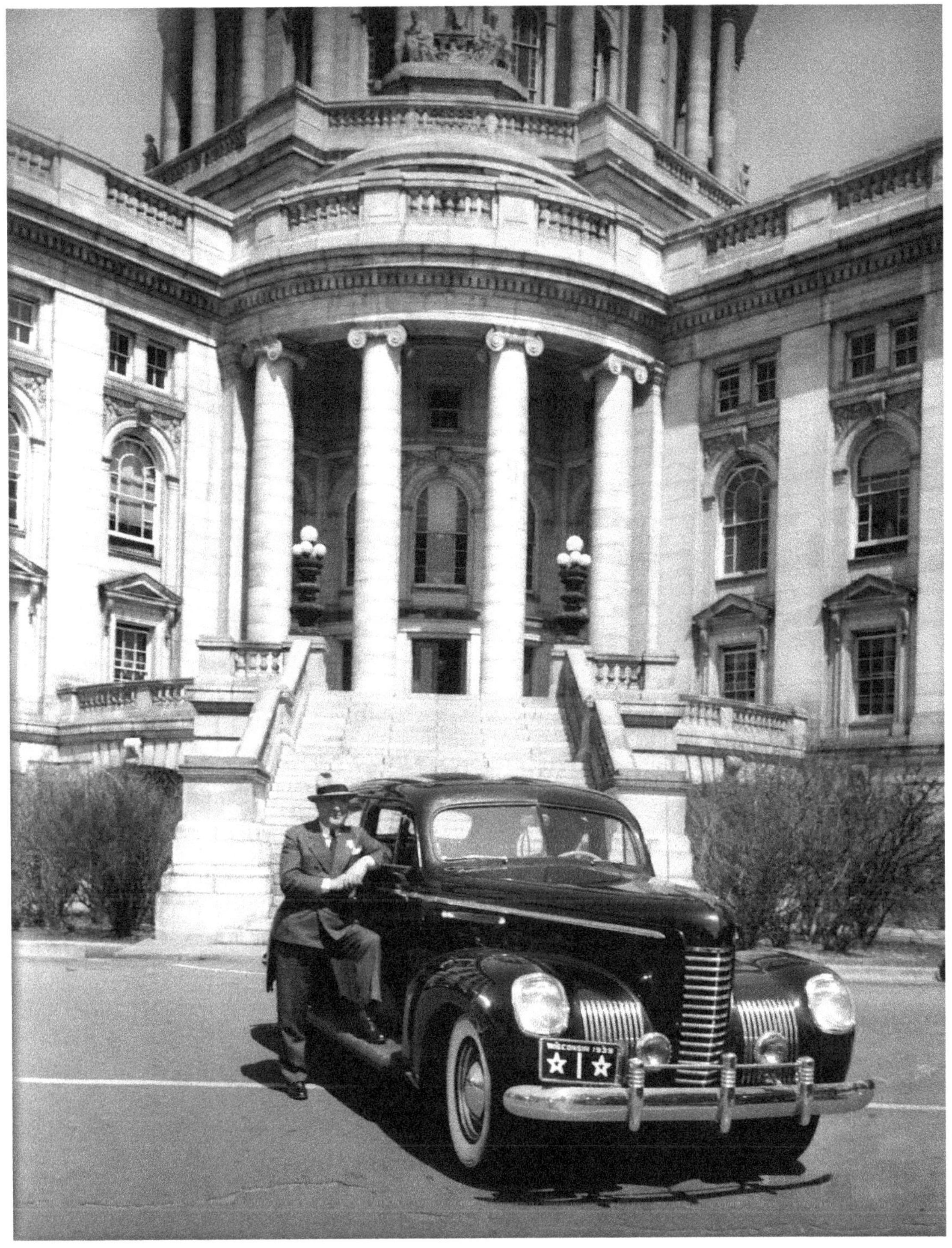

The man and the automobile represent two manufacturing giants from Wisconsin. Governor Julius Heil poses with his official car, a Nash, in 1939. Heil was the founder of Heil Co. in 1906, which eventually grew into a leading manufacturer of dump-truck bodies, storage and transport tanks, road machinery, and home heating units. The Nash started out as Rambler in 1902, the second mass-produced automobile in America. The company, owned by the Jeffery family, was sold to Charles W. Nash, a former president of General Motors, in 1916, who renamed it Nash Motors Company.

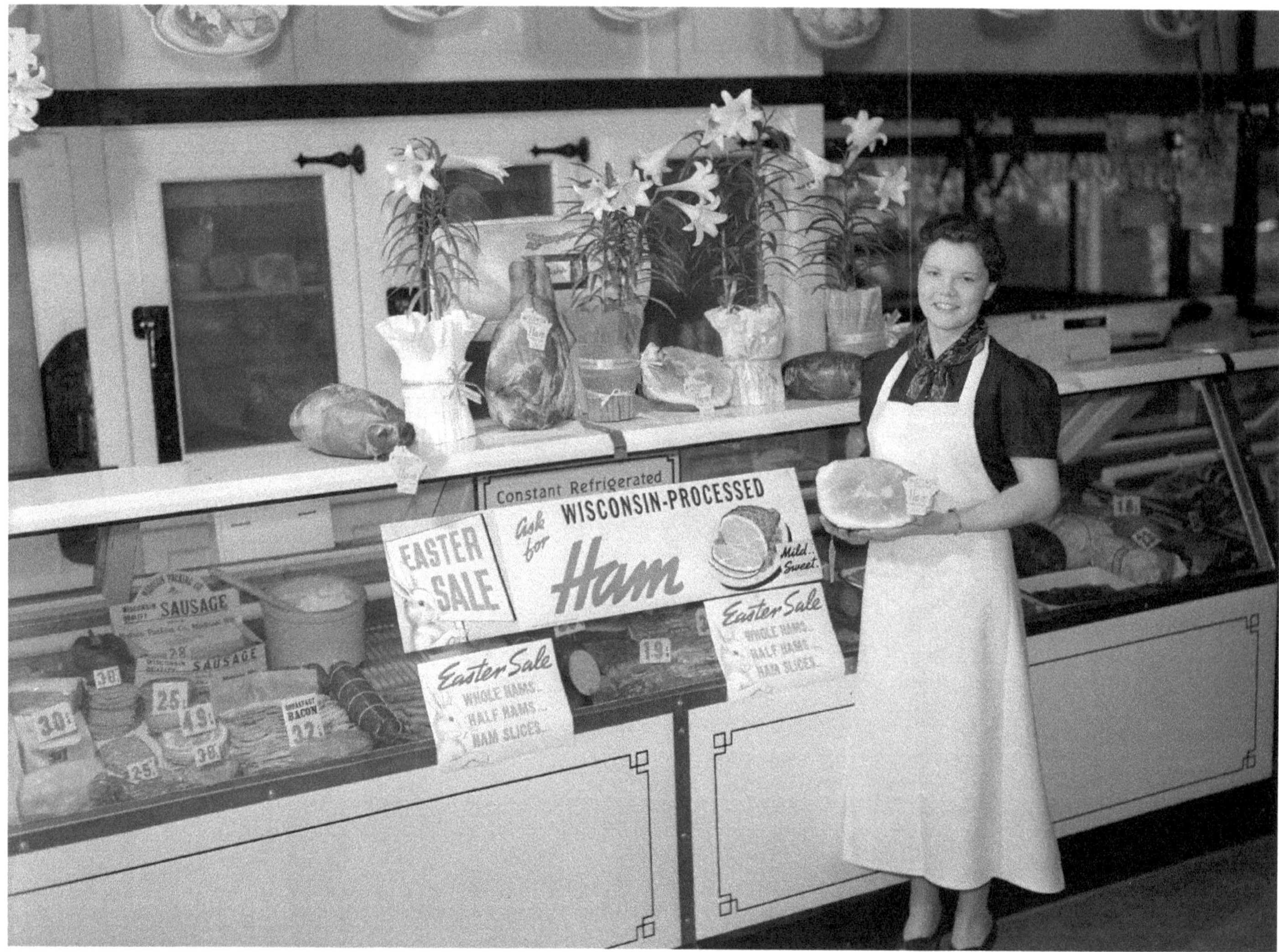

This 1939 meat market display was photographed by Melvin E. Diemer, whose collection of more than 6,000 negatives is housed in the Wisconsin Historical Society. Diemer earned a doctorate in chemistry from the University of Wisconsin and worked in photography at the U.S. Forest Products Laboratory in Madison, becoming head of the university's photo lab in 1931. He set up his own business in 1933 and retired twenty-two years later to concentrate on education and science with a special interest in nature photography and rural scenes.

Years of Change

(1940–1970)

At the start of the 1940s, unemployment across the nation stood at more than 8 million, the federal minimum wage was 30 cents an hour, and just a little more than half of U.S. homes had indoor plumbing. The onset of World War II pulled the nation out of the Great Depression and away from isolationism. Change became the norm.

Gender roles altered as women entered factories and offices to replace men at war. By 1944, more than 400,000 of 1.2 million Wisconsin women had paid employment, nearly double what it had been just four years before. Women constituted the majority of the work force at Ray-O-Vac, the Madison battery company founded in partnership with a University of Wisconsin faculty member.

The end of the war brought soldiers home and into the University of Wisconsin in numbers so great and so suddenly—tripling the student population between 1944 and 1947—that Quonset huts and trailers had to be moved onto campus as housing and as classrooms. Some veterans enrolling as students lived in tents in Madison. In 1949, three times as many college degrees were conferred across the nation as in 1940. College became available to the capable rather than to just the privileged few.

Although movies were still popular, by the end of 1948, America had four major television networks and television ownership had jumped from 9,000 to 125,000 during that year. By 1960, ownership of television sets had reached 87 percent across the nation, and Madison had launched its own local television stations WMTV, WISC, WKOW, and WHA.

Growing prosperity blanketed the nation during the 1950s forward, but the city entered an era of questions in the 1960s as civil rights issues and U.S. involvement in the Vietnam War raised debates that rapidly became visceral.

In 1970, Madison entered the decade at the center of a national debate over war, and, as they had done in times past, Madisonians took divergent positions, not shrinking from the discourse, a historic responsibility tied to the city's namesake.

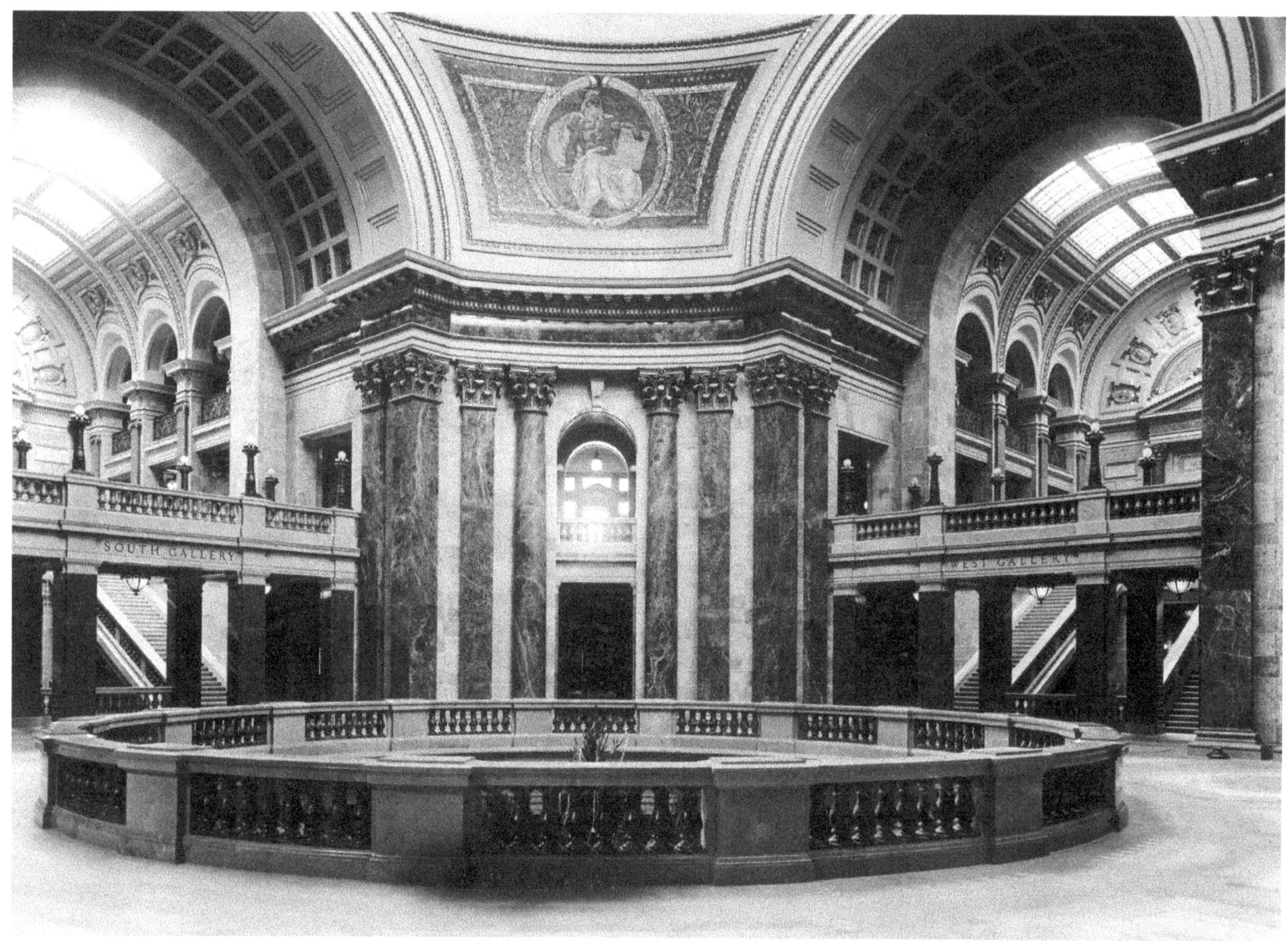

This image from the early 1940s shows the pendentive (the structure between the arches) in the Capitol rotunda at the entrances of the South and West galleries. Each of the four pendentives of the rotunda is decorated with glass mosaics designed by Kenyon Cox (1856–1919), an American painter, draftsman, and art critic. He also painted murals for the Library of Congress and the capitols of Iowa and Minnesota. The twelve-foot by twenty-four-foot panels in the Capitol consist of approximately 100,000 pieces of glass tile and represent Wisconsin's three branches of government (the legislative, the executive, and the judicial) and liberty. Shown here is "Legislation," represented by a powerful old man with a long beard. His left hand rests upon a stone tablet; his right hand holds a stylus. The photo was apparently taken during the Christmas season, since the top of a tree from the first floor can be seen peeking through the balcony opening.

Madison's first public Flag Day was celebrated June 14, 1940. Boy Scouts and others stand for the Pledge of Allegiance during a ceremony held at the University of Wisconsin football stadium.

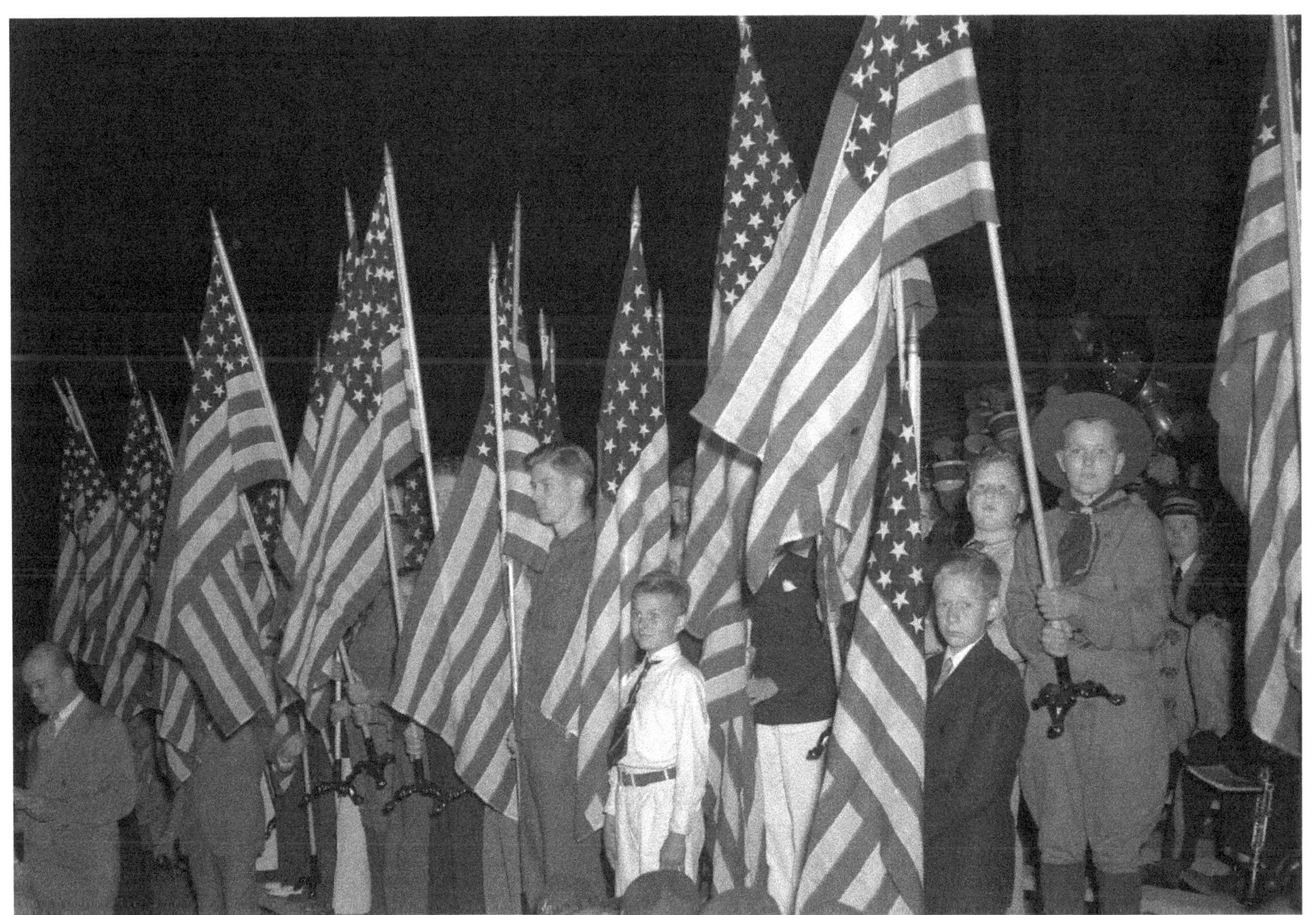

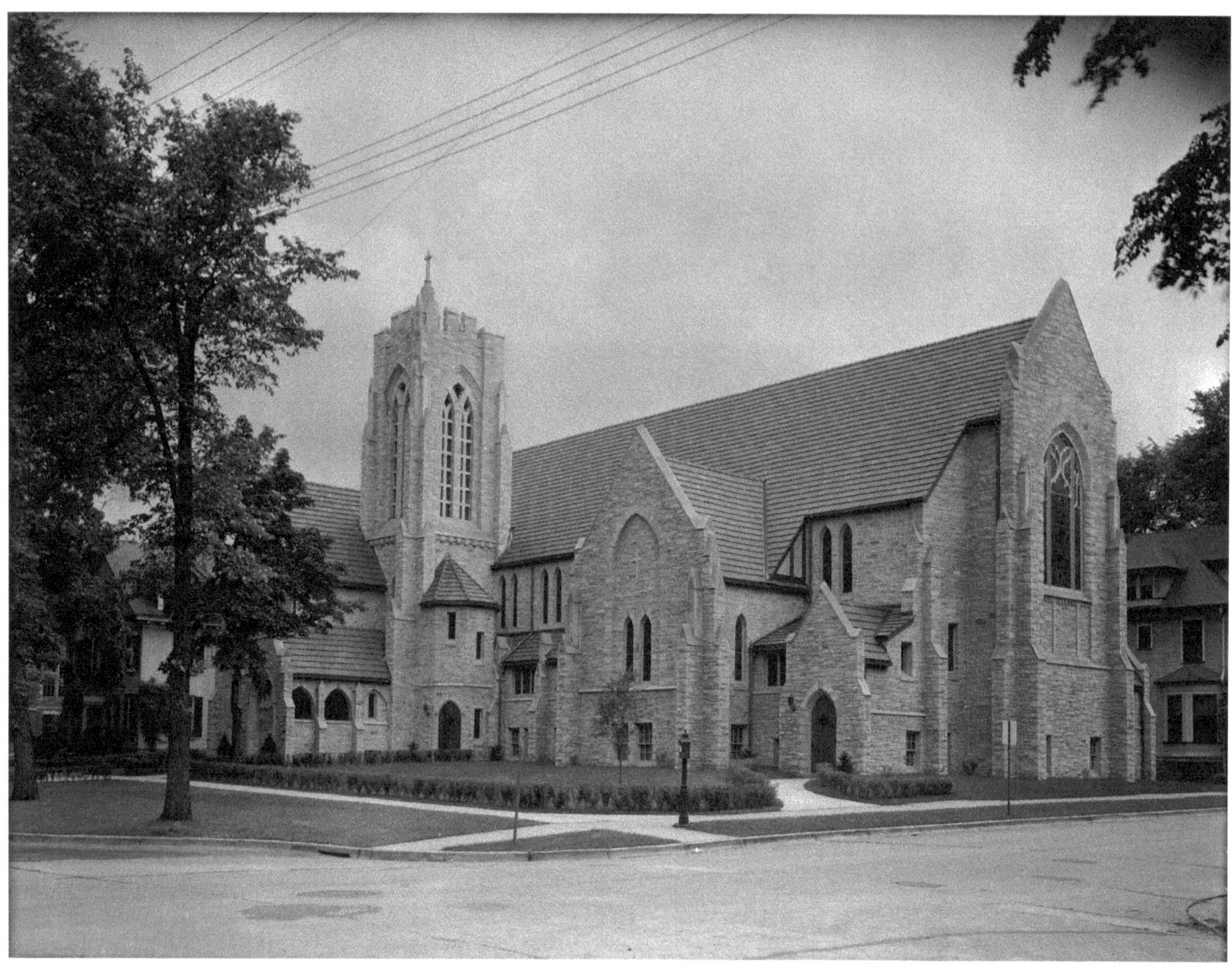

This June 22, 1941, photo shows the exterior view of the Bethel Lutheran Church, 318 Wisconsin Avenue, three weeks after the first services were held in the new building. The congregation dates to 1855 when the number of Norwegian settlers in Madison began to grow. Norwegian continued to be the language spoken during services at the church until 1929.

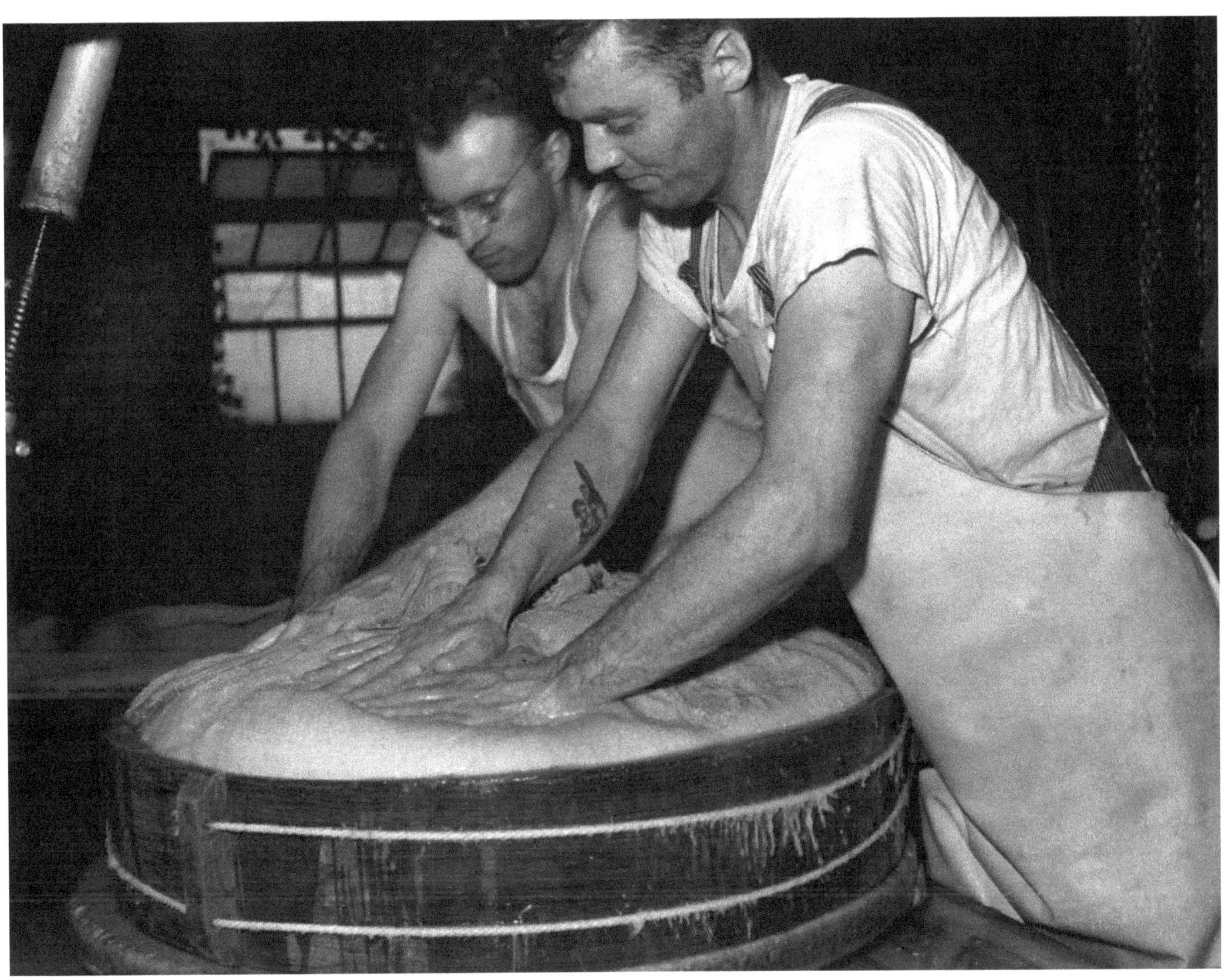

Two men press curd into a form at the Swiss Cheese Factory in 1941. The 200-pound wheel of cheese measures roughly three feet in diameter and several inches thick. Wisconsin had become known for its Swiss cheese more than half a century before this image was recorded.

Businesses on the odd-numbered side of the 100 block of King Street. At far left is the Majestic Theater, 115-17 King Street, where Jack London's *Sign of the Wolf* was playing. Just up the street is Charlier & Son Jewelers, at 107 King Street. At the corner is Fidelity Assurance Association, 101 King Street, facing the Capitol Square.

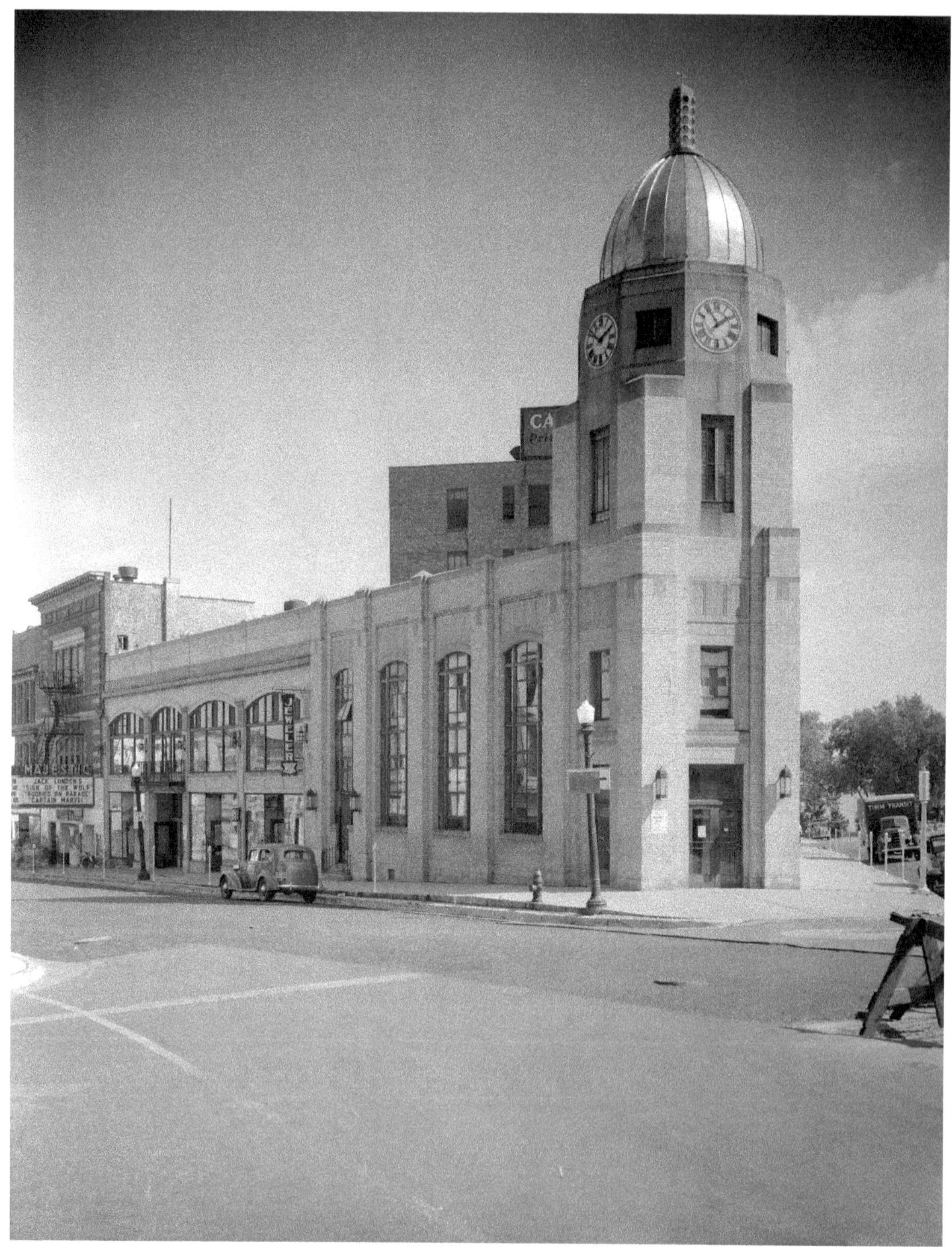

A man and woman in a basement Credit Union National Association (CUNA) office talk with a clerk about buying war savings bonds and stamps in January 1942, one month after the United States entered World War II. CUNA had been organized eight years before as a federation of state leagues. The bond denominations ranged from $25 to $1,000 and paid 2.9 percent interest. Savings stamps, introduced during World War I, re-emerged in denominations ranging from 10 cents to $5. They bore no interest, but purchasers could accumulate them and exchange them for bonds.

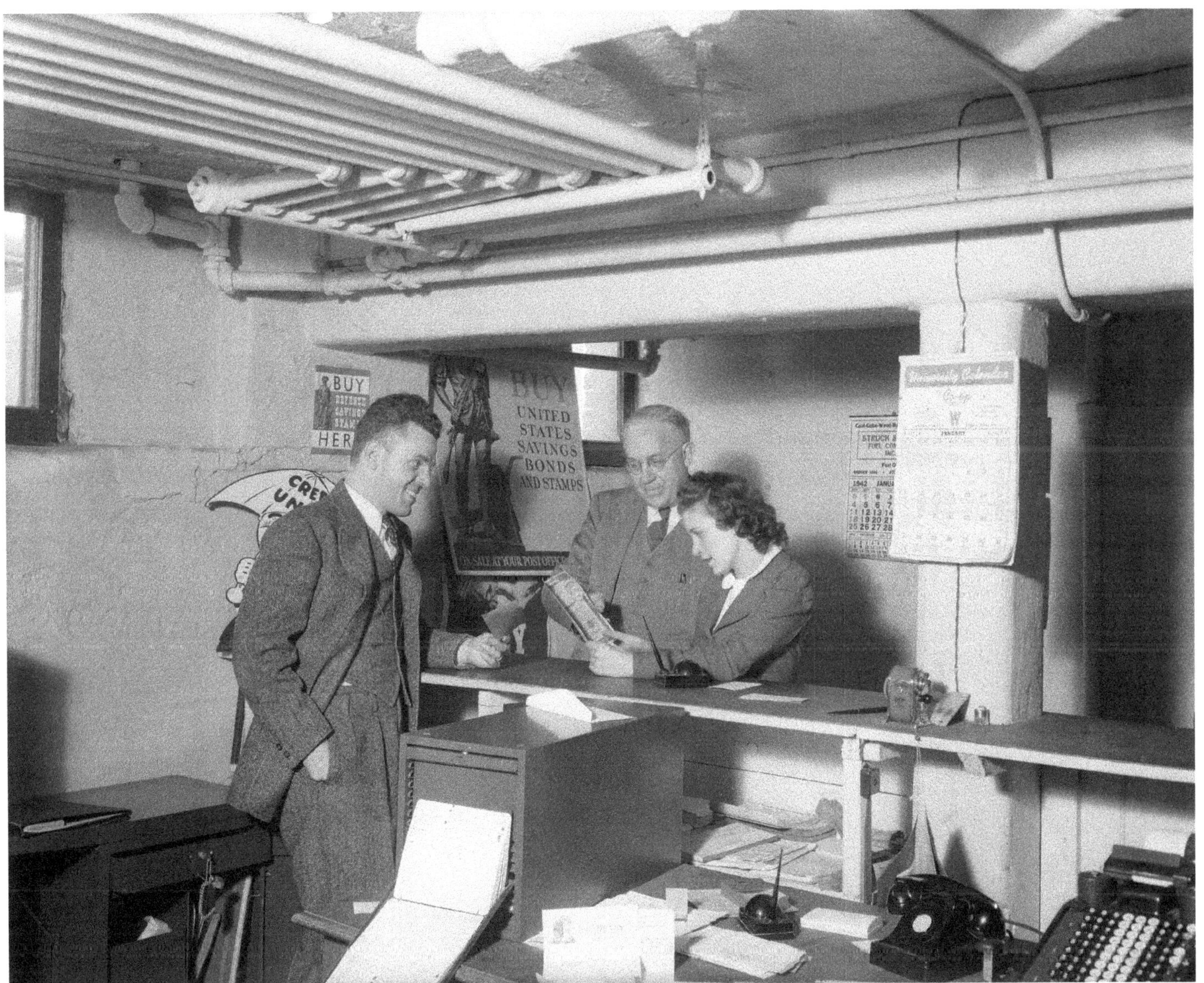

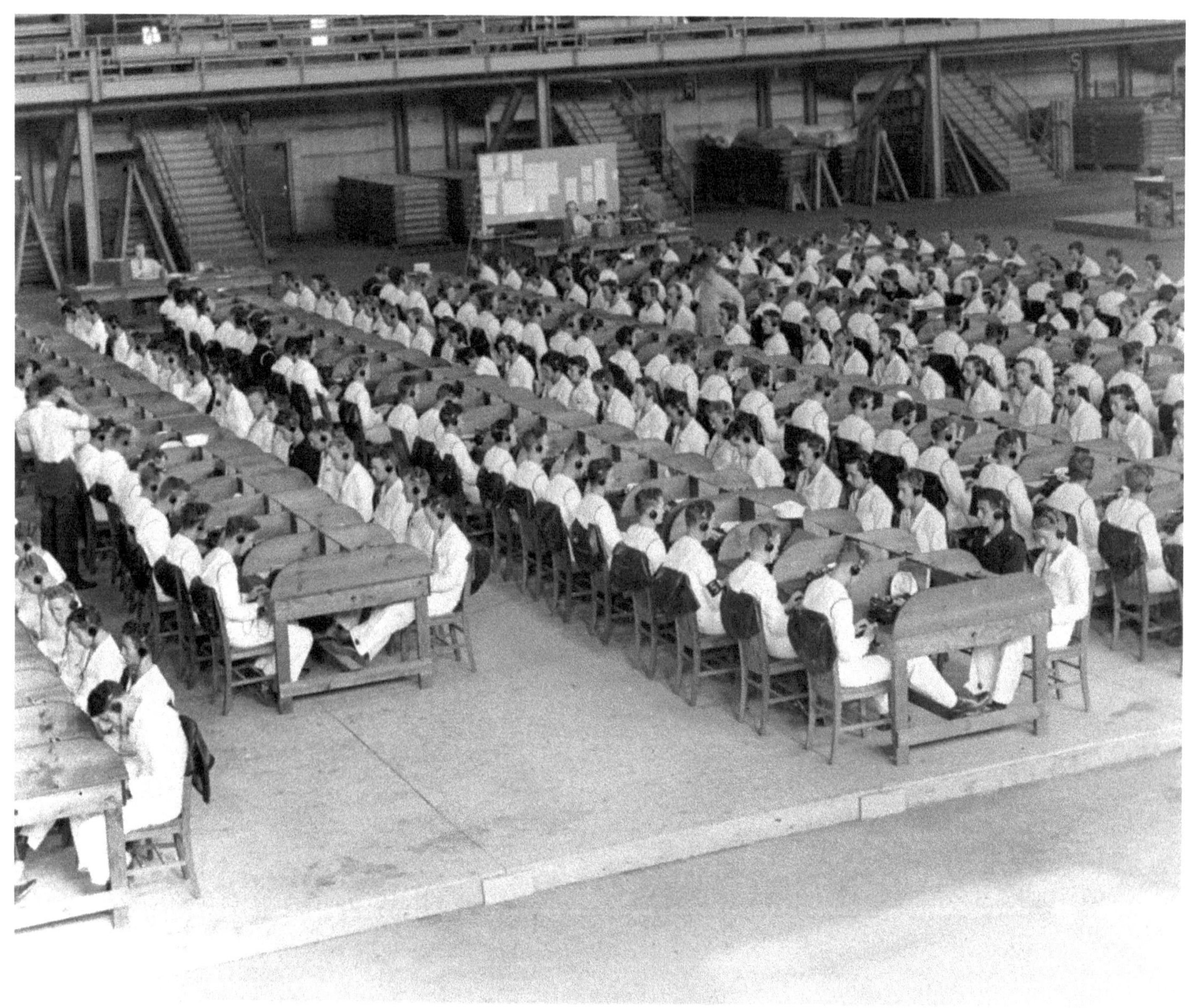

Navy personnel wearing headphones learn code while working at typewriters, around 1943. The sailors are probably in the Field House on the University of Wisconsin campus.

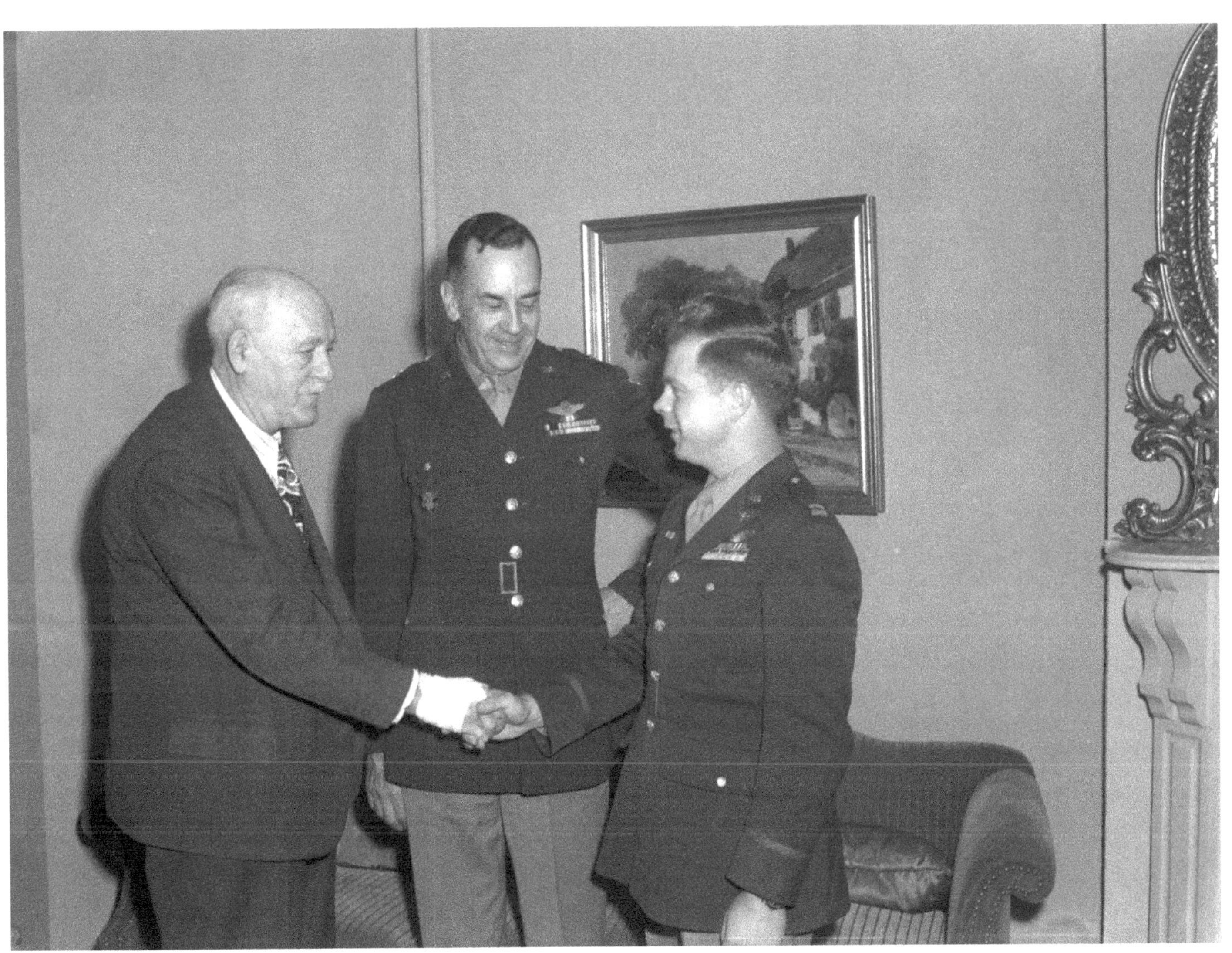

Army Air Force major Richard I. Bong, the World War II ace credited with knocking out forty Japanese planes in the South Pacific, shakes hands in December 1944 with Governor Walter Goodland at the governor's mansion. The commanding officer of Truax Field Air Force Base in Madison, Brigadier General S. W. Fitzgerald, stands at center. Bong had just been awarded the Congressional Medal of Honor that month. He died eight months later while test piloting a Lockheed P-80 Shooting Star, the first operational jet fighter in the United States.

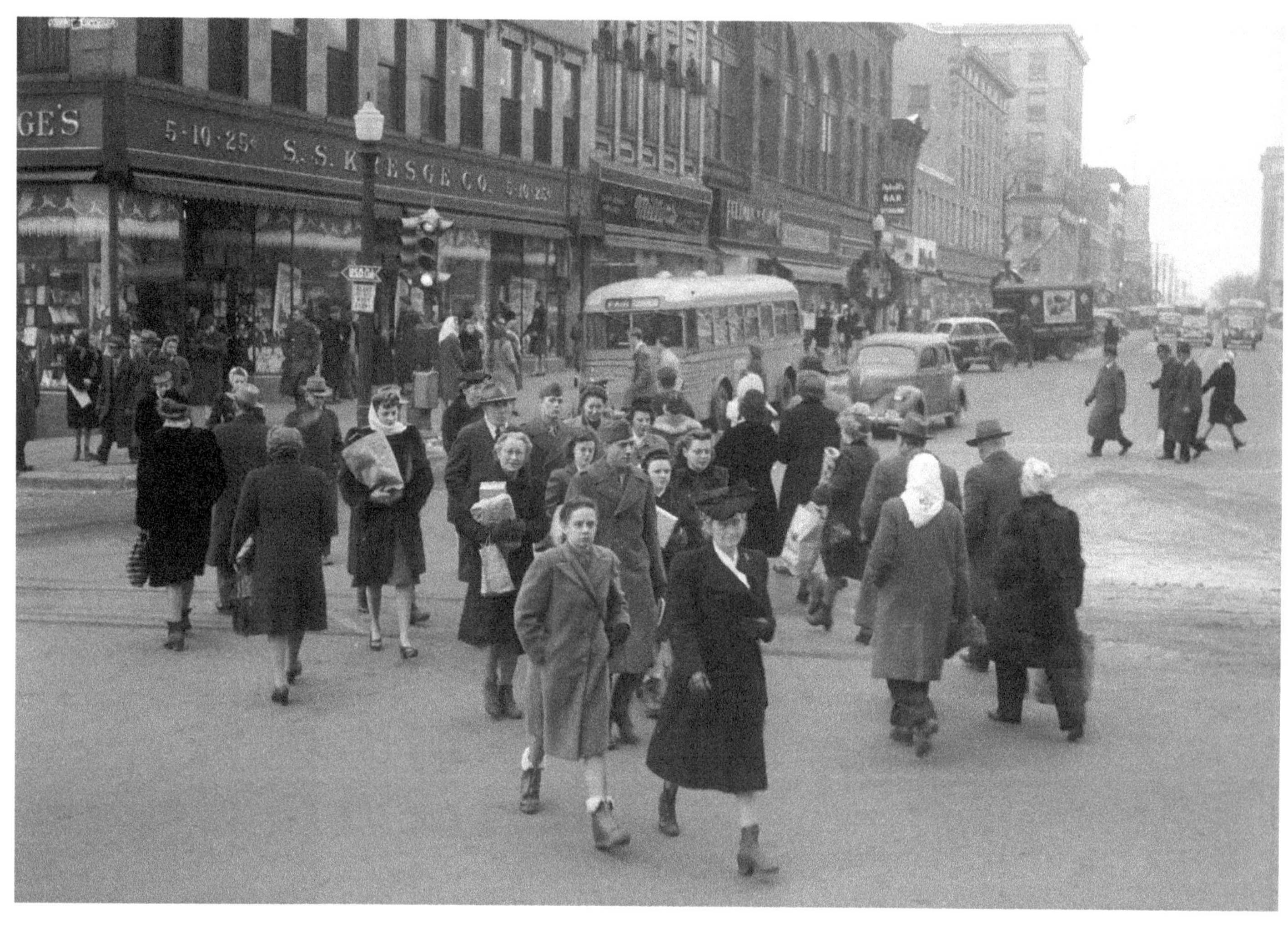

In this December 1944 photo, Christmas shoppers cross the street at the corner of King Street on the Capitol Square in front of Kresge's, at 25-27 East Main Street.

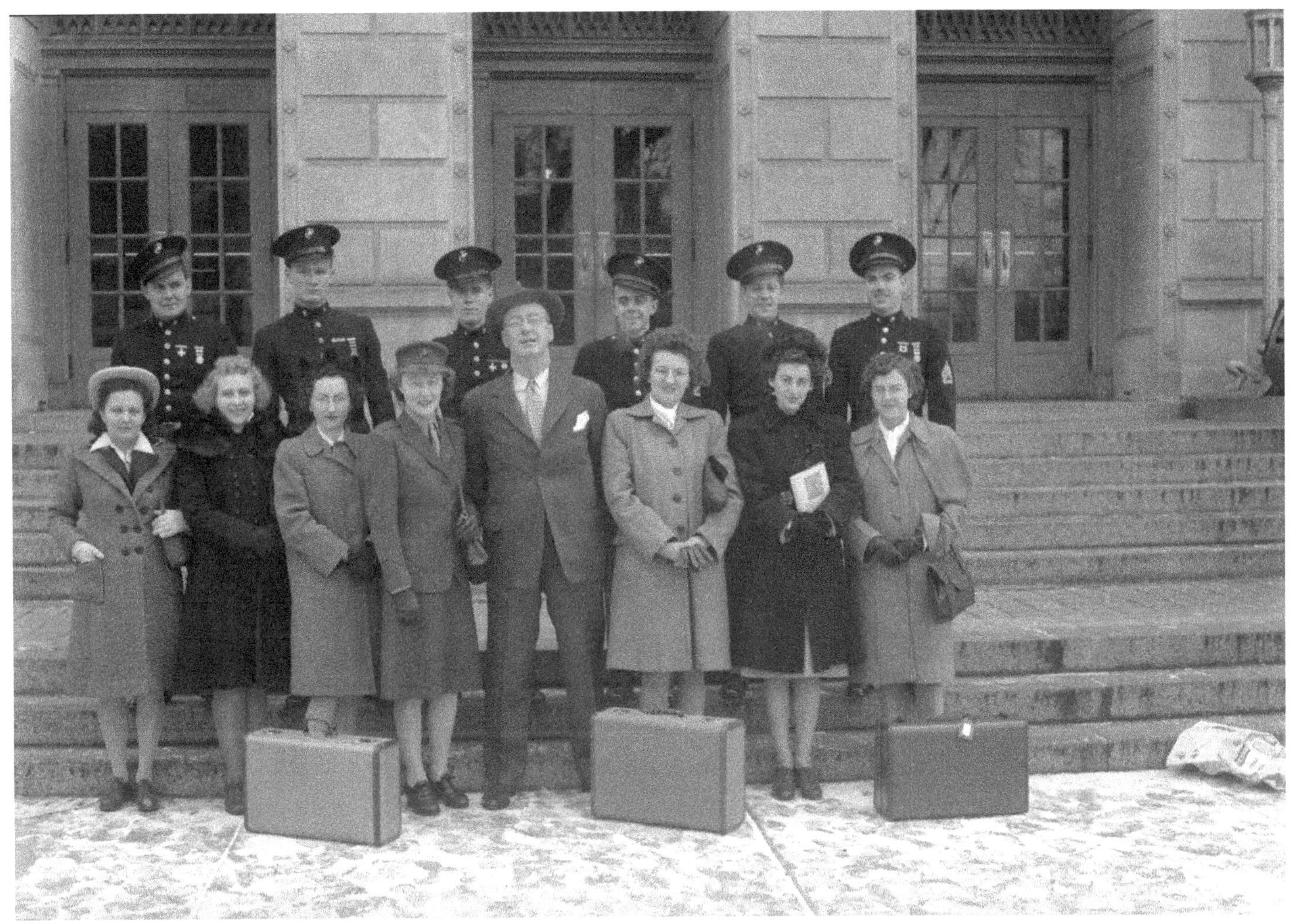

In February 1944, six new members of the Marine Corps Women's Reservists pose for a photo prior to their departure for Camp Lejeune, New River, North Carolina. At center is "Roundy" Coughlin and his ward, Corporal Elizabeth Sullivan. Coughlin was in his twenty-first year as a popular sports columnist for the *Wisconsin State Journal.* Standing behind them are six Marines stationed at Truax Field.

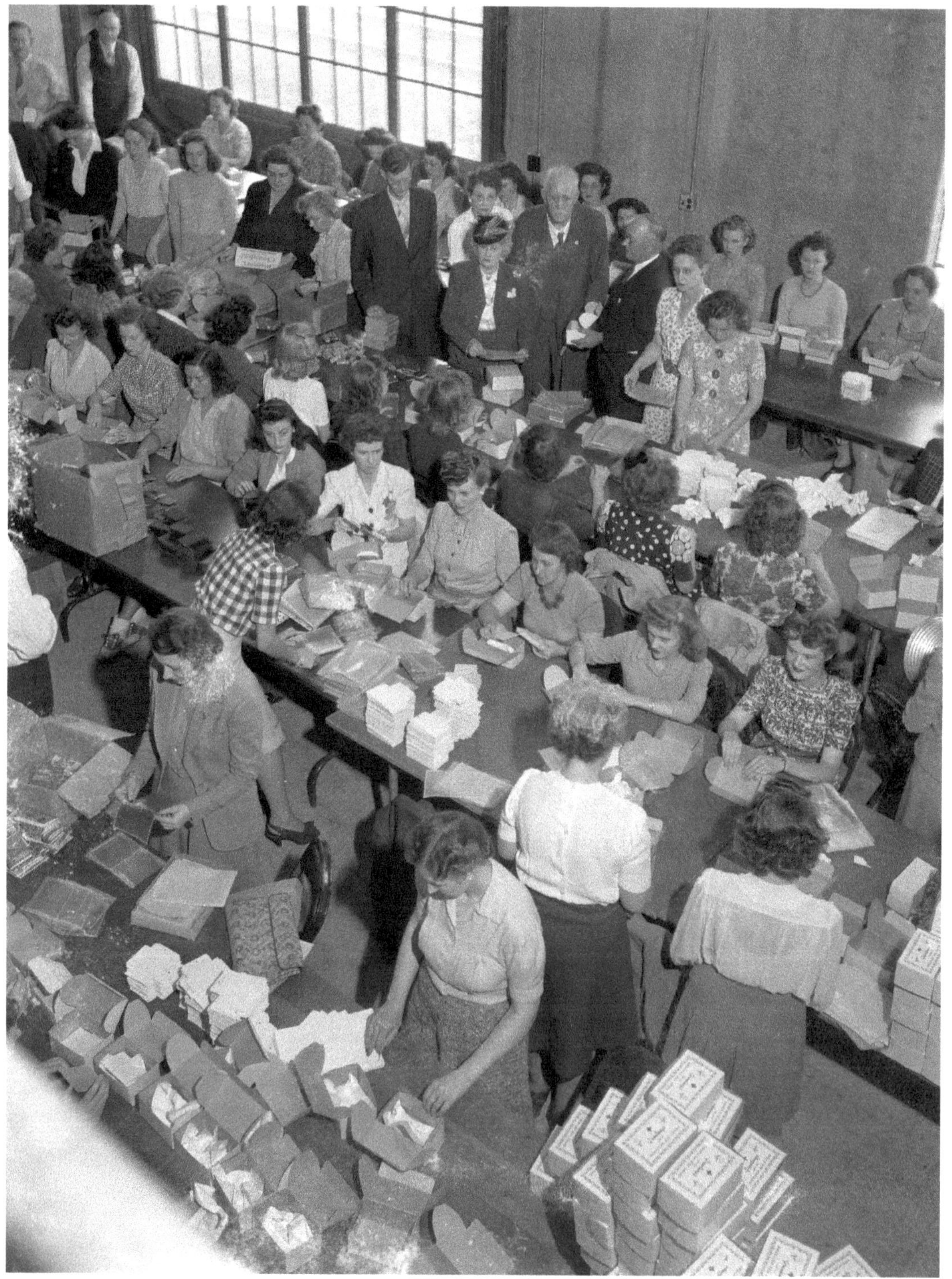

State employees work at long tables in the basement at the rear of the lakeside State Office Building on West Wilson Street in 1944 packing Red Cross Christmas boxes for soldiers. Governor Walter Goodland and his wife can be seen near the rear window viewing the work.

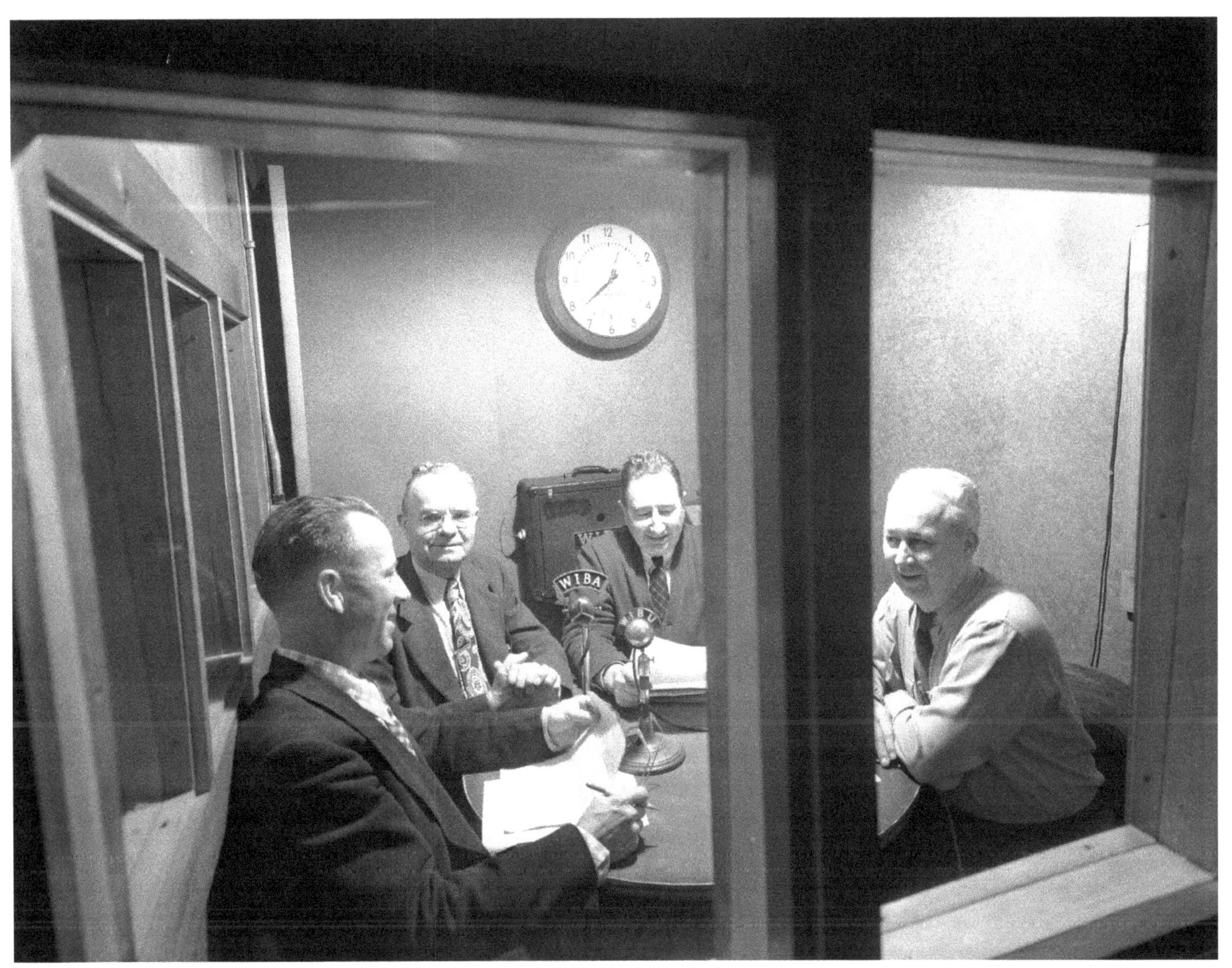

Four men sit at WIBA and WIBU radio microphones in 1945 in the broadcast booth at Oscar Mayer.

Shown here in 1945 is the entrance to the Madison Free Library at 206 North Carroll Street. The library building, which opened its doors in 1906, was among sixty-four libraries in Wisconsin built with gifts from Andrew Carnegie. The University of Wisconsin's library school shared the building for thirty-two years.

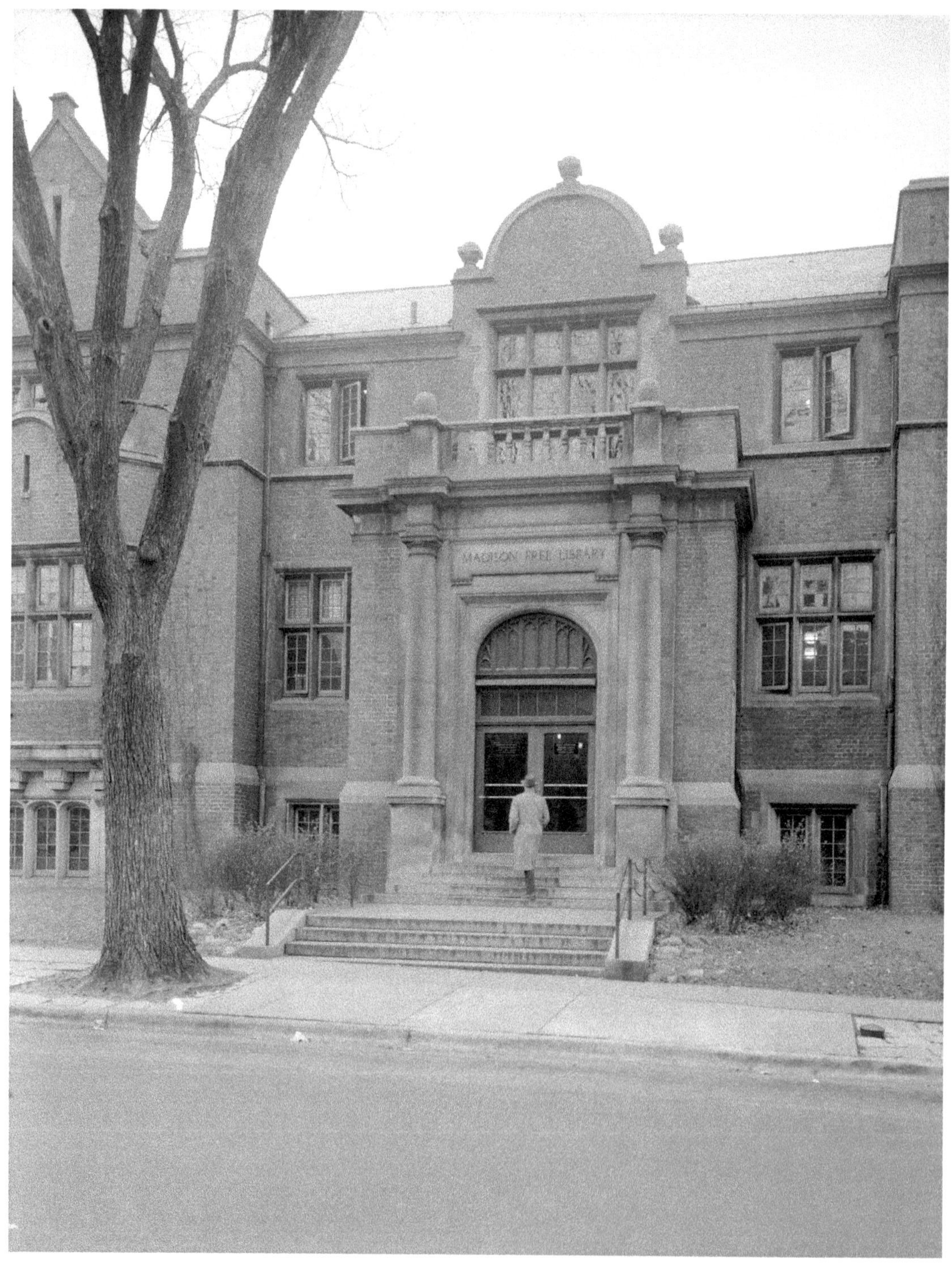

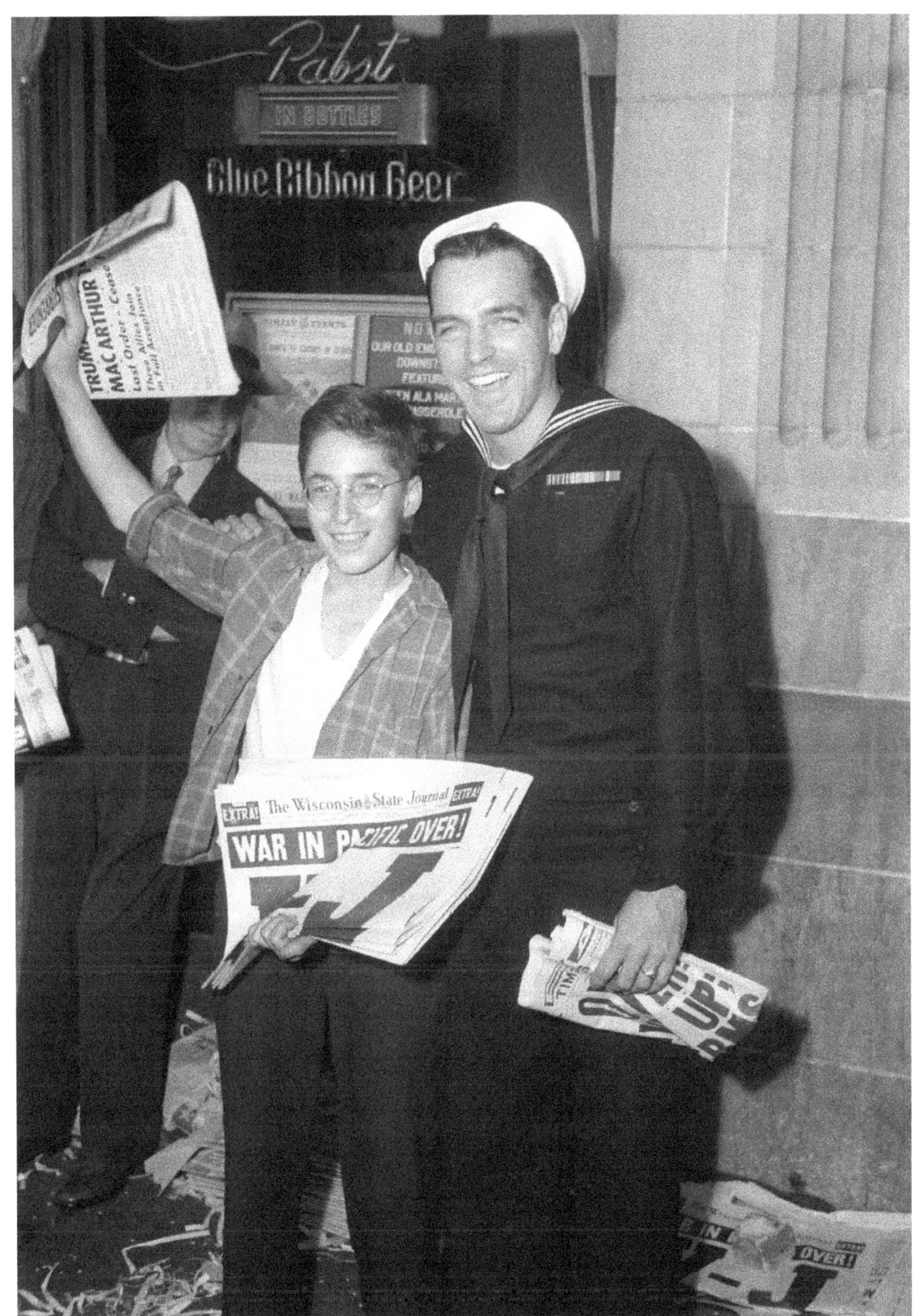

On August 15, 1945, the Allies announced the surrender of Japanese forces and the end of World War II. Seaman 1st class Tom Teeley and newsboy Bernard Ehrmann hold the *Wisconsin State Journal* with headline declaring "War in Pacific Over."

Traffic jams the Capitol Square in a spontaneous outpouring of glee to news on August 15, 1945, that World War II was over. Cars turn from North Pinckney Street onto East Mifflin Street. The car loaded with people riding on the fenders and running boards at lower right was the first to circle the square in the course of the hours-long celebration.

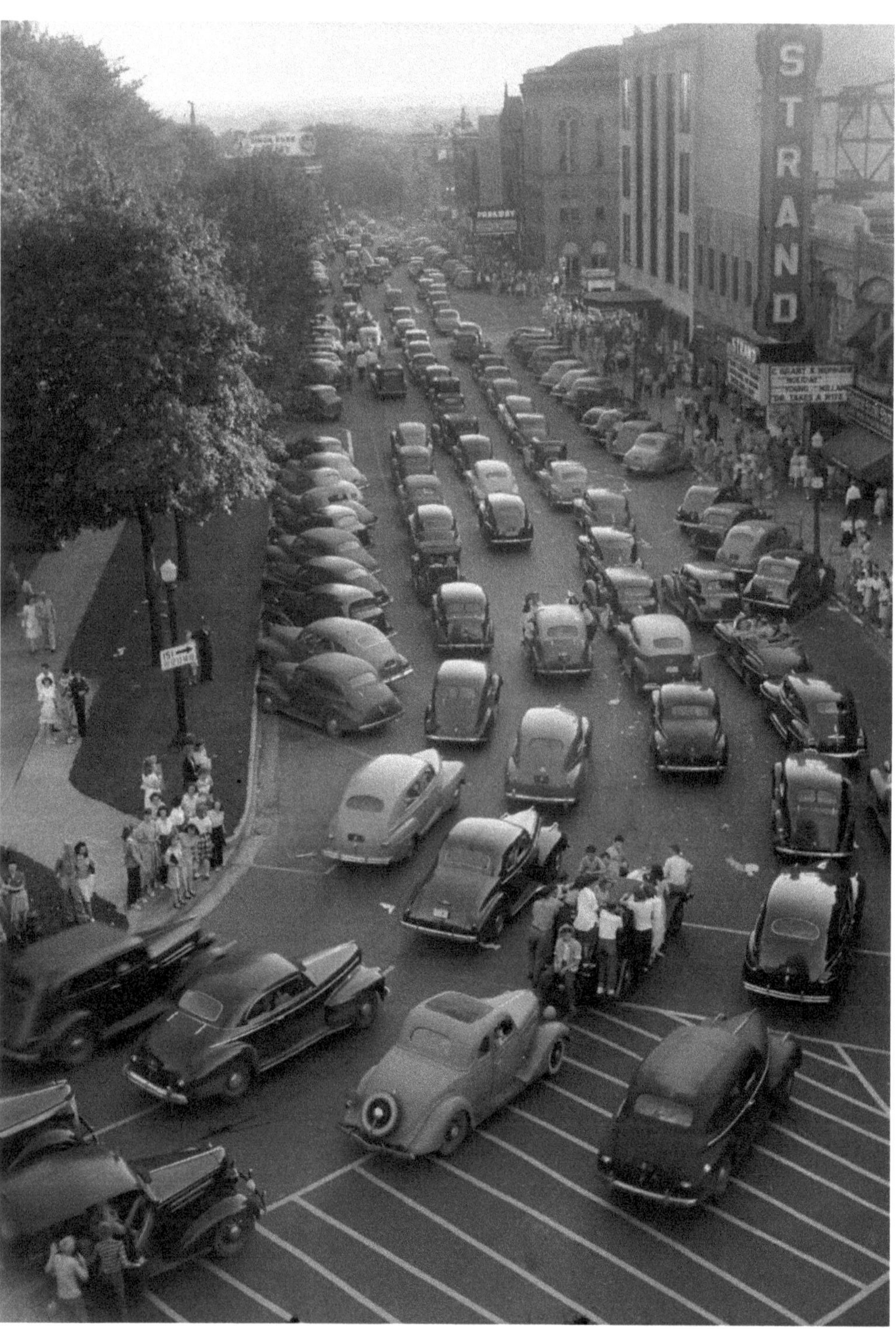

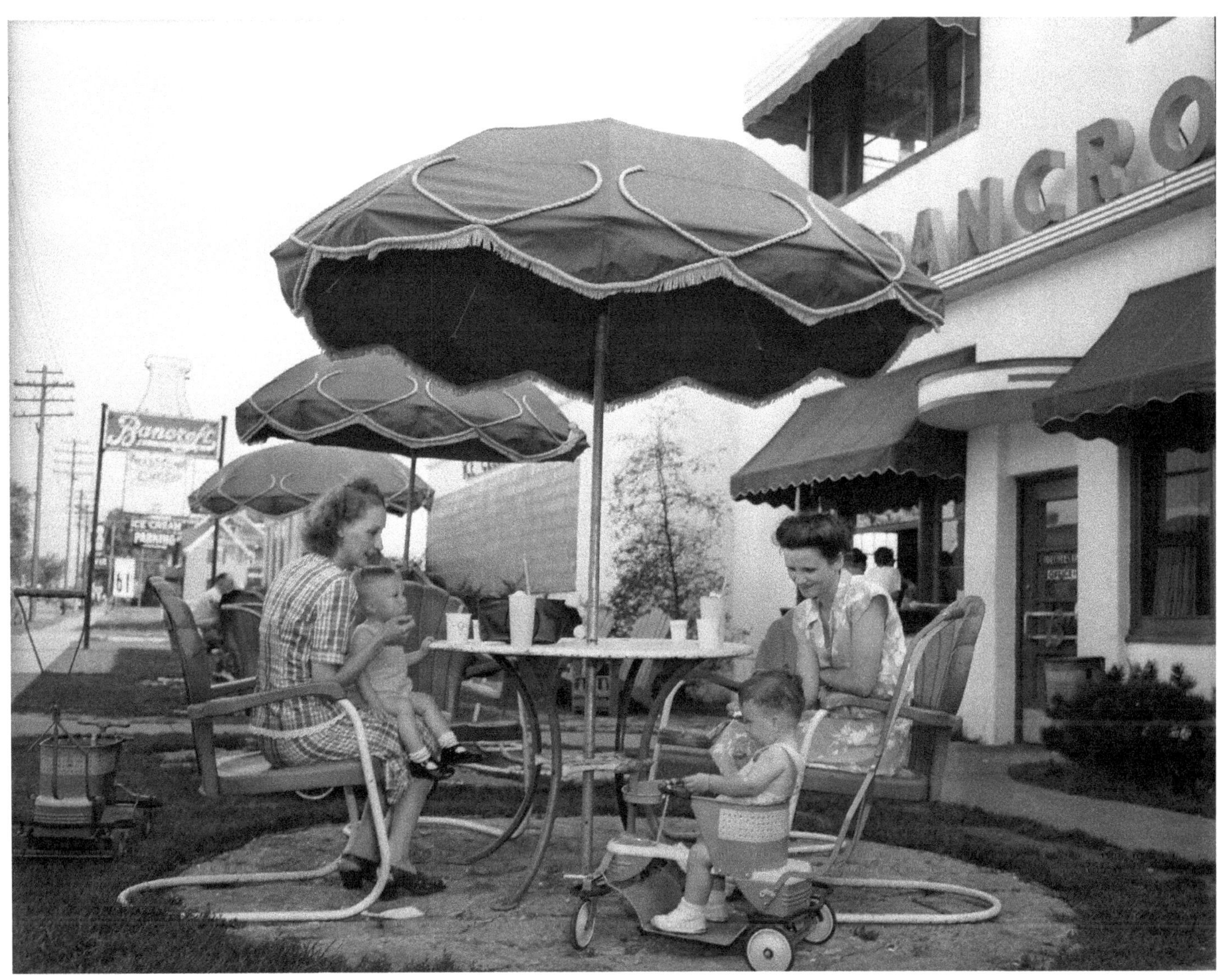

In summer 1946, two women and their children sit at the Bancroft Dairy "sidewalk fountain," at 1010 South Park Street. "This is the first summer since the close of the war that we have been able to serve on the lawn," explained A. J. Sticha, manager, who said the service was abandoned during the war years because of the scarcity of ice cream.

Grace Episcopal Church, shown here in 1946, is the oldest remaining building on the Capitol Square. It was built in 1855 on the designs of Milwaukee architect James Douglas. Behind the church at 6 North Carroll Street is the Wisconsin Power and Light Building, at 122 West Washington Avenue, and the Gay Building, at 16 North Carroll Street. The nine-story Gay Building, constructed in 1911, was Madison's first skyscraper.

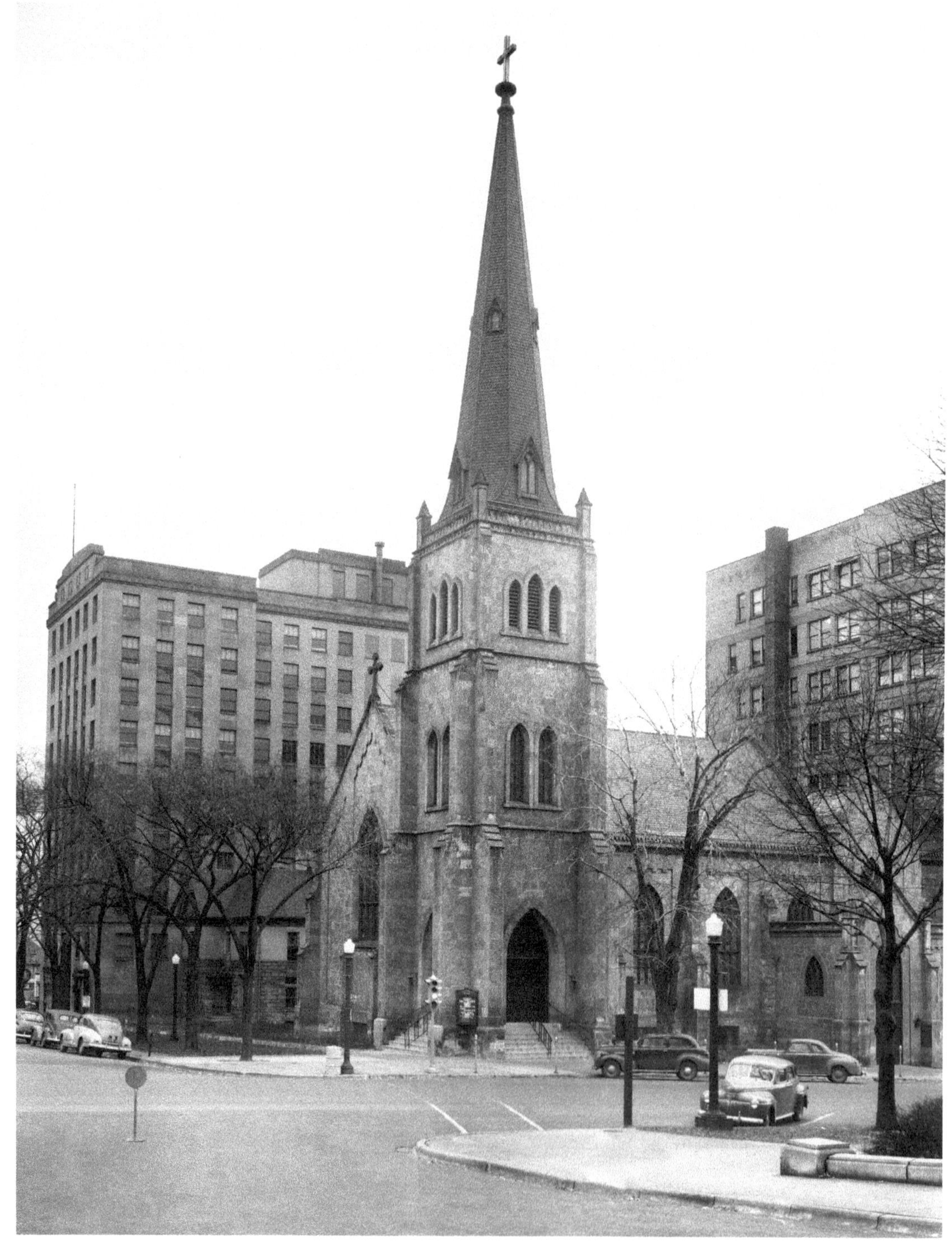

Dignitaries wait in May 1946 for a ceremony to begin for the Major Richard Ira Bong (1920–1945) Memorial dedication. The World War II flying ace from Poplar, Wisconsin, was one of the nation's most decorated war heroes. He became an army test pilot and was killed in the crash of a P-80 Shooting Star in California on the same day the atomic bomb was dropped on Hiroshima, marking the end of the war. In addition to a Congressional Medal of Honor, he received the Distinguished Service Cross, Silver Star, Distinguished Flying Cross, and Air Medal. Those pictured, from left to right, are Bong's mother, Wisconsin chief justice Marvin Rosenberry, First Lady Madge Goodland, Governor Walter Goodland, Marge Bong (Bong's widow), Bong's father, Rosa Fred, and University of Wisconsin president E. B. Fred.

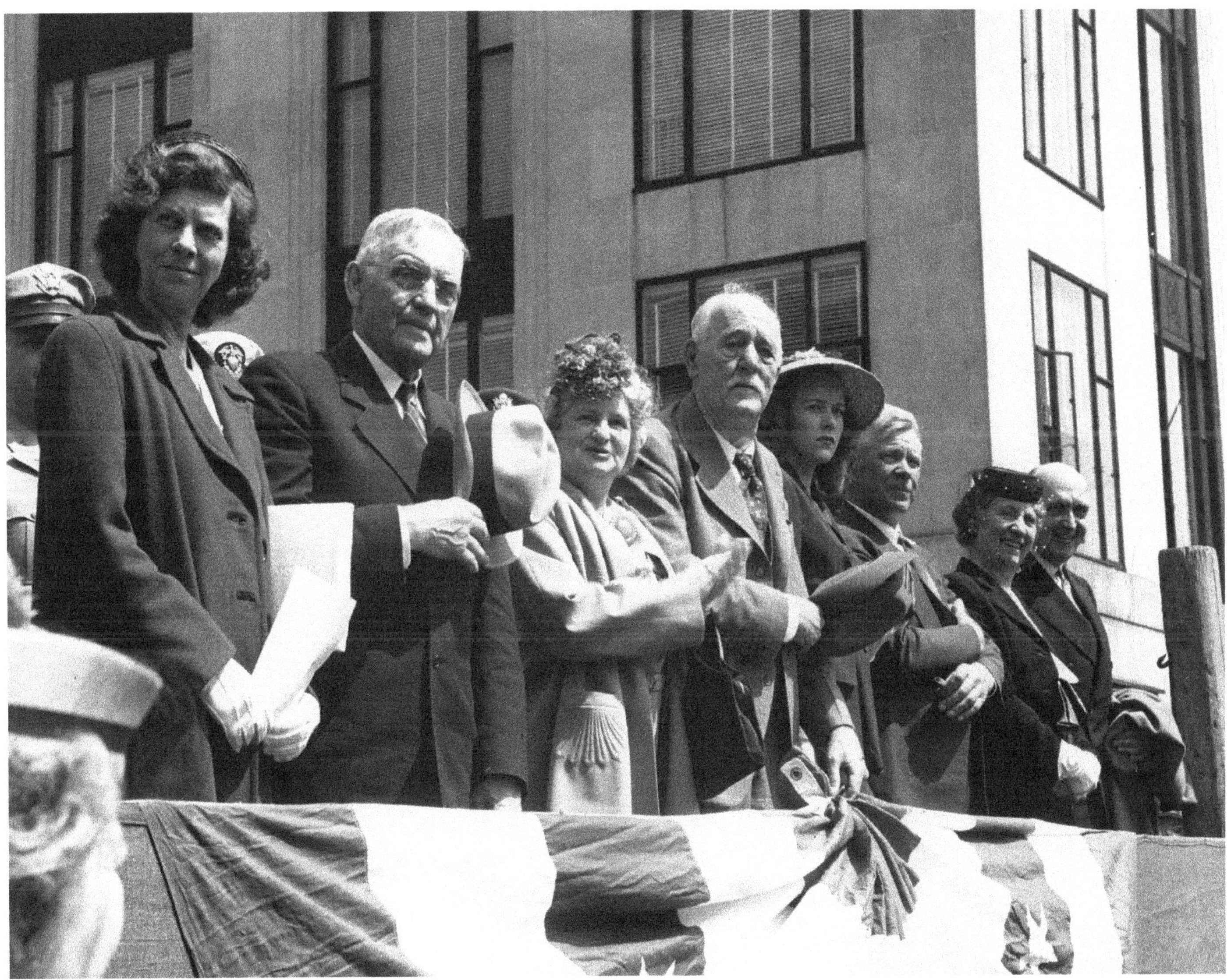

The first shipment of 1946 DeSoto automobiles, known for their "airflow" design for maximum efficiency, arrives in Madison on January 7. Civilian production of automobiles had just resumed in late 1945. Four men pose with the cars as they come off a train onto a loading dock for Stadium Garage Plymouth and DeSoto Sales and Service, at 1501 Monroe Street. The DeSoto, named for the sixteenth-century Spaniard who discovered the Mississippi River, echoed a theme sounded by parent company Chrysler's other new brand, Plymouth. After thirty-two years, DeSoto production came to an abrupt halt on November 30, 1960. The Madison dealer was notified by telegram.

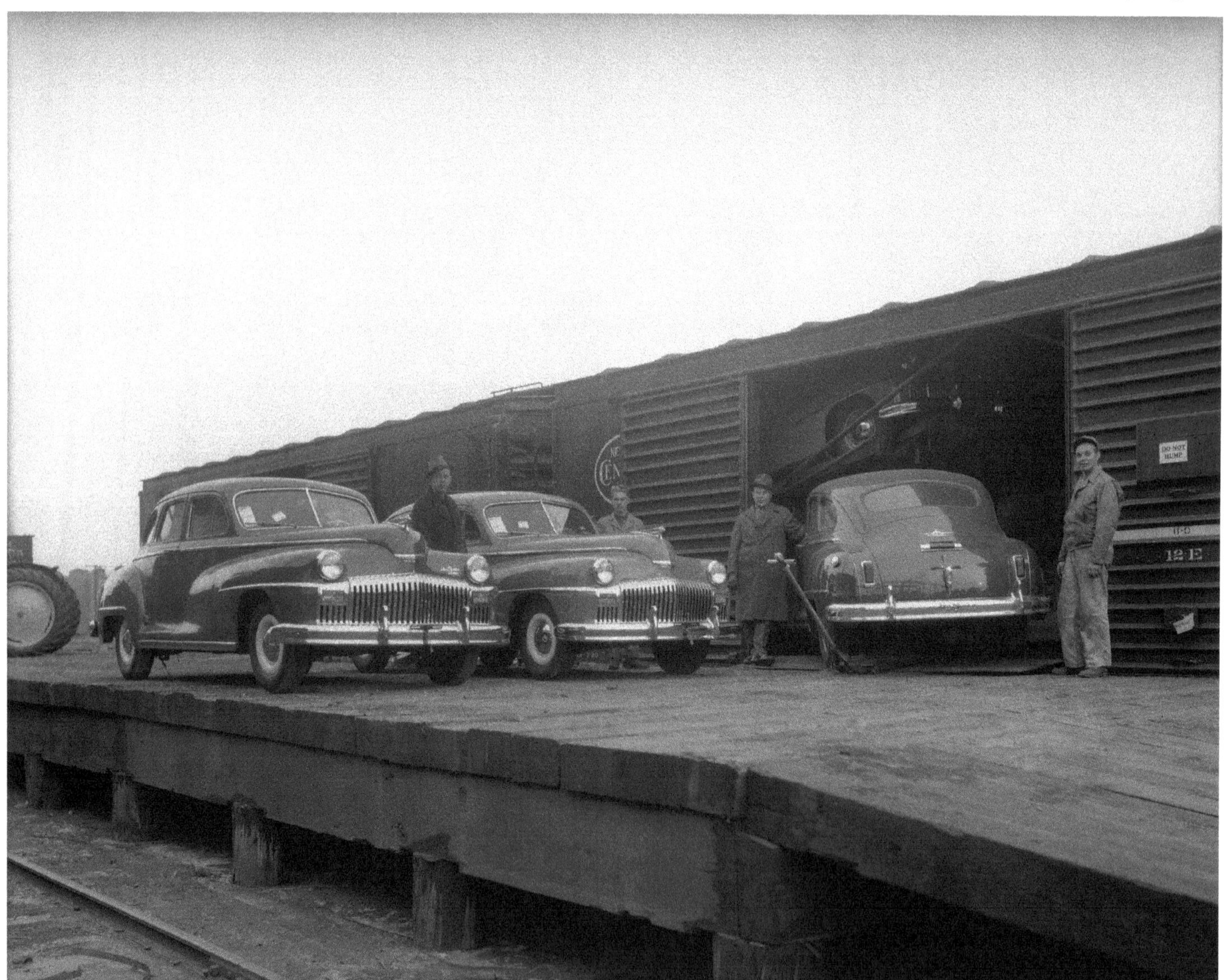

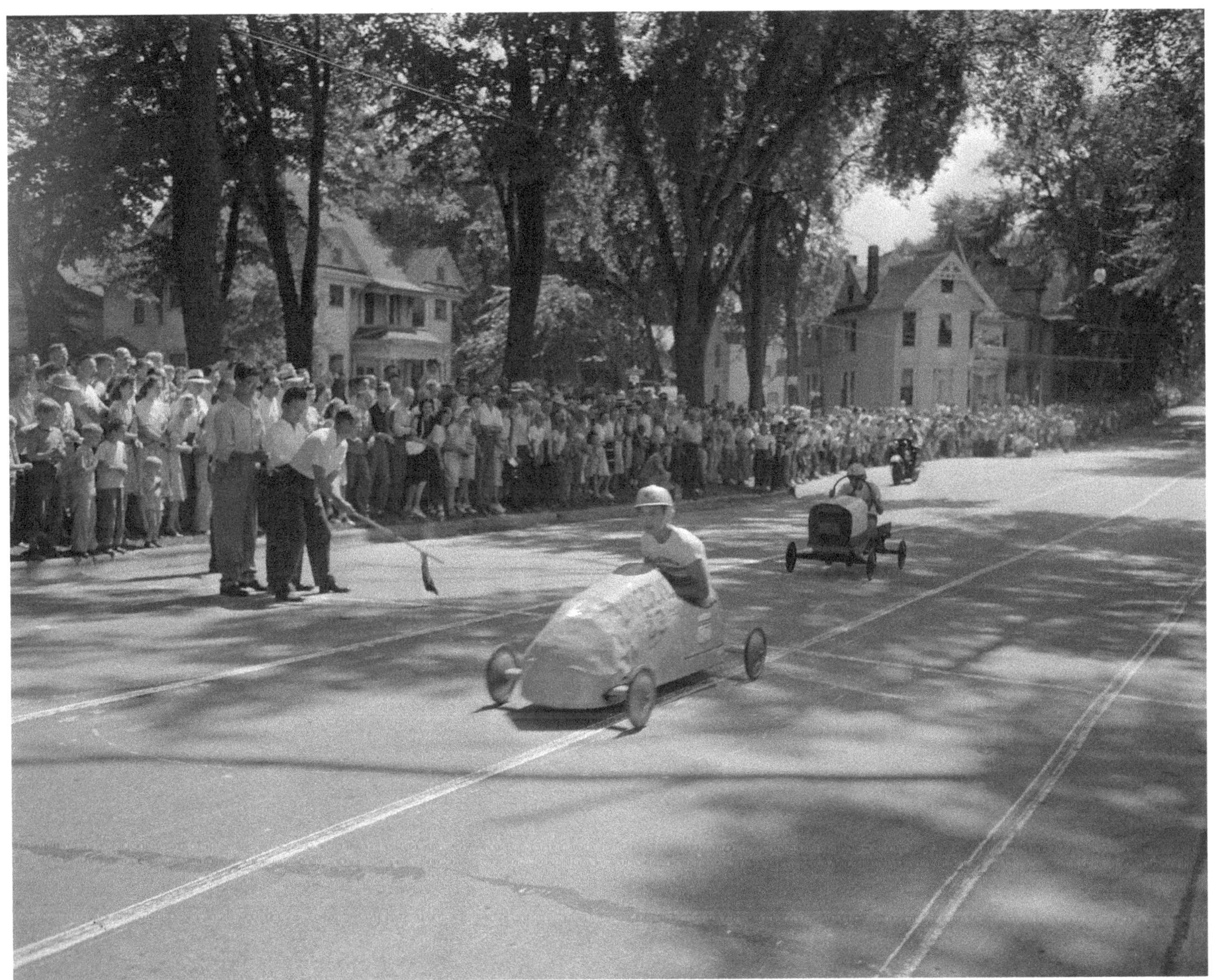

Soap Box Derby cars cross the finish line on East Gorham Street on July 26, 1947, about ten years after the national movement of local races began. The gravity-driven soapbox cars were originally built from soap crates and roller-skate wheels, but became more sophisticated over time.

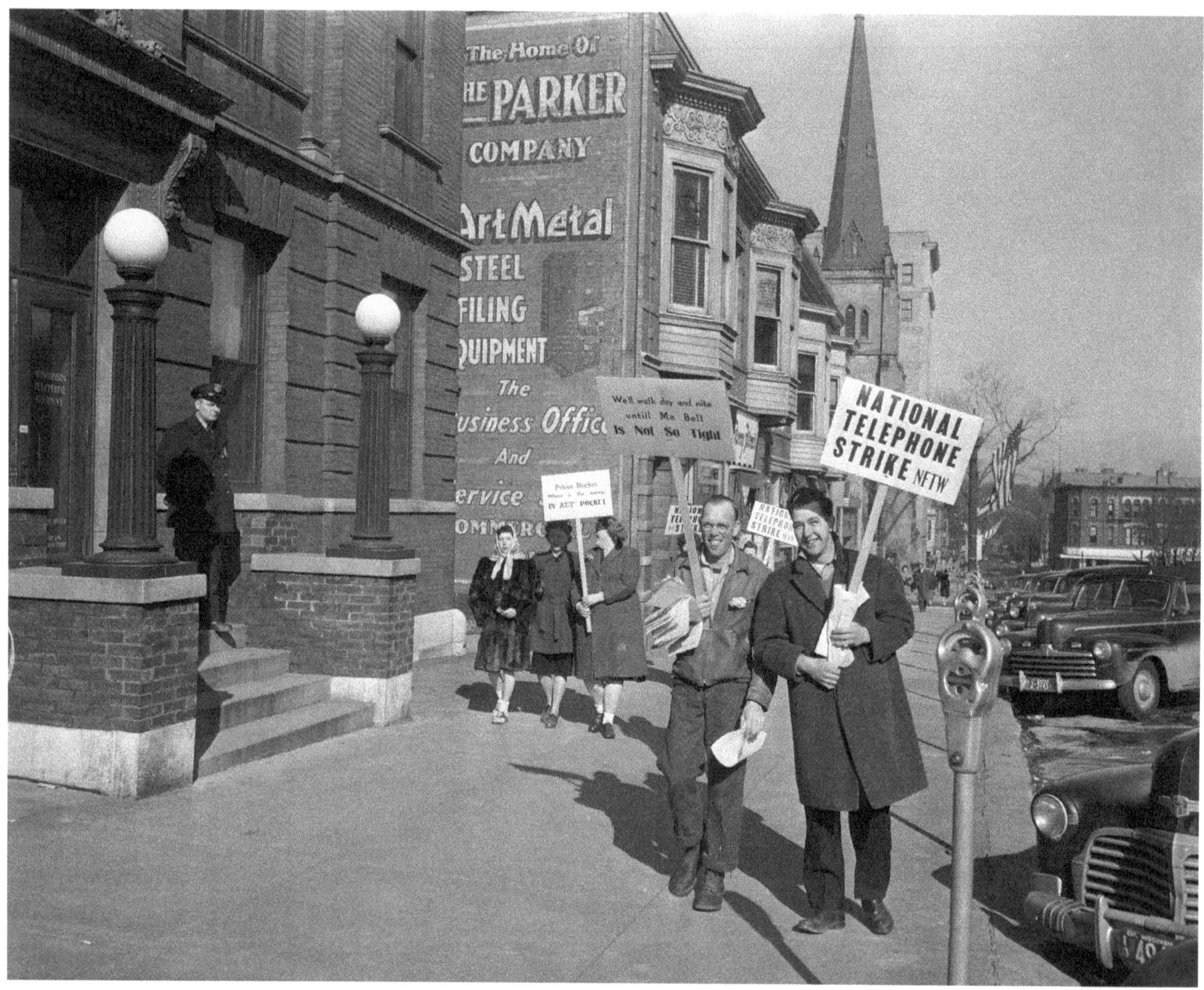

Telephone workers picket at the telephone exchange on Capitol Square, near the corner of West Main and South Carroll streets. Seven hundred Madison telephone employees participated in the country's first nationwide telephone strike. Picket signs include "We'll walk day and nite until Ma Bell Is Not So Tight." Although the National Federation of Telephone Workers lost the 1947 strike, the work stoppage helped to bring telephone workers together. The rank and file reorganized the chain of local chapters into a national organization called the Communication Workers of America (CWA). By 1950, the CWA had 180,000 members.

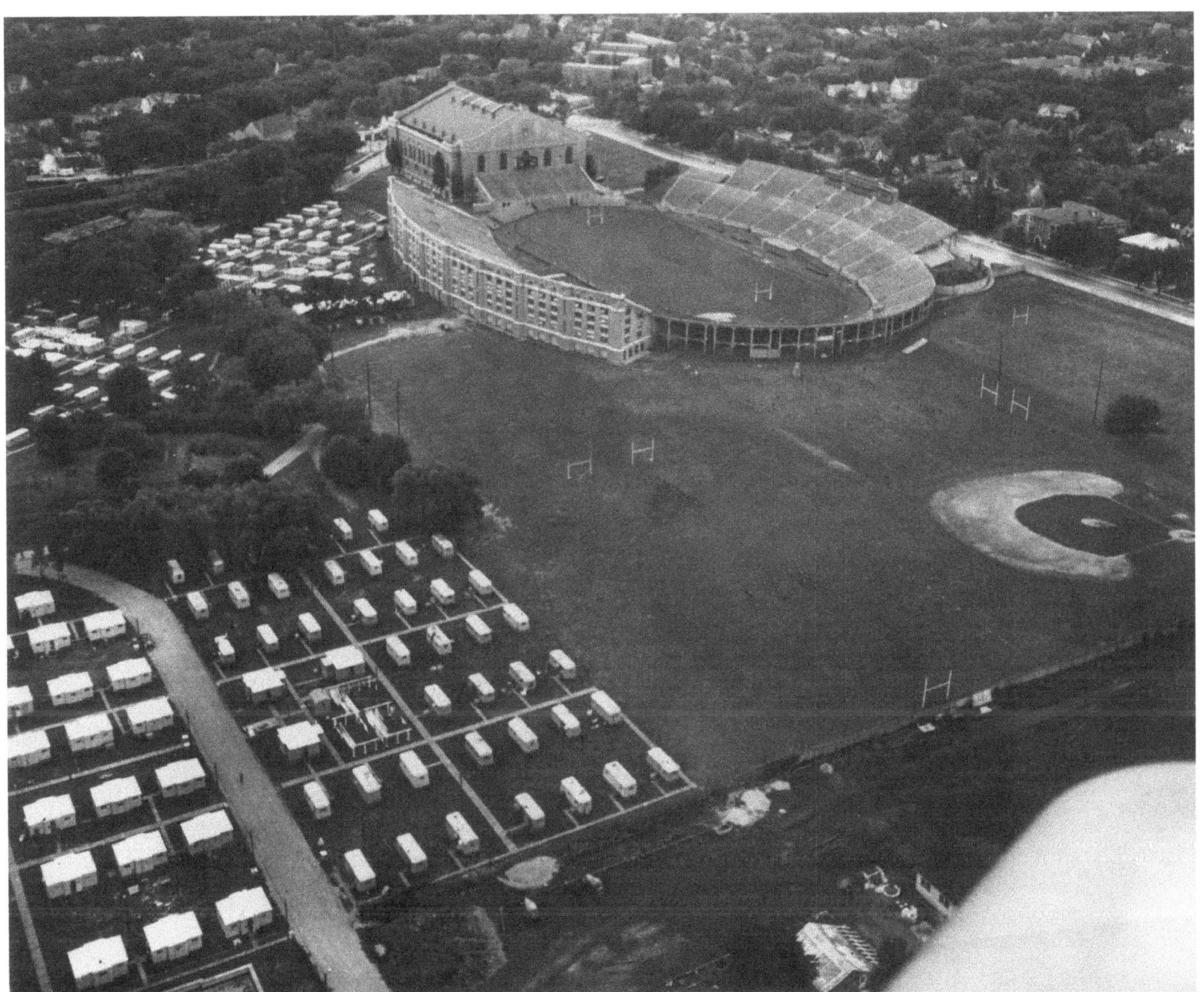

This 1947 aerial view of Camp Randall shows the prefabricated and trailer housing for married veterans installed by the University of Wisconsin to accommodate the surge of students when soldiers returned from service after World War II. Enrollment rose from 6,500 in 1944 to 20,000 in 1947. Of those 20,000, nearly 60 percent were veterans.

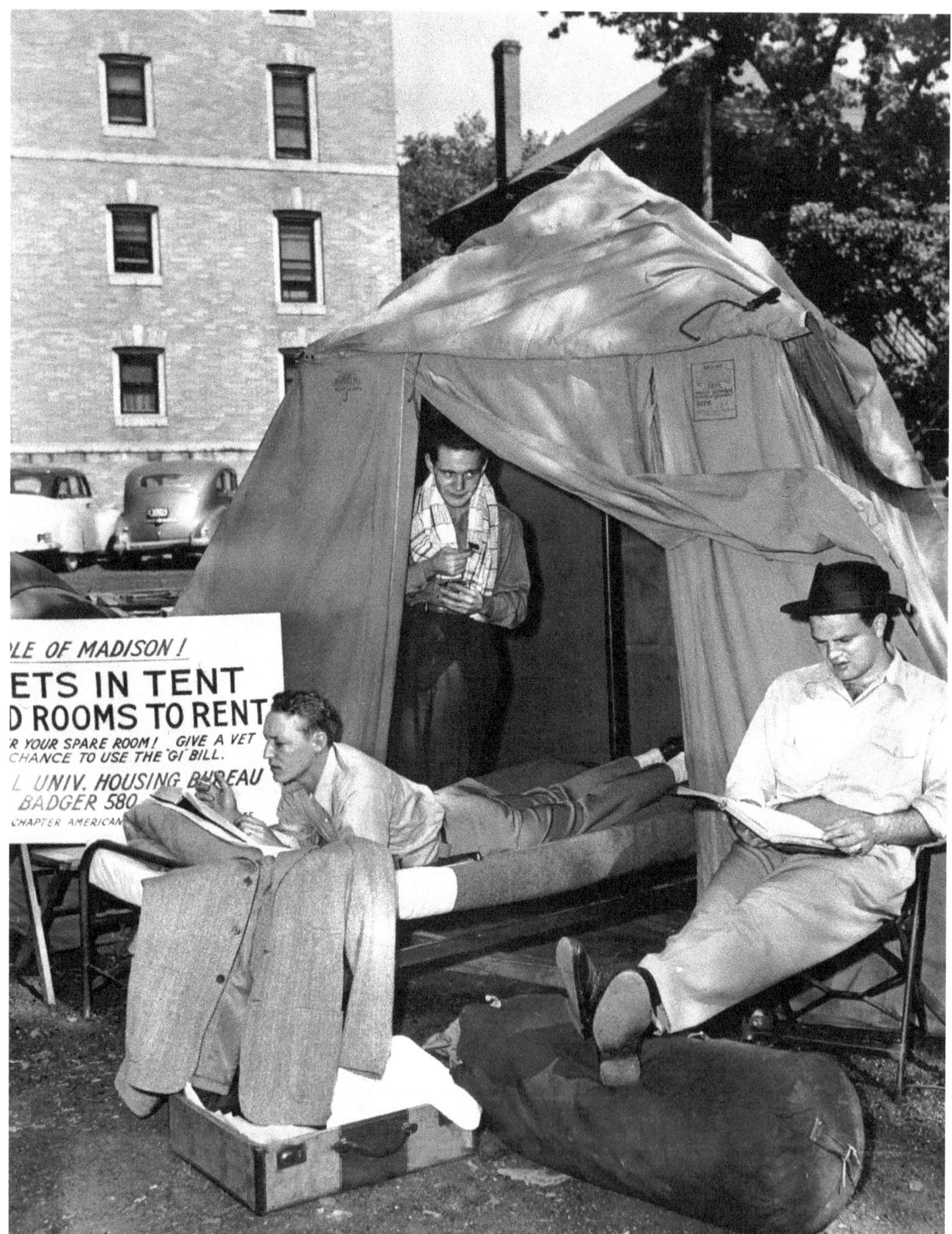

The housing shortage for veterans taking advantage of the G.I. Bill is underscored in this 1947 image. Three men in a tent at the University of Wisconsin repose beside a sign that reads "People of Madison! Vets in tents need rooms to rent . . . Call Univ. Housing."

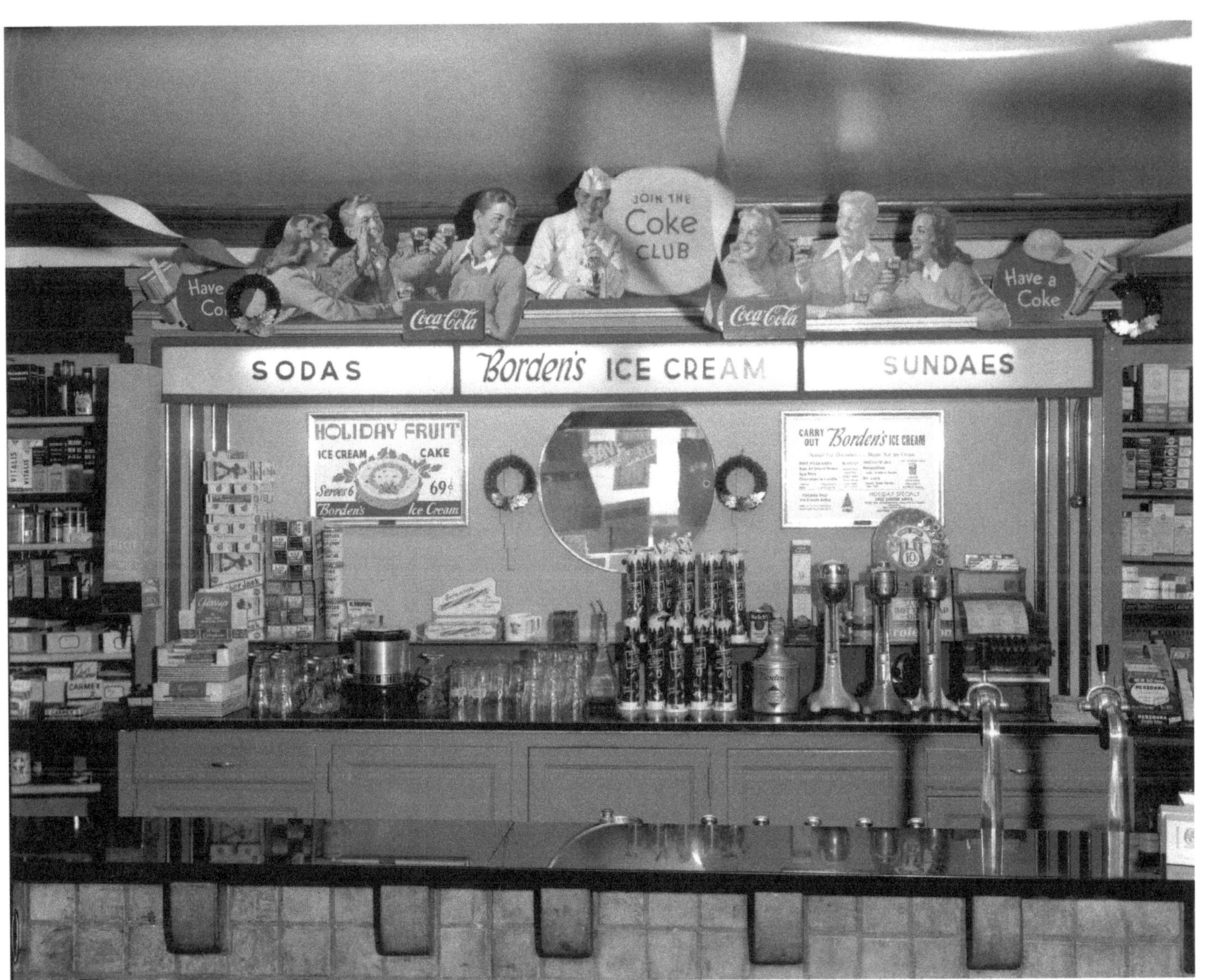

The interior of the White Cross Pharmacy Soda Fountain, at 920 East Johnson Street, in December 1947.

Scores of ice fishermen scatter across Lake Mendota just after New Year's Day in 1948.

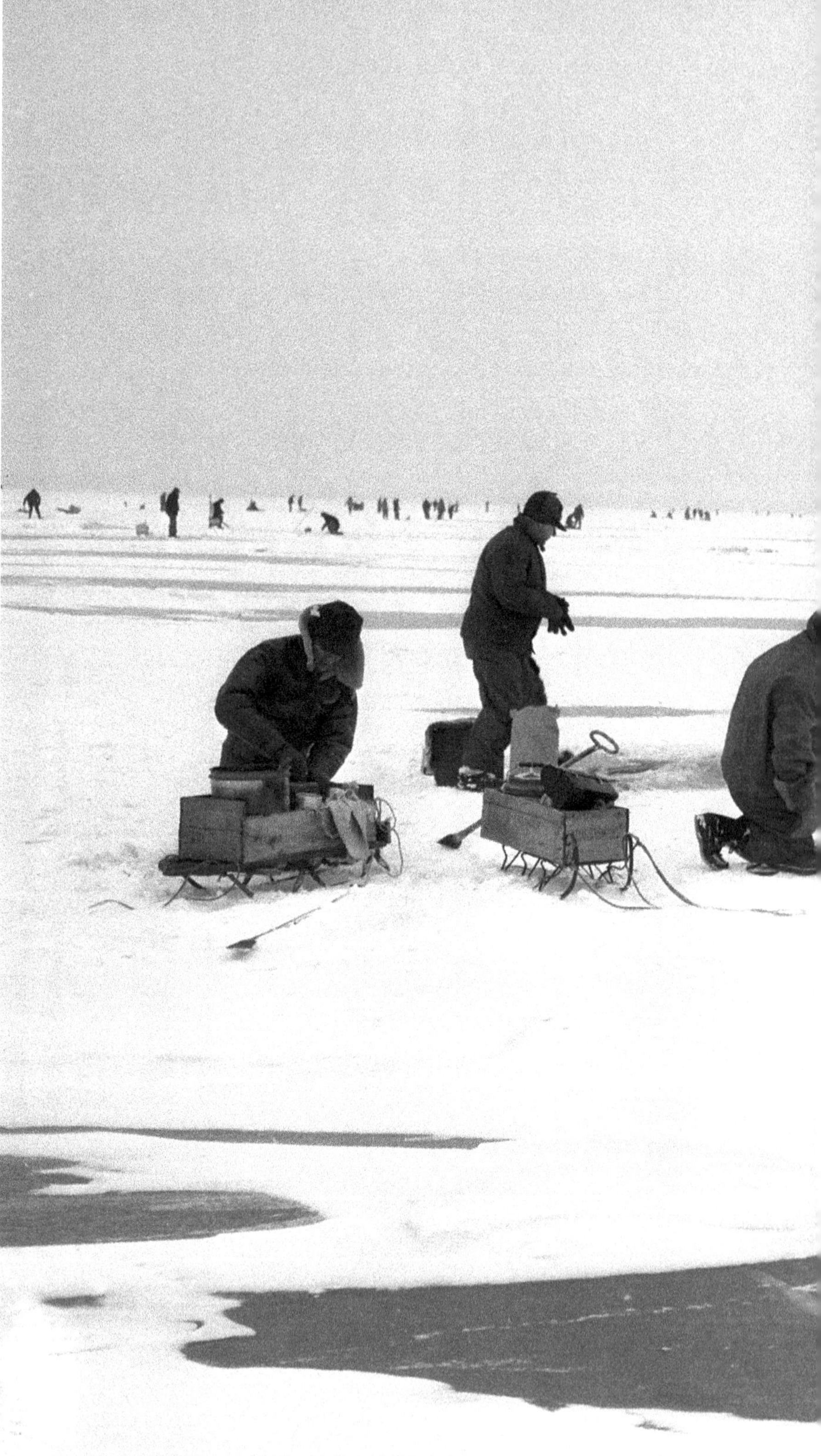

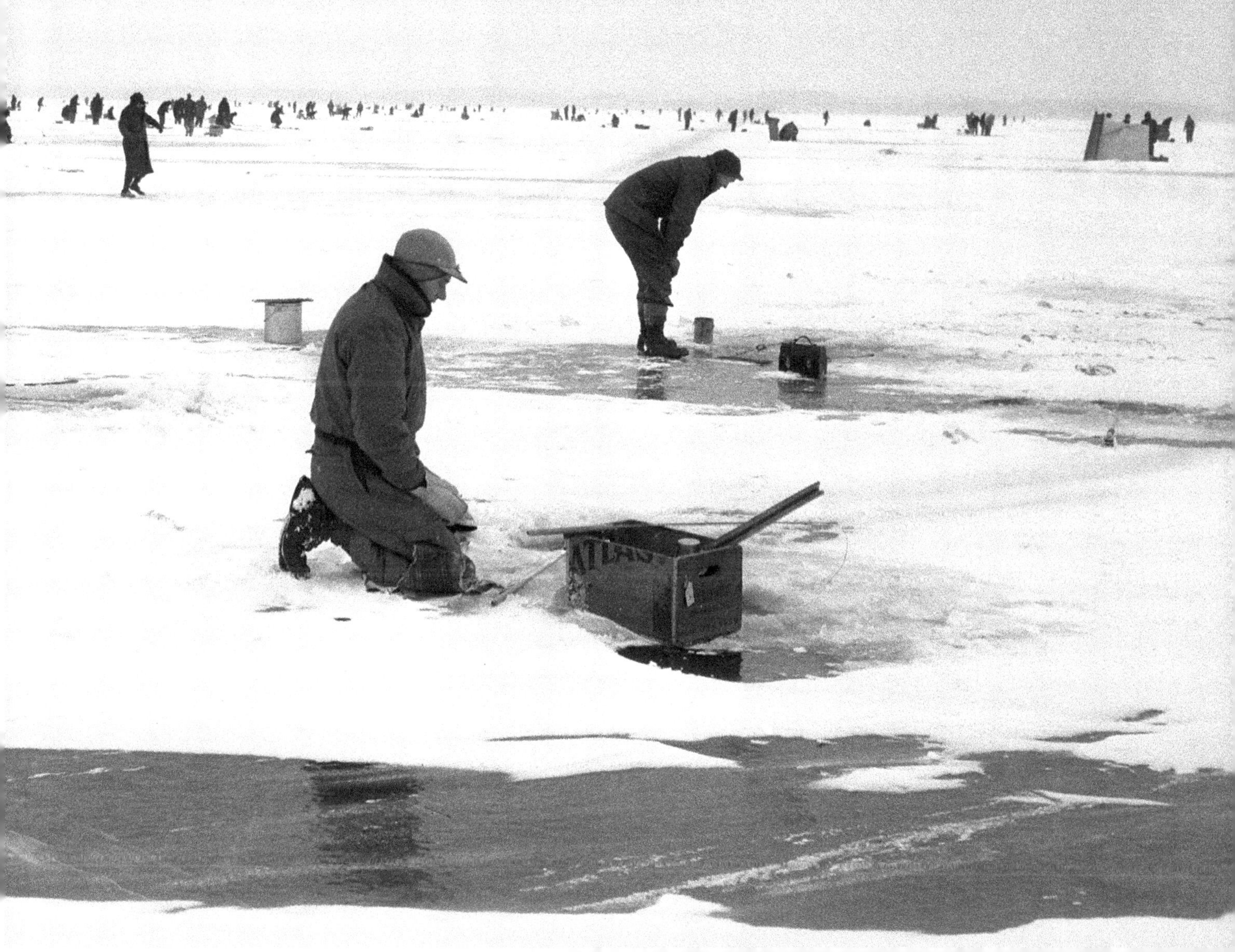

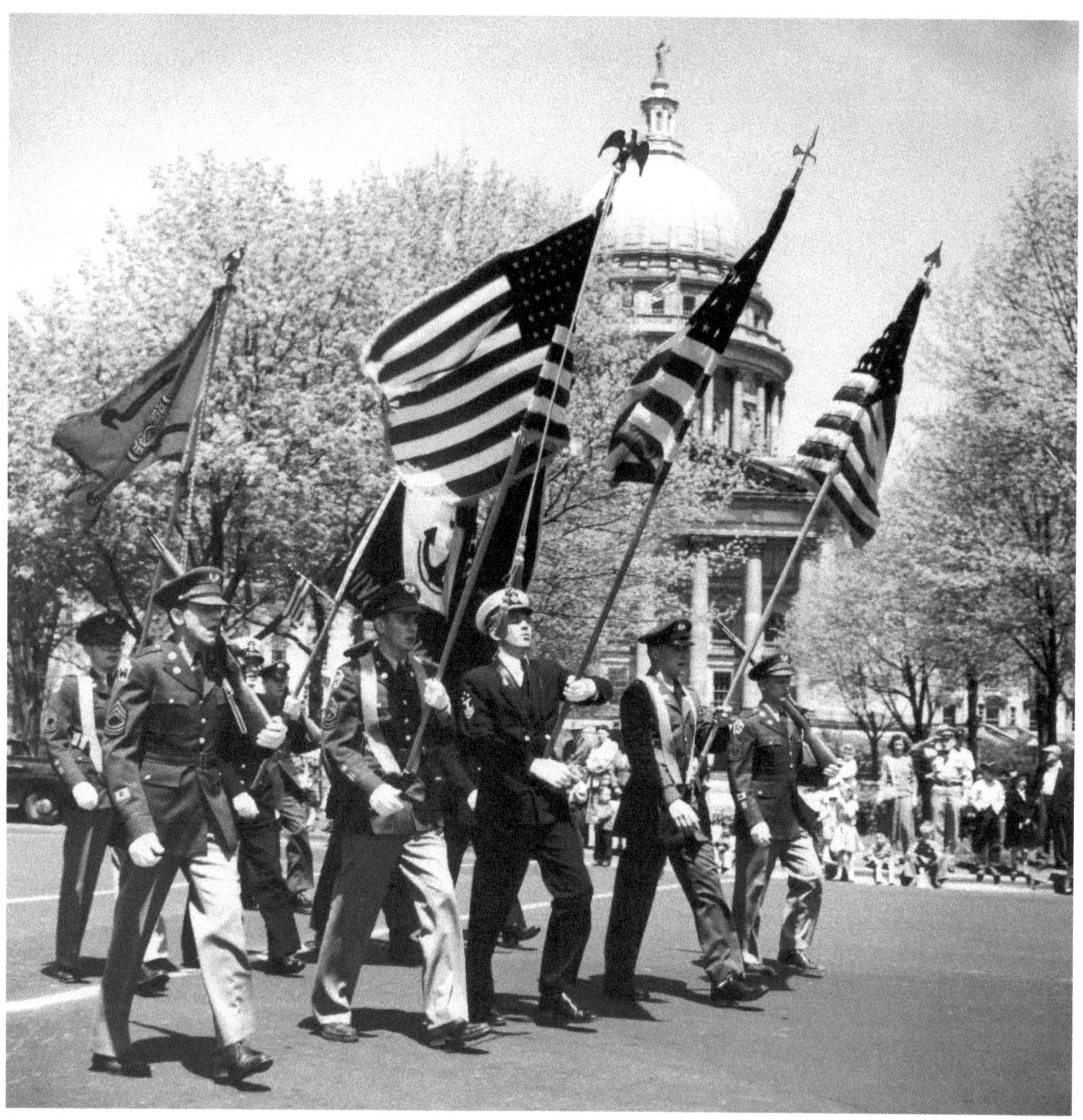

Color guards carrying flags march past the Wisconsin Capitol on the nation's first Armed Forces Day on Saturday, May 20, 1950, as a crowd looks on. The national theme was "Teamed for Defense." The combined celebration was declared by President Harry Truman in August 1949 to replace separate events held for each of the military branches and to mark the creation of a single overarching Department of Defense.

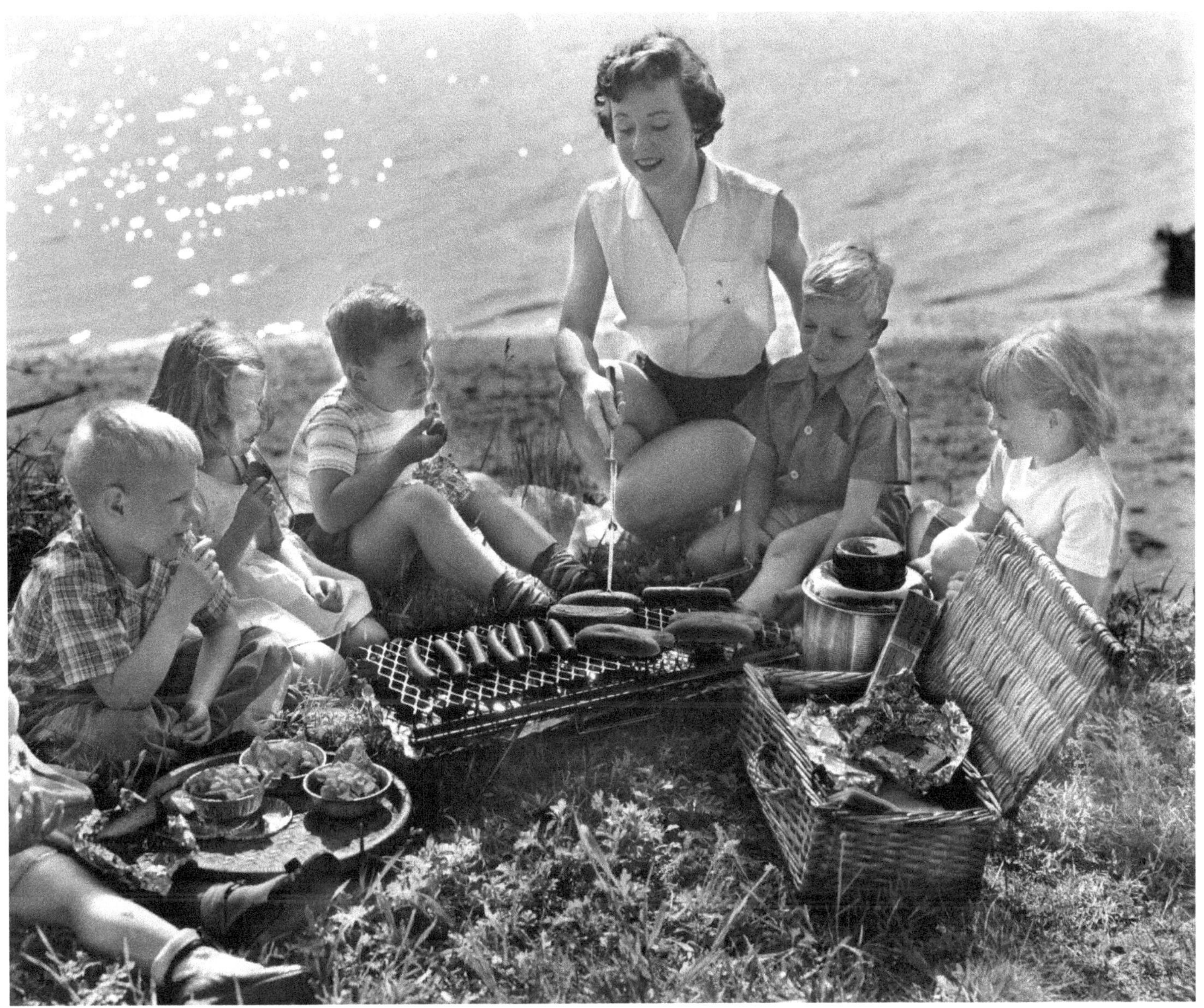

A woman with children grills hot dogs at one of Madison's beaches around 1950. Although not part of the original series, the photo recalls a 1948 *Life* magazine piece, "The Good Life in Madison," extolling the virtues of the city. The magazine declared Madison to be the best city in the United States in which to live. Photographer Alfred Eisenstaedt, the "father of photojournalism" who created such iconography as the famous image of the sailor kissing a nurse in Times Square on VJ Day, illustrated the *Life* article.

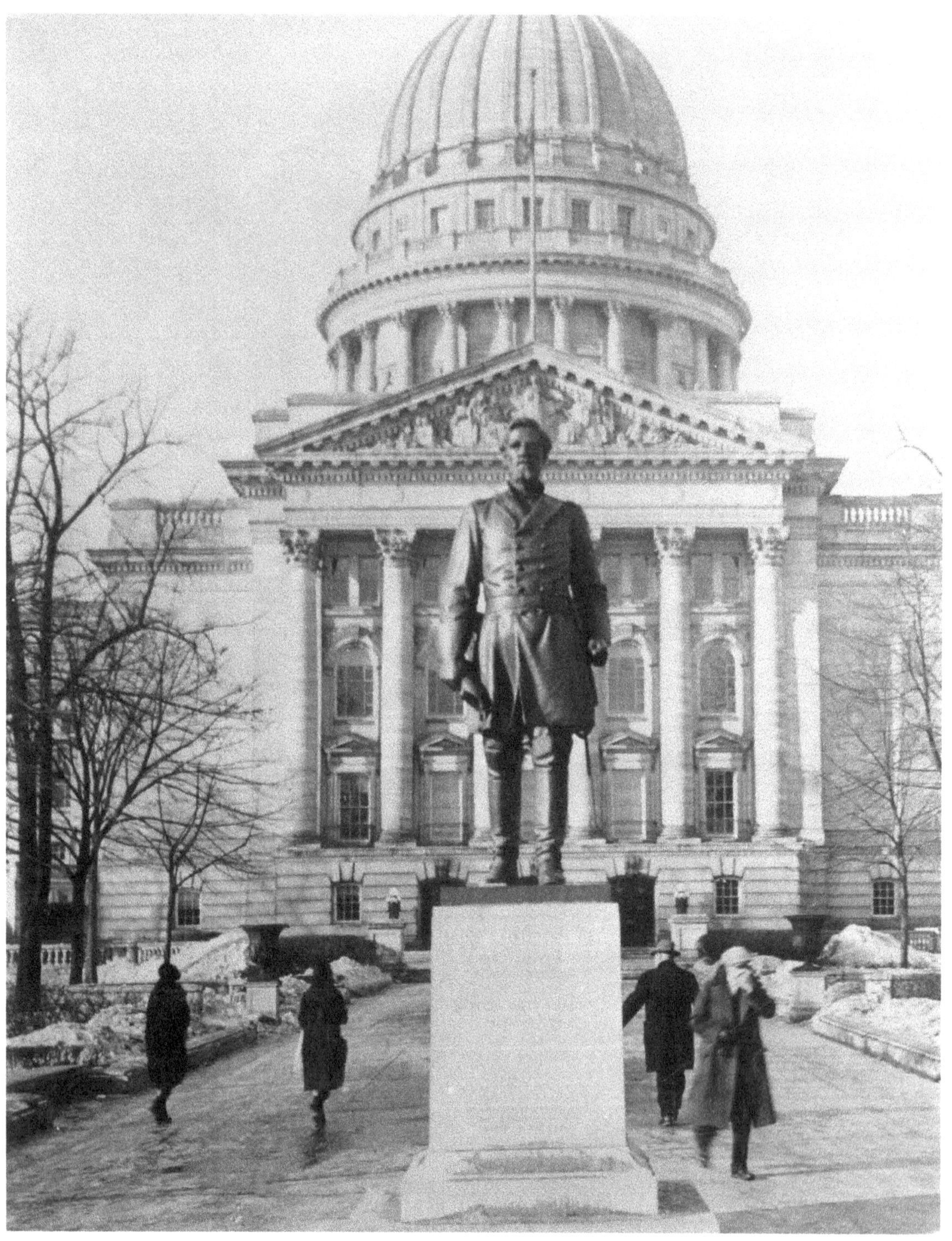

The statue of Colonel Hans Christian Heg (1829–1863), commander of the 15th Wisconsin Volunteer Infantry in the Civil War, stands in front of the Wisconsin State Capitol in 1950. The regiment served in Tennessee, the Atlanta Campaign, and Chickamauga, where Heg was killed in action. About $25,000 in contributions in 1920 paid for the statue as well as a counterpart in Dramen, Norway, where Heg was born. Heg's father, who came to Wisconsin in 1840 with a group of Norwegian immigrants, was one of the founders and publishers of *Nordlyset* (1847), the first newspaper in America published for Norwegian-born settlers.

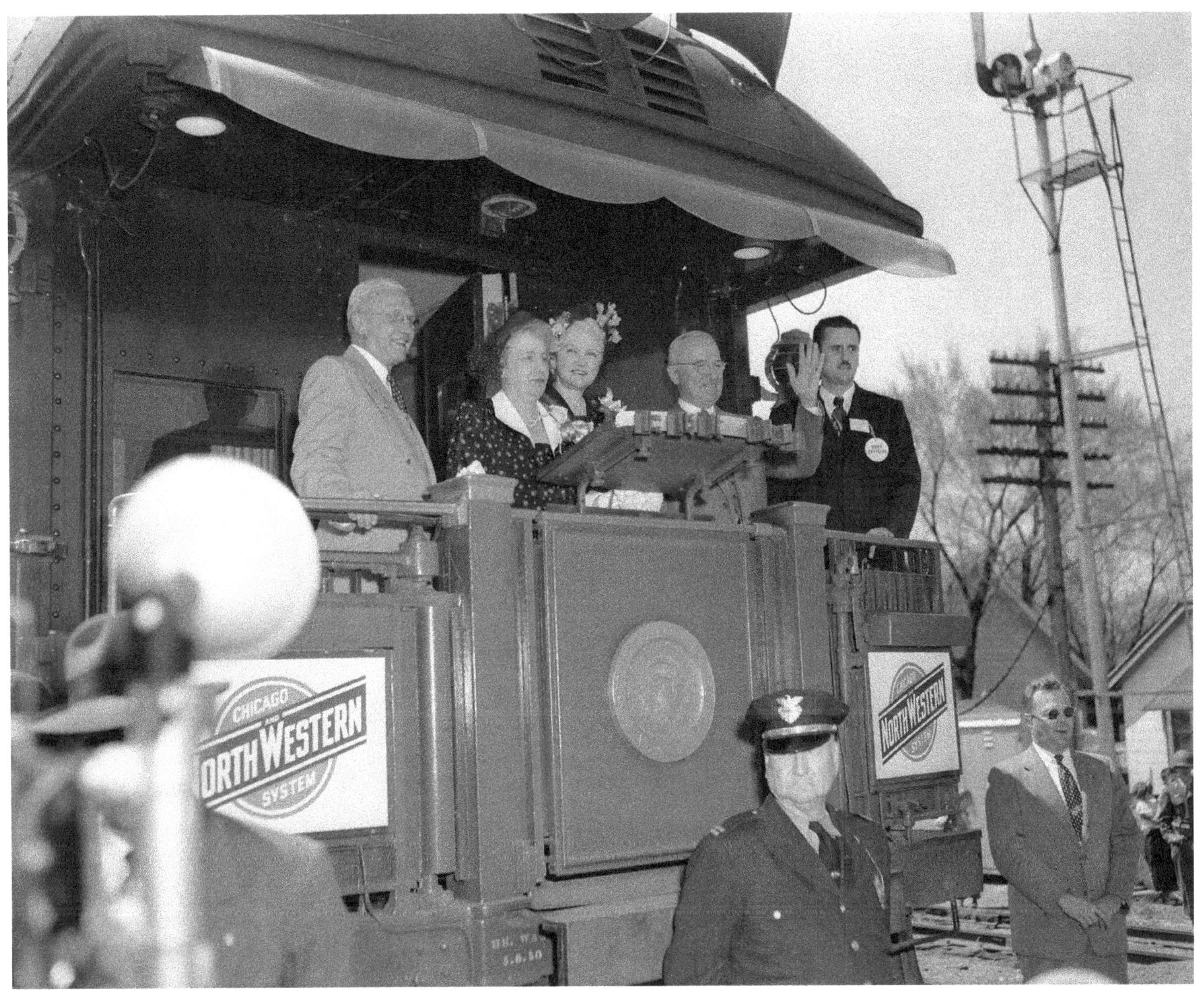

In June 1950, President Harry S Truman greets a crowd from the back platform of a Northwestern train in Madison. From the left are Governor Oscar Rennebohm, Bess Truman, and Mary Oscar Rennebohm.

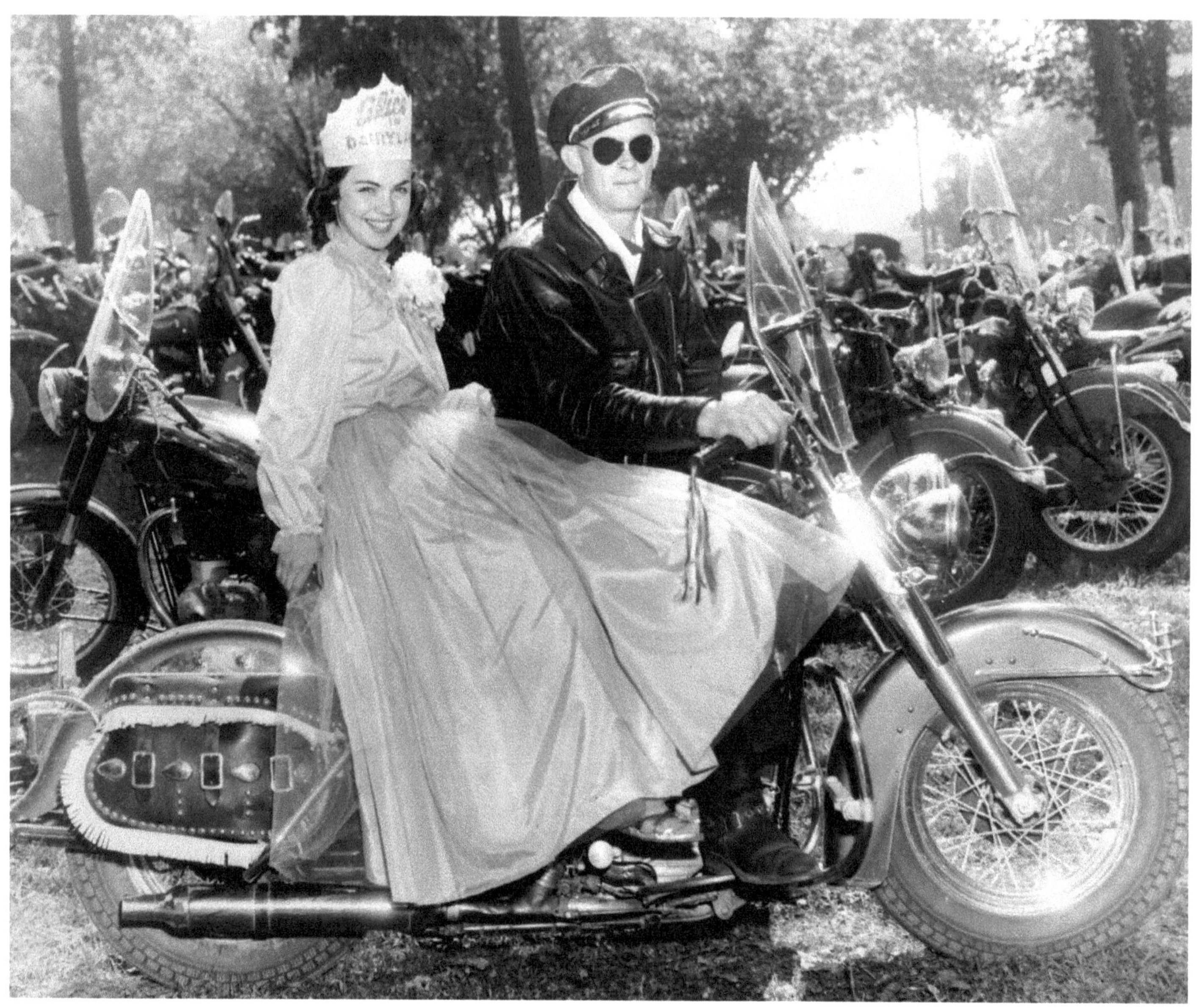

"Alice in Dairyland," Margean Czerwinski, in tiara and gown, rides on the back of a Harley-Davidson motorcycle in 1951. During Wisconsin's centennial year of 1948, state officials started a program to promote Wisconsin's dairy industry nationwide. Every year since, a young woman from Wisconsin has been chosen to be Alice in Dairyland. One of the most recognizable spokespersons of Wisconsin agriculture, "Alice" is a public relations professional working for the Wisconsin Department of Agriculture, Trade and Consumer Protection. "Alice" travels the state, nation, and world to promote Wisconsin products.

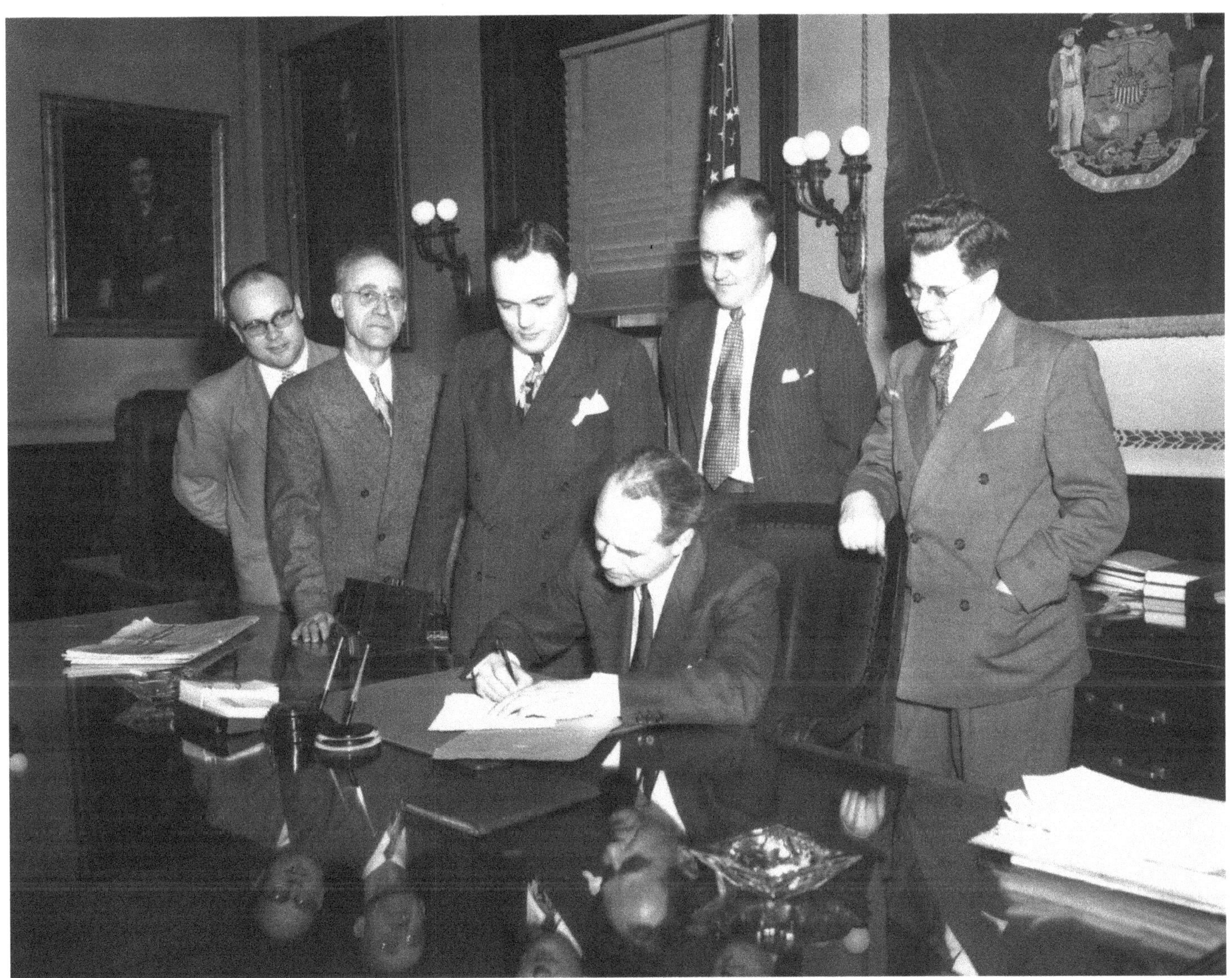

In March 1951, Governor Walter J. Kohler, Jr., signs a bill to liberalize state housing loans to veterans. The legislators around him are, left to right, Theodore Jones, Martin Howard, Roy Sengstock, Melvin Laird (later a U.S. congressman and secretary of defense), directly behind the governor, and Arthur Lenroot. The Republican Kohler was elected governor of Wisconsin in 1950 and was re-elected in 1952 and 1954.

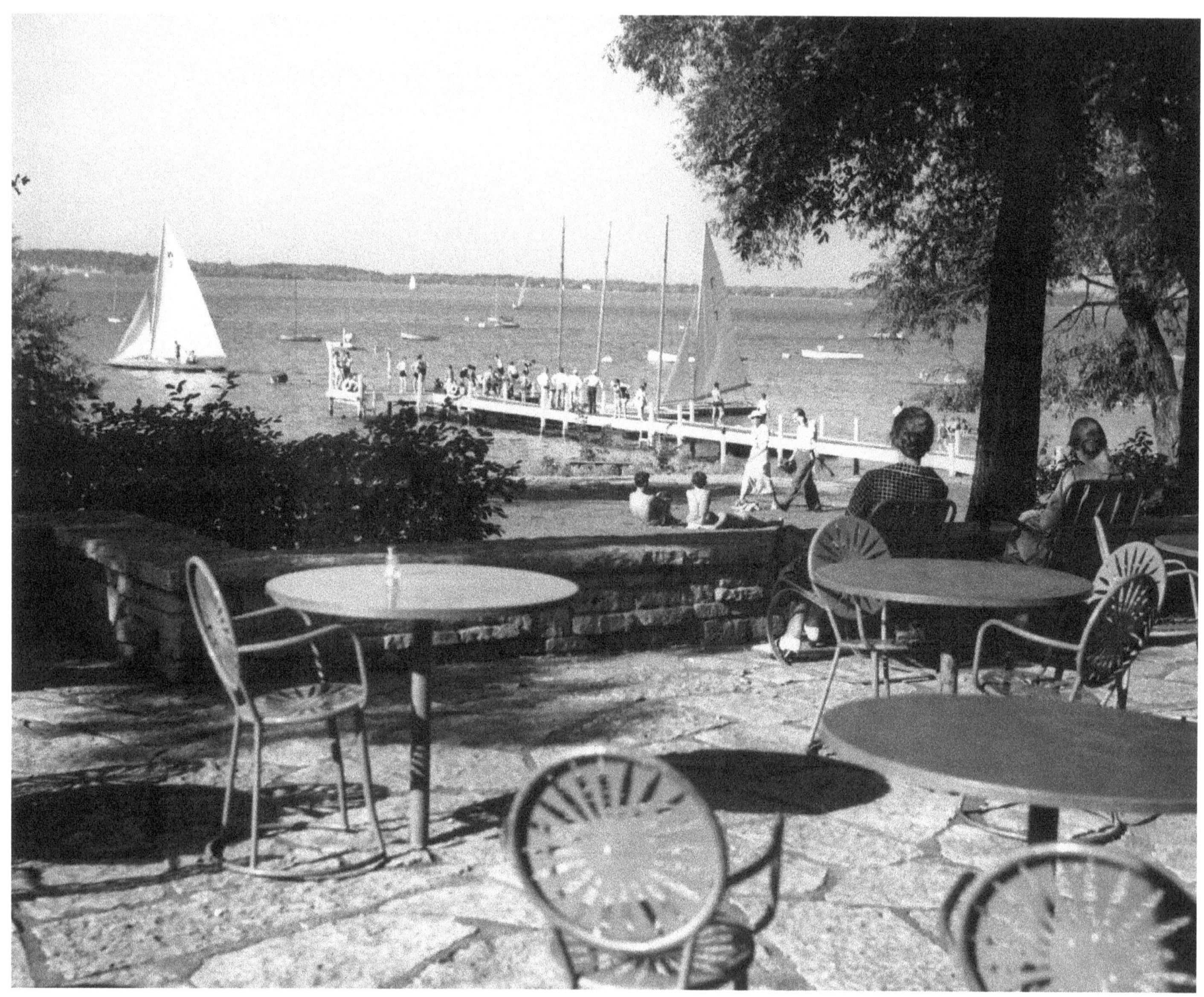

The University of Wisconsin's Memorial Union Terrace, with Lake Mendota and sailboats in the background in 1952. The terrace and the view remain relatively unchanged more than half a century later. The famous, ever-present trademarked Union chairs are in the foreground. When the company that manufactured the metal chairs went bankrupt, the Union purchased the tool and die to continue manufacturing the chairs. A miniature replica of a terrace chair was added to the objects sealed in a Madison sesquicentennial time capsule in the city's new Overture Center in 2006.

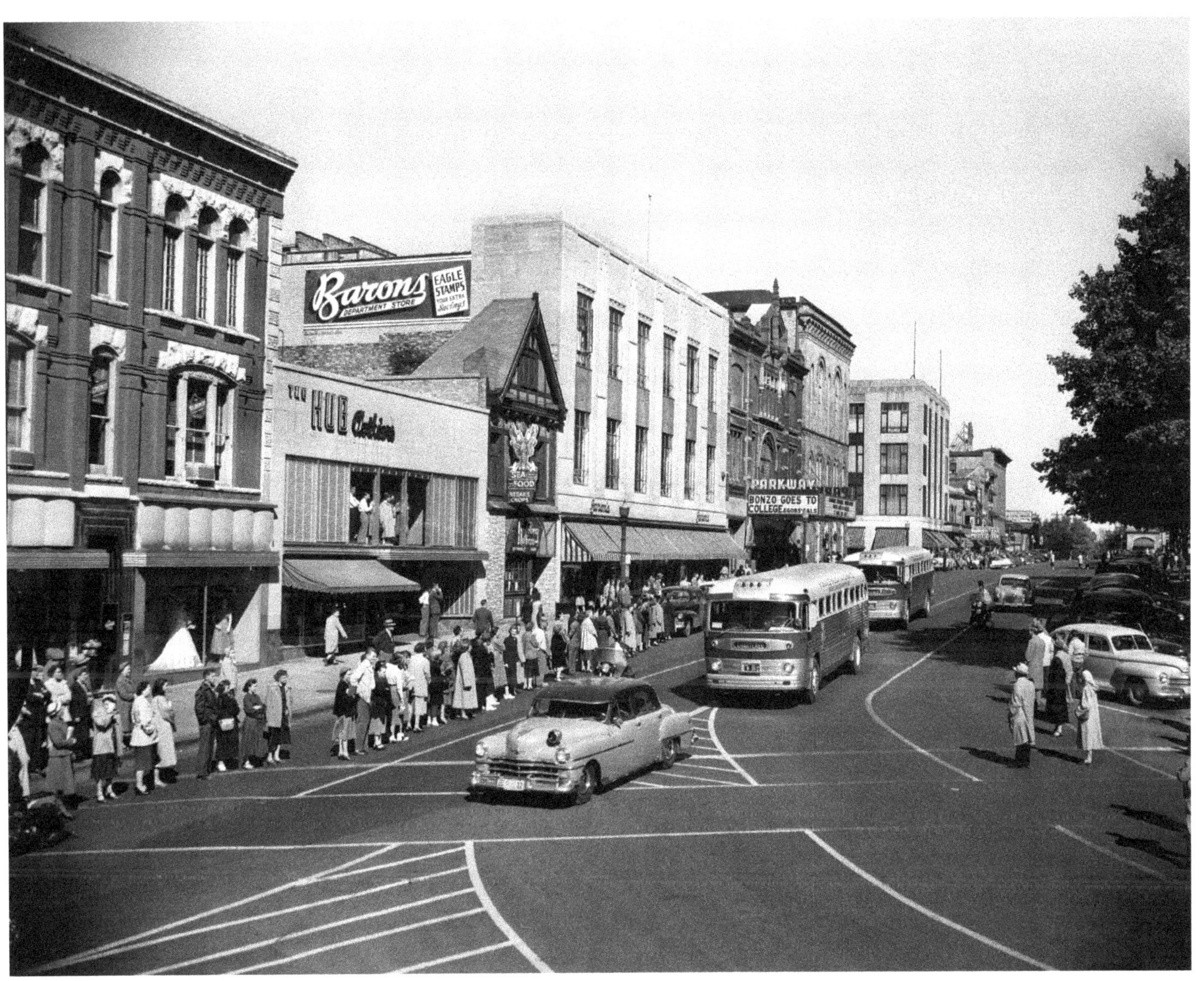

People gather on the Capitol Square to celebrate a visit by Adlai Stevenson, Democratic candidate for president in 1952.

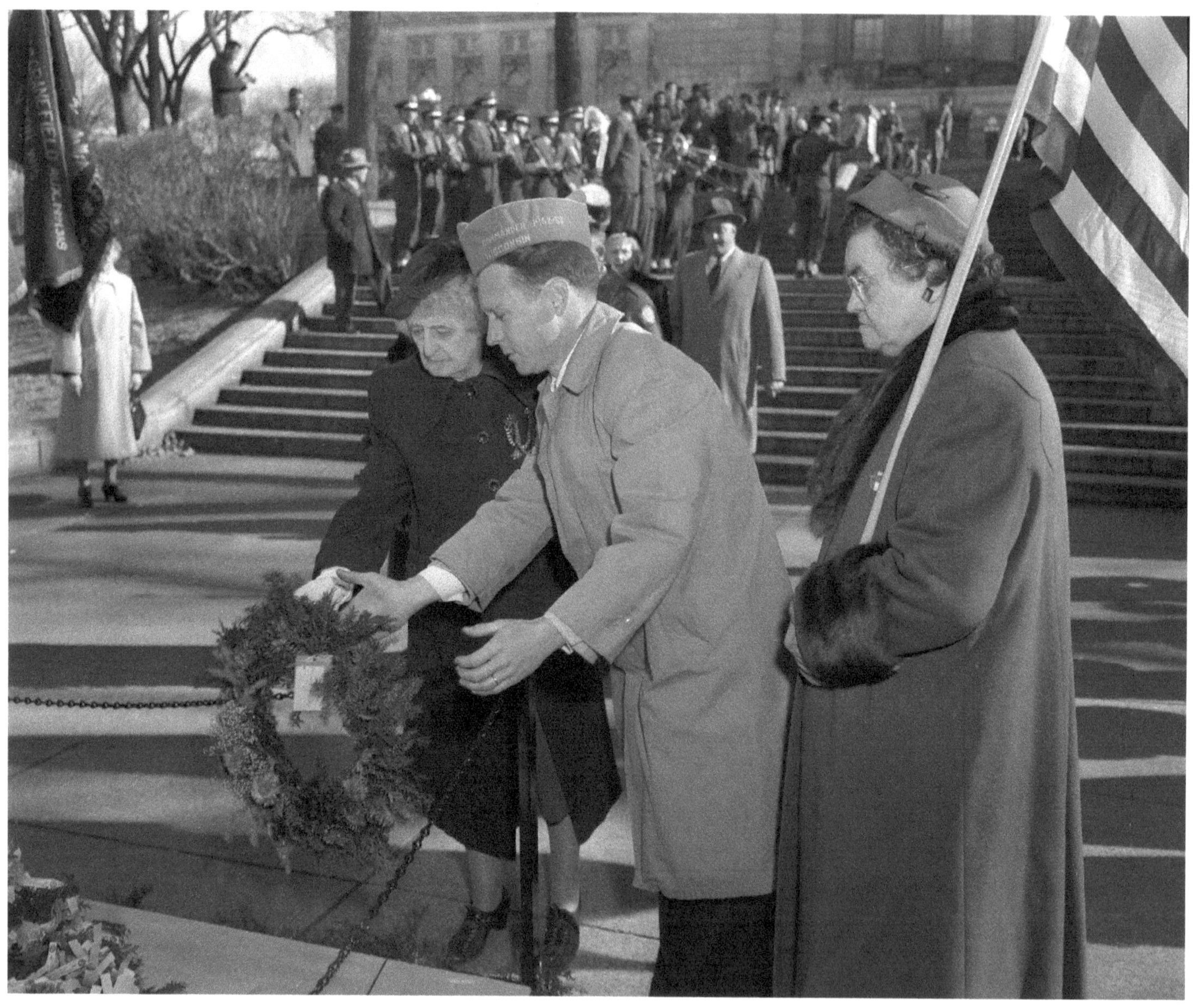

On Veterans Day 1952, Nena Aylward (left) of the Women's Relief Corps places a wreath on the cenotaph in Armistice Day ceremonies in Capitol Park. She is assisted by Clarence R. Starr, Madison Veterans of Foreign Wars commander, and Elsie Jensen of the Women's Relief Corps color guard. World War I formally ended at the eleventh hour of the eleventh day of the eleventh month of 1918 when the Germans signed the Armistice. The occasion has been recognized annually since 1938.

In 1952, a little girl rides her tricycle in front of the Spot Lunch diner, a former streetcar, at 640 Williamson Street, owned by John B. Hanson.

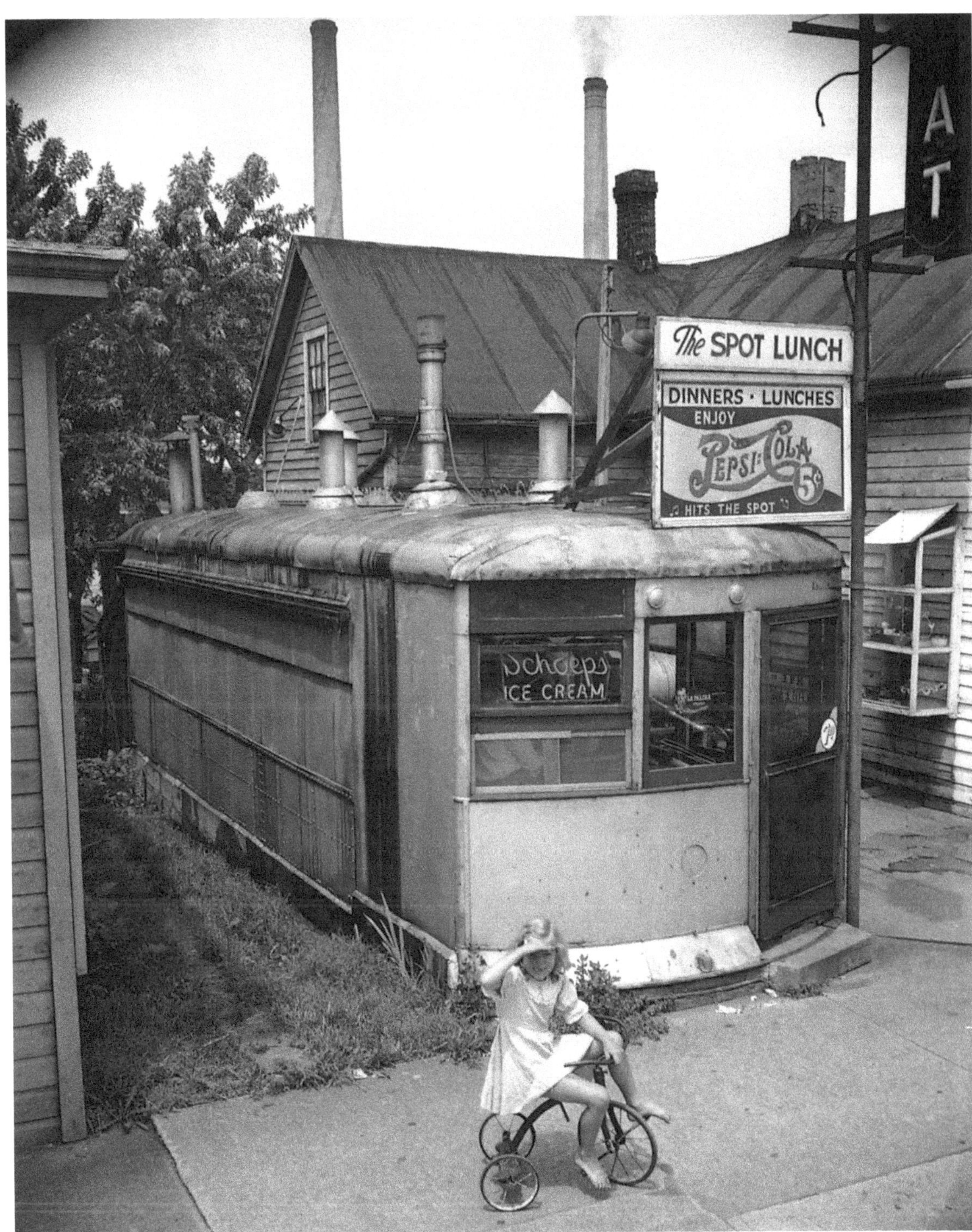

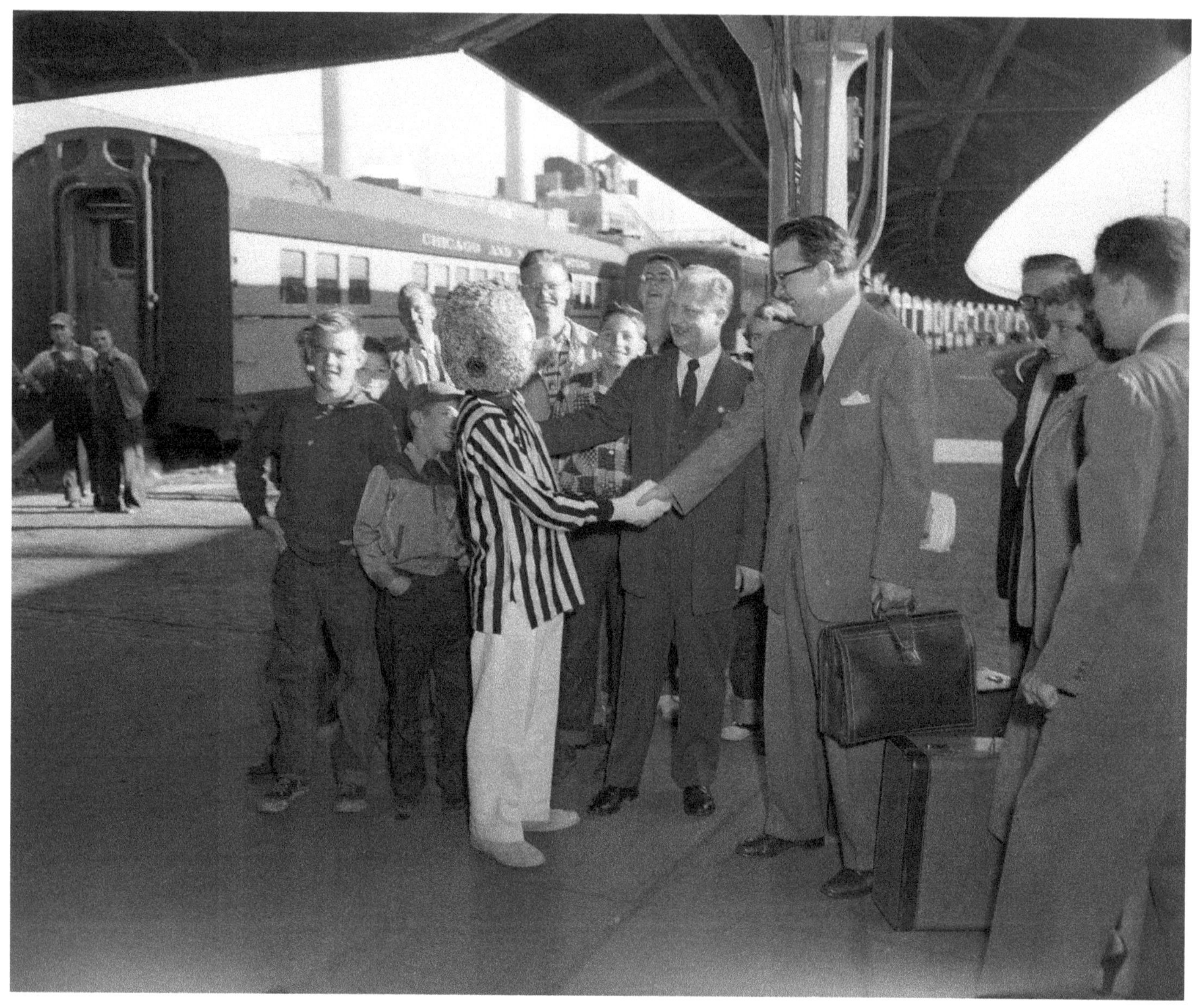

Cartoonist Walt Kelly, arriving in Madison at the Chicago & North Western depot, is met by a person dressed as Pogo, one of his cartoon characters. Pogo's most famous words were "We have met the enemy and he is us," a rallying cry for a generation of environmentalists.

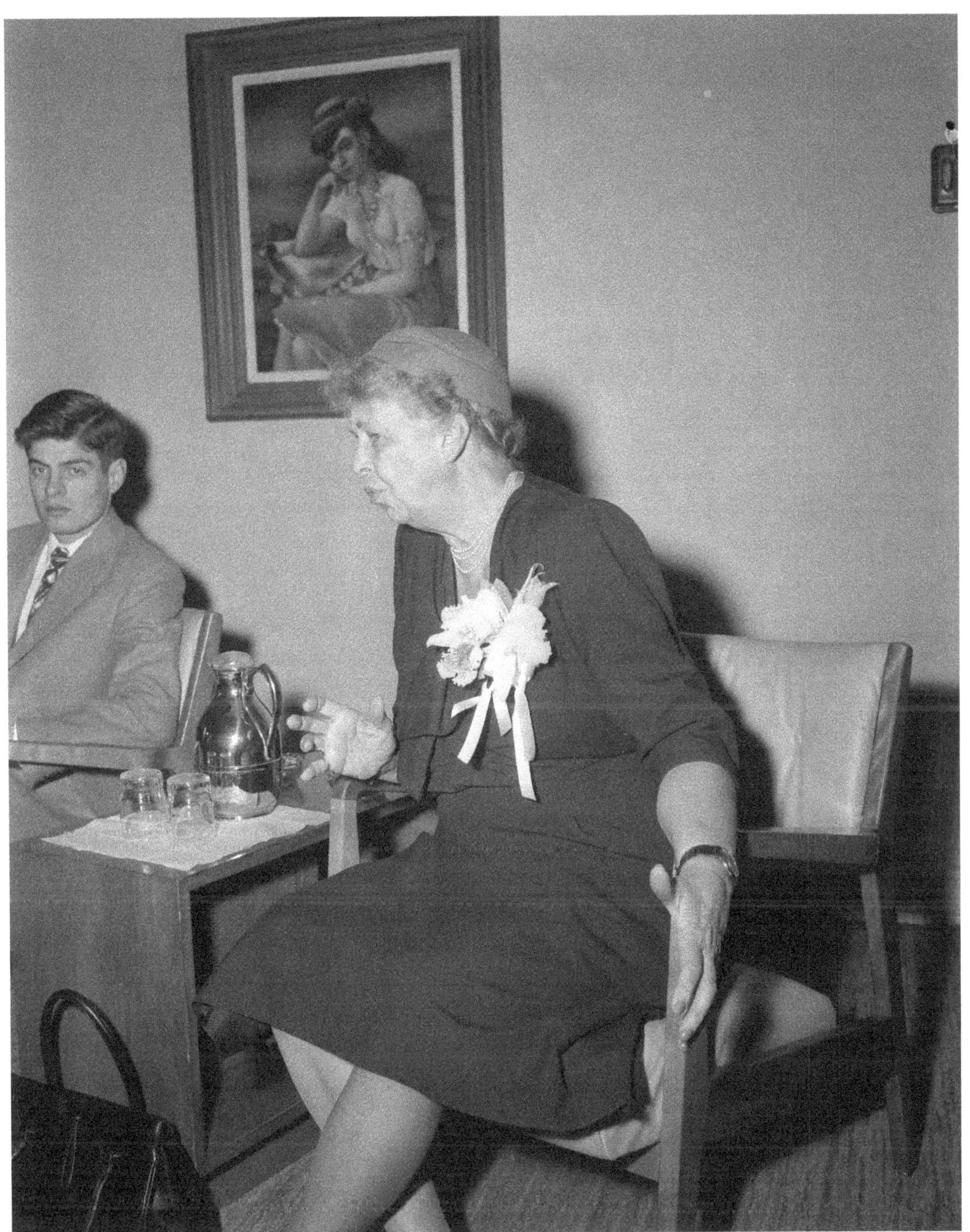

Eleanor Roosevelt talks with reporters prior to her Sunday afternoon talk in the University of Wisconsin Memorial Union Theater on January 18, 1953.

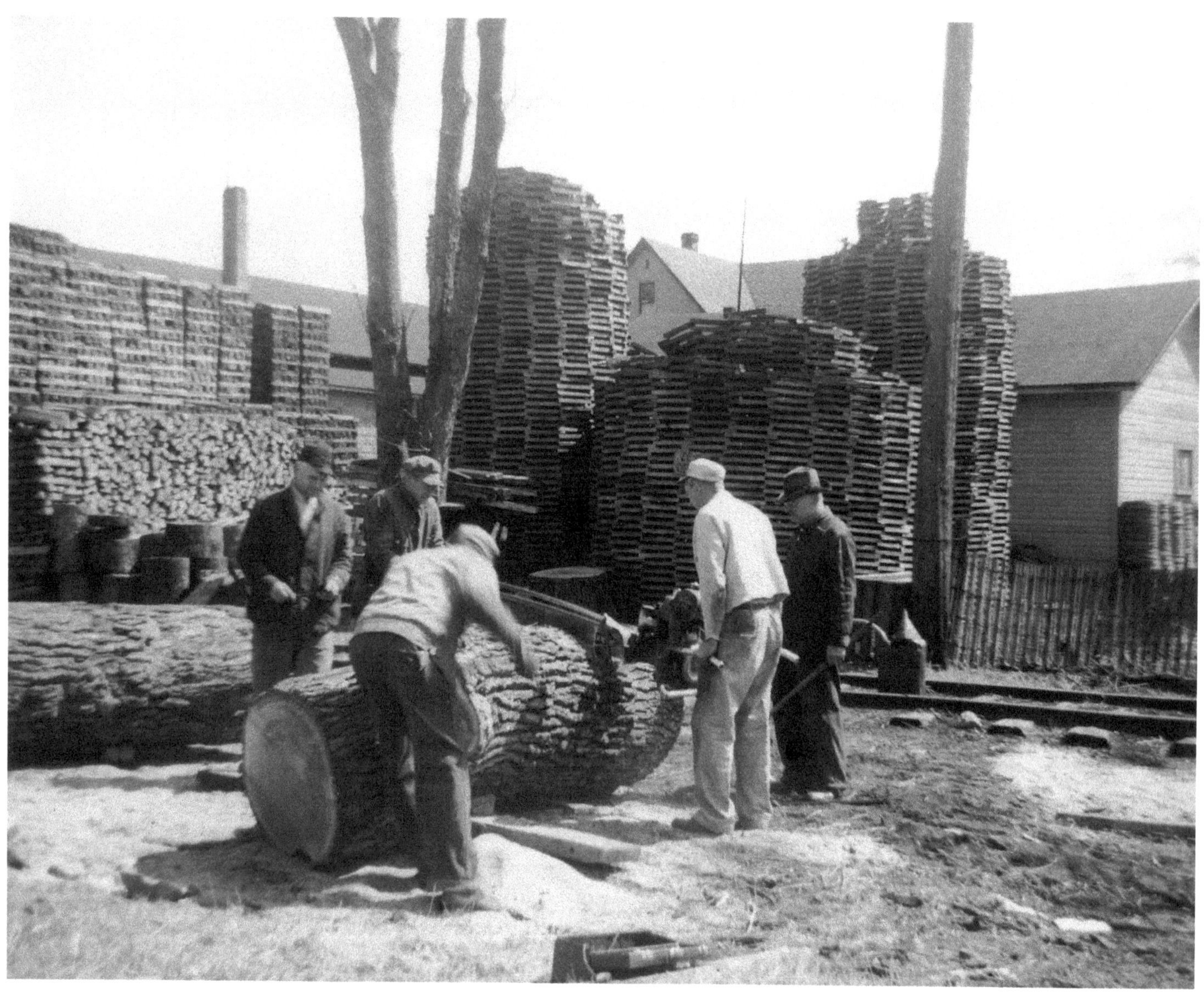

Five workers at the Hess Cooperage cut a large oak log to header length for barrels. The cooperage was near the 1900 block of East Main Street. In 1900, Henry Fauerbach of Fauerbach Brewery persuaded Frank Hess to relocate his operation to Madison. Hess Cooperage, which continued in operation until 1966, was the longest and last running oak beer-barrel cooperage in the United States.

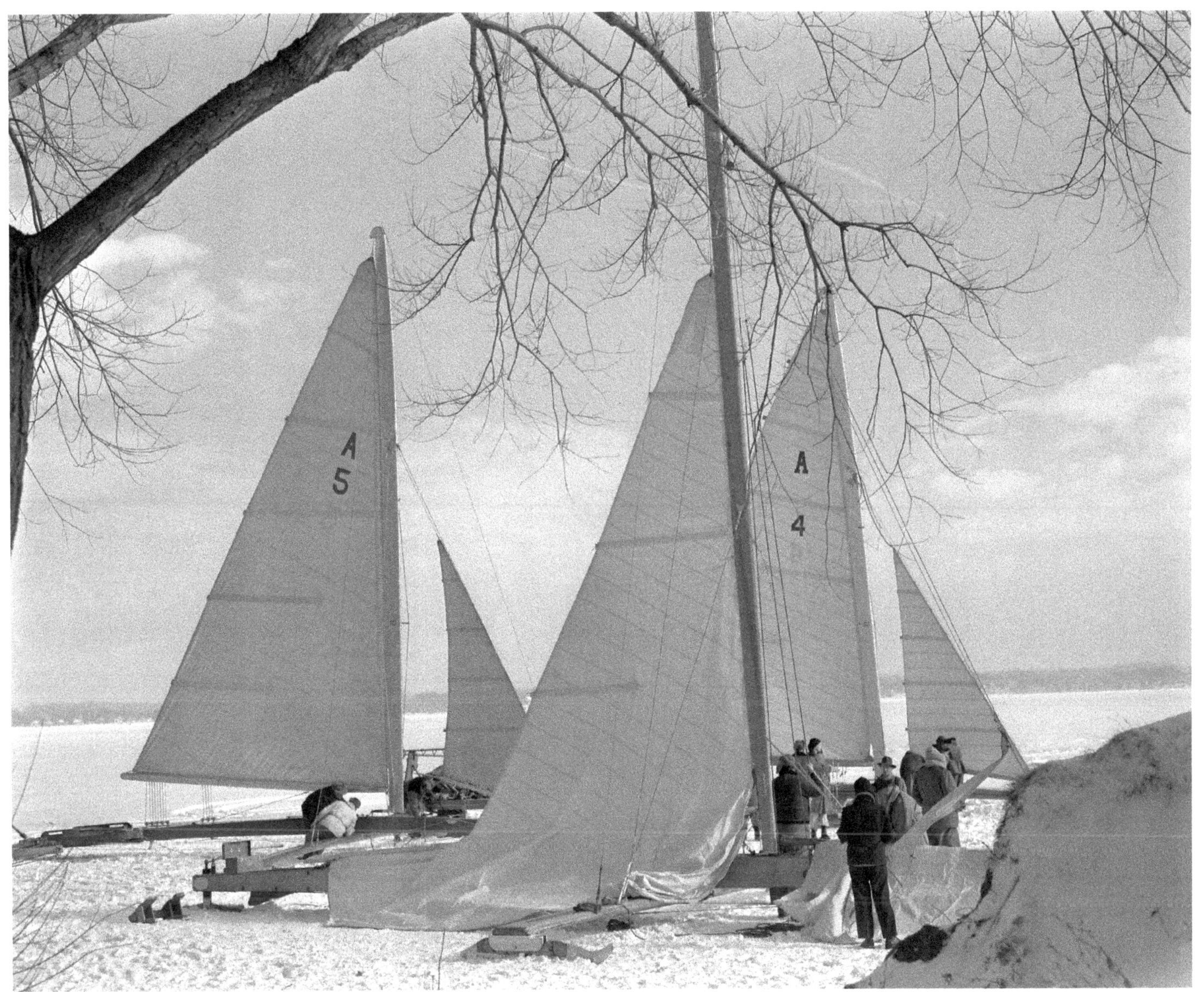

Iceboaters prepare to set sail on one of Madison's lakes in January 1954.

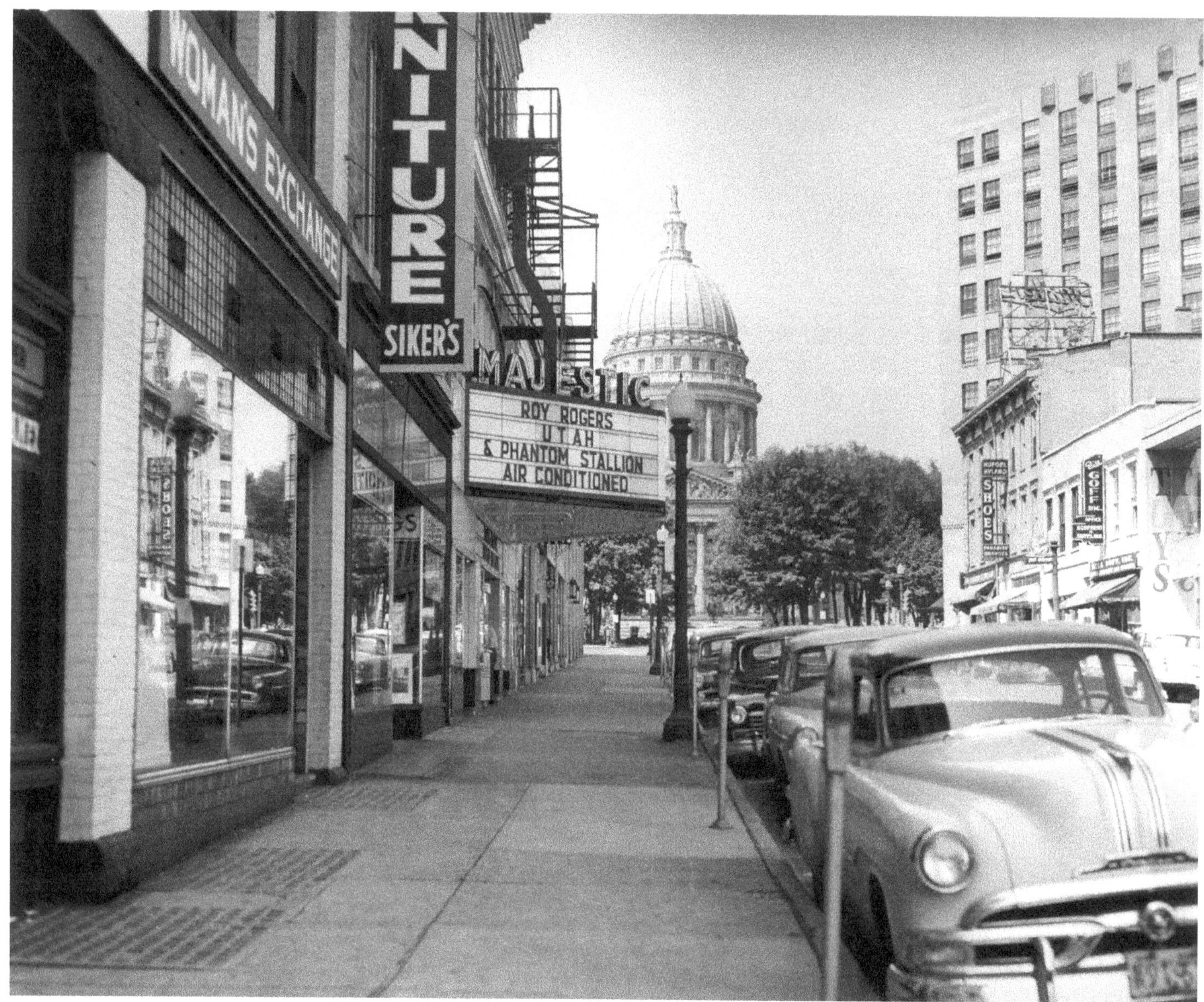

This view of the Capitol, taken in 1954, looks up King Street past the Majestic Theater, a Madison landmark built in 1906 as a two-story vaudeville theater by the Biederstaedt brothers. It was the Madison home of a touring company known as the Majestic Players, which included Melvyn Douglas and Ralph Bellamy among other noted actors.

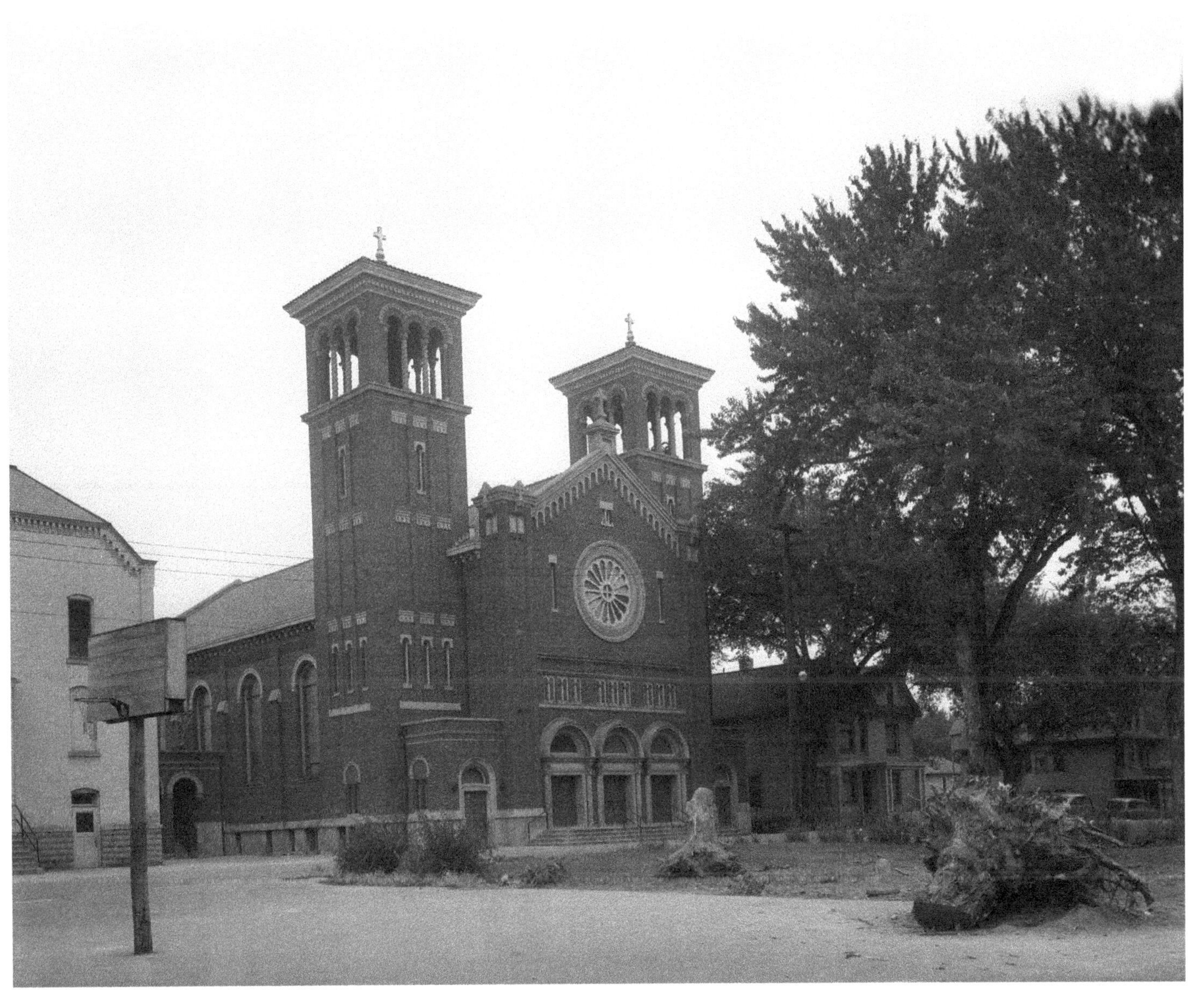

St. James Catholic Church at 1130 St. James Court on October 5, 1955, apparently after a heavy storm took down a tree. The building opened in July 1924.

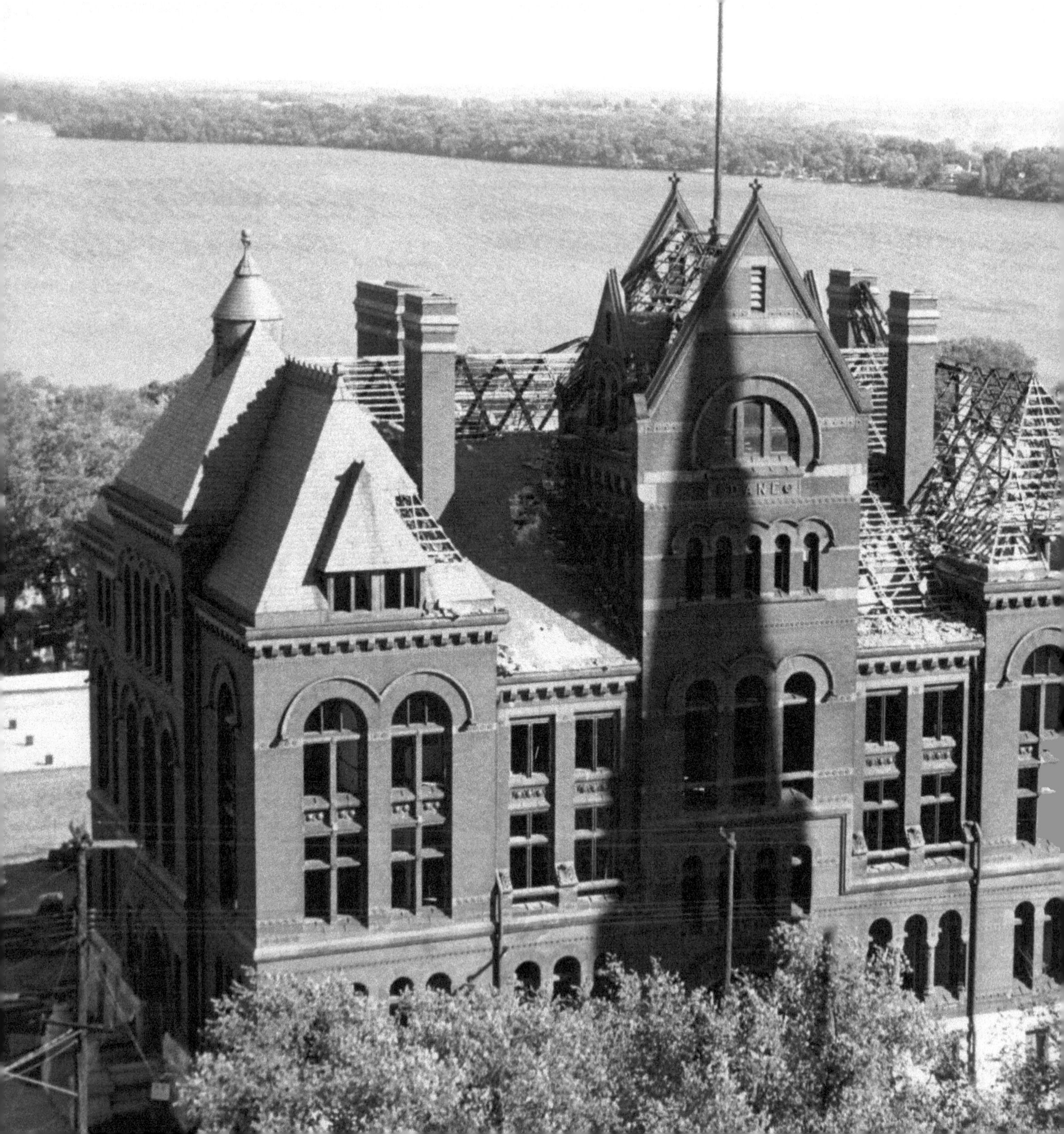

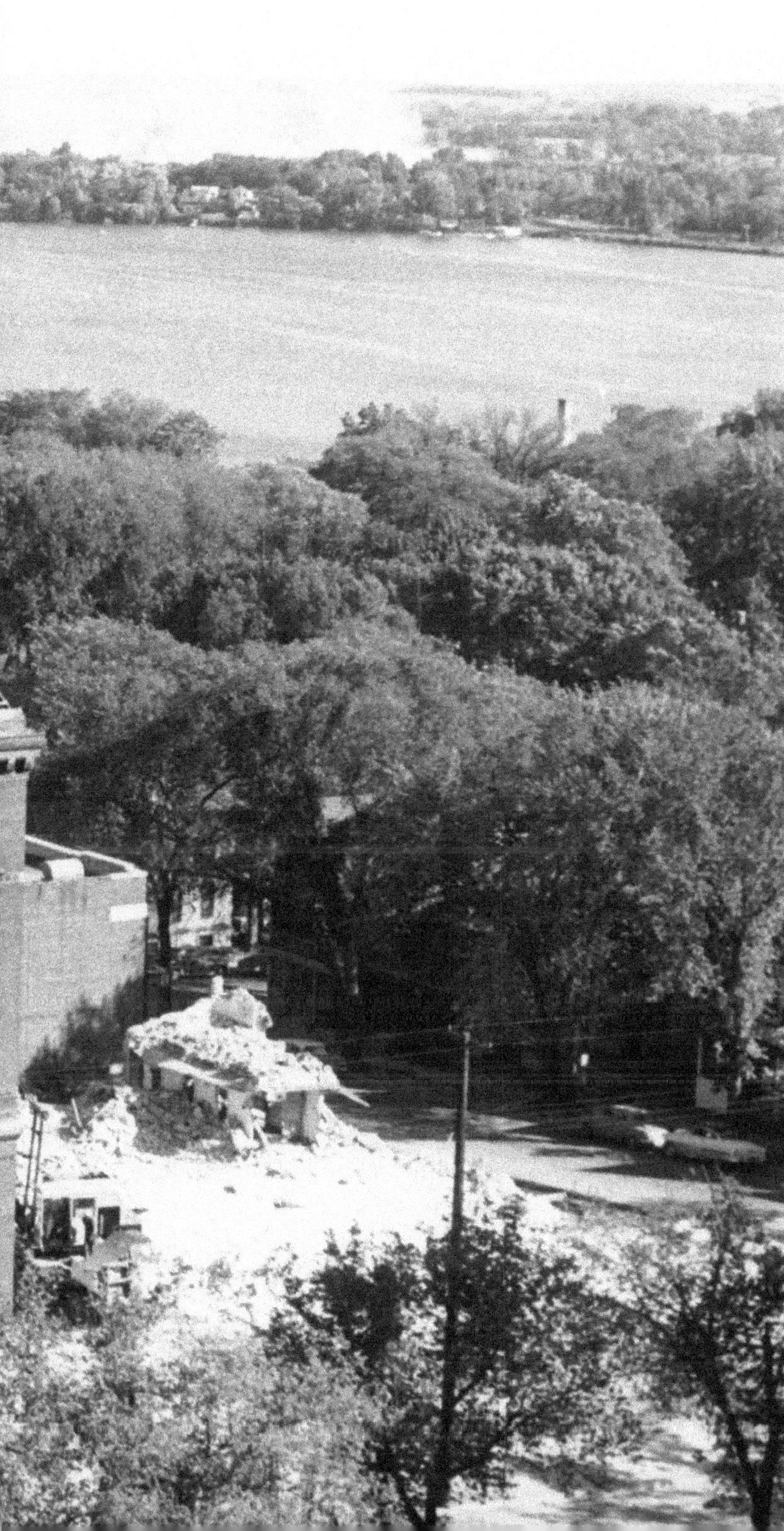

This aerial view of the Dane County Courthouse, built in 1885 at 207 West Main Street, shows the building being razed in 1958.

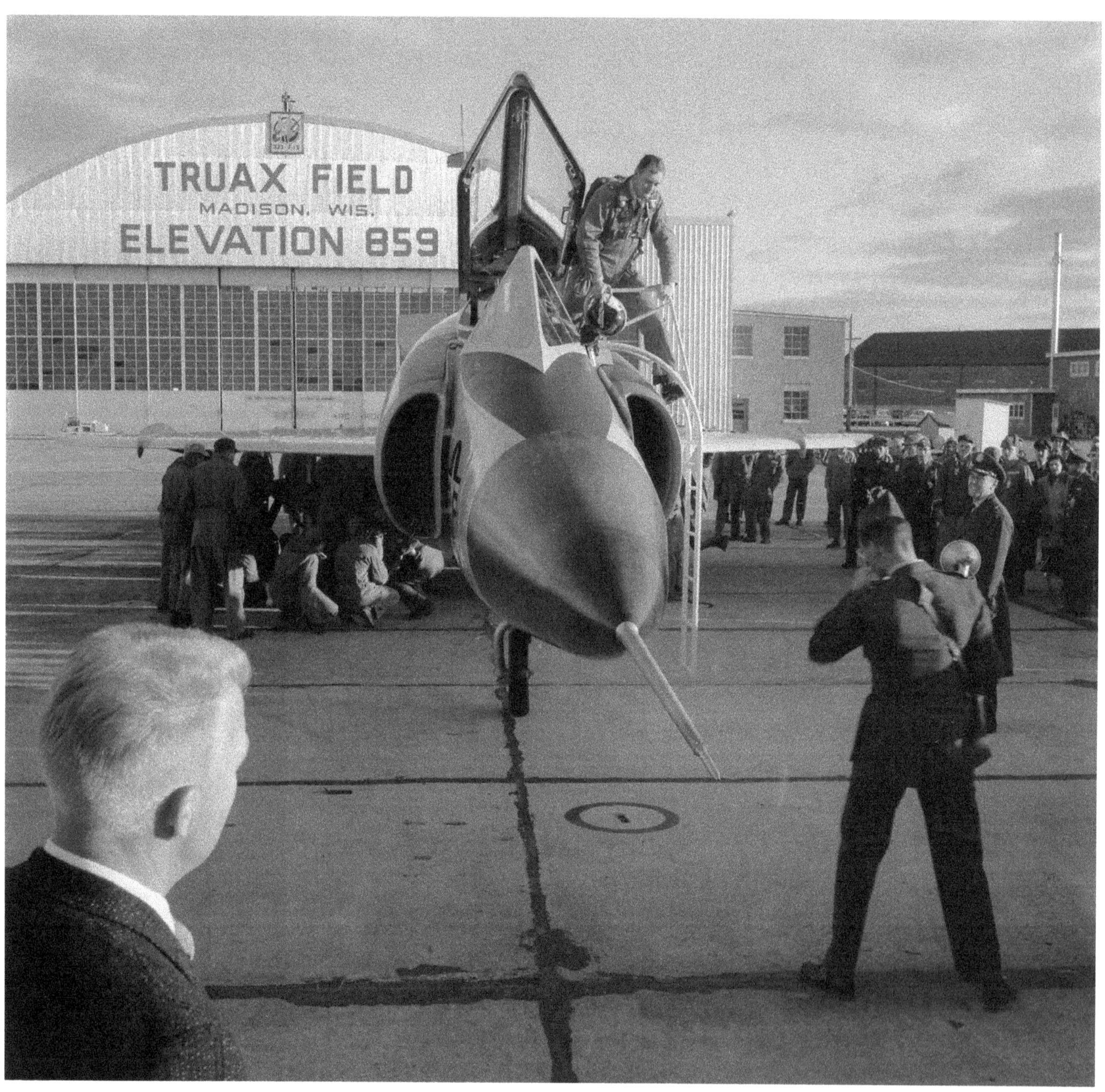

The first delta-winged F-102 jet arrives at Truax Field in Madison on November 8, 1956. Truax Field, located at the Dane County Regional Airport in northeast Madison, was created as an Army air base in June 1942 and deactivated as an active military base in 1968, when it was taken over by the Wisconsin Air National Guard. It was named in honor of Lieutenant Thomas L. Truax, a Wisconsin native, who was killed in a P-40 training accident in November 1941.

This rally for presidential candidate John F. Kennedy was held in Madison October 23, 1960. Kennedy had completed the fourth televised presidential debate just two days before.

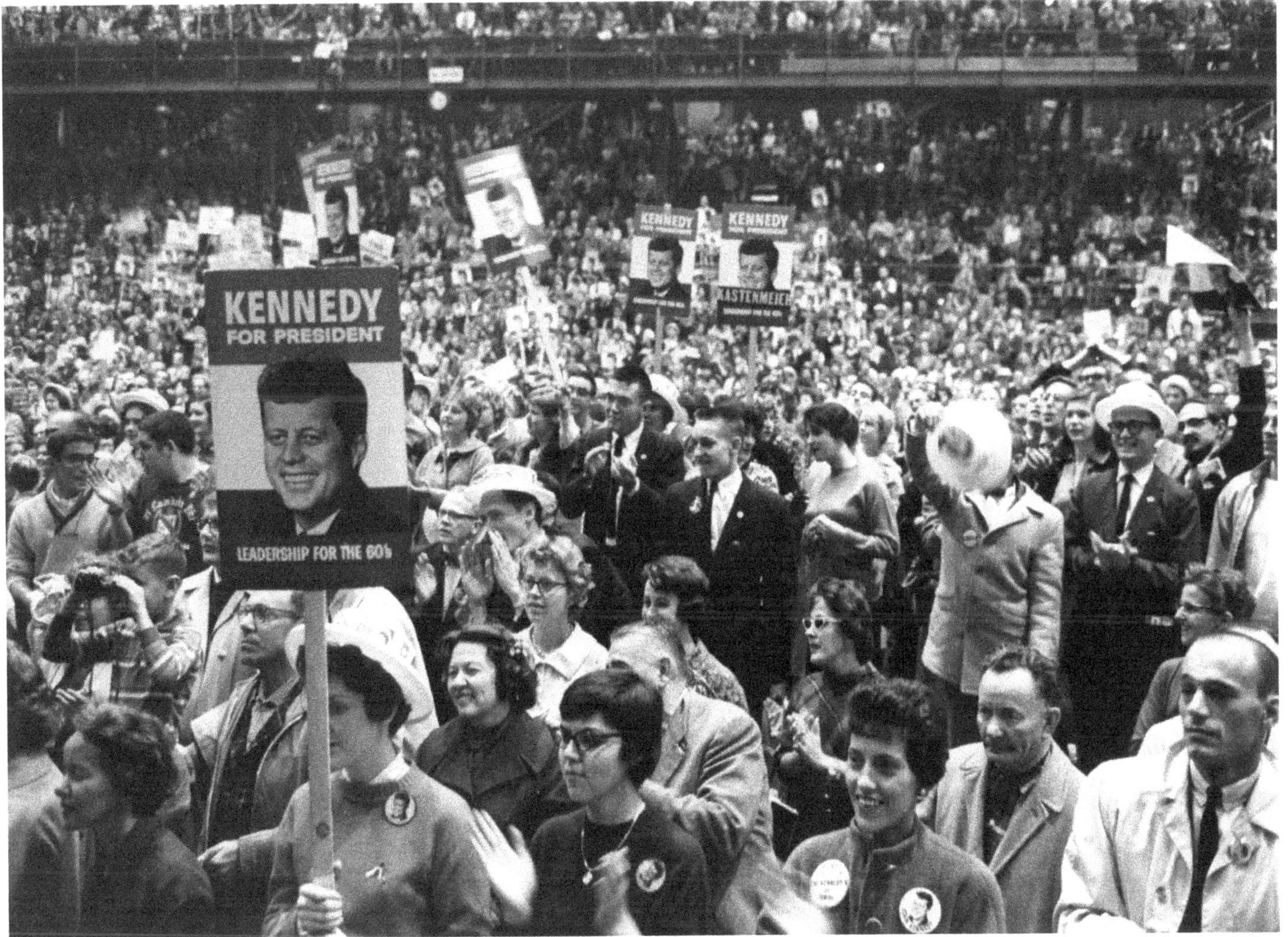

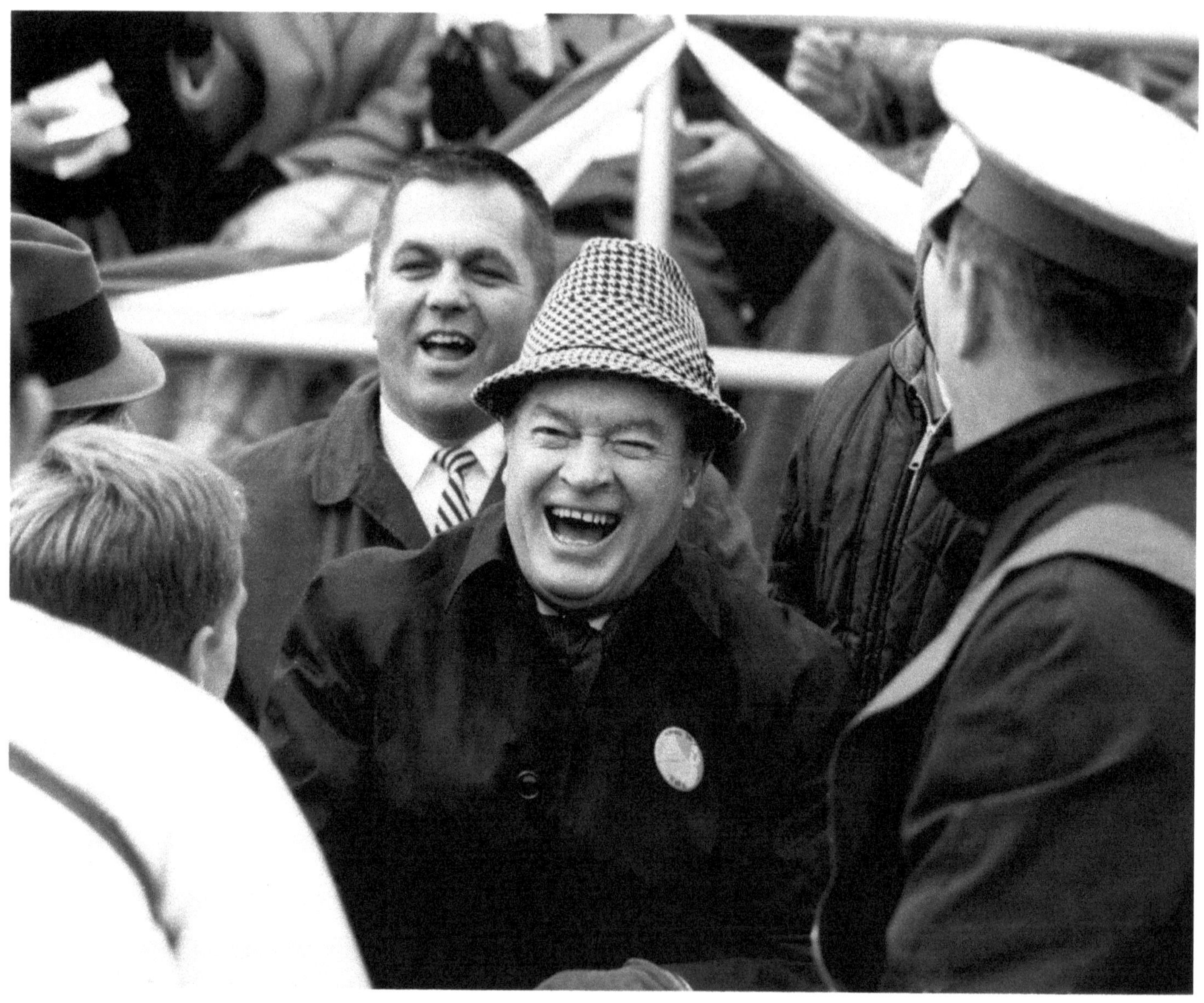

Bob Hope enjoys a laugh at the University of Wisconsin homecoming football game. Wisconsin was playing against Ohio State, Hope's alma mater, on October 23, 1965. Ohio won 20-10.

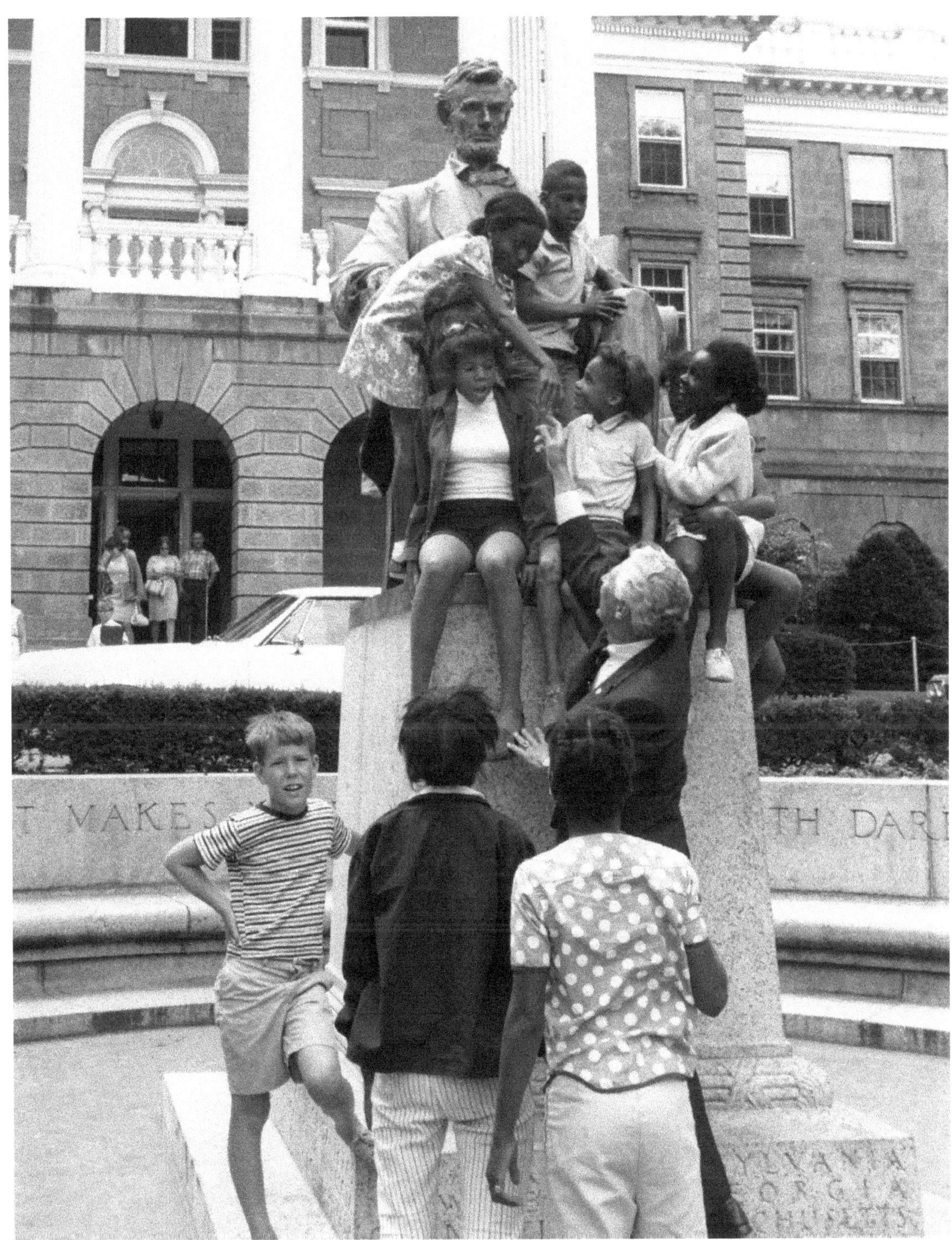

Governor Warren Knowles reaches up to touch the hand of a girl in a cluster of children climbing on the Lincoln Memorial on the University of Wisconsin campus in 1964. Knowles was elected governor in 1964 and re-elected in 1966 and in 1968. The Lincoln statue was created by sculptor Adolph Weinman in 1909. Lincoln is considered a patron of the university because he signed the Morrill Act in 1862 to provide federal aid to land-grant colleges like UW.

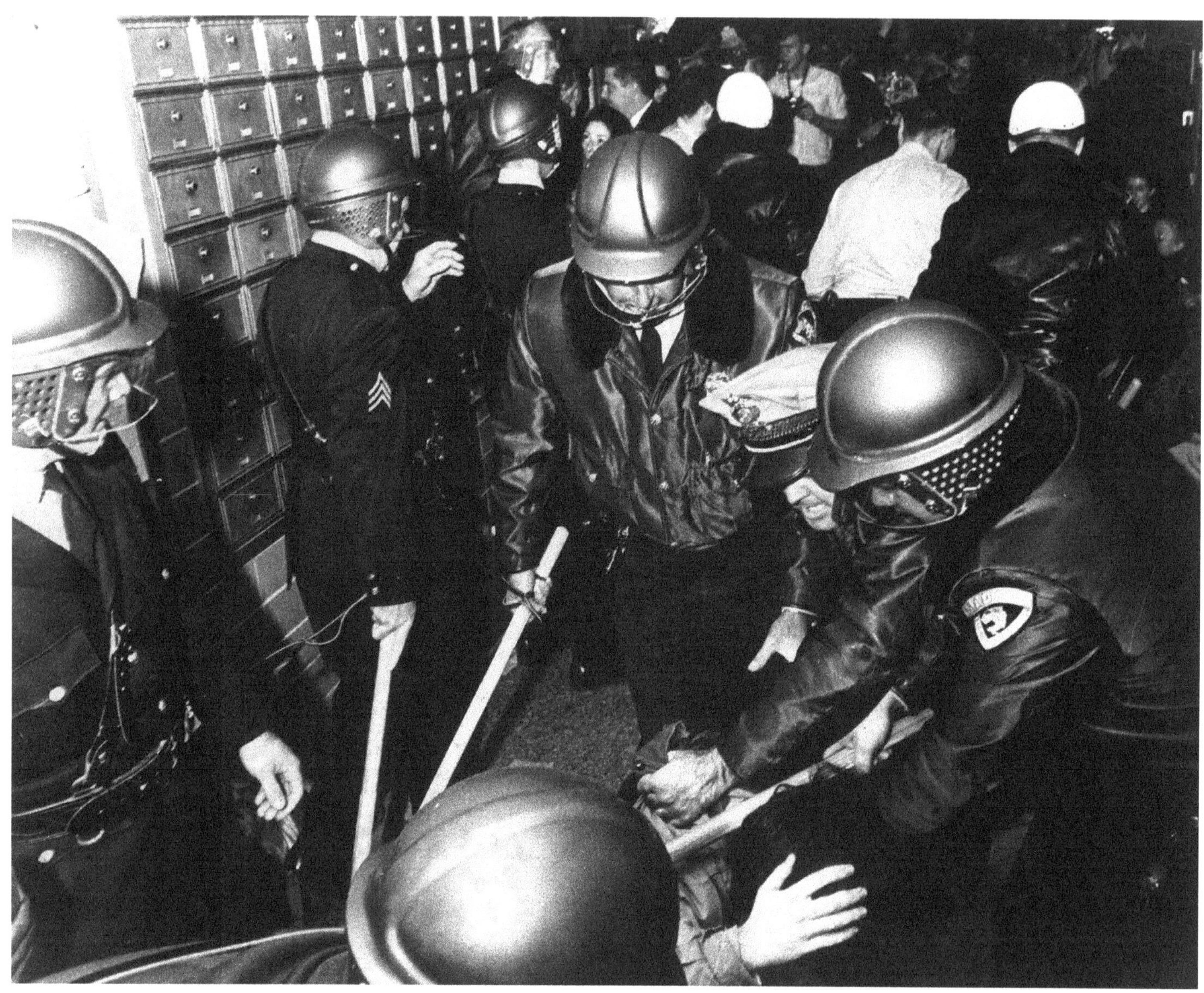

In a turning point of student protest against the Vietnam War in October 1967, University of Wisconsin students clash with riot police during a campus protest against the maker of the fiery weapon napalm—Dow Chemical Company—which was recruiting on the Madison campus. During the 1960s, the UW gained a reputation as one of the nation's most radical campuses. Events led to protest marches, draft card burning, and confrontations with army recruiters.

The intense protest movement on the University of Wisconsin campus against the Vietnam War took an ironic, deadly turn on August 24, 1970. A group of young men, who called themselves "the New Years Gang," detonated 2,000 pounds of ammonium nitrate in a van outside the east wing of Sterling Hall, home to the Mathematics Research Center, a U.S. Army–funded facility that many protesters believed contributed to the death and destruction in Vietnam. Until the Oklahoma City bombing in 1995, this was considered the single most destructive act of sabotage in United States history. The explosion killed physics researcher Robert Fassnacht and injured four others. Although it was feared that tensions would escalate and more violence would follow, the bombing had the opposite effect.

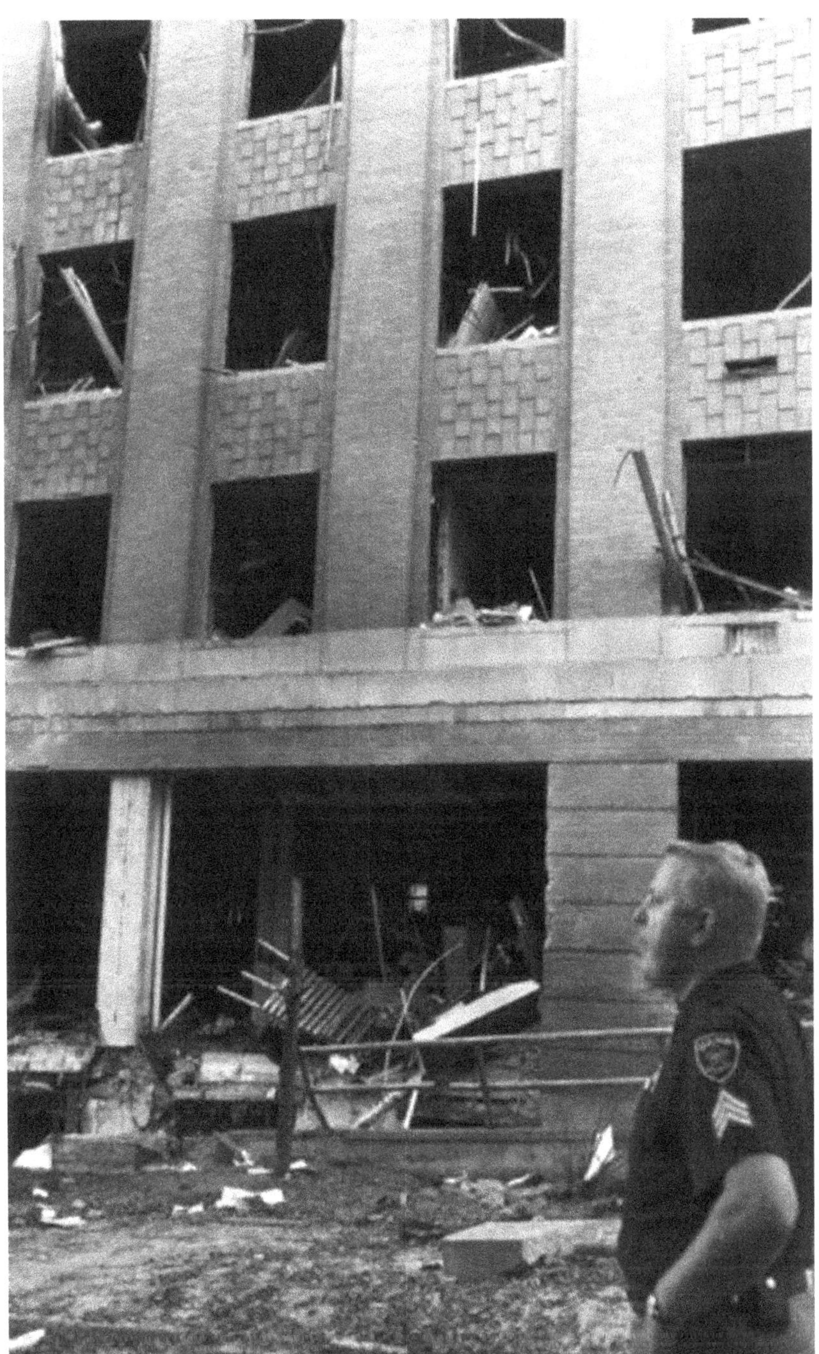

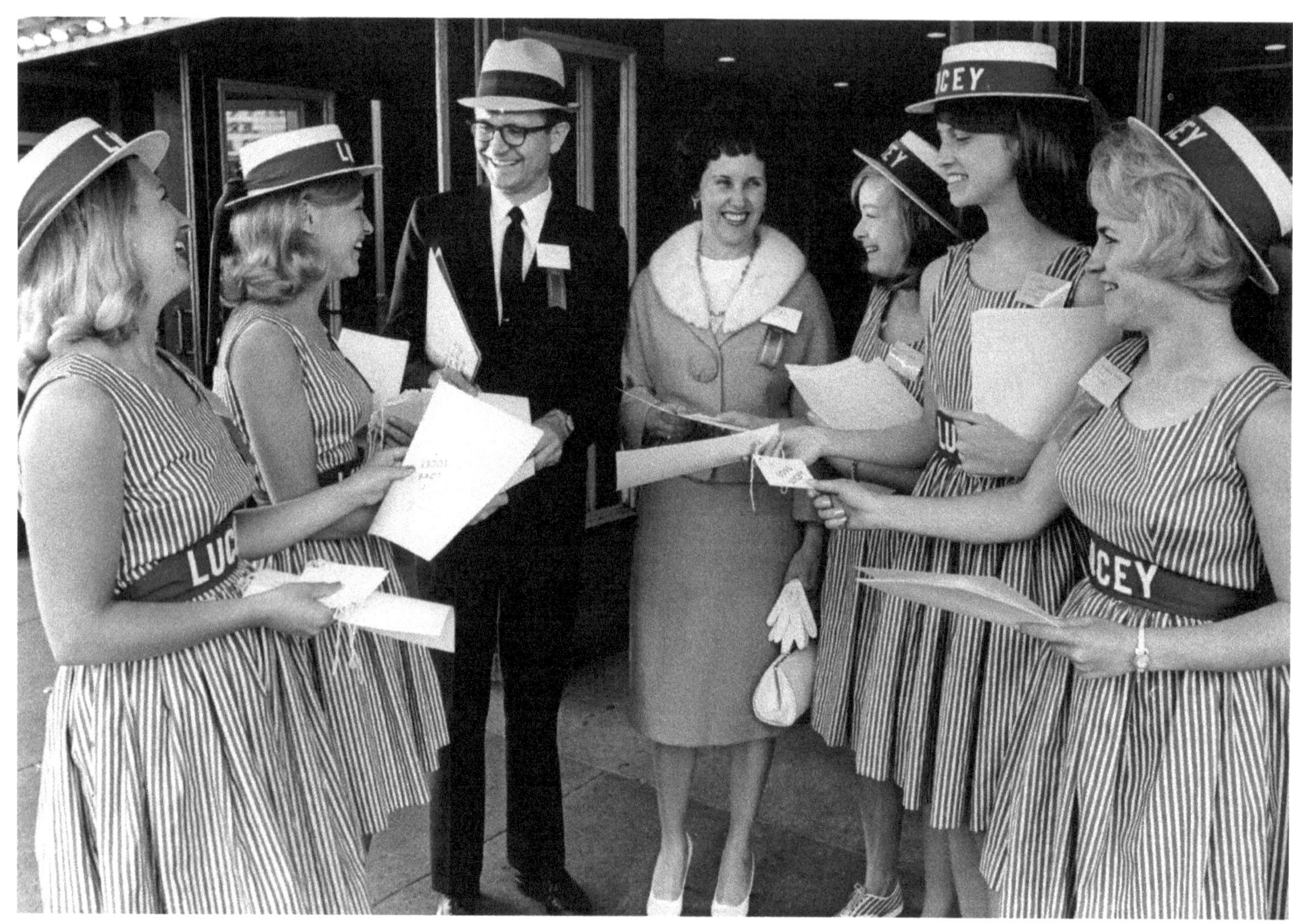

Supporters of Patrick J. Lucey for governor in 1966 distribute fliers and buttons to promote his campaign. Lucey served as governor of Wisconsin from 1970 until he resigned in 1977 to serve as the United States ambassador to Mexico.

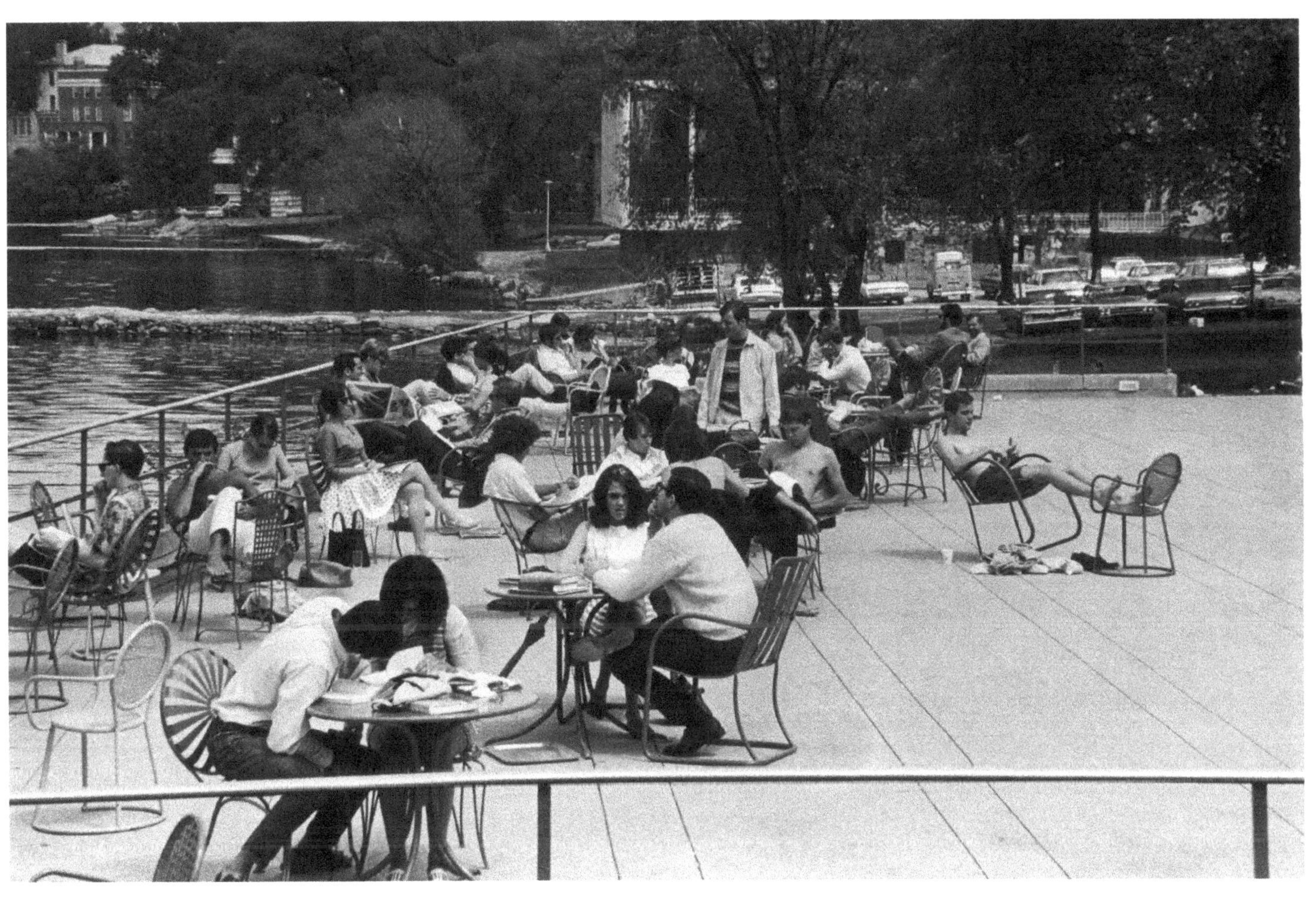

Students and faculty study and relax on the University of Wisconsin Memorial Union Terrace on Lake Mendota during final exams in May 1968.

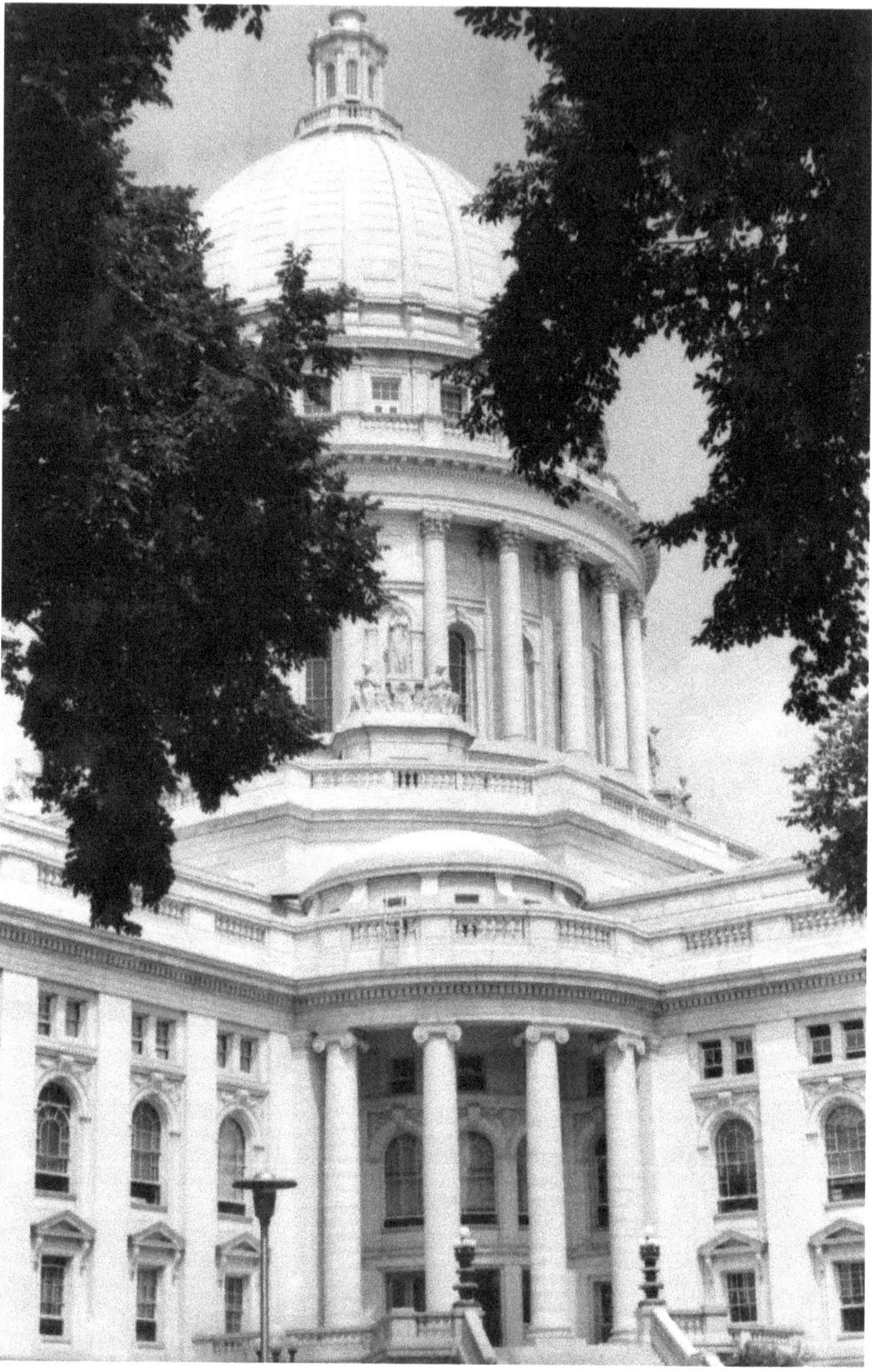

This view through tree branches of the Wisconsin State Capitol dome was recorded in 1969. Starting in 1980, a complete renovation of the capitol to its original architectural integrity began. The 21-year project, costing $145 million, involved restoration of the building as well as its murals, mosaics, and statuary. The exterior was cleaned with a sponge jetting process, the granite was repaired, and the joints were tuck pointed. The work was completed in November 2001, the same year the capitol was designated a National Historic Landmark.

NOTES ON THE PHOTOGRAPHS

These notes, listed by page number, attempt to include all aspects known of the photographs. Each of the photographs is identified by the page number, photograph's title or description, photographer and collection, archive, and call or box number when applicable. Although every attempt was made to collect all available data, in some cases complete data was unavailable due to the age and condition of some of the photographs and records.

II **WISCONSIN CAPITOL (THIRD) FROM WISCONSIN AVENUE**
Wisconsin Historical Society
11036

VI **CAPITOL STEPS REUNION**
Wisconsin Historical Society
23206

X **LABOR DAY PARADE**
Wisconsin Historical Society
36026

2 **CAPITOL (SECOND) VIEWED FROM BASCOM HILL**
Wisconsin Historical Society
10487

3 **CORNER OF MAIN AND S. CARROLL STREETS**
Wisconsin Historical Society
24924

4 **VAN SLYKE RESIDENCE**
Wisconsin Historical Society
32063

5 **CAPITOL (THIRD) WITHOUT DOME**
Wisconsin Historical Society
3133

6 **FIRE COMPANY WAGON**
Wisconsin Historical Society
23462

7 **LAKESIDE HOUSE**
Wisconsin Historical Society
38335

8 **CAPITOL (THIRD) DOME UNDER CONSTRUCTION**
Wisconsin Historical Society
23183

9 **UNIVERSITY OF WISCONSIN STUDENTS**
Wisconsin Historical Society
27716

10 **SOLDIERS' ORPHANS HOME**
Wisconsin Historical Society
2690

11 **PARK HOTEL**
Wisconsin Historical Society
11267

12 **NORWEGIAN FAMILY WITH POSSESSIONS**
Wisconsin Historical Society
1972

13 **WISCONSIN STATE HOSPITAL FOR THE INSANE**
Wisconsin Historical Society
27192

14 **GROUP BY CENTENNIAL FOUNTAIN ON CAPITOL SQUARE**
Wisconsin Historical Society
27129

15 **N. PINCKNEY STREET**
Wisconsin Historical Society
8656

16 **DEPOT ON WEST WASHINGTON**
Wisconsin Historical Society
11653

17 **FAMILY AND FARM**
Wisconsin Historical Society
25050

18 **CONGREGATIONALIST CHURCH**
Wisconsin Historical Society
27570

19 **FORMAL GROUP ON STEAMBOAT**
Wisconsin Historical Society
27189

20 **THE AMERICAN HOUSE HOTEL**
Wisconsin Historical Society
25470

21 **FARWELL'S MILL**
Wisconsin Historical Society
35418

22 **VIEW OF WISCONSIN STATE CAPITOL**
Wisconsin Historical Society
23347

23 **WASHBURN OBSERVATORY**
Wisconsin Historical Society
26709

24 **CAPITOL INTERIOR—QUARTERS OF THE HISTORICAL SOCIETY**
Wisconsin Historical Society
23291

25 **THE CASINO**
Wisconsin Historical Society
11225

26 **LEVI VILAS HOUSE**
Wisconsin Historical Society
35735

27 **Capitol Grounds Gate**
Wisconsin Historical Society
34431

28 **Schadauer Tobacco Store**
Wisconsin Historical Society
3155

29 **Capitol (Third) Construction**
Wisconsin Historical Society
10480

30 **View of Entrance to 508 State Street**
Wisconsin Historical Society
25234

31 **Fauerbach's Brewery**
Wisconsin Historical Society
3056

32 **Capitol Square Parade**
Wisconsin Historical Society
23921

33 **Railroad Depot**
Wisconsin Historical Society
32148

34 **Horseback Riders on Langdon Street**
Wisconsin Historical Society
41117

35 **Hollister's Pharmacy**
Wisconsin Historical Society
5495

36 **Fire Wagon in Action**
Wisconsin Historical Society
23469

37 **City Hall and the Fuller Opera House in Madison**
Wisconsin Historical Society
11305

38 **Hausmann Brewery Bar**
Wisconsin Historical Society
3054

39 **Water Tower at East Washington Avenue**
Wisconsin Historical Society
4648

40 **Capitol Funeral for Fairchild**
Wisconsin Historical Society
23247

41 **W. A. Oppel Grocery**
Wisconsin Historical Society
27246

42 **Iceboats on Lake Mendota**
Wisconsin Historical Society
2074

44 **Mifflin Street**
Wisconsin Historical Society
40205

45 **Construction Workers at Wisconsin Historical Society**
Wisconsin Historical Society
28582

46 **Madison McCormick Dealership**
Wisconsin Historical Society
9707

48 **Capitol Steps Dancers' Living Flag**
Wisconsin Historical Society
23127

49 **Fuller Opera House Interior**
Wisconsin Historical Society
26550

50 **UW Women's Carpentry Class**
Wisconsin Historical Society
10323

51 **Dane County Jail**
Wisconsin Historical Society
34615

52 **Fire Station**
Wisconsin Historical Society
23434

53 **Side Porch of House at 104 East Gilman Street**
Wisconsin Historical Society
41092

54 **Surveying the Fire's Damage**
Wisconsin Historical Society
23340

55 **Construction of Streetcar Tracks**
Wisconsin Historical Society
11040

56 **Children at Brittingham Park**
Wisconsin Historical Society
11074

57 **Sumner's Drugstore**
Wisconsin Historical Society
5449

58 **Fred Schenk Grocery Store**
Wisconsin Historical Society
6530

59 **The Wisconsin Building**
Wisconsin Historical Society
10596

60 **C & NW Passenger Station**
Wisconsin Historical Society
2258

62 **Third Capitol Demolition**
Wisconsin Historical Society
23346

63 **Crowd on East Washington Avenue**
Wisconsin Historical Society
27144

64 **Fair Oaks Trolley**
Wisconsin Historical Society
24965

65 **Madison Market**
Wisconsin Historical Society
2259

66 **Harry McDaniel Motorcycle and Bike Shop**
Wisconsin Historical Society
2245

68 **Parade on the Capitol Square**
Wisconsin Historical Society
3158

69 **Railroad Freight Wagons**
Wisconsin Historical Society
23447

70 **Goldenberger Wurst Roast**
Wisconsin Historical Society
1971

71 **Dedication of the Camp Randall Memorial Arch**
Wisconsin Historical Society
11270

72 **Ringling Circus Wagon and Clowns**
Wisconsin Historical Society
23000

73 **Conklin Ice House**
Wisconsin Historical Society
11341

74 **American Express Wagons**
Wisconsin Historical Society
1913

75 **Rising Wisconsin**
Wisconsin Historical Society
9566

76 **Railroad Depot**
Wisconsin Historical Society
32147

77 **Loyalty Day Parade**
Wisconsin Historical Society
24522

78 **Drafted Man at Chicago & North Western Station**
Wisconsin Historical Society
11039

79 **Training World War I**
Wisconsin Historical Society
40911

80 **Selling Dried Corn at the Municipal Market**
Wisconsin Historical Society
11070

81 **Labor Day Parade**
Wisconsin Historical Society
36026

82 **UW Division Class**
Wisconsin Historical Society
10324

84 **First Dairy School**
Wisconsin Historical Society
28340

85 **University of Wisconsin Coeds**
Wisconsin Historical Society
24429

86 **W. J. Hyland Plumbing Truck**
Wisconsin Historical Society
2378

87 **U.S. Sugar Company**
Wisconsin Historical Society
11038

88 **House Chamber**
Wisconsin Historical Society
4906

89 **Armory—Red Gym**
Wisconsin Historical Society
3207

90 **Viewing Casket of Robert M. La Follette, Sr.**
Wisconsin Historical Society
28380

91 **Masonic Temple**
Wisconsin Historical Society
22417

92 **University Methodist Church**
Wisconsin Historical Society
21225

93 **Alpha Kappa Lambda Fraternity Christmas Party**
Wisconsin Historical Society
22362

94 **Democratic Printing Company Building**
Wisconsin Historical Society
6359

95 **Lindbergh Returns**
Wisconsin Historical Society
5126

96 **Madison Oriental Rug Company**
Wisconsin Historical Society
6360

97 **U.S. Post Office and Federal Courthouse Under Construction**
Wisconsin Historical Society
3865

98 **Morey's Flying Billboard**
Wisconsin Historical Society
10864

99 **Threshing Outfit**
Wisconsin Historical Society
21665

100 **Progressive Republicans at the Park Hotel**
Wisconsin Historical Society
21551

101 **Woolworth's Variety Store**
Wisconsin Historical Society
21857

102 **Airplane Delivery**
Wisconsin Historical Society
20837

103 **Capital Buick Body Shop**
Wisconsin Historical Society
20871

104 **Civil War Cannon in Snow**
Wisconsin Historical Society
31898

105 **Central High School Band**
Wisconsin Historical Society
21270

106 **Christ Presbyterian Church**
Wisconsin Historical Society
3848

107 **Paul E. Stark Company**
Wisconsin Historical Society
21221

108 Children Sledding
Wisconsin Historical Society
35720

109 Automobile Accident
Wisconsin Historical Society
20230

110 Amos 'n' Andy on the Capitol Theatre Marquee
Wisconsin Historical Society
19901

111 Bock Oil Burner Company
Wisconsin Historical Society
20232

112 Dodge 8 Marathon Car
Wisconsin Historical Society
20225

113 Fall Festival Entertainers
Wisconsin Historical Society
6371

114 Hammersley for Governor Campaigners
Wisconsin Historical Society
19891

115 Parade of the Knights Templar
Wisconsin Historical Society
19958

116 University of Wisconsin Dairy Barn
Wisconsin Historical Society
2115

117 Stunt Car at the Dane County Fair
Wisconsin Historical Society
20149

118 Traffic on State Street
Wisconsin Historical Society
25153

119 Champion Wisconsin Cattle Judging Team
Wisconsin Historical Society
18352

120 A&W Rootbeer Stand
Wisconsin Historical Society
18489

121 Around-the-world Telephone Call
Wisconsin Historical Society
19224

122 Fleet of Trucks
Wisconsin Historical Society
18478

123 Champion Cow Milker
Wisconsin Historical Society
18359

124 Chanticleer Orchestra
Wisconsin Historical Society
19414

125 Dane County Motor Police
Wisconsin Historical Society
19219

126 East High School Football Players
Wisconsin Historical Society
18467

127 Baron Brothers Department Store
Wisconsin Historical Society
17987

128 Lie Detector Test
Wisconsin Historical Society
18265

129 University of Wisconsin Crew Team
Wisconsin Historical Society
4709

130 Golf Stunt
Wisconsin Historical Society
17867

131 Herbert Hoover and Governor Kohler
Wisconsin Historical Society
35034

132 Kroger Grocery Store
Wisconsin Historical Society
6395

133 Alpha Epsilon Phi Dinner
Wisconsin Historical Society
17277

134 Baptism in Lake Monona
Wisconsin Historical Society
17285

135 Celebrating the End of Prohibition
Wisconsin Historical Society
1956

136 Niglis Implement Store
Wisconsin Historical Society
15776

137 State Street View
Wisconsin Historical Society
1935

138 Babe Ruth
Wisconsin Historical Society
16271

139 Reed Sound Service Car
Wisconsin Historical Society
15214

140 Bartenders Pouring Drinks
Wisconsin Historical Society
15193

141 Retreaded Tires
Wisconsin Historical Society
14891

142 Iron Country Liquor Company Truck
Wisconsin Historical Society
15139

143 Rudy Vallee & SAE Group
Wisconsin Historical Society
15227

144 L. C. Smith Typewriter Display
Wisconsin Historical Society
15025

145 Governor Heil and Nash
Wisconsin Historical Society
14442

146 Meat Market Display
Wisconsin Historical Society
2035

148 Capitol Rotunda
Wisconsin Historical Society
7051

149 Flag Day Events
Wisconsin Historical Society
9943

150 Bethel Lutheran Church
Wisconsin Historical Society
13790

151 Pressing Curd
Wisconsin Historical Society
2168

152 Capitol City Bank Building
Wisconsin Historical Society
13930

153 Selling Defense Savings Bonds
Wisconsin Historical Society
13806

154 Naval Training Class
Wisconsin Historical Society
25160

155 Bong and Goodland
Wisconsin Historical Society
27739

156 Crowds on Capitol Square
Wisconsin Historical Society
34465

157 Marines and Marine Corps Women Reservists
Wisconsin Historical Society
38251

158 Packing Christmas Boxes for Soldiers
Wisconsin Historical Society
13296

159 Radio Broadcast Booth at Oscar Mayer
Wisconsin Historical Society
12788

160 Madison Free Library Entrance
Wisconsin Historical Society
12733

161 V-J Day Celebration
Wisconsin Historical Society
1869

162 V-J Day Celebration
Wisconsin Historical Society
34316

163 Bancroft Dairy Outdoor Bar
Wisconsin Historical Society
34461

164 Grace Episcopal Church
Wisconsin Historical Society
6433

165 Richard Bong Memorial Dedication
Wisconsin Historical Society
26948

166 New DeSoto Automobiles
Wisconsin Historical Society
12630

167 Soap Box Derby Competition
Wisconsin Historical Society
34439

168 Telephone Strike
Wisconsin Historical Society
34564

169 Aerial View of Camp Randall
Wisconsin Historical Society
42827

170 Vet Housing
Wisconsin Historical Society
3338

171 White Cross Pharmacy Soda Fountain
Wisconsin Historical Society
4965

172 Ice Fishing
Wisconsin Historical Society
34482

174 Armed Forces Day
Wisconsin Historical Society
3454

175 Children's Picnic at the Beach
Wisconsin Historical Society
8477

176 Hans Heg Statue
Wisconsin Historical Society
34301

177 Harry Truman on Train
Wisconsin Historical Society
35026

178 Alice in Dairyland
Wisconsin Historical Society
2000

179 Kohler Signing Housing Bill
Wisconsin Historical Society
33111

180 Memorial Union Terrace
Wisconsin Historical Society
42913

181 Parade on the Square
Wisconsin Historical Society
25797

182 Presenting Wreath on Armistice Day
Wisconsin Historical Society
34473

183 The Spot Lunch Diner
Wisconsin Historical Society
24415

184 Walt Kelly and Pogo on Book Tour
Wisconsin Historical Society
35562

185 Eleanor Roosevelt at Press Conference
Wisconsin Historical Society
35829

186 Employees Cutting Log to Header Length
Wisconsin Historical Society
32268

187 Iceboats on Madison Lake
Wisconsin Historical Society
33110

188 King Street Looking Toward the Capitol
Wisconsin Historical Society
3257

189 St. James Catholic Church
Wisconsin Historical Society
35808

190 Dane County Courthouse Being Razed
Wisconsin Historical Society
5626

192 Wisconsin Air National Guard F-102
Wisconsin Historical Society
11722

193 Rally for John F. Kennedy
Wisconsin Historical Society
8619

194 Bob Hope
Wisconsin Historical Society
9418

195 Touching Hands
Wisconsin Historical Society
25346

196 Dow Chemical Demonstration
Wisconsin Historical Society
2289

197 Sterling Hall Bombing
Wisconsin Historical Society
33885

198 Lucey Supporters
Wisconsin Historical Society
25349

199 Students at the Memorial Union Terrace
Wisconsin Historical Society
42829

200 Wisconsin State Capitol Dome
Wisconsin Historical Society
34302

HISTORIC PHOTOS OF MADISON

By the late nineteenth century, the city of Madison was a vibrant cultural center of the West. Through changing fortunes, Madison has continued to grow and prosper by overcoming adversity and maintaining the strong, independent culture of its citizens.

Historic Photos of Madison captures this journey through still photography selected from the finest archives. From Mansion Hill to the *Capital Times*, Madison's second daily newspaper, the industrialist John Johnson's founding of Gisholt Manufacturing to the Stearling Hall Bombing, *Historic Photos of Madison* follows life, government, education, and events throughout the city's history.

This volume captures unique and rare scenes through the lens of hundreds of historic photographs. Published in striking black and white, these images communicate historic events and everyday life of two centuries of people building a unique and prosperous city.

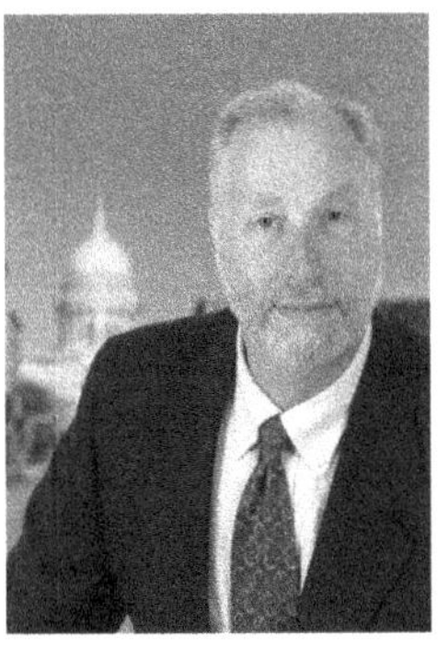

Donald J. Johnson is a lifelong Madison resident, a graduate of East High School and of the University of Wisconsin-Madison. He is a senior editor and heads communications at the UW-Madison Libraries. He has been a professional writer and editor throughout his career. He has also worked in public broadcasting and taught news writing, advertising, and social science research methods. Much of his work has been in magazine editing, starting in New York at McGraw-Hill and later starting magazines at the Cleveland Clinic Foundation, Beloit College, and the UW-Madison. He has been a partner with his wife in Johnson & Johnson Consulting since 1994. Johnson is president of the Wisconsin Center for the Book, an affiliate of the Library of Congress.

WWW.TURNERPUBLISHING.COM

www.ingramcontent.com/pod-product-compliance
Lightning Source LLC
LaVergne TN
LVHW060610110826
845154LV00003B/67

9781683369493